Deep Dive into the Power Platform in the Age of Generative AI

Architectural Insights and Best Practices for Intelligent Business Solutions

Biswa Pujarini Mohapatra
Gaurav Aroraa
Yash Agarwal

Deep Dive into the Power Platform in the Age of Generative AI:
Architectural Insights and Best Practices for Intelligent Business Solutions

Biswa Pujarini Mohapatra
Hyderabad, Telangana, India

Gaurav Aroraa
Delhi, Delhi, India

Yash Agarwal
Hyderabad, Telangana, India

ISBN-13 (pbk): 979-8-8688-0898-2
https://doi.org/10.1007/979-8-8688-0899-9

ISBN-13 (electronic): 979-8-8688-0899-9

Copyright © 2024 by Biswa Pujarini Mohapatra, Gaurav Aroraa, Yash Agarwal

This work is subject to copyright. All rights are reserved by the Publisher, whether the whole or part of the material is concerned, specifically the rights of translation, reprinting, reuse of illustrations, recitation, broadcasting, reproduction on microfilms or in any other physical way, and transmission or information storage and retrieval, electronic adaptation, computer software, or by similar or dissimilar methodology now known or hereafter developed.

Trademarked names, logos, and images may appear in this book. Rather than use a trademark symbol with every occurrence of a trademarked name, logo, or image we use the names, logos, and images only in an editorial fashion and to the benefit of the trademark owner, with no intention of infringement of the trademark.

The use in this publication of trade names, trademarks, service marks, and similar terms, even if they are not identified as such, is not to be taken as an expression of opinion as to whether or not they are subject to proprietary rights.

While the advice and information in this book are believed to be true and accurate at the date of publication, neither the authors nor the editors nor the publisher can accept any legal responsibility for any errors or omissions that may be made. The publisher makes no warranty, express or implied, with respect to the material contained herein.

    Managing Director, Apress Media LLC: Welmoed Spahr
    Acquisitions Editor: Smriti Srivastava
    Development Editor: Laura Berendson
    Editorial Assistant: Kripa Joseph

Cover designed by eStudioCalamar

Cover image is by Unsplash

Distributed to the book trade worldwide by Springer Science+Business Media New York, 1 New York Plaza, Suite 4600, New York, NY 10004-1562, USA. Phone 1-800-SPRINGER, fax (201) 348-4505, e-mail orders-ny@springer-sbm.com, or visit www.springeronline.com. Apress Media, LLC is a California LLC and the sole member (owner) is Springer Science + Business Media Finance Inc (SSBM Finance Inc). SSBM Finance Inc is a **Delaware** corporation.

For information on translations, please e-mail booktranslations@springernature.com; for reprint, paperback, or audio rights, please e-mail bookpermissions@springernature.com.

Apress titles may be purchased in bulk for academic, corporate, or promotional use. eBook versions and licenses are also available for most titles. For more information, reference our Print and eBook Bulk Sales web page at http://www.apress.com/bulk-sales.

Any source code or other supplementary material referenced by the author in this book is available to readers on GitHub. For more detailed information, please visit https://www.apress.com/gp/services/source-code.

If disposing of this product, please recycle the paper

*To my father Mr. Bibhuti Bhusan Mohapatra,
daughter Priyansi, and my son Mivan.*
—*Pujarini Mohapatra*

*To my family, whose love and support give me strength
and purpose.*
—*Gaurav*

Table of Contents

About the Authors xix

About the Technical Reviewers xxi

Acknowledgments xxiii

Introduction xxv

Part I: Getting started, Security, Governance and Compliance 1

Chapter 1: Power Platform Overview 3

Overview 3

Introduction to the Power Platform 5

    Definition and Scope 5

    Brief History and Evolution 5

Why Do Organizations Use the Power Platform? 6

High-Level Overview of the Platform 7

Chapter 2: Power Platform Administration and Governance 57

Overview 57

Power Platform Admin Roles and Responsibilities 57

    Understanding the Role of Admin 57

    Understanding the Role of Power Platform Admin Roles and Responsibilities 58

    Difference Between Global Admin and Power Platform Admin 60

    Security Layers in the Power Platform 63

v

TABLE OF CONTENTS

Environment Strategy 64
    Explore Types of Environments... 66
    Best Practices for Developing an Environment Strategy 68
Managed Environment 71
    Managed Environments Capabilities 72
Security and Data Governance... 81
    Managing Environmental Security.. 86
    Overview of Dataverse Security 87
    Data Loss Prevention Policy (DLP) 93
    Overview of Connectors 96
Analytics and Auditing 101
    Tenant-Level Analytics... 103
    Analyze Telemetry with Application Insights 105
    Data Export to Data Lake 107
    Overview of Auditing 109
Best Practices and Tools 112
    Center of Excellence (COE) Kit 112
    PowerShell Scripts 113
    Managed Environments 114

Chapter 3: Dataverse Capabilities in Power Platform 115

Dataverse Overview 115
Brief History and Evolution of Microsoft Dataverse 116
Why Should Organizations Use Microsoft Dataverse? 117
Overview of Dataverse Layers 120
    Presentation Layer... 120
    Service Layer.. 122
    Business Logic Layer.. 122
    Data Layer 123

TABLE OF CONTENTS

Security Layer 124
Key Components of Microsoft Dataverse 125
Use Cases and Applications of Dataverse 153
Summary 157

Chapter 4: Data Integration, Data Export, and Analytics in Dataverse 159

Introduction to Dataflows 159
    Key Features 160
    Purpose and Benefits of Dataflows 161
    Benefits of Dataflows 162
    Disadvantages of Power Apps Dataflows 164
    Use-Case Scenarios for Dataflows 166
    Creating and Configuring Dataflows 167
    Transformations and Data Preparation 171
Integration with Power Query 175
    Data Transformation and Cleansing 176
    Advanced Dataflow Scenarios 176
Dataflow Scheduling and Automation 177
    Dataflow Scheduling 178
    Dataflow Automation 179
    Benefits of Dataflow Scheduling and Automation 180
    Monitoring and Managing Dataflow Execution 180
Azure Synapse Link for Dataverse 184
    Introduction to Azure Synapse Link 186
    Overview of Near-Real-Time Insights 187
Enabling Near-Real-Time Analytics 188
    Prerequisites 189
    Configuring and Activating Azure Synapse Link 190

vii

TABLE OF CONTENTS

Enable Change Tracking to Control Data Synchronization 191
Azure Synapse Link with Delta Lake 193
Connecting Dataverse to Synapse Workspace and Exporting Data in
Delta Lake Format 195
Monitor Azure Synapse Link 196
Real-Time Data Sync Mechanisms Using Microsoft Fabric 198
Comparing Link to Fabric with Azure Synapse Link for Dataverse 200

Dataverse Plugins and Custom APIs 201
Plugins 201
Custom APIs 204

Integration with External Services 206
Learn How to Integrate Power Platform with External Services
for Enhanced Data Capabilities 207
Common Integration Scenarios and Solutions 209

Power BI Integration with Microsoft Dataverse 211
Significance of Visualizing Microsoft Dataverse Data 212
Integrating Power BI with Microsoft Dataverse 213
Dataverse Connectors in Power BI 217
Embedding Power BI Reports 218
Tabular Data Stream (TDS) Endpoint 220

Tools 222
Key Features of Dataverse Accelerator 222
Benefits of Using Dataverse Accelerator 223

Chapter 5: Dataverse Connectors and Gateway 225

Introduction to Dataverse Connectors 225
Types of Connectors 226
Connecting to Cloud-Based Data Sources 233
On-Premises Data Connectivity with Gateway Clusters 238

TABLE OF CONTENTS

Troubleshooting Data Source Connectivity Issues 248
Scaling and Growth Considerations 254
    Scaling Dataverse Connectors... 255
    Scaling On-Premises Data Gateways 257
Real-World Use Cases.. 261
Summary... 267

Chapter 6: Modern App Design with Power Apps 269

Introduction to Modern App Design 269
Responsive Design Essentials... 272
    Best Practices for Responsive Design in Power Platform 277
Introduction to App Development in Power Platform 281
    Key Concepts in Power Platform App Development 282
    Application Development Lifecycle in Power Platform 285
    Benefits of Using Power Platform for App Development 287
Building Canvas Apps.. 289
    Key Features of Canvas Apps 289
    Getting Started with Canvas Apps 292
    Best Practices for Building Canvas Apps 298
    Use Cases for Canvas Apps 301
Model-Driven App Development 302
    Key Features of Model-Driven Apps 303
    Getting Started with Model-Driven Apps 306
    Best Practices for Building Model-Driven Apps... 311
    Use Cases for Model-Driven Apps 314
Customizing Themes and Branding 316
    Customizing Themes and Branding in Canvas Apps................................ 317
    Customizing Themes and Branding in Model-Driven Apps...................... 319
    Best Practices for Branding and Custom Themes 322

ix

TABLE OF CONTENTS

Accessibility Considerations 324
    Accessibility Considerations for Canvas Apps 325
    Accessibility Considerations for Model-Driven Apps 327
    Tools for Testing and Validating Accessibility 329
    Best Practices for Accessibility in Power Platform Apps 330

Integration with Power Automate and Copilots 332
    Integrating Power Apps with Power Automate 332
    Integrating Power Apps with AI Copilots 335
    Use Cases of Integrating Power Apps with Power Automate and AI Copilots 336
    Best Practices for Integrating Power Apps with Power Automate and AI Copilots 338

Data Visualization Techniques 340
    Built-in Visualization Controls in Canvas Apps 341
    Bulit-In Visualization Controls in Model-Driven Apps 342
    Integration with Power BI 344
    Custom Visualizations Using JavaScript Libraries 344
    Use Cases for Data Visualization in Power Apps 345
    Best Practices for Data Visualization in Power Apps 346

Testing and Debugging Modern Apps 348
    Testing Canvas Apps 348
    Types of Testing in Canvas Apps 348
    Tools and Techniques for Testing Canvas Apps 349
    Testing Model-Driven Apps 351
    Types of Testing for Model-Driven Apps 351
    Tools and Techniques for Testing Model-Driven Apps 352
    Common Debugging Scenarios and Solutions 354
    Best Practices for Debugging and Testing 355

Summary 357

TABLE OF CONTENTS

Part II: Power Platform Components and Real-world Use cases 359

Chapter 7: Microsoft Copilot Studio 361

Introduction to Microsoft Copilot Studio 361
    Building Custom Copilots with Copilot Studio 362
    Grounding Your Copilot in Data 365
    Generative Actions 365
    Custom Development and Integration 365
    Publishing Your Copilot 366
    Performance Monitoring and Management 366
    Use Cases 366

Security and Governance 367
    Compliance and Trust 367

Getting Started with Generative AI 372
    Overview of Generative AI in Copilot Studio 373
    Generative Answers 375
    Key Features of Generative Answers 375
    Getting Started with Generative Answers 377
    Prompting in Copilot Studio 378
    Use of Custom Data sources 379

Enhancing Copilot with Connectors 380
    Key Features of Connectors 380
    Benefits of Using Connectors 381
    Implementing Connectors in Copilot Studio 382
    Examples of Connectors in Action 384
    Enhancing Security and Governance with Connectors 386
    Conclusion 386

TABLE OF CONTENTS

Generative Actions in Copilot Studio 387
    Key Features of Generative Actions 387
    Implementing Generative Actions 389
    Examples of Generative Actions 391
    Benefits of Generative Actions 391
Copilot Studio Architecture 392
    Overview of Copilot Studio Architecture 393
Monitoring and Diagnosing 396
    Monitoring Tools and Capabilities 396
    Diagnostic Capabilities 397
    Diagnostic Events and Auditing 398
    Comprehensive Analytics 399
    Reporting and Analytics 399
Publish and Integrate Copilots 404
    Tools for Monitoring and Diagnosing 408
    Auditing and Troubleshooting Practices 408
Tools—Power CAT Copilot Studio Kit 409
    Testing Capabilities 409
    Copilot KPIs 410
Summary 410

Chapter 8: Workflow Automation Using Power Automate 411

Getting Started with Power Automate 411
    Power Automate Overview 411
    Different Types of Flows in Power Automate 415
    Advanced Features in Power Automate 421
    Use Cases for Power Automate 422

TABLE OF CONTENTS

Create Flows Using Power Automate 424
    Creating Cloud Flows in Power Automate 425
    Creating Desktop Flows in Power Automate 427
Advanced Flow Design Using Copilots 429
    Overview of Copilots in Power Automate 430
    Key Features of Copilots in Power Automate 430
    Designing Advanced Flows with Copilots 432
    Example: Automating Employee Onboarding 433
    Best Practices for Flow Design Using Copilots 435
Integration with Power Apps 438
    Benefits of Integrating Power Automate with Power Apps 438
    Integration Scenarios 440
    Steps to Integrate Power Automate with Power Apps 441
    Best Practices for Integrating Power Automate with Power Apps 443
Data Connectivity and Transformations 446
    Data Connectivity in Power Automate 446
    Data Transformation in Power Automate 449
    Data Manipulation in Power Automate 452
    Workflow Example 453
    Best Practices for Data Connectivity, Transformation, and
    Manipulation in Power Automate 455
Error Handling and Troubleshooting in Power Automate 457
    Examples of Error Handling 460
    Troubleshooting in Power Automate 460
    Debugging Tools and Techniques 463
    Best Practices for Troubleshooting and Error Handling in Power
    Automate 464
Power Automate Best Practices 466
Summary 472

xiii

TABLE OF CONTENTS

Chapter 9: Integrating AI with Power Platform: AI Builder 475
Key Learning Outcomes 475
Introduction to AI Builder 477
    The Power of AI in Business 477
    The History of AI 477
    Key Milestones in AI History 481
Understanding AI Builder 481
    Transformative Impact on Business Processes 482
    Examples of Few Real-World Applications 483
Role of AI in the Power Platform 483
    AI Builder Key Features 484
    Use Cases 484
AI Builder vs. Azure AI Studio: Key Differences 485
    Target Audience and Usability 485
    Functionality and Features 486
    Integration and Ecosystem 486
    Customization and Control 487
Introduction to Prompt Engineering 488
    Key Elements of a Prompt 488
    Types of Prompts 489
AI Builder Prompts 492
    Using Prompts for Automation 493
    Prerequisites 494
    Prebuilt AI Prompts 494
    Custom Prompts 495
    Use Your Own Data in a Prompt 498
    Summary 500

TABLE OF CONTENTS

AI Builder Models 500
    Prebuilt AI Models...504
    Custom AI Models...505
    Common Business Scenarios with AI Builder Models 507
    Summary...511

AI Builder Architecture and Integration 511
    Overview of AI Builder Architecture..511
    AI Builder Integration in Power Automate......................................513
    AI Builder Integration in Power App..514
    AI Builder Integration in Copilot Studio..517
    AI Builder Integration in Dataverse Plugins....................................519
    Summary...520

Security and Governance 520
    Overview..520
    Personas and Roles 520
    Data Security and Privacy...521
    Model Accessibility and Permissions 521
    Roles and Permissions Mapping 522
    Data Loss Prevention (DLP) 522
    Model Lifecycle Management...522
    Capacity Management..523
    Monitoring and Compliance..523

Responsible AI...524
Summary..525

Chapter 10: Solutions Overview and ALM Strategy 527

Introduction to Application Lifecycle Management (ALM)...................527
    Key Areas of ALM..528
    Application Lifecycle...529

TABLE OF CONTENTS

ALM for Power Apps, Power Automate, Microsoft Copilot Studio, and Dataverse 530

Solutions..531

Dataverse 531

Source Control..531

Continuous Integration and Continuous Delivery (CI/CD)..........................532

Benefits of ALM..532

ALM Basics with Microsoft Power Platform...533

Environments..533

Solutions..536

ALM Strategy in Power Platform...543

Challenges in the Implementation of ALM in Power Platform 543

Automate Deployments with Pipelines for Power Platform 547

Overview of Pipelines...548

Key Components..548

Setting Up Pipelines 549

Benefits of Pipelines..550

Practical Use Cases Based on Persona 551

Summary...552

Best Practices for ALM with Solutions..553

Tools...555

Summary..558

Chapter 11: Power Pages for External Websites 561

Power Pages for External Websites 561

Understanding Power Pages—An Overview..565

Key Features of Microsoft Power Pages...567

Low-Code Design Principles 576

User-Centric Design...577

TABLE OF CONTENTS

Modular and Reusable Components	578
Data-Driven Design	578
Responsive Design	578
Security and Compliance	579
Scalability and Performance	579
Integration with Other Services	579
Continuous Improvement	580
High-Level Architectural Overview	580
Key Components	582
Why Use Power Pages?	584
Business Benefits	585
User Experience	588
Security Governance	589
Zero Trust Security	590
Built-In Security Features	593
Compliance and Standards	607
Integration with External Websites	608
Connecting to Third-Party Services	609
Embedding External Content	610
Configuring for Cross-Browser Capability	612
Responsive Design	612
Cross-Browser Testing	612
Performance Optimization	613
Challenges of Using Power Pages for External Websites	614
Customization Limitations	614
Learning Curve for Professional Developers	615
Integration Complexities	615
Performance and Scalability Concerns	615

TABLE OF CONTENTS

Security and Compliance Management..615
Cost Management 616
Dependency on the Microsoft Ecosystem 616
Limited Offline Functionality...616
Complexity in Role-Based Access Control (RBAC)..616
Support and Documentation...617
Summary..617
Key Takeaways...620
References..621

Chapter 12: Real-World Use Cases and Success Stories...................623

Unveiling Power Platform Impact...625
Role of Low Code in Modern Business Solutions 626
Success Stories 629
Healthcare Industry 630
Retail Industry 631
Finance industry...633
Use Case: Manufacturing Industry 634
Problem Statement..635
Expected Solution..636
Transformation Journey Using Power Platform.......................................637
Leveraging Power Platform...638
Automate and Get the Alert Using Power Automate 639
Summary..641
Key Takeaways...642

Index..643

About the Authors

Pujarini Moahpatra is a seasoned technology leader with over 18 years of IT experience. She is currently serving as the Principal Engineering Manager at Microsoft. She leads a global team in designing and implementing scalable solutions using the Power Platform and Azure. Her expertise spans artificial intelligence, low-code/power platform, cloud computing, leadership, management, and enterprise architecture.

Gaurav Aroraa is a Microsoft MVP award recipient. He is a Mentor of Change with AIM NITI Aayog, Govt. of India; Business Coach with Business Blaster, Govt. of NCT of Delhi, India; and President, Open AI Enth. India. He is a lifetime member of the Computer Society of India (CSI), an advisory member and senior mentor at IndiaMentor, certified as a Scrum trainer and coach, ITIL-F-certified, and PRINCE-F- and PRINCE-P-certified. Gaurav is an open-source developer and a contributor to the Microsoft TechNet community. He has authored books across technologies, including *Cloud Debugging and Profiling in Microsoft Azure* (Apress) and *Hands-on Azure Cognitive Services* (Apress). Recently, Gaurav has been recognized as a world record holder for writing books in exceptional technologies.

ABOUT THE AUTHORS

Yash Agarwal is a Power Platform solution architect with experience working on Microsoft Power Apps, Power Automate, and Copilot Studio. He is a 5× Microsoft MVP and MCT for business applications. He has experience working in domains such as healthcare, banking and finance, education, automotive, etc.. He can be reached at his blog, bythedevs.com.

About the Technical Reviewers

Dipti Jaiswal is the Partner Director of Engineering at Power Pages responsible for all maker, end-user, administration, governance, and security experiences in Power Pages. The Power Pages team is focused on building modern, intelligent experiences that revolutionize how end users interact with websites. Dipti also leads engineering for Power Apps Mobile platform that powers mobile native experiences for Power Apps.

Mehdi Slaoui Andaloussi is a Principal Engineering Manager on the Power CAT team within the Power Platform engineering organization at Microsoft. In his official role as Solution Architect and unofficial role as Chief Designer on the team, he has advised hundreds of enterprise customers on how to make their Power Apps solutions look better, run faster, and scale to work for hundreds of thousands of users in Fortune 500 organizations. He regularly shares his learnings and tips on Power Platform blogs, product docs, and the Power CAT Live channel.

Anand Narayanaswamy works as an author, reviewer, and blogger based in Thiruvananthapuram, Kerala, India. He was recognized as a Microsoft MVP from 2002 to 2011 and Windows Insider MVP from 2019 to 2023 and is currently a Microsoft MVP in Windows and Devices. Anand contributes articles to leading online and print publications. He runs his blogs

ABOUT THE TECHNICAL REVIEWERS

(netans.com and surfacebuzzer.com) and actively helps the Windows community on Quora. In his spare time, Anand loves to dig the old gadgets such as Microsoft Zune, iPod, and iPod Classic. He can be reached via X at @visualanand and Instagram at @netanstech.

Acknowledgments

I would like to express my deepest gratitude to my co-authors, Gaurav Aroraa and Yash Agarwal. Their insights and collaboration have been invaluable throughout this journey.

I am deeply appreciative of my mentors, Saurabh Pant, Marc Schweigert, Mehdi Slaoui Andaloussi, Dipti Jaiswal, and Prabhat Ranjan, for their continuous guidance, wisdom, and encouragement.

A special acknowledgment to my husband, Balakrushna Swain, whose unwavering support and love have been my greatest source of strength and inspiration.

I also wish to express my sincere thanks to my father, Bibhuti Bhusan Mohapatra, my mother, Kiranbala Mohapatra, my sister, Biswabijaini, and my brother Biswaranjan, for their endless love, encouragement, and support throughout my life.

Thanks to Apress for giving us this platform to share knowledge. Finally, I would like to thank all the readers for their interest in this book. I hope it serves as a valuable resource and provides you with insights and knowledge that will be beneficial in your endeavors.

—Biswa Pujarini Mohapatra

Introduction

In the rapidly evolving landscape of digital transformation, organizations across the globe are constantly seeking ways to streamline processes, enhance productivity, and drive innovation. The emergence of Generative AI has added a new dimension to this transformation, offering unprecedented capabilities to automate, innovate, and personalize business solutions. The Power Platform, a powerful suite of tools from Microsoft, stands at the forefront of this revolution, providing the essential building blocks for creating intelligent, scalable, and customizable applications. *Deep Dive into the Power Platform in the Age of Generative AI* is a comprehensive guide designed to help professionals navigate this dynamic ecosystem, harnessing the full potential of the Power Platform in the context of Generative AI.

This book is structured to offer both a foundational understanding and an in-depth exploration of the Power Platform's capabilities. It starts by introducing readers to the core components of the Power Platform, laying the groundwork for a more detailed examination of its applications and potential. The opening chapter, "Power Platform Overview," provides a broad introduction, setting the stage by explaining the platform's purpose, its key features, and how it fits into the broader Microsoft ecosystem. This chapter is crucial for those new to the Power Platform, offering a solid base of knowledge before diving into more complex topics.

Following the overview, the book delves into "Power Platform Administration and Governance." This chapter is essential for IT professionals and administrators responsible for managing and maintaining Power Platform environments. It covers the critical aspects of governance, including setting up environments, managing security,

INTRODUCTION

and ensuring compliance with organizational policies. The emphasis on governance reflects the increasing need for businesses to manage their digital tools effectively, particularly in an age where data security and regulatory compliance are paramount.

"Dataverse Capabilities in Power Platform" is the focus of the third chapter, where readers are introduced to Dataverse, the underlying data platform that powers the Power Platform. Dataverse is more than just a data repository; it is a sophisticated data service that enables the integration, management, and analysis of business data. This chapter explores its capabilities, demonstrating how Dataverse can be used to build powerful, data-driven applications that are both scalable and secure. The discussion extends to topics such as data modeling, security, and the role of Dataverse in supporting advanced features like AI and automation.

The exploration continues with "Data Integration, Data Export, and Analytics in Dataverse," a chapter dedicated to the critical aspects of data management. In today's data-driven world, the ability to integrate, export, and analyze data is vital. This chapter covers the various tools and techniques available within the Power Platform for managing data across different systems. It provides practical insights into how businesses can leverage these tools to gain actionable insights, improve decision-making, and enhance operational efficiency. The integration of data from multiple sources, coupled with powerful analytics, forms the backbone of modern business intelligence, making this chapter particularly relevant for organizations looking to maximize the value of their data.

The fifth chapter, "Dataverse Connectors and Gateway," expands on the integration capabilities of the Power Platform by exploring the use of connectors and gateways. Connectors are essential for linking the Power Platform to external systems and services, enabling seamless data flow and integration across diverse platforms. This chapter provides a detailed examination of how connectors work, the different types available, and how they can be used to extend the functionality of Power Apps, Power

INTRODUCTION

Automate, and other components of the Power Platform. The use of gateways for secure on-premises data access is also discussed, highlighting the importance of connectivity in building robust and scalable solutions.

As the book progresses, the focus shifts to application development with "Modern App Design with Power Apps." This chapter is particularly valuable for developers and solution architects who want to create user-friendly and visually appealing applications. It covers the principles of modern app design, exploring the features and capabilities of Power Apps in creating custom applications that meet specific business needs. The chapter emphasizes the importance of user experience (UX) and user interface (UI) design in building applications that are not only functional but also intuitive and engaging.

A significant portion of the book is dedicated to exploring the capabilities of Generative AI within the Power Platform, starting with "Microsoft Copilot Studio." CoPilot Studio represents a groundbreaking advancement in how AI can be integrated into the development process, providing tools that assist in the creation and enhancement of applications. This chapter explores the various features of CoPilot Studio, including how it can be used to generate code, suggest improvements, and automate repetitive tasks. The role of Generative AI in augmenting human creativity and productivity is a central theme, demonstrating how AI can be leveraged to accelerate development and reduce time-to-market.

"Workflow Automation Using Power Automate" follows, offering readers a deep dive into the automation capabilities of the Power Platform. Power Automate is a powerful tool for automating business processes, enabling organizations to streamline operations and reduce manual effort. This chapter provides practical guidance on creating automated workflows, integrating AI into these workflows, and using Power Automate to drive efficiency across the organization. The integration of AI in automation processes is particularly emphasized, showcasing how businesses can achieve new levels of productivity and innovation.

INTRODUCTION

The intelligence of AI is further explored in "Integrating AI with Power Platform: AI Builder." AI Builder is a key component of the Power Platform that allows users to incorporate AI into their applications without requiring extensive coding knowledge. This chapter provides a comprehensive overview of the capabilities of AI Builder, including how it can be used to create predictive models, automate decision-making, and enhance the intelligence of applications. The chapter is particularly relevant for businesses looking to harness the power of AI to gain a competitive edge, offering practical examples of how AI can be integrated into real-world applications.

As the book approaches its conclusion, "Solutions Overview and ALM Strategy" offers insights into best practices for solution management and application lifecycle management (ALM). This chapter is crucial for organizations that need to manage the development, deployment, and maintenance of their applications efficiently. It covers the tools and methodologies available within the Power Platform for managing the entire lifecycle of an application, from development to production. The focus on ALM reflects the importance of maintaining quality and consistency in software development, particularly in large and complex environments.

"Power Pages for External Websites" explores the use of Power Pages for creating external-facing websites. This chapter is particularly relevant for businesses that need to engage with customers, partners, and other external stakeholders through web applications. It covers the features of Power Pages, including how they can be used to create secure, scalable, and user-friendly websites that integrate seamlessly with the Power Platform. The chapter emphasizes the importance of web presence in the digital age and how Power Pages can be leveraged to create impactful online experiences.

Finally, the book concludes with "Real-World Use Cases and Success Stories," a chapter that brings together the concepts and tools discussed throughout the book by showcasing real-world examples of how the Power

Platform has been used to drive success in various industries. These case studies provide valuable insights into how organizations have applied the Power Platform to solve complex challenges, improve operations, and achieve their business goals. The success stories serve as inspiration and proof of the transformative power of the Power Platform in the age of Generative AI, demonstrating the platform's versatility and potential to drive innovation across diverse sectors.

Deep Dive into the Power Platform in the Age of Generative AI is not just a technical guide; it is a roadmap for navigating the future of business application development in a world increasingly shaped by AI. Whether you are a developer, administrator, or business leader, this book offers the insights and knowledge needed to harness the full potential of the Power Platform, empowering you to build intelligent, scalable, and impactful solutions that meet the demands of the modern business landscape.

PART I

Getting started, Security, Governance and Compliance

CHAPTER 1

Power Platform Overview

This chapter provides a detailed overview of various aspects involved with Power Platform, introducing readers to its core components, functionalities, and the tra Power Pages, offering authors nsformative capabilities it offers for building business applications and automating processes.

Overview

In this introductory chapter, we embark on a journey to unravel the multifaceted Power Platform. We start by defining the Power Platform and delving into its historical evolution, setting the stage for a comprehensive exploration.

The first subtopic, "Introduction to the Power Platform," aims to provide readers with a clear understanding of the platform's purpose and scope. We explore its evolution over time, highlighting key milestones that have contributed to its current significance. Additionally, a high-level overview introduces the core components—Power Apps, Power Automate, AI Builder, Copilot Studio, Dataverse, and Power Pages.

CHAPTER 1   POWER PLATFORM OVERVIEW

We dedicate sections to each major component, beginning with "Introduction to Power Apps." Here, we familiarize readers with Power Apps' role in building custom applications, distinguishing between canvas apps and model-driven apps. The discussion extends to how Power Apps simplifies development for users with varying technical expertise.

The third subtopic, "Introduction to Power Automate," delves into the platform's role in automating business processes. We explore connectors, integrations, and provide practical examples to illustrate the power of workflow automation using Power Automate.

"Introduction to AI Builder" follows, shedding light on the fundamentals, core features, and real-world use cases. This section aims to demystify AI Builder's capabilities, showcasing its impact on various applications.

"Introduction to Copilot Studio" provides a comprehensive overview of this innovative tool, delving into its foundational principles and key functionalities. This segment aims to elucidate Copilot Studio's role in revolutionizing chatbot customization, highlighting its intuitive interface, seamless integration capabilities, and transformative impact on conversational AI solutions.

Our exploration continues with "Introduction to Power Pages," where we uncover the potential of Power Pages for external-facing websites. Core features, capabilities, and considerations such as security and governance are addressed.

"Introduction to Dataverse" offers an overview of Microsoft Dataverse, exploring its tables, relationships, plugins, and connectors. The discussion extends to roles and security within Dataverse.

Through this chapter, readers will gain a solid foundation in Power Platform's components, setting the stage for a deeper dive into each element in subsequent chapters.

Introduction to the Power Platform

The Power Platform stands as a transformative force in the realm of business applications and process automation. Defined as a comprehensive suite of tools, the Power Platform empowers organizations to create custom solutions, automate workflows, and infuse artificial intelligence into their processes. This introductory section aims to provide readers with a foundational understanding of the Power Platform, encompassing its definition, historical evolution, and a high-level overview of its core components.

Definition and Scope

Power Platform is a product family that delivers innovative business solutions across one seamlessly integrated platform. Power BI, Power Apps, Power Automate, Power Pages, and Microsoft Copilot Studio allow any business to analyze and visualize real-time business performance, quickly and easily build custom apps, automate workflows, deliver business websites, and integrate AI capabilities.

Brief History and Evolution

The Power Platform has undergone a significant evolution since its inception, starting with the introduction of Power Apps, Flows, Dataverse (Formerly CDS), and Power BI. It has now developed into a comprehensive suite featuring Power Apps, Power Automate, AI Builder, Dataverse, Copilot studio, and Power Pages. Each stage of evolution has been driven by the changing needs of businesses, making the Power Platform a dynamic and adaptable solution.

By providing a low-code interface, the Power Platform enables users to swiftly create custom apps, while also offering robust tools for professional developers. This dual approach facilitates the development of integrated and innovative solutions spanning Azure, Microsoft 365, Dynamics 365, and standalone applications. For enterprises, the platform acts as a fundamental "agility layer," empowering organizations to rapidly build new applications and experiences while capitalizing on the data and services offered by core business systems such as SAP or Salesforce. At the convergence of these products lies digital transformation, empowering customers to innovate anywhere while unlocking value everywhere.

Why Do Organizations Use the Power Platform?

The Power Platform provides organizations with a level of capability, security, and supportability that enables them to swiftly build, test, and deploy applications and solutions while leveraging their existing data and systems. This agility layer offers a cost-effective means for developing and testing new ideas and services within an organization.

A notable feature of the Power Platform is its user-friendly nature. With all tools being low-code to no-code, users can create functional solutions without the need for extensive coding. With appropriate governance measures in place, this results in the rapid production of standardized, supportable solutions with fewer bugs, ready for quick deployment to end-users for testing and validation.

Another benefit of the Power Platform is its seamless integration with enterprise data. Whether building an order tracking app utilizing SAP data or an employee feedback app drawing from HR files in Workday, the Power Platform effortlessly integrates with enterprise data sources without requiring migrations or synchronizations.

To address concerns about shadow IT, where business units or individuals create unofficial IT solutions, the Power Platform offers a solution. By empowering users to develop solutions within a controlled environment, organizations can harness innovation without compromising

CHAPTER 1 POWER PLATFORM OVERVIEW

on data security, compliance, or system integration. This balance between user empowerment and IT governance ensures that innovation flourishes while aligning with organizational standards and best practices.

Finally, organizations choose the Power Platform for its simplicity and scalability. Unlike traditional software development and operation, which involve various technical complexities, the Power Platform offers a standardized, reliable solution that eliminates the burdens of building, deploying, and maintaining coded applications. This simplicity enables individual makers to create and deploy solutions with ease, providing organizations with a reliable platform for innovation and growth.

High-Level Overview of the Platform

The Power Platform comprises five core components, each serving a distinct purpose:

> **Power Apps**: Facilitates the creation of custom applications through both canvas and model-driven approaches, catering to users with varying technical expertise.
>
> **Power Automate**: Streamlines business processes by automating workflows, integrating with a wide array of applications through connectors.
>
> **AI Builder**: Infuses artificial intelligence into applications, making it accessible for organizations to leverage machine learning capabilities without extensive technical expertise.
>
> **Copilot Studio**: Copilot Studio is a low-code tool for customizing Microsoft Copilot, offering a comprehensive suite of conversational capabilities, from custom prompts to generative AI plugins

and manual topics. It streamlines the design, development, and publishing process of chatbots, empowering users with no-code graphical interface and seamless integration with other Power Platform technologies.

Dataverse: Serves as a unified data platform, allowing for the management of data entities, relationships, and security.

Power Pages: Extends the platform's capabilities to create external-facing websites with an emphasis on user experience, security, and governance.

Managed Environments: Managed environments are a premium capability of the Power Platform designed to enable best practices in governance and solution delivery. They offer features such as sharing limitations, ALM pipelines, and enhanced administration tools, empowering organizations to scale their governance and optimize performance across various environments.

Connectors: Connectors serve as bridges between different services within the Power Platform, facilitating seamless data flow across applications, databases, and services. With prebuilt connectors for popular services and the ability to create custom connectors, they simplify data integration and offer unparalleled flexibility to organizations.

This introduction lays the groundwork for a deeper exploration of each Power Platform component in subsequent sections, providing readers with a comprehensive understanding of the platform's capabilities and its potential impact on organizational efficiency and innovation.

Figure 1-1 shows various products within the Power Platform landscape.

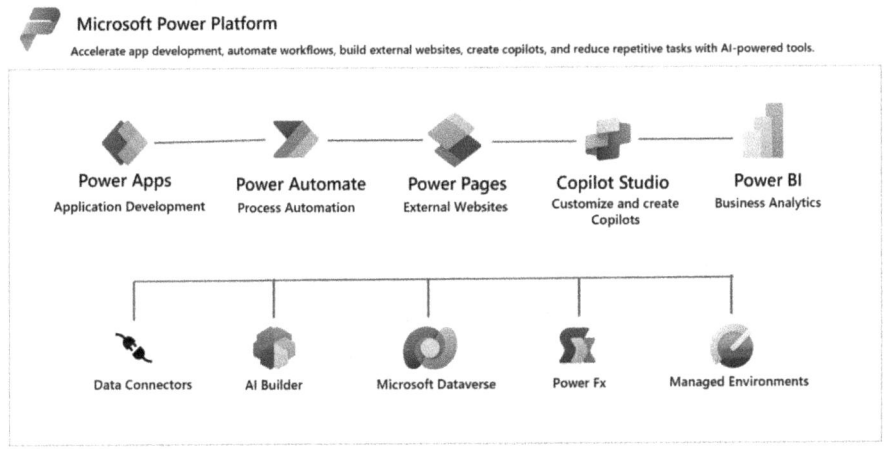

Figure 1-1. *Power Platform landscape*

1. Introduction to Power Apps

    a. Introduction to Power Apps for Building Custom Applications

    Power Apps is a Microsoft platform that empowers users to build custom applications without the need for extensive coding expertise. It opens application development to a broader audience, allowing business users to create tailored solutions that address specific needs. The intuitive interface and drag-and-drop functionality enable users to design applications that streamline processes and enhance efficiency. Power Apps serves as a cornerstone within the Power Platform, offering a platform for swift application development tailored for both business users and professional developers. Designed to expedite the creation of business applications, Power Apps seeks to bridge the divide between IT departments and other business units, streamlining the traditionally cumbersome and time-consuming app development process.

A key feature of Power Apps is its low-code approach to application development. Users can construct fully functional apps with minimal coding using an intuitive, drag-and-drop interface. This low-code environment empowers not only professional developers but also business users, often referred to as "makers," to craft customized applications to meet their specific requirements without enduring lengthy development cycles.

Another distinguishing aspect of Power Apps is its seamless integration with other components of the Power Platform, particularly Dataverse. This integration enables apps to effortlessly store, retrieve, and interact with data, ensuring consistency and reliability in data management. Additionally, Power Apps can connect with an extensive array of external data sources, including SharePoint Online, SQL Server, and various third-party services, leveraging the diverse connectors available within the Power Platform ecosystem.

Power Apps prioritizes mobility, recognizing the growing importance of mobile platforms in modern business operations. By enabling the creation of responsive apps that function seamlessly across devices, including desktops, tablets, and smartphones, Power Apps ensures uninterrupted business processes regardless of the user's device or location. This flexibility promotes efficiency and adaptability within organizations.

b. Overview of Canvas Apps and Model-Driven Apps

Power Apps offers two primary approaches to application development: canvas apps and model-driven apps.

Canvas Apps: These apps provide a blank canvas where users can design applications visually by placing elements like buttons, text boxes, and galleries. Canvas apps are highly customizable, offering flexibility in design and functionality.

Model-Driven Apps: These apps are built on a data model, with the user interface dynamically generated based on the underlying data structure. Model-Driven Apps are particularly beneficial when working with complex data relationships and scenarios.

Understanding the distinction between canvas apps and model-driven apps allows users to choose the most suitable approach based on their specific application requirements.

c. How Power Apps Simplifies App Development for Users with Varying Technical Expertise?

Power Apps democratizes app development by simplifying the process for users with varying technical backgrounds.

No-/Low-Code Development: Power Apps operates on a no-/low-code philosophy, allowing users to create applications through a visual interface. This reduces the reliance on traditional coding, making app development more accessible to individuals with limited programming knowledge.

Templates and Connectors: Power Apps provides templates and connectors that facilitate the integration of data from various sources. Users can leverage prebuilt components and connections, speeding up the development process and reducing the learning curve.

User-Friendly Interface: The platform's user-friendly interface ensures that designing applications is an intuitive experience. Users can drag and drop elements, set properties, and define logic without delving into complex coding syntax.

To get started with Power Apps, users can navigate to https://make.powerapps.com/. Refer home page screenshot in Figure 1-2.

CHAPTER 1   POWER PLATFORM OVERVIEW

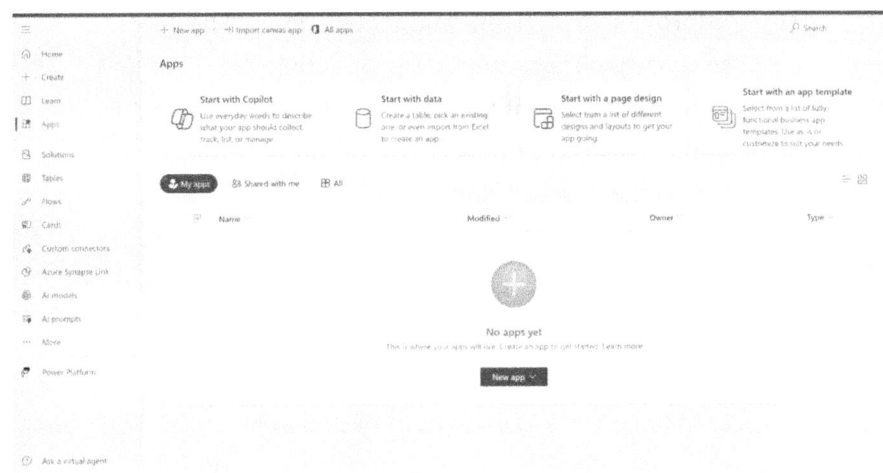

Figure 1-2. *Power Apps maker portal*

In summary, Power Apps introduces users to a new era of application development where creating custom solutions is not confined to traditional developers. The platform's versatility, offering both canvas apps and model-driven apps, coupled with its no-/low-code approach, empowers a diverse range of users to contribute to the development of applications tailored to their specific business needs.

2. Introduction to Power Automate

   a. Understanding the Role of Power Automate in Automating Business Processes

   Power Automate serves as a robust automation platform within the Microsoft Power Platform, designed to streamline and automate business processes. It enables users to create automated workflows that connect various applications and services, eliminating manual tasks and improving overall operational efficiency. The primary goal is to enhance productivity by automating repetitive processes, reducing errors, and ensuring a smoother flow of information across the organization.

Power Automate stands as a crucial component within the Power Platform, designed to streamline workflows and automate tasks across various applications and services. Its core purpose is to drive automation in business processes, thereby enhancing efficiency and reducing manual effort and the risk of errors.

Central to Power Automate is its extensive library of prebuilt connectors, enabling users to establish automated workflows between a wide range of services. Whether within Microsoft's ecosystem, including SharePoint, Dynamics 365, and Microsoft 365, or with third-party applications like Twitter, Dropbox, and Google Workspace, these connectors ensure that Power Automate serves as a central hub for automating workflows, regardless of the diverse technologies employed by a business.

The versatility of Power Automate is evident in its ability to address both simple and complex automation scenarios. Users can rely on templates for straightforward tasks, offering predefined workflows tailored for common use cases. For example, users can quickly configure a flow to save email attachments from Outlook to

CHAPTER 1   POWER PLATFORM OVERVIEW

OneDrive. For more intricate workflows, Power Automate provides advanced logic capabilities such as conditions, loops, and switches, enabling the creation of nuanced automations tailored to specific business needs.

Security and compliance are prioritized within Power Automate due to the potential sensitivity of data involved in automated processes. The platform seamlessly integrates with Microsoft's security infrastructure to ensure secure and compliant data handling throughout its journey. Detailed audit logs are provided, enabling administrators to monitor and review all automation activities effectively.

b. Overview of Connectors and Integrations with Various Applications

Connectors are the bridges that allow Power Automate to seamlessly integrate with a wide array of applications and services. Power Automate supports an extensive library of connectors for popular apps such as Microsoft 365, SharePoint, OneDrive, as well as third-party applications like Salesforce, X (formerly known as Twitter), and more. This enables users to create workflows that span across different platforms, consolidating data and actions into unified, automated processes. The ability to integrate with various applications enhances the adaptability and versatility of Power Automate in addressing diverse business needs.

c. Practical Examples of Workflow Automation Using Power Automate

To illustrate the practical applications of Power Automate, this section provides concrete examples of workflow automation scenarios. These examples showcase how businesses can leverage Power Automate to enhance efficiency and reduce manual intervention. Examples may include

Email Notification Workflow: Demonstrating how Power Automate can be used to automatically send email notifications based on specific triggers or conditions.

Document Approval Process: Illustrating the creation of automated workflows for document approval, where documents move through a predefined approval process without manual intervention.

Data Synchronization Between Applications: Highlighting the ability to synchronize data between different applications, ensuring consistency across platforms.

To get started with Power Automate, users can navigate to https://make.powerautomate.com/, where they can explore the platform, create workflows, and become familiar with its functionalities. Additionally, users are encouraged to explore prebuilt templates available on the platform. These templates serve as valuable learning resources, providing insights into best practices and common use cases. By leveraging prebuilt templates, users can accelerate their understanding of Power Automate and quickly apply automation to their specific business scenarios.

The Power Automate home page screenshot is shown in Figure 1-3.

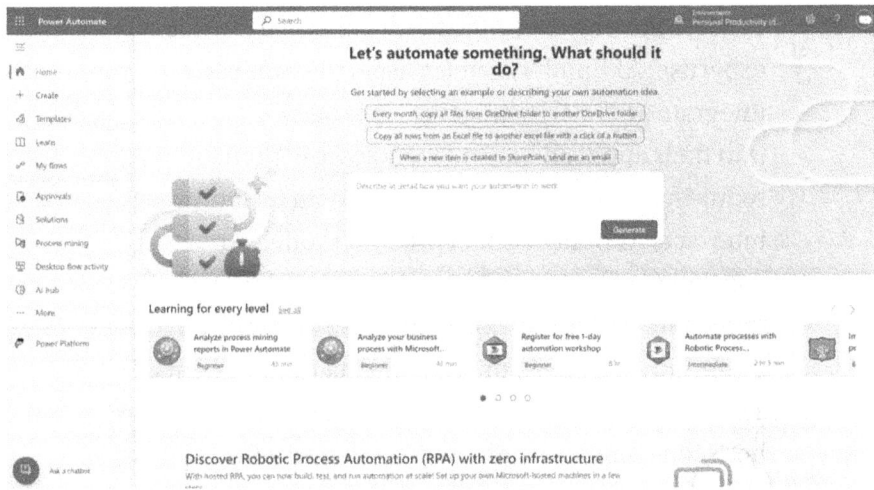

Figure 1-3. *Power Automate*

In conclusion, this segment of the chapter not only provides a comprehensive introduction to Power Automate but also offers practical guidance for users to initiate their journey by exploring the platform and leveraging prebuilt templates for accelerated learning.

3. Introduction to AI Builder

   a. Understanding the Fundamentals of AI Builder

AI Builder, a feature within the Microsoft Power Platform, revolutionizes the integration of artificial intelligence into business processes. With AI Builder, users can effortlessly create and deploy AI models, optimizing processes and gaining valuable insights. This section introduces readers to the fundamental principles of AI Builder, emphasizing its no-code/low-code environment that empowers users to harness the power of AI without extensive technical expertise. AI Builder enables users to seamlessly integrate artificial intelligence capabilities into their applications and workflows without requiring extensive AI knowledge. With its intuitive interface, AI Builder offers prebuilt models for common scenarios such as form processing, object detection, and prediction, while also allowing for customization based on unique data requirements. This tool democratizes AI, bridging the divide between complex AI processes and everyday business applications, empowering organizations to leverage AI-driven insights and automation effortlessly.

b. Exploring the Core Features and Capabilities of AI Builder

AI Builder offers a rich set of features and capabilities, including

Model Types: Users can choose from a diverse set of AI solutions, ranging from prebuilt models suitable for common business scenarios to the creation of custom models tailored to specific needs.

Integration with Power Apps and Power Automate: AI Builder seamlessly integrates with Power Apps and Power Automate, providing an intuitive environment for incorporating AI capabilities into applications and automated workflows.

c. Unveiling Real-World Use Cases Showcasing AI Builder's Impact

To illustrate the practical application of AI Builder, real-world use cases showcase its transformative impact:

> **Automated Document Processing:** AI Builder can automate the extraction of information from documents, enhancing efficiency in data entry processes within Power Automate.
>
> **Customer Sentiment Analysis:** Implementing sentiment analysis in customer feedback using Power Apps, allowing businesses to gain insights into customer satisfaction.
>
> **Image Classification in Retail:** Leveraging AI Builder for image classification in Power Apps, facilitating inventory management and enhancing the customer experience.

d. Integration with Power Apps and Power Automate

AI Builder seamlessly integrates with Power Apps and Power Automate, making the utilization of AI within these platforms straightforward. Here's how you can add intelligence to your business:

Choose an AI Model Type: Select the model type that aligns with your business needs, either opting for prebuilt models for common scenarios or creating custom models as required.

Connect Data: Tailor your AI model by selecting business-specific data, ensuring relevance and accuracy in predictions.

Tailor Your AI Model: Adjust custom models to enhance performance and address specific business requirements.

Train Your AI Model: The automatic training process teaches your AI model how to address business problems based on tailored data, allowing it to generate insights and predictions.

Use Insights from Your AI Model: Apply the results from your AI model across Power Platform to create solutions without coding skills. For instance, automate document processing in Power Automate or predict supplier compliance in a Power Apps application.

The AI Builder home page screenshot is shown in Figure 1-4.

CHAPTER 1 POWER PLATFORM OVERVIEW

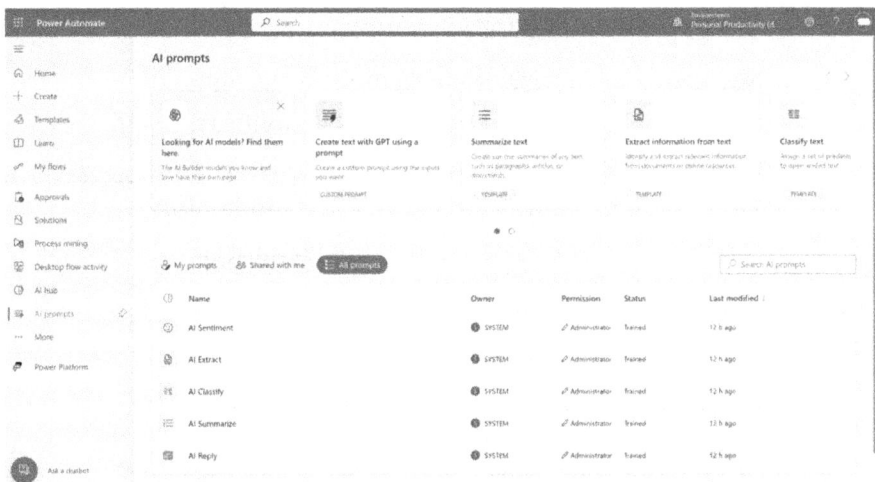

Figure 1-4. *AI hub*

e. Download: AI Builder No-Code AI Cheat Sheet

Enhance your journey into the realm of AI with the AI Builder No-Code AI Cheat Sheet – your go-to resource for demystifying AI model selection within the Power Platform. This cheat sheet, available as a downloadable landscape poster, is crafted for ease of use and informed decision-making.

Guide Download Link: https://aka.ms/ aibuildercheatsheet

About the Cheat Sheet
Practical Guidance

This cheat sheet serves as a practical guide for individuals exploring AI capabilities within the Power Platform. Whether you are a seasoned professional or just beginning your AI journey, this resource is tailored to be your companion in understanding and leveraging AI Builder's potential.

21

Demystifying AI Model Selection

Navigating the intricacies of AI model selection can be challenging. The cheat sheet simplifies this process, breaking down model types and providing clear insights into when to use prebuilt models for common scenarios and when to opt for custom models tailored to specific business needs.

Handy and Accessible

Download and print the AI Builder No-Code AI Cheat Sheet to keep it handy at your workspace. Its landscape format ensures a comprehensive overview, allowing you to make informed decisions on AI model selection without navigating through complex documentation.

Decision-Making Support

As you explore the diverse AI solutions offered by AI Builder, this cheat sheet acts as a quick reference, aiding your decision-making process. It empowers you to choose the right AI model type based on your business requirements, promoting efficiency and accuracy in your AI endeavors.

In summary, AI Builder within the Microsoft Power Platform serves as a gateway for businesses to infuse intelligence into their processes, offering a user-friendly and accessible approach to AI integration for users of varying technical expertise.

CHAPTER 1   POWER PLATFORM OVERVIEW

4. Introduction to Power Pages

    a. Overview of Power Pages for External-Facing Websites

    Power Pages extends the capabilities of the Power Platform beyond internal operations, providing a comprehensive solution for building external-facing websites. This section introduces readers to the concept of Power Pages, emphasizing its role in creating visually appealing and functional websites that cater to external audiences. Power Pages leverages Power Platform's capabilities to deliver a seamless and engaging user experience for visitors accessing content outside the organization. Its user-friendly low-code interface expedites the design, development, and publishing process, catering to both makers and seasoned developers alike.

    Like other components within the Power Platform, Power Pages seamlessly taps into shared business data stored in the Dataverse. This enables creators to fashion a comprehensive array of applications, workflows, intelligent virtual agents, and analytics visualizations that seamlessly integrate with Power Pages.

    Security and governance lie at the heart of Power Pages, offering authors the means to safeguard business data. Leveraging site authentication with various providers, Power Pages grants precise authorization scopes to business data. Moreover, it adheres to modern Transport Layer Security (TLS) standards and operates on the

Azure App Service platform, fortified with an array of compliance accreditations such as ISO, SOC, and PCI DSS described below.

ISO (International Organization for Standardization)

ISO is an independent, nongovernmental international organization that develops and publishes standards to ensure the quality, safety, efficiency, and interoperability of products, services, and systems. The standards cover various industries and sectors, including information security, environmental management, quality management, and more.

- **ISO 9001**: Focuses on quality management systems (QMS) and aims to help organizations ensure that they meet customer and other stakeholder needs within statutory and regulatory requirements related to a product or service.

- **ISO 27001**: Specifies the requirements for establishing, implementing, maintaining, and continuously improving an information security management system (ISMS). It helps organizations manage the security of assets such as financial information, intellectual property, employee details, or information entrusted by third parties.

SOC (System and Organization Controls)

SOC reports are a series of standards designed to help measure how well a given service organization conducts and regulates its information. These reports are provided by certified public accountants (CPAs) and are part of the American Institute of Certified Public Accountants (AICPA) framework.

- **SOC 1**: Focuses on internal controls over financial reporting. It's typically relevant for organizations that handle financial transactions or impact financial statements of their clients.

- **SOC 2**: Concerns the controls at a service organization relevant to security, availability, processing integrity, confidentiality, and privacy. It's crucial for technology and cloud computing organizations that store customer data.

- **SOC 3**: Similar to SOC 2 but provides a less detailed report that can be freely distributed and is intended for a general audience.

PCI DSS (Payment Card Industry Data Security Standard)

PCI DSS is a set of security standards designed to ensure that all companies that accept, process, store, or transmit credit card information maintain a secure environment. It was created to increase controls around cardholder data and reduce credit card fraud.

PCI DSS Requirements: There are 12 primary requirements organized into six categories:

- Build and Maintain a Secure Network and Systems
  - Install and maintain a firewall configuration to protect cardholder data.
  - Do not use vendor-supplied defaults for system passwords and other security parameters.
- Protect Cardholder Data
  - Protect stored cardholder data.
  - Encrypt transmission of cardholder data across open, public networks.
- Maintain a Vulnerability Management Program
  - Protect all systems against malware and regularly update antivirus software or programs.
  - Develop and maintain secure systems and applications.
- Implement Strong Access Control Measures
  - Restrict access to cardholder data by business need to know.
  - Identify and authenticate access to system components.
  - Restrict physical access to cardholder data.
- Regularly Monitor and Test Networks
  - Track and monitor all access to network resources and cardholder data.

- Regularly test security systems and processes.

- Maintain an Information Security Policy

  - Maintain a policy that addresses information security for employees and contractors.

These standards and frameworks are essential for organizations to ensure compliance, protect sensitive information, and maintain customer trust.

For organizations catering to international, high-traffic websites, Power Pages can be configured to leverage content delivery networks, web application firewalls, and edge caching. Integration with Azure Front Door facilitates the provision of global, low-latency business websites, leveraging the Software-as-a-Service (SaaS) model.

Formerly known as Power Apps Portals and Dynamics 365 Portals, Power Pages incorporates the portal features previously available in these platforms. This integration ensures compatibility with tools such as the Power Pages Design Studio, Portals Management App, and the Power Platform Command-Line Interface (CLI).

The Power Pages home page screenshot is shown in Figure 1-5.

CHAPTER 1   POWER PLATFORM OVERVIEW

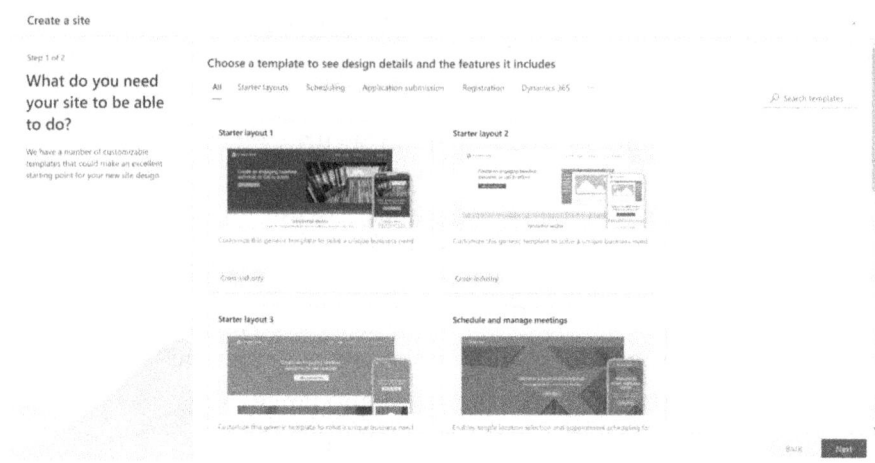

Figure 1-5. *Power Pages: Templates*

More information is available at https://learn.microsoft.com/en-us/power-pages/getting-started/create-manage.

  b. Exploring the Core Features and Capabilities of Power Pages

   This subsection delves into the essential features and capabilities that define Power Pages.

   Create a Power Pages Site

   Makers can easily create Power Pages sites by utilizing the Design Studio, offering a powerful and code-free environment. The design studio encompasses four workspaces:

   Pages Workspace: Create, design, and arrange web pages effortlessly.

   Styling Workspace: Apply styles and themes to your site for an engaging design.

CHAPTER 1   POWER PLATFORM OVERVIEW

Data Workspace: Modify Microsoft Dataverse tables used in data-driven web applications.

SetUp Workspace: Administer and manage your site seamlessly.

The Power Pages create website screenshot is shown in Figure 1-6.

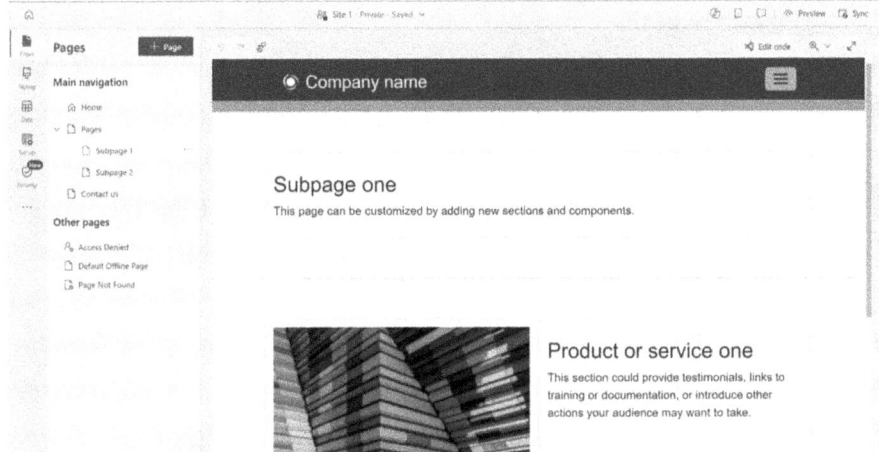

Figure 1-6. *Power Pages: Create site*

Drag-and-Drop Design: Power Pages offers a user-friendly interface with drag-and-drop functionality, allowing users to design web pages intuitively without intricate coding requirements.

Integration with Power Platform Components: Users can seamlessly integrate Power Pages with other Power Platform components, such as Power Apps and Power Automate, to enhance the website's functionality and interactivity.

Responsive Design: Power Pages is designed to be responsive, ensuring a consistent and optimal user experience across various devices, including desktops, tablets, and mobile phones.

Rich Content Elements: Users can incorporate a variety of content elements, including text, images, videos, and forms, to create dynamic and engaging web pages.

Advanced Development Capabilities for Pro Developers: For advanced development, makers can collaborate with pro developers using Visual Studio Code and Microsoft Power Platform CLI. This collaboration allows for the creation of powerful business application websites with extended functionality.

c. Power Pages Security and Governance:

The security and governance aspects of Power Pages are crucial to maintaining control over external-facing content:

Role-Based Access Control (RBAC): Power Pages incorporates RBAC, allowing organizations to control access to different parts of the website based on roles and responsibilities.

Authentication and Authorization: Power Pages supports various authentication methods, including Azure Active Directory, ensuring secure access to web pages for authorized users.

Data Privacy and Compliance: Power Pages adheres to data privacy and compliance standards, ensuring that external-facing content aligns with regulatory requirements and organizational policies.

Version Control: Implementing version control mechanisms ensures that changes to Power Pages are tracked, providing an audit trail and facilitating rollback in case of unintended modifications.

Powerful Security Features: Power Pages offers robust inbuilt security features, enabling organizations to control access securely through authorization rules.

Compliance and Standards: Hosted as Azure App Service, Power Pages complies with ISO, SOC, and PCI DSS standards, ensuring data security and regulatory compliance.

Web Security Measures: Power Pages supports modern TLS crypto standards (TLS 1.2), Azure DDoS protection, dynamic IP restriction, and configuration-driven mechanisms to address top web security vulnerabilities.

In conclusion, this section provides a comprehensive introduction to Power Pages, covering their purpose in external-facing websites, exploring core features for design and functionality, and addressing critical aspects of security and governance. Power Pages empower organizations to extend their digital presence, fostering engagement with external audiences while maintaining control and compliance.

CHAPTER 1   POWER PLATFORM OVERVIEW

5. Introduction to Dataverse

   a. Overview of Microsoft Dataverse

   Microsoft Dataverse serves as a robust and scalable data platform within the Power Platform ecosystem. It provides a unified and secure foundation for storing and managing data used by various applications. Dataverse facilitates seamless integration between Power Platform components, ensuring a consistent and organized approach to data management. Power Platform applications like Power Apps, Power Automate, and Power BI seamlessly utilize Dataverse to store and manage data, forming a crucial part of the unified ecosystem for business application development.

   A key aspect of Dataverse is its capability to store data in a relational manner, enabling the management of complex relationships, hierarchies, and structures essential for sophisticated business applications. Data in Dataverse is organized into tables, akin to tables in other relational databases such as SQL, allowing for multiple columns and relationships with other tables. Additionally, the platform enables the establishment of business rules and logic at the data layer, ensuring adherence to business-specific constraints and conditions during data operations.

   Dataverse also boasts a robust set of security mechanisms to ensure data integrity and protection. This includes fine-grained permissions, role-based access control, and field-level security, thereby restricting access or modification of specific data sets to authorized users only. Integration with Entra further enhances its security capabilities by aligning with a widely recognized identity service.

Dataverse is highly extensible and facilitates integration with other systems. Developers can utilize its APIs to interact with data, enabling the creation of custom applications or integration with external systems. This extensibility is complemented by a comprehensive set of connectors provided by the Power Platform, enabling seamless integration with a plethora of applications and services, ranging from Microsoft products like Dynamics 365, SharePoint Online, and Azure services to third-party solutions.

b. Overview of Tables, Relationships, Plugins, and Connectors

Tables: In Dataverse, data is organized into tables, representing entities that hold specific types of information. Tables act as containers for records, each resembling a single instance of the entity. Users can define tables to suit their business needs, creating a structured data environment.

Relationships: Dataverse supports the establishment of relationships between tables, reflecting real-world associations. This ensures data integrity and allows for the creation of complex data models. Relationship types include one-to-many, many-to-one, and many-to-many, enabling flexibility in data representation.

One-to-Many: One record in a table relates to multiple records in another table (e.g., a single customer has many orders).

Many-to-One: Multiple records in a table relate to a single record in another table (e.g., many orders belong to one customer).

Many-to-Many: Multiple records in a table relate to multiple records in another table, often implemented through a junction table (e.g., students and courses where students can enroll in many courses and courses can have many students).

Plugins: Plugins are custom business logic components that can be integrated into Dataverse to automate processes. They execute in response to predefined events such as record creation, update, or deletion. Plugins enhance the functionality of Dataverse by allowing users to tailor the system to specific business requirements.

Connectors: Dataverse supports a variety of connectors, enabling seamless integration with external systems and data sources. These connectors facilitate data exchange and interoperability, allowing organizations to leverage their existing data investments.

CHAPTER 1 POWER PLATFORM OVERVIEW

c. Dataverse Roles and Security

In this section, we will delve into the intricate web of security measures that Microsoft Power Apps employs to ensure a robust and controlled environment for users. Authentication, licensing, and role-based access form the backbone of Power Apps security, allowing organizations to tailor their app and data access to meet specific needs.

1. **Authentication with Microsoft Entra ID**: Users are authenticated through Microsoft Entra ID (formerly Azure AD), ensuring a secure and standardized process for accessing Power Apps components.

2. **Licensing As the First Control-Gate**: Licensing serves as the primary control-gate, regulating access to Power Apps components. Proper licensing is a prerequisite for users to engage with the platform.

3. **Role-Based Access in Environments**: The ability to create applications and flows is governed by security roles within the context of environments. Environments act as security boundaries, allowing for tailored security measures in each environment.

4. **Application Sharing**: Users' visibility and usage of apps are controlled through the sharing mechanism. Canvas apps are shared directly with users or Microsoft Entra groups, subject to Dataverse security roles. Model-driven apps are shared through Dataverse security roles.

5. **Dataverse Security Roles for Model-Driven Apps**: Security roles within Dataverse are pivotal in controlling access to model-driven apps, providing a structured and role-based approach to application sharing.

6. **Connector Permissions**: Flows and canvas apps utilize connectors, with specific connection credentials determining permissions. Service entitlements associated with connectors play a crucial role in governing these permissions.

7. **Advanced Security Models with Dataverse**: Environments integrated with Dataverse introduce more advanced security models, specifically designed to control access to data and services within the Dataverse database.

8. **System Administrator Role in Dataverse**: To manage security settings effectively, individuals must possess the role of a system administrator in Dataverse. This role grants the necessary privileges to configure and maintain security settings.

Figure 1-7 depicts Dataverse authentication layers

CHAPTER 1　POWER PLATFORM OVERVIEW

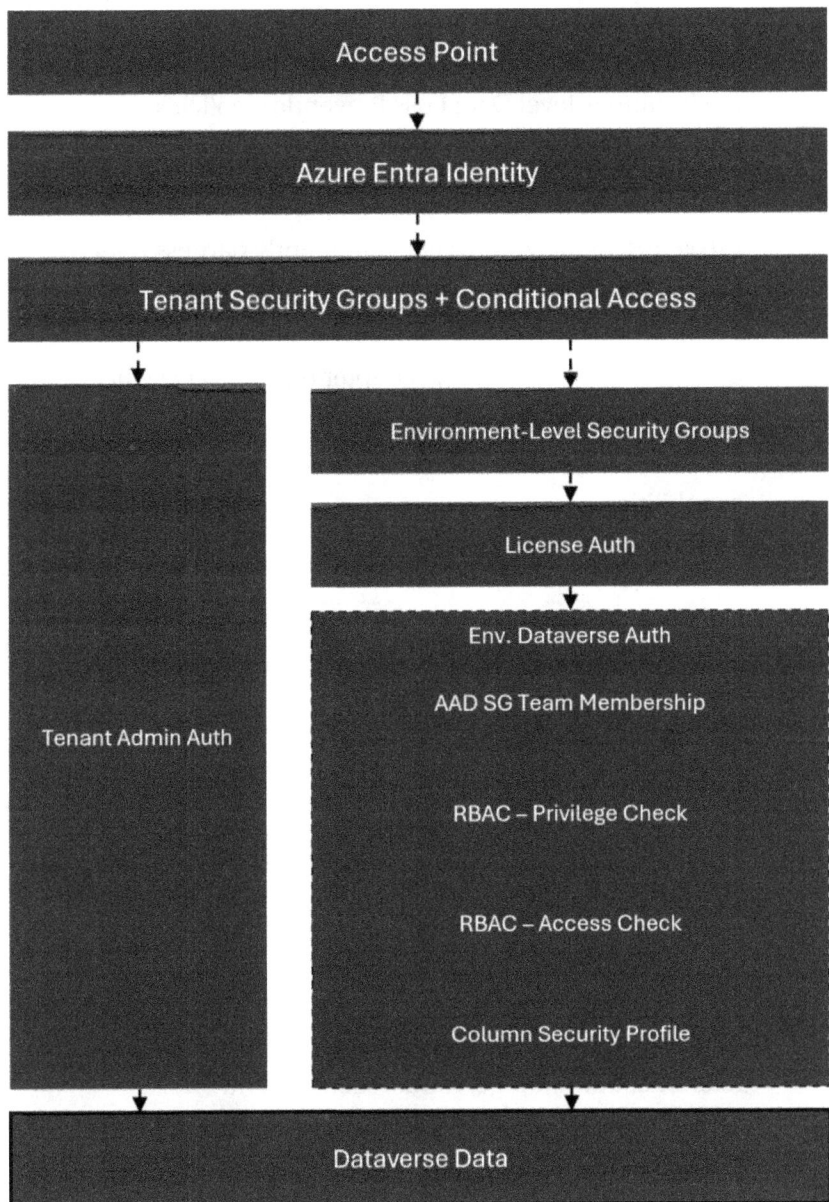

Figure 1-7. *Dataverse authentication*

Security Layers: There are five layers of security, including tenant-level Azure AD Conditional Access, environment-level Data Loss Prevention policies, and resource-level Resource permissions.

By understanding and implementing these security measures, organizations can confidently harness the capabilities of Microsoft Power Apps while maintaining the integrity and confidentiality of their data and applications. The chapter on Dataverse will explain in depth the security layers and roles. Figure 1-8 depicts the Dataverse landscape and capabilities.

Figure 1-8. *Microsoft Dataverse capabilities*

In summary, Dataverse's core features, including relational data storage, robust security, and extensibility, position it as a critical asset within the Power Platform ecosystem.

6. Introduction to CoPilot Studio

Introduction

In a significant leap forward, the capabilities and features of Power Virtual Agents are now seamlessly integrated into Microsoft Copilot Studio. Microsoft Copilot Studio is a low-code tool designed for customizing Microsoft Copilot, offering a comprehensive suite of conversational capabilities, from custom prompts to generative AI plugins and manual topics. It simplifies the process of tailoring Copilot for Microsoft 365 to suit the specific scenarios of your organization.

With Copilot Studio, users can swiftly build, test, and publish standalone Copilots and custom GPTs, all while managing and securing their customizations with precise access controls, data management, user permissions, and analytics tracking.

Leveraging the foundational elements of Power Virtual Agents and other Microsoft Power Platform technologies, Copilot Studio seamlessly integrates with Microsoft Azure OpenAI Studio, Azure Cognitive Services, Azure Bot Service, and other Microsoft conversational AI tools. This ensures compatibility with the needs of both IT professionals and nontechnical makers.

A standout feature of Copilot Studio is its intuitive no-code graphical interface, enabling users of all technical backgrounds to design intricate chatbot flows effortlessly by simply dragging and dropping elements. This empowers subject matter experts to lead chatbot creation, crafting meaningful dialogues that align with the nuances of the business or service provided, without relying on developers for every step.

Integration is another key strength of Copilot Studio, seamlessly connecting with the broader Power Platform ecosystem, particularly Power Automate. This enables chatbots to trigger workflows or actions in other systems, extending their capabilities beyond mere conversation to enhance user interactions and streamline processes.

Copilot Studio offers robust analytics capabilities, empowering organizations to continuously improve their chatbots by analyzing user interactions, identifying frequently asked questions, and addressing areas of user dissatisfaction or drop-off. This iterative refinement process ensures that chatbots perform optimally over time.

Key Features

Generative AI: Microsoft Copilot Studio is powered by advanced generative AI, allowing users to create powerful copilots capable of handling a wide range of requests. From simple answers to complex conversations, Copilot Studio leverages generative AI for intelligent and context-aware interactions.

Integration Across Microsoft Copilot: The integration of Power Virtual Agents' capabilities into Copilot Studio ensures a cohesive and unified experience. Users can transition seamlessly between the familiar features of Power Virtual Agents and the enhanced capabilities of Copilot Studio.

CHAPTER 1   POWER PLATFORM OVERVIEW

Multilingual Support: Copilot Studio enables engagement with customers and employees in multiple languages. Whether it's on websites, mobile apps, Facebook, Microsoft Teams, or any channel supported by the Azure Bot Framework, Copilot Studio ensures a consistent and language-friendly interaction.

Maker-Friendly: Creating copilots with Copilot Studio is designed to be user-friendly and doesn't require the expertise of data scientists or developers. This democratizes the process, allowing a broader range of users to build powerful AI-driven copilots. Figure 1-9 shows a screenshot of Copilot Studio home page.

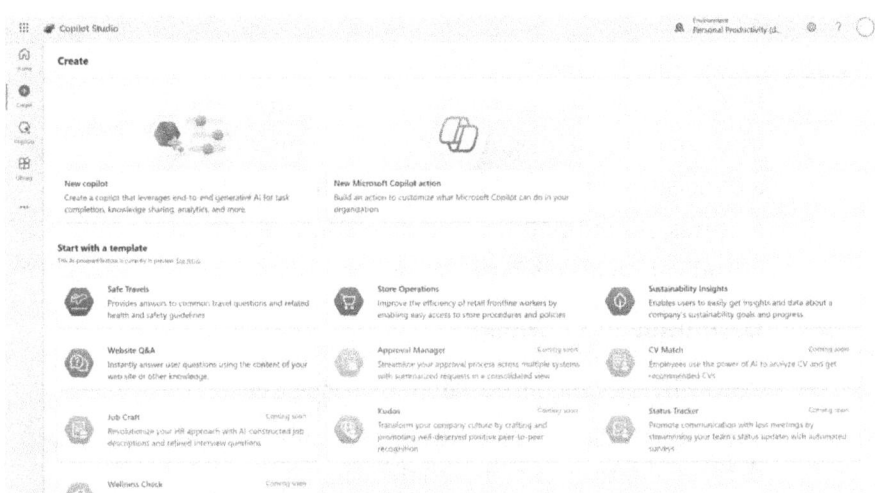

Figure 1-9. *Copilot Studio: Home page*

Conclusion

Microsoft Copilot Studio represents a leap forward in AI conversational capabilities, seamlessly integrating Power Virtual Agents' features. With its ease of use, multilingual support, and versatility in addressing a spectrum of scenarios, Copilot Studio empowers users to create AI-driven copilots that enhance customer and employee engagement across various channels.

The purpose of this book is not to give a lot of details about Power BI, but a brief overview of Power BI could help the readers to understand some features of Power BI.

7. Introduction to Power BI

Power BI, developed by Microsoft, is a powerful business analytics tool that transforms raw data into meaningful insights. This section provides a concise overview of Power BI, outlining its key features, functionalities, and its pivotal role in data visualization and decision-making.

Definition and Purpose

Power BI is a business analytics service that empowers organizations to visualize and analyze data, facilitating data-driven decision-making. It enables users to connect to a wide range of data sources, create interactive reports and dashboards, and share compelling insights across the organization.

Key Features

Data Connectivity: Power BI allows seamless integration with various data sources, including databases, cloud services, and spreadsheets, providing a holistic view of organizational data.

Data Transformation and Modeling: Users can transform raw data into a structured and comprehensible format using Power BI's data modeling capabilities. This includes data cleaning, shaping, and creating relationships between different datasets.

Visualization: One of Power BI's strengths lies in its rich visualization capabilities. Users can create compelling charts, graphs, and interactive dashboards to represent data trends and patterns.

Power Query: Power BI incorporates Power Query, a data connection and transformation tool, enabling users to shape and manipulate data before it enters the report or dashboard.

DAX (Data Analysis Expressions): Power BI employs DAX, a formula language, for creating custom calculations and aggregations, enhancing the depth of data analysis.

Sharing and Collaboration: Power BI allows users to share reports and dashboards with stakeholders, fostering collaboration and ensuring that insights are accessible across the organization.

Mobile Accessibility: The platform offers mobile applications, ensuring that users can access reports and dashboards on-the-go, promoting real-time decision-making.

Use Cases: Power BI finds applications across various industries and business functions. It is utilized for financial reporting, performance tracking, sales analytics, and much more. Organizations leverage Power BI to transform complex data into actionable insights, driving strategic initiatives and improving overall operational efficiency.

Conclusion

As a comprehensive business intelligence tool, Power BI stands at the forefront of modern data analysis. Its intuitive interface, robust features, and integration capabilities make it a vital asset for organizations seeking to harness the full potential of their data for informed decision-making.

8. Power FX Overview

Introduction to Power FX

Power FX is a low-code programming language developed by Microsoft, specifically designed for building business applications within the Power Platform. As a formula language, Power FX simplifies the process of expressing logic, calculations, and data manipulations, making it accessible to a wide range of users, including those with no traditional coding background.

Key Characteristics of Power FX

No-Code/Low-Code Philosophy: Power FX adheres to the no-code/low-code philosophy, empowering users to build applications with minimal reliance on traditional coding practices. This makes it inclusive for business users and citizen developers.

Excel-like Syntax: Power FX adopts a syntax that is reminiscent of Microsoft Excel formulas. This familiarity allows users with spreadsheet experience to transition smoothly into application development.

Declarative Language: Power FX is a declarative language, meaning that users define what they want to achieve rather than specifying step-by-step instructions. This approach simplifies the development process, making it more intuitive.

Integration with Power Platform Services: Power FX seamlessly integrates with other Power Platform services, including Power Apps, Power Automate, and Power Pages. This integration facilitates the creation of end-to-end solutions with data, logic, and AI-driven capabilities.

Expressions and Functions: Power FX includes a wide array of built-in functions and expressions that users can leverage to perform various tasks. These functions cover areas such as data manipulation, filtering, and calculations.

Use Cases of Power FX

Power Apps: Power FX is extensively used in Power Apps for defining logic and behavior within the applications. It allows users to create responsive and dynamic user interfaces by specifying rules and calculations.

Power Automate: Within Power Automate, Power FX can be used to define expressions for conditional logic, data transformations, and other automation tasks. This extends the capabilities of workflow automation.

Benefits of Power FX

User-Friendly: The Excel-like syntax and no-code/low-code approach make Power FX user-friendly, enabling a broader audience to participate in application development.

Rapid Application Development: With Power FX, applications can be developed rapidly due to its simplicity and declarative nature. This accelerates the development life cycle.

Consistency Across Power Platform: Since Power FX is a common language across the Power Platform, users can leverage their knowledge and skills consistently in Power Apps, Power Automate, and Power Virtual Agents.

Accessible to Nondevelopers: By providing a familiar environment for expressing logic and calculations, Power FX opens up application development to users who might not have a traditional programming background.

In conclusion, Power FX plays a crucial role in democratizing app development within the Power Platform. Its user-friendly nature, Excel-like syntax, and seamless integration contribute to making the Power Platform accessible and empowering users to create custom business solutions efficiently.

9. Managed Environments Overview

Introduction

Managed Environments is a comprehensive suite of premium capabilities designed to empower administrators in efficiently managing the Power Platform at scale. This suite provides enhanced control, reduced administrative effort, and deeper insights, offering a seamless experience for administrators across various types of environments. Once enabled, Managed Environments unlocks additional features, contributing to a more robust and streamlined management approach within the Power Platform.

Key Features of Managed Environments

Limit Sharing: Managed Environments introduces the capability to limit sharing, providing administrators with greater control over data access and sharing settings within the Power Platform.

Weekly Usage Insights: Administrators gain access to weekly usage insights, allowing them to monitor and analyze the usage patterns of environments. This feature aids in optimizing resource allocation and identifying potential efficiency improvements.

Data Policies: Managed Environments enables the configuration of data policies, ensuring adherence to data governance standards and regulatory requirements.

Pipelines in Power Platform: This feature allows administrators to manage and execute data pipelines seamlessly within the Power Platform, enhancing data integration and transformation capabilities.

Maker Welcome Content: Managed Environments enhances the onboarding experience by providing the ability to configure welcome content for makers, ensuring a smoother transition into the Power Platform environment.

Solution Checker: Administrators can utilize the Solution Checker to perform comprehensive checks on solutions, ensuring adherence to best practices and minimizing potential issues during deployment.

IP Firewall: Managed Environments introduces IP Firewall capabilities, allowing administrators to control and restrict access based on IP addresses, enhancing security measures.

IP Cookie Binding: This feature enhances security by binding cookies to specific IP addresses, adding an additional layer of authentication for users within Managed Environments.

Customer-Managed Key (CMK): Administrators can leverage Customer-Managed Keys for enhanced control over encryption keys, contributing to heightened security measures.

Lockbox: Managed Environments provides a Lockbox feature for added security, allowing administrators to control and monitor access to sensitive operations.

Extended Backup: Administrators can utilize extended backup capabilities, ensuring comprehensive data protection and recovery options within Managed Environments.

DLP for Desktop Flow: Data Loss Prevention (DLP) measures are extended to include Desktop Flows within Managed Environments, adding an additional layer of protection for sensitive data.

Export Data to Azure Application Insights: Managed Environments allows for seamless integration with Azure Application Insights, enabling administrators to export and analyze data for deeper insights.

Catalog in Power Platform: This feature enhances data cataloging capabilities, making it easier for administrators to organize and manage datasets within the Power Platform.

Default Environment Routing: Administrators can configure default environment routing, streamlining the flow of data and processes within Managed Environments.

Power Platform Advisor: In the dynamic landscape of Power Platform, staying optimized and secure is crucial for seamless operations. Power Platform Advisor, currently in preview, emerges as a personalized guide, offering tailored recommendations to enhance the efficiency, security, and reliability of your Power Platform tenant.

Power Platform Advisor encompasses the following key capabilities:

- **Proactive Recommendations**: Receive proactive, best practice recommendations tailored to your Power Platform tenant, ensuring you stay ahead of potential issues.

- **Overall Health Improvement**: Leverage the insights provided by Power Platform Advisor to enhance the overall health and performance of your Power Platform environment.

- **Inline Actions and Automation**: Take immediate, inline actions based on the recommendations, or automate actions using cloud flows to streamline optimization processes.

Enable or edit Managed Environments in the admin center as follows:

- In the Power Platform admin center (https://aka.ms/ppac), in the left panel, select Environments.

- Select the check mark to the left of an environment.

- On the command bar, select Enable Managed Environments. If the environment is already managed, select Edit Managed Environments.

Figure 1-10 shows a screenshot of how to enable Managed Environments in the Power Platform admin center.

Enable Managed Environments

Increase visibility and control for ContosoOps. Learn more

ⓘ Once enabled, end users will need standalone Power Apps or Power Automate licenses to run apps and flows in this environment (preview).

View licensing details

Limit sharing

Help reduce risk by limiting how widely canvas apps can be shared. Learn more

◉ Don't set limits

○ Exclude sharing with security groups

☐ Limit total individuals who can be shared to   No limit

Usage insights

Get adoption insights, like top apps and flows, in this environment. Learn more

☑ Include insights for this environment in the weekly email digest

☐ Add additional recipients for the weekly email digest

Data policies

Help safeguard your organizational data by limiting the connectors available. Learn more

☐ See active data policies for this environment

[Enable] [Cancel]

Figure 1-10. Enable Managed Environments

CHAPTER 1   POWER PLATFORM OVERVIEW

10. Connectors

Introduction

Data Connectors serve as the bridge between the Power Platform and various external data sources, enabling seamless integration and data exchange. These connectors are instrumental in empowering users to bring data into their Power Platform applications, facilitating the creation of dynamic and robust solutions. With an extensive library of connectors, users can connect to a wide range of data sources, from common business applications to custom APIs, databases, and cloud services. Connectors act as bridges, facilitating seamless data flow across various applications, databases, and services within the Power Platform. Regardless of whether data originates from cloud-based solutions, on-premises systems, or third-party platforms, connectors ensure the platform's data integration capabilities remain versatile and expansive.

A standout characteristic of connectors is their prebuilt functionality. Microsoft offers an extensive array of ready-made connectors for the Power Platform, covering popular services like SharePoint, Dynamics 365, Azure SQL, Salesforce, Google Workspace, and more. These connectors significantly streamline the data integration process, enabling users to establish connections with external systems effortlessly, without delving into complex API intricacies.

In addition to the prebuilt connectors, the Power Platform also offers the ability to create custom connectors. Recognizing that businesses may utilize unique or niche systems not covered by preexisting connectors, the platform provides tools for users to develop their own connectors. This ensures that even proprietary or less common systems can seamlessly integrate with the Power Platform, offering businesses unparalleled flexibility in data integration.

Key Characteristics of Connectors

Diverse Integration: Data Connectors support integration with a wide array of external data sources, allowing users to bring in data from Microsoft 365, Dynamics 365, Azure services, third-party applications, and more.

No-Code/Low-Code Approach: The Power Platform adopts a no-code/low-code philosophy, and Data Connectors align with this approach. Users can seamlessly integrate data without extensive coding, making it accessible to a broad audience.

Prebuilt Connectors: The Power Platform offers a rich library of prebuilt connectors for popular applications and services. These connectors simplify the integration process, enabling users to quickly connect to commonly used data sources.

Custom Connectors: For unique or specialized data sources, users can create custom connectors. This flexibility allows organizations to integrate with proprietary systems, APIs, and other tailored data solutions.

Real-Time and Batch Data Exchange: Data Connectors support both real-time and batch data exchange, catering to different use cases and ensuring the availability of up-to-date information.

Prebuilt Actions and Triggers: Leveraging the power of prebuilt actions and triggers, users can expedite app and workflow development. This feature simplifies the process, enabling even those with limited coding expertise to create sophisticated applications.

Types of Connectors

Standard Connectors: These are prebuilt connectors provided by Microsoft for commonly used applications such as SharePoint, OneDrive, SQL Server, and others.

Premium Connectors: Premium connectors offer advanced functionality and are often associated with premium licensing. Examples include connectors for Salesforce, Adobe Sign, and others.

Custom Connectors: Organizations can create custom connectors using Power Platform's custom connector capability. This allows integration with proprietary systems, databases, or APIs.

Use Cases of Connectors

Data Integration: Data Connectors facilitate the integration of external data into Power Platform applications, enabling a unified view of information.

Workflow Automation: Connectors play a crucial role in workflow automation, allowing users to trigger actions based on data changes in external systems.

Business Intelligence: Power BI utilizes data connectors to pull in data from various sources, enabling users to create insightful visualizations and reports.

Application Development: Power Apps leverage connectors to interact with backend data, making it possible to create custom applications that seamlessly interact with existing data sources.

Process Automation: Power Automate relies on connectors to automate processes by connecting to different applications and services.

Popular Connectors in the Ecosystem

Examples of widely used connectors within the ecosystem include

- **Salesforce**: Streamlining integration with customer relationship management (CRM) data
- **Microsoft 365**: Enabling seamless connectivity with Microsoft's suite of productivity tools
- **X (Formerly Twitter)**: Integrating social media interactions into applications and workflows
- **Dropbox**: Facilitating the incorporation of file-sharing capabilities
- **Google Services**: Connecting with various Google applications and services

CHAPTER 1 POWER PLATFORM OVERVIEW

Enabling Connectivity

Users can easily connect to data sources by selecting the appropriate connector within Power Apps, Power Automate, or Power BI. The platform provides a user-friendly interface for configuring connections, making it accessible to both technical and nontechnical users.

Conclusion

Connectors play a pivotal role in extending the capabilities of the Power Platform, enabling users to integrate, analyze, and act upon data from diverse sources. Whether utilizing prebuilt connectors or creating custom ones, the flexibility and ease of use provided by Data Connectors contribute to Power Platform's effectiveness in creating comprehensive business solutions.

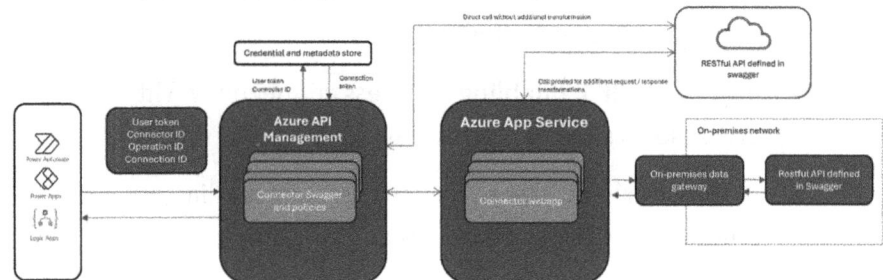

Figure 1-11. Connectors Architecture runtime flow

CHAPTER 2

Power Platform Administration and Governance

Overview

This chapter provides comprehensive coverage of various aspects related to Power Platform administration and governance, including roles and responsibilities, environment strategy, data governance, security best practices, monitoring, auditing, and best practices with relevant tools.

Power Platform Admin Roles and Responsibilities

Understanding the Role of Admin

The role of a Power Platform admin encompasses a broad spectrum of responsibilities, primarily focused on the effective governance and management of the Power Platform environments within an organization.

Understanding the Role of Power Platform Admin Roles and Responsibilities

Daily Management of Environments

The Power Platform admin is primarily responsible for the everyday management of the platform's environments. This involves ensuring that the environments are running smoothly, efficiently, and securely.

Assignment of Environment Admins

It is a best practice to assign at least three environment admins to each environment. This practice helps ensure that there is always someone available who can manage and make decisions for each environment. This is crucial for maintaining operational continuity and security.

Environment Creation and Deletion

The Power Platform admin has the authority to create and delete environments. This power is typically reserved for Global admins and Dynamics 365 service admins as well, marking the significance of the role in terms of its capacity to influence the structure and scale of the platform within the organization.

Monitoring and Compliance

Another critical responsibility of the Power Platform admin is to monitor the environments to ensure they comply with organizational policies and external regulations. This includes managing data security and user access, ensuring that the environments do not deviate from compliance requirements.

Strategic Role

Beyond technical management, the Power Platform admin also plays a strategic role in planning the use of the platform to align with the organization's overall IT strategy. This involves making decisions about the creation of new environments based on needs assessment and strategic direction.

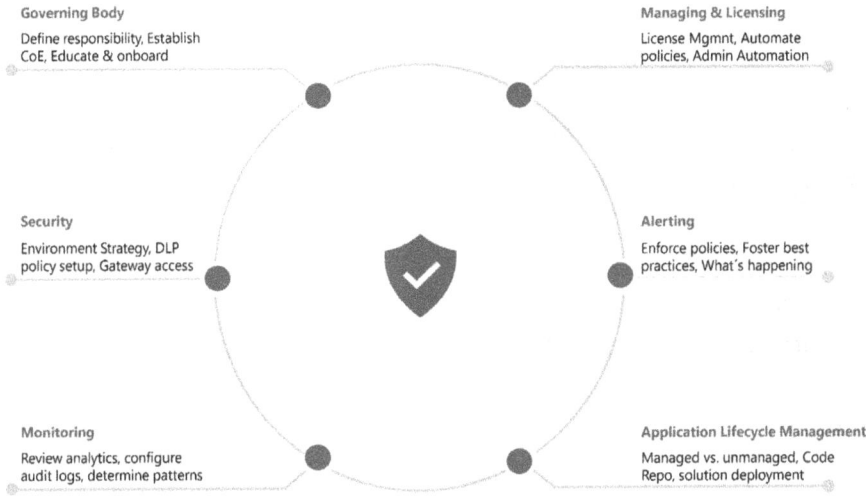

Figure 2-1. *Power Platform areas of governance*

The role of a Power Platform admin, as shown in Figure 2-1, is pivotal in ensuring the effective and efficient use of the Power Platform in alignment with broader organizational goals and compliance requirements. This role demands a combination of technical skills, strategic thinking, and a deep understanding of both the platform and the operating environment of the organization.

CHAPTER 2   POWER PLATFORM ADMINISTRATION AND GOVERNANCE

Various Options to Govern the Platform

- Using the Power Platform admin center: https://aka.ms/ppac
- Enabling Managed Environments
- Using the CoE Starter Kit
- Extending via dedicated tools/scripts/APIs

Difference Between Global Admin and Power Platform Admin

The Microsoft Power Platform allows for governance and administration at various levels through different roles, mainly Global admin and Power Platform admin. Understanding the distinction between these roles is crucial for effective management and security of the Power Platform within an organization.

Global Admin

The Global admin has the highest level of privileges across all administrative roles within the Microsoft cloud services, including Microsoft 365, Dynamics 365, and the Power Platform. This role can access and manage all features in the Microsoft 365 admin center and other admin centers.

Key Responsibilities

User and License Management: Global admins are responsible for adding and removing users, assigning roles across the platform, and managing subscriptions and licenses.

Security and Compliance: They oversee security policies across all services, implementing compliance requirements, guarding against security threats, and managing data governance.

Full Environment Control: Unlike role-specific admins, Global admins can manage settings and policies across all environments within the tenant, regardless of the specific service.

Use Cases

- Implementing company-wide security measures
- Managing comprehensive access control and user permissions
- Overseeing the integration and configuration of all Microsoft cloud services

Power Platform Admin

The Power Platform admin role is specific to the Microsoft Power Platform. It includes administrative access over Power Apps, Power Automate, Power Virtual Agents, and Power BI within the tenant.

Key Responsibilities

Platform-Specific Management: This admin manages the creation, modification, and deletion of environments within the Power Platform and controls who can enter these environments.

Data Policies and DLP: Implements data policies and Data Loss Prevention (DLP) strategies specific to the Power Platform to ensure data is handled securely and in compliance with organizational policies.

Resource Monitoring: Monitors and manages resources used by the Power Platform, ensuring optimal performance and cost-efficiency.

User Training and Support: Often responsible for training users on the Power Platform and providing support for platform-specific issues.

Use Cases

- Setting up new environments for specific departmental needs
- Implementing and monitoring environment strategies
- Conducting training sessions on Power Apps and Power Automate for organizational users

Figure 2-2 describes different types of roles and how Power Platform administrator derives from the Global administrator role.

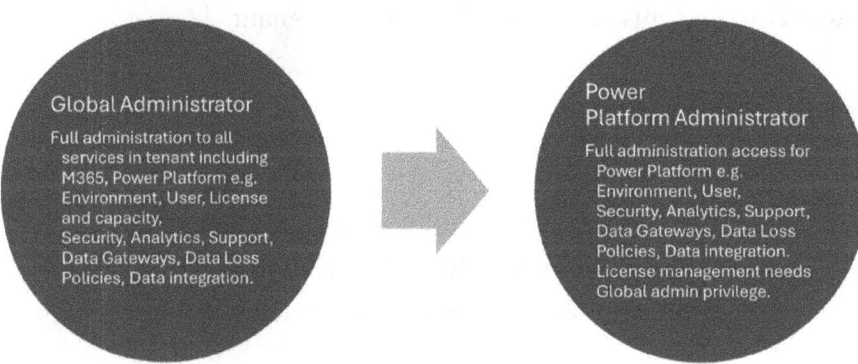

Figure 2-2. *Power Platform roles*

Conclusion

Assigning the correct admin roles in an organization is critical to maintaining operational efficiency, security, and compliance. The distinction between Global admin and Power Platform admin is significant, with each role playing a critical part in the administration of Microsoft's varied services and platforms. Understanding these roles helps ensure that the administration of the organization's IT resources is aligned with its goals and regulatory requirements.

Security Layers in the Power Platform

- **Tenant Level**: Azure Entra seamlessly integrates with the Power Platform, enabling conditional access.
- **Environment Security**: Environments serve as management containers with built-in security roles for permissions control.
- **Resource-Level Permissions**: Administrators can manage user privileges for creating resources like apps, flows, and connectors.
- **Dataverse Security**: Dataverse provides role-based security, allowing for the grouping of privileges and enforcing record- and field-level security.

Tenant Isolation for Data Exfiltration Control

Tenant isolation is indeed crucial for data exfiltration control, particularly in multitenant environments like Azure. By implementing robust isolation mechanisms such as network segmentation, role-based access controls, and encryption, organizations can mitigate the risk of unauthorized access and data breaches across tenants. This helps ensure regulatory compliance and enhances overall security posture.

Adding features like allowing admins to govern cross-tenant access for Azure Active Directory (AAD)-based connections, implementing allow list support for individual tenants in inbound, outbound, or both directions, and providing unique data exfiltration governance capabilities scoped to Power Platform connections can further strengthen data protection measures. These additional capabilities offer finer control over access permissions and enhance the ability to prevent unauthorized data access or exfiltration incidents.

Go to Power platform admin center (https://admin.powerplatform.microsoft.com/) ➤ click "Tenant Isolation." Refer to the screenshot in Figure 2-3 to enable/disable Tenant isolation.

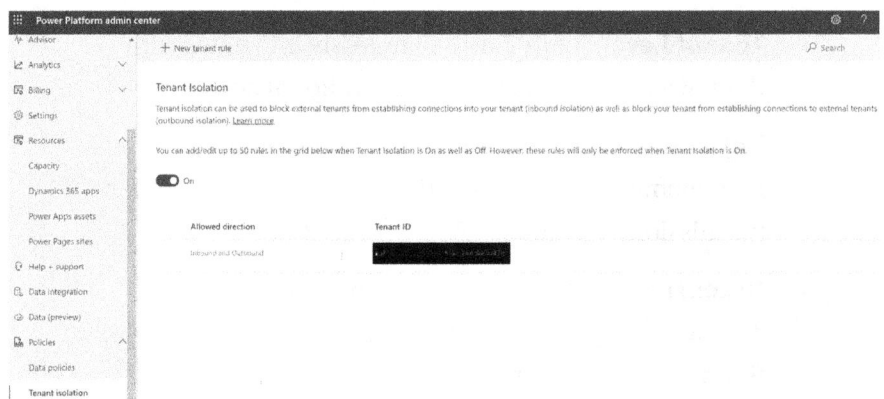

Figure 2-3. *Tenant isolation with inbound and outbound rules*

Environment Strategy

An environment strategy in the Power Platform involves planning and organizing the various environments used for application development, testing, and production deployment. It typically includes the following elements:

Environment Types: Defining different types of environments such as development, testing, sandbox, and production to facilitate the software development lifecycle

Environment Lifecycle Management: Establishing policies and procedures for environment provisioning, cloning, backup, and decommissioning to ensure efficient utilization and minimize risk

Governance and Security: Implementing security measures, role-based access controls, and compliance policies to safeguard data and applications within each environment

Resource Isolation: Ensuring segregation of resources and data between environments to prevent unauthorized access and minimize the impact of issues or failures

Integration and Collaboration: Facilitating collaboration among development teams by enabling seamless integration with version control systems, project management tools, and collaboration platforms

Monitoring and Performance: Implementing monitoring and performance management capabilities to track resource utilization, identify bottlenecks, and optimize environment performance

Cost Management: Optimizing costs associated with environment usage by monitoring resource consumption, implementing cost allocation mechanisms, and leveraging automation for resource optimization

Overall, a well-defined environment strategy helps organizations effectively manage and govern their Power Platform environments to support agile development, ensure security and compliance, and optimize resource utilization and costs.

Explore Types of Environments

In the Power Platform, there are several types of environments designed to support different stages of application development and deployment:

Default Environment

- Open to all makers
- Intended for individual and small team productivity apps
- No Application Lifecycle Management (ALM) features
- Features a restrictive Data Loss Prevention (DLP) policy
- Supports standard connectors

Development Environment

- Used by developers for creating and testing applications
- Where initial development work takes place
- Typically separate from the production environment to prevent unintended disruptions to live applications
- Supports ALM for development

Sandbox Environment

Isolated instances for developers to experiment, configure, test new features, or troubleshoot issues.

- No impact on production or other environments
- Often used for training purposes
- Supports ALM for experimentation and testing

Production Environment

- Meant for hosting live applications accessible to end-users
- Where finalized and thoroughly tested solutions are deployed for everyday use
- Reserved for mission-critical applications
- Accessible by request only
- Requires ALM for deployment and management
- Enforces the most restrictive DLP policy
- Supports premium, standard, and custom connectors

Trial Environment:

Temporary environments provided by Microsoft for exploration and evaluation of the Power Platform.

- Limited capabilities
- Intended for demonstration and learning purposes
- Supports standard connectors

Each type of environment serves a specific purpose in the application life cycle, from initial development and testing to deployment and production use. Proper management and segregation of these environments help ensure efficient development processes and maintain the stability and reliability of applications deployed on the Power Platform.

Best Practices for Developing an Environment Strategy

Developing a robust environment strategy within the Power Platform involves configuring environments and implementing layers of data security to support productive development while ensuring the security and organization of resources. A well-defined strategy for managing environment provisioning, access control, and resource management is crucial to

1. Secure data and access.
2. Properly utilize the default environment.
3. Manage the optimal number of environments to prevent sprawl and conserve capacity.
4. Facilitate application life cycle management (ALM).
5. Organize resources effectively within logical partitions.
6. Assist operations and helpdesk in identifying production apps by housing them in dedicated environments.
7. Ensure data is stored and transmitted in acceptable geographic regions for performance and compliance reasons.
8. Maintain isolation of applications under development.

CHAPTER 2 POWER PLATFORM ADMINISTRATION AND GOVERNANCE

Key facts about environments and security include

- Environments are associated with a specific geographic location configured during creation.
- They can serve different audiences or purposes such as development, testing, and production.
- Data Loss Prevention (DLP) policies can be applied at the environment or tenant level.
- Each tenant has a default environment.
- Nondefault environments can be created by licensed users and offer more control over permissions.
- An environment can have zero or one Microsoft Dataverse instance.
- Predefined security roles in environments align with security best practices.
- Default environment routing is a premium feature allowing automatic redirection of new makers to personal developer environments.

Types of environments to consider include

- Development, testing, and production environments for specific business groups or applications
- Individual-use environments for proof of concepts and training workshops

To develop an effective environment strategy, consider the following steps:

- Assign appropriate admin roles like Microsoft Power Platform service admin or Dynamics 365 service admin.

CHAPTER 2   POWER PLATFORM ADMINISTRATION AND GOVERNANCE

- Restrict the creation of new production environments to admins to maintain control and prevent unnecessary consumption.

- Treat the default environment as a user and team productivity environment, renaming it through the admin center for clarity.

- Establish a process for requesting access to or creation of environments to ensure clear communication and support between developers and admins.

- Implement tenant- and environment-level Data Loss Prevention (DLP) policies to prevent unintentional data exposure and protect information security.

Optimizing Resource Utilization

Monitor and manage environment usage to optimize resource utilization. Identify and resolve resource bottlenecks, optimize costs, and scale resources as needed to support application development and deployment.

Promoting Collaboration and Communication

Encourage collaboration among development teams, stakeholders, and IT operations by providing communication tools, documentation, and knowledge-sharing platforms. Foster collaboration and feedback to drive continuous improvement.

Educating and Training Users

Provide comprehensive training and resources to users, developers, and administrators to ensure understanding of best practices, security guidelines, and governance policies. Cultivate a culture of learning and improvement.

By adhering to these guidelines, organizations can proactively manage their Power Platform environments, fostering efficient development, governance, and deployment practices while safeguarding data and resources.

Managed Environment

Managed Environments represent a suite of premium capabilities empowering administrators to efficiently oversee Power Platform operations at scale, requiring less effort while offering enhanced control and insights. Compatible with any environment type, Managed Environments unlock additional features upon activation and can be configured to tailor specific functionalities.

Key components of Managed Environments include

- Environment groups for streamlined organization.
- Sharing limitations to maintain data security.
- Weekly usage insights for informed decision-making.
- Data policies for comprehensive data management.
- Pipelines in Power Platform for automated workflows.
- Maker welcomes content for user guidance.
- Solution checker for ensuring quality.
- IP Firewall and IP cookie binding for enhanced security.
- Customer Managed Key (CMK) and Lockbox for added data protection.
- Extended backup capabilities for improved data retention.

- Desktop flow Data Loss Prevention (DLP) for heightened security.

- Export data to Azure Application Insights for advanced analytics.

- Catalog in Power Platform for efficient resource discovery.

- Default environment routing for seamless navigation.

- Create an app description with Copilot.

Leverage Managed Environments to streamline operations, enhance security, and gain deeper insights into Power Platform usage.

Managed Environments Capabilities

Admins can enable, disable, and edit Managed Environments in the Power Platform admin center. Admins can also use PowerShell to disable Managed Environments.

- In the Power Platform admin center (https://admin.powerplatform.microsoft.com/), in the left panel, select Environments.

- Select the check mark to the left of an environment.

- On the command bar, select Enable Managed Environments. If the environment is already managed, select Edit Managed Environments.

- Configure the settings, and then select Enable or Save.

Refer Figure 2-4 to configure Managed Environments within the Power Platform admin center.

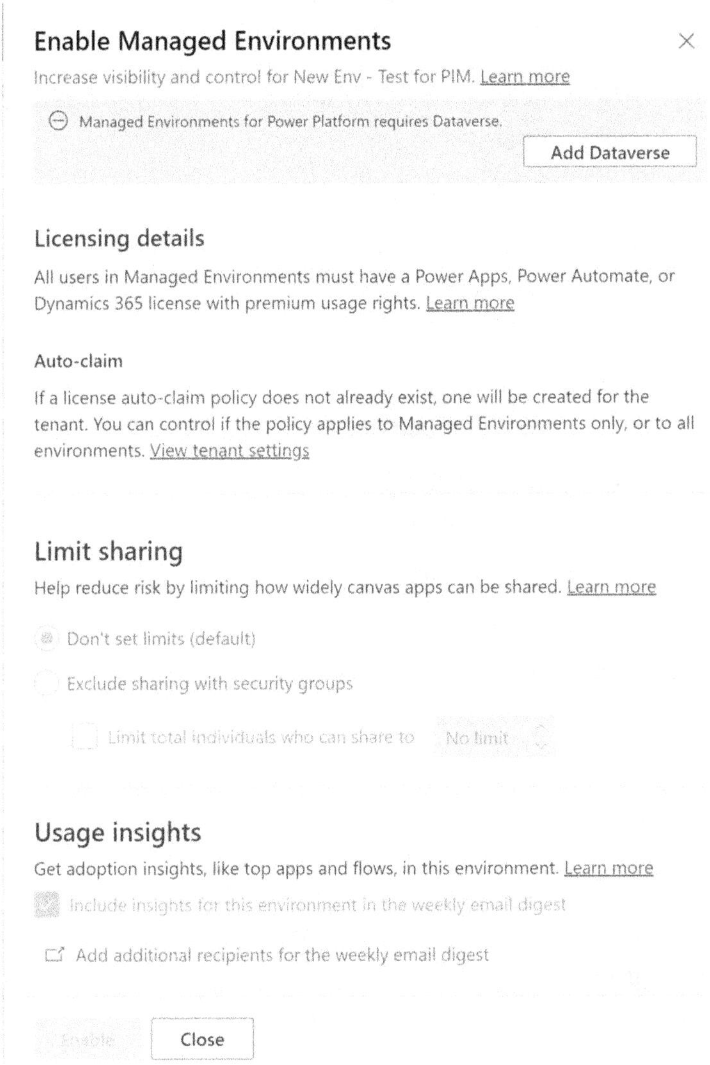

CHAPTER 2   POWER PLATFORM ADMINISTRATION AND GOVERNANCE

Enable Managed Environments

Increase visibility and control for New Env - Test for PIM. Learn more

⊖ Managed Environments for Power Platform requires Dataverse.

Add Dataverse

Licensing details

All users in Managed Environments must have a Power Apps, Power Automate, or Dynamics 365 license with premium usage rights. Learn more

Auto-claim

If a license auto-claim policy does not already exist, one will be created for the tenant. You can control if the policy applies to Managed Environments only, or to all environments. View tenant settings

Limit sharing

Help reduce risk by limiting how widely canvas apps can be shared. Learn more

◉ Don't set limits (default)

○ Exclude sharing with security groups

☐ Limit total individuals who can share to   No limit

Usage insights

Get adoption insights, like top apps and flows, in this environment. Learn more

☐ Include insights for this environment in the weekly email digest

☐ Add additional recipients for the weekly email digest

[Enable]   [Close]

Figure 2-4. *Managed Environments*

CHAPTER 2   POWER PLATFORM ADMINISTRATION AND GOVERNANCE

Setting	Description
Limit sharing	Help reduce risk by limiting how widely canvas apps can be shared.
Don't set limits	Select to not limit sharing of canvas apps.
Exclude sharing with security groups	Select if makers aren't allowed to share canvas apps with any security groups. Admins may share with a limit on who an app can be shared with.
Limit total individuals who can be shared to	Exclude sharing with security groups is selected to limit the number of people that makers can share canvas apps with.
Usage insights	Select to include insights for this environment in the weekly email digest.
Data policies	Help safeguard your organizational data by limiting the connectors available.
See active data policies for this environment	View the policies that define the consumer connectors that specific data can be shared with.

Environment Groups

These act like folders to help administrators organize their environments based on criteria such as business unit, project, or location. Rules can be applied to groups for bulk governance, reducing manual effort and ensuring consistency across environments.

Sharing Limitations

Admins can control how widely canvas apps can be shared within Managed Environments, enhancing data security by restricting sharing permissions.

Weekly Usage Insights

Power Platform provides admins with weekly analytics, offering insights into top apps, impactful makers, and inactive resources, facilitating informed decision-making and resource optimization.

Data Policies

Managed Environments allows admins to easily manage data policies, ensuring uniform data management across the organization and preventing accidental data exposure to unauthorized connectors like social media platforms. Refer Figure 2-5 to configure DLP within the Power Platform admin center.

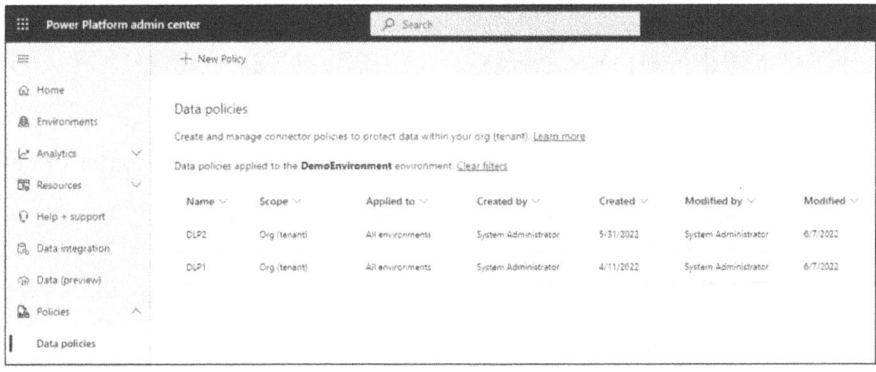

Figure 2-5. Power Platform admin center: Data policies

Pipelines in Power Platform

These aim to democratize application life cycle management (ALM) by bringing automation and continuous integration/continuous delivery (CI/CD) capabilities to Power Platform and Dynamics 365 customers, making ALM more approachable for all users. Refer Figure 2-6 to configure pipelines within the maker portal.

CHAPTER 2   POWER PLATFORM ADMINISTRATION AND GOVERNANCE

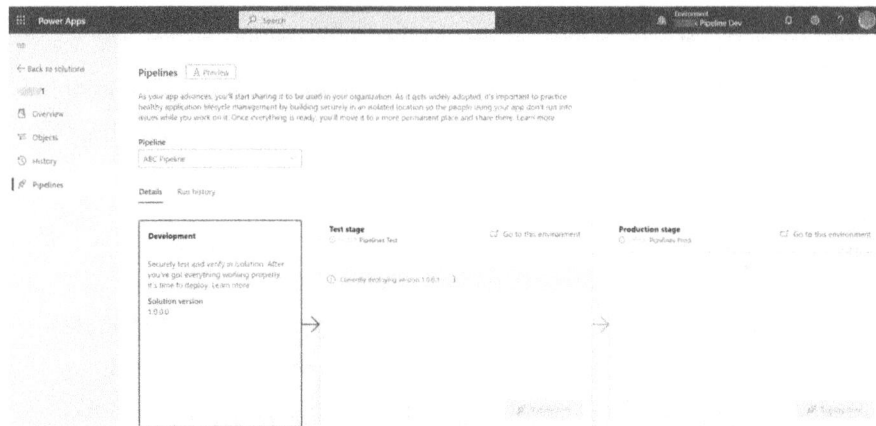

Figure 2-6. *Power Platform Pipelines*

Maker Welcome Content

Admins can provide customized welcome content to help makers get started with Power Apps, replacing the default first-time help experience with personalized guidance upon sign-in.

Solution Checker

Used to enforce static analysis checks on solutions against best practice rules; the solution checker in Managed Environments identifies problematic patterns and ensures solution quality.

IP Firewall and IP Cookie Binding

These features enhance data protection by restricting access to Microsoft Dataverse based on allowed IP locations, preventing unauthorized access in real time.

Lockbox

Lockbox provides additional data protection by limiting access to customer data and providing customers with an interface to review and approve data access requests, ensuring transparency and control over data access.

Customer Managed Key (CMK)

Customer Managed Key (CMK) provides customers with the ability to enhance data privacy and compliance by encrypting their data at-rest within the Power Platform. This encryption ensures that in the event of a data breach or unauthorized access, the stolen data remains protected and unusable without the encryption key.

By default, all customer data stored in Power Platform is encrypted at-rest using strong Microsoft-managed encryption keys. However, CMK allows customers to self-manage the database encryption key associated with their Microsoft Dataverse environment. This gives them control over their data encryption process, including the ability to rotate or swap encryption keys as needed.

Data Loss Prevention (DLP) for Desktop Flows

Power Automate enables the creation and enforcement of policies to classify desktop flow modules and individual module actions as Business, Nonbusiness, or Blocked. This classification prevents makers from combining modules and actions from different categories into a desktop flow or between a cloud flow and the desktop flows it utilizes. By implementing these policies, organizations can control the types of actions performed within desktop flows, ensuring compliance with security and data protection regulations while minimizing the risk of data loss or unauthorized access. Refer Figure 2-7 to configure or edit DLP within the Power Platform admin center.

CHAPTER 2   POWER PLATFORM ADMINISTRATION AND GOVERNANCE

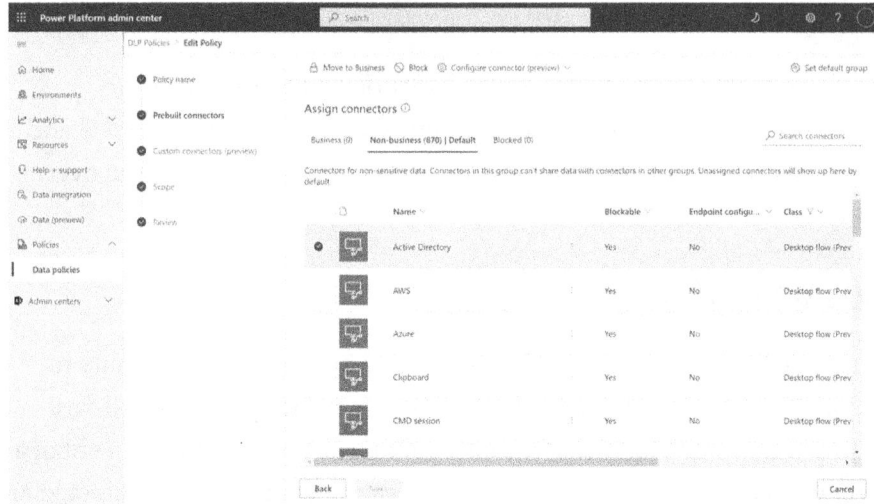

Figure 2-7. *Power platform admin center: DLP*

Catalog in Power Platform

Power Platform's catalog facilitates the easy crowd-sourcing and discovery of templates and code components within an organization, fostering collaboration and innovation among developers and makers. Users can quickly find and install the latest and most authoritative versions of components, enabling them to leverage prebuilt solutions and accelerate development. This centralized repository allows organizations to maximize the value of Power Platform by promoting reuse and collaboration across diverse teams and environments.

In thriving organizations, a fusion team's approach is embraced, where professional developers, makers, and administrators collaborate to maximize the benefits of the Power Platform for all employees. Fusion teams promote the reuse of components and templates.

Components encompass various elements such as

- Custom connectors
- Controls within the Power Apps component framework
- Flows in Power Automate
- Canvas apps
- Model-driven apps

Templates serve as advanced starting points for components, connecting to enterprise systems and resources while utilizing the organization's themes.

Environment Routing

This functionality empowers Power Platform administrators to automatically guide new or existing makers to their personalized developer environments upon visiting make.powerapps.com. Environment routing provides makers with an individual, secure environment within Microsoft Dataverse, ensuring that their apps and data are inaccessible to others. Refer Figure 2-8 to get a high-level understanding on environment routing.

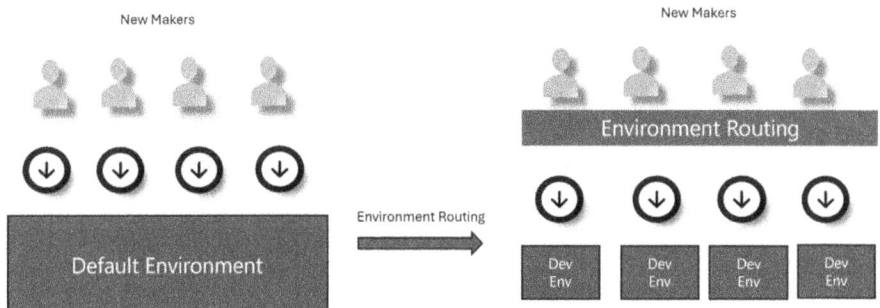

Figure 2-8. Environment routing

When environment routing is activated in the Power Platform admin center, makers are directed to their personal developer environments instead of the default environment. These personal developer environments function as dedicated workspaces akin to OneDrive, facilitating makers to initiate app and solution development securely and efficiently without the need to select a specific environment.

Power Platform Advisor

It serves as your personalized guide, providing tailored recommendations to optimize your Power Platform tenant. By analyzing Managed Environments and the associated apps within your tenant, Advisor offers solutions to bolster security, reliability, and overall health.

Key capabilities of Advisor for administrators include

> **Proactive Recommendations**: Receive proactive guidance and best practice recommendations to enhance the performance and efficiency of your Power Platform tenant.
>
> **Health Improvement**: Implement suggestions from Advisor to improve the overall health and stability of your Power Platform environment, ensuring smooth operation and optimal performance.
>
> **Inline and Automated Actions**: Take immediate actions directly within Advisor or automate tasks using cloud flows, streamlining management processes and ensuring prompt resolution of identified issues.

Refer Figure 2-9 for Power Advisor within the Power Platform admin center.

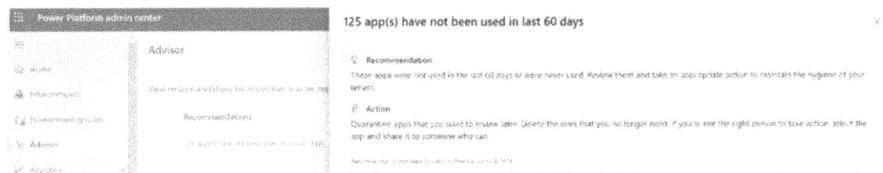

Figure 2-9. *Power platform admin center : Power Advisor*

Security and Data Governance

Security and data governance are paramount in the Power Platform to ensure the protection, integrity, and regulatory compliance of organizational data and applications.

Security in the Power Platform operates across multiple layers, ensuring comprehensive protection for organizational data:

> **Tenant-Level Security**: Security begins at the tenant level, where native integration with Azure Active Directory (AAD) provides built-in support for conditional access to the Power Platform. This integration includes roles for Power Platform-specific service admins and tenant isolation capabilities for authorized connections.
>
> **Environment Security**: Environments, also referred to as management containers, have their own built-in security roles that control access within each environment. All policies and settings can be managed at the environment level, providing granular control over resources and access.

Resource-Level Permissions: Users' privileges to create resources such as apps, flows, custom connectors, and connections can be controlled through resource-level permissions. This ensures that only authorized users can create and manage resources within the Power Platform.

Connection Authentication and Authorization: The Power Platform includes mechanisms for authenticating and authorizing connections in the user context, ensuring that only authenticated users can access data and resources. Additionally, extensive data loss prevention measures are implemented at the connector and content levels, with provisions for gateway security and email exfiltration controls.

Dataverse Security Model: Dataverse offers a robust security model that includes role-based security, allowing administrators to group privileges together and assign them to specific roles. This model supports both record-level and field-level security, ensuring that sensitive data is protected from unauthorized access.

Refer Figure 2-10 to get an understanding of various Dataverse security model layers.

CHAPTER 2   POWER PLATFORM ADMINISTRATION AND GOVERNANCE

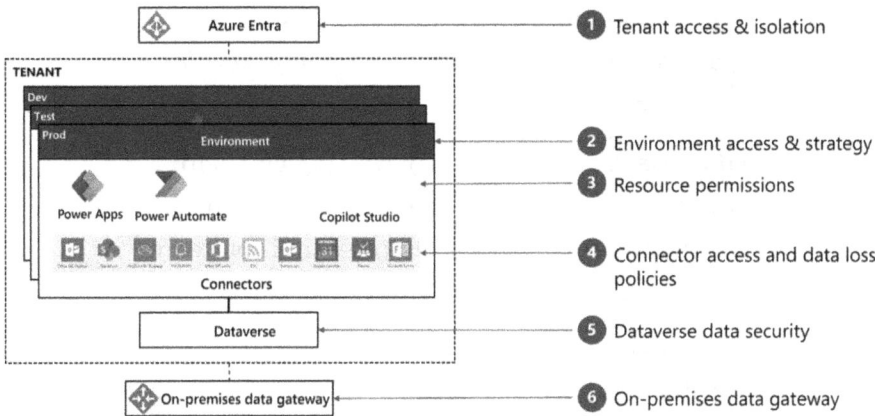

Figure 2-10. Layers of security in Power Platform

By implementing security measures across these layers, organizations can safeguard their data and ensure compliance with regulatory requirements while leveraging the capabilities of the Power Platform for business operations.

Here's an overview of key aspects of security and data governance in the Power Platform:

> **Access Control**: Role-based access control (RBAC) allows administrators to define roles and permissions for users based on their responsibilities and access needs.
>
> Conditional Access policies enable administrators to enforce access controls based on specific conditions such as user location, device compliance, and risk level.
>
> **Data Protection**: Encryption at rest and in transit ensures that data stored in the Power Platform is safeguarded from unauthorized access.

Customer Managed Keys (CMK): These allow organizations to manage their encryption keys for added control over data security.

Data Loss Prevention (DLP): DLP policies help prevent the accidental or unauthorized sharing of sensitive information by monitoring and controlling the flow of data within the Power Platform.

DLP rules can classify data, restrict sharing based on sensitivity labels, and block or monitor actions that may pose a risk to data security.

Compliance and Auditing: Compliance features ensure that the Power Platform adheres to industry regulations and standards such as GDPR, HIPAA, and SOC.

Audit logs track user activity and changes within the Power Platform, providing visibility into who accessed what data and when.

Environment Management: Managed Environments provide a controlled environment for app development and deployment, allowing administrators to enforce governance policies and monitor resource usage.

Environment Lifecycle Management enables administrators to manage the creation, provisioning, and decommissioning of environments to maintain security and compliance.

Integration with Azure Entra: Integration with AAD allows organizations to leverage existing identity management policies and controls, including multifactor authentication (MFA) and conditional access.

Figure 2-11 shows all types of access and data protection options available.

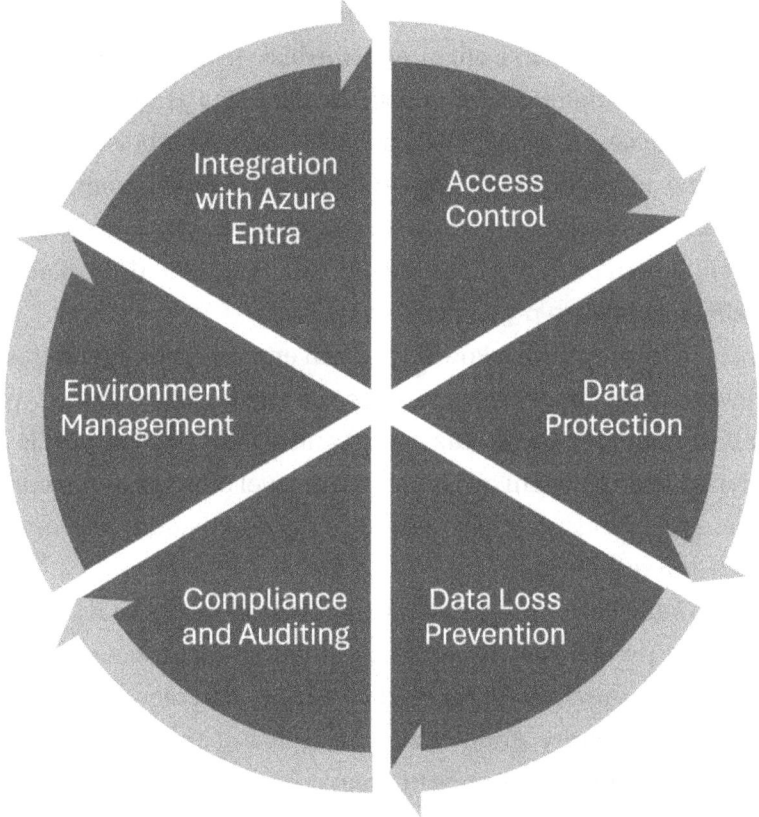

Figure 2-11. *Power Platform access control*

By implementing robust security and data governance practices in the Power Platform, organizations can mitigate risks, protect sensitive information, and ensure compliance with regulatory requirements, ultimately fostering trust and confidence in the platform's capabilities.

Managing Environmental Security

Power Apps and Power Automate prioritize data security by ensuring that users can only access data assets for which they have appropriate permissions. This principle aligns with the least privilege access model, where users are granted access only to the data they genuinely need.

Network Access Control (NAC) policies can further bolster security by regulating access to Power Apps and Power Automate from within the network. By blocking access to specific sites or sign-on pages, organizations can prevent unauthorized connections to these platforms, enhancing overall data protection.

Access control within a Power Platform environment operates across three levels: environment roles, resource permissions (for Power Apps, Power Automate, etc.), and Dataverse security roles (if Dataverse is provisioned within the environment). Each level offers granular control over user access, ensuring that only authorized individuals can interact with data and resources.

When Dataverse is integrated into an environment, Dataverse security roles become pivotal in controlling access within that environment. These roles dictate permissions related to data entities and records, effectively managing data security. Additionally, migration of environment admins and makers ensures consistency in access control policies across the platform.

Environment type	Role	Principal type (Microsoft Entra ID)
Environment without Dataverse	Environment role	User, group, tenant
	Resource permission: Canvas app	User, group, tenant
	Resource permission: Power Automate, Custom Connector, Gateways, Connections	User, group
Environment with Dataverse	Environment role	User
	Resource permission: Canvas app	User, group, tenant
	Resource permission: Power Automate, Custom Connector, Gateways, Connections1	User, group
	Dataverse role (applies to all model-driven apps and components)	User

Overview of Dataverse Security

Microsoft Dataverse, the underlying data platform for Power Platform components, implements a robust security model to ensure that users can effectively perform their tasks while safeguarding data and services. The security model ranges from simple to highly complex, allowing organizations to tailor access controls according to their specific needs.

Here's a high-level overview of how security is implemented in Dataverse:

User Authentication: Users are authenticated using Microsoft Entra ID, ensuring that only authorized individuals can access the platform.

Licensing: Licensing serves as the initial control gate, determining which users have access to Power Apps components based on their licensing agreements.

Security Roles: The ability to create applications and flows is controlled by security roles within the context of environments. These roles define the actions that users can perform within the environment.

App Sharing: Users' access to apps is managed by sharing the application with them. Canvas apps can be shared directly with individual users or Microsoft Entra groups, subject to Dataverse security roles. Model-driven apps are shared via Dataverse security roles.

Environments: Environments serve as security boundaries, allowing organizations to implement different security configurations in each environment based on their specific requirements.

Connectors: Flows and canvas apps utilize connectors, and the permissions granted to users are determined by the specific connection credentials and associated service entitlements when using these connectors.

Dataverse Security Models: Environments with Dataverse integration support advanced security models tailored to control access to data and services within the environment's Dataverse database. These models provide granular control over record- and field-level access, ensuring data security and compliance.

By leveraging these security features, organizations can effectively manage access to data and services within their Power Platform environments, balancing user productivity with data protection and compliance requirements.

Dataverse Security Models

Environments integrated with Dataverse support sophisticated security models designed to manage access to data and services stored within the environment's Dataverse database. These models offer precise control over access at both the record and field levels, enhancing data security and enabling compliance with regulatory requirements.

Dataverse Hierarchy Structure

The Dataverse hierarchy structure consists of several key components:

Organization

- At the root of the hierarchy is the organization, which represents the highest level entity.
- Organizations can be used to isolate users from different organizations, especially in multitenant applications.
- Users can only access records belonging to the same organization as them.

Business Unit

- Under the organization are business units (BUs), which are used to build a security hierarchy.
- Users can only belong to one BU at a time, and privileges can be granted at this level.
- Each organization has at least one default business unit, named similarly to the organization.

Team

- Teams can be created within business units.
- Users can be members of multiple teams, even across business units, with their privileges being cumulative.
- There are three types of teams: Owner, Access, and Azure AD Group.

Users

- Users represent actual end-users, services, or applications.
- They belong to an organization, are part of a business unit, and can be members of teams.

Permissions and Privileges

In Dataverse, access to records is controlled through various privileges, each granting specific permissions:

1. **Create:** Allows the creation of new records

2. **Write**: Permits the modification of existing records

3. **Read**: Enables the viewing of existing records

4. **Delete**: Allows the deletion of existing records

5. **Append**: Permits the establishment of relationships between records at the child level

6. **Append To**: Allows the establishment of relationships between records at the parent level

7. **Assign**: Grants permissions to reassign a record to another user or team

8. **Share**: Allows a user to share a record with an access team

Privileges are assigned at different levels and are associated with specific entities, forming access rights. Dataverse also provides record-level and field-level permissions for granular control.

Security roles are used to group access rights and are assigned to users and teams. These roles must be configured for each custom entity, and access rights can be modified in built-in roles for standard entities as depicted in Figure 2-12. The security area in advanced settings provides access to security-related configurations, including the assignment of access rights to roles for each entity and permission. Each column represents a permission, each line represents an entity, and their intersection represents a privilege.

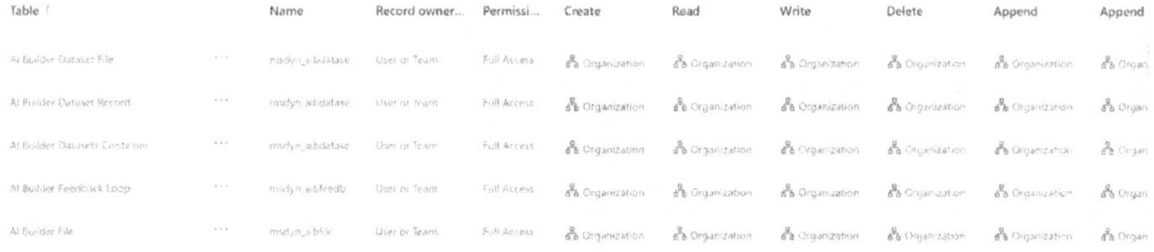

Table		Name	Record owner...	Permissi...	Create	Read	Write	Delete	Append	Append
AI Builder Dataset File	···	msdyn_aibdatase	User or Team	Full Access	Organization	Organization	Organization	Organization	Organization	Organ
AI Builder Dataset Record	···	msdyn_aibdatase	User or Team	Full Access	Organization	Organization	Organization	Organization	Organization	Organ
AI Builder Datasets Container	···	msdyn_aibdatase	User or Team	Full Access	Organization	Organization	Organization	Organization	Organization	Organ
AI Builder Feedback Loop	···	msdyn_aibfeedb	User or Team	Full Access	Organization	Organization	Organization	Organization	Organization	Organ
AI Builder File	···	msdyn_aibfile	User or Team	Full Access	Organization	Organization	Organization	Organization	Organization	Organ

__Figure 2-12.__ Power Platform roles and Privileges

Security Level

In Dataverse, security can be enforced at various levels to control access to records and fields.

Environment-Level Security

Access rights at this level provide permissions to users from one environment on all records of the entity owned by the same organization.

Business Unit-Level Security

Access rights at this level provide permissions to users from one business unit on all records of the entity owned by the same business unit. Additionally, access rights can be extended to records owned by business units located under the user's business unit.

User- and Team-Level Security

This level grants access rights to a user on every record that the user owns or, in the case of team ownership records, on records owned by one of the user's teams.

Record-Level Security

Users granted the Share permission on an entity can share specific records of that entity with the members of an access team, specifying the permissions they will receive on each record.

Field-Level Security

Field-level security is applied using field security profiles. Administrators can add teams or individual users to the profile and control the field permissions.

The role-based access control provided by Dataverse offers flexibility and can accommodate various organizational structures and security requirements, ranging from simple configurations using out-of-the-box roles to complex setups involving business units and teams.

Data Loss Prevention Policy (DLP)

Your organization's data holds significant value, and protecting it is a key responsibility as an administrator. Utilizing Power Apps and Power Automate enables swift development and deployment of essential applications, allowing users to access and act on data in real time. As these applications and automations increasingly integrate with various data sources and services, including external platforms and social networks, there's a heightened risk of unintended data exposure.

To mitigate this risk, you can implement Data Loss Prevention (DLP) policies, which serve as guardrails to prevent inadvertent data leaks. These policies can be tailored at either the environment or tenant level, providing flexibility to establish rules that balance protection and productivity effectively. Tenant-level policies can be applied universally across all environments, specific environments, or exempted environments, as per your requirements. Meanwhile, environment-level policies offer granular control within individual environments.

DLP policies enforce rules governing which connectors can be utilized together, categorizing them as either Business or Nonbusiness. Connectors classified as Business can only be used alongside other Business connectors in an application or flow. Additionally, certain connectors can be entirely blocked from usage by designating them as Blocked, ensuring sensitive data remains secure.

Managing Data Loss Prevention Policies

Data Loss Prevention (DLP) in the Power Platform involves setting up policies to prevent unintentional exposure of sensitive organizational data.

These policies help classify connectors and data sources as **Business**, **Nonbusiness**, or **Blocked**, ensuring that only authorized connections are used within apps and flows.

Here's how to group business, nonbusiness data, and blocked connectors in the context of DLP in the Power Platform.

Business Data

Business data refers to connectors and data sources that are approved for use within the organization and are compliant with data protection policies. These connectors are typically used for accessing organizational data or approved third-party services that meet security standards. Examples of business data sources include internal databases, enterprise applications, and trusted cloud services.

Connectors and data sources classified as Business are grouped together based on their intended use and level of trustworthiness. This grouping ensures that only authorized connectors are used together within apps and flows, minimizing the risk of data leakage.

Nonbusiness Data

Nonbusiness data encompasses connectors and data sources that are not approved for use within the organization or do not meet security and compliance standards. These connectors may pose risks to data security and privacy if used in conjunction with business data sources. Examples of nonbusiness data sources include personal cloud storage accounts, social media platforms, and unapproved third-party applications.

Connectors and data sources classified as nonbusiness are grouped separately from business data sources. These connectors are restricted from being used together with business data sources in apps and flows to prevent unauthorized access or exposure of sensitive information.

Blocked Connectors

Blocked connectors are those that are explicitly prohibited from being used within the organization due to security, compliance, or regulatory reasons. These connectors pose significant risks to data security and should be restricted from accessing organizational data or interacting with other services.

Connectors classified as Blocked are explicitly prohibited from being used within apps and flows in the Power Platform environment. Any attempts to use these connectors will be blocked by the DLP policies, preventing potential data breaches or unauthorized access to sensitive information.

Refer Figure 2-13 to get a high-level understanding of DLP grouping based on data classification.

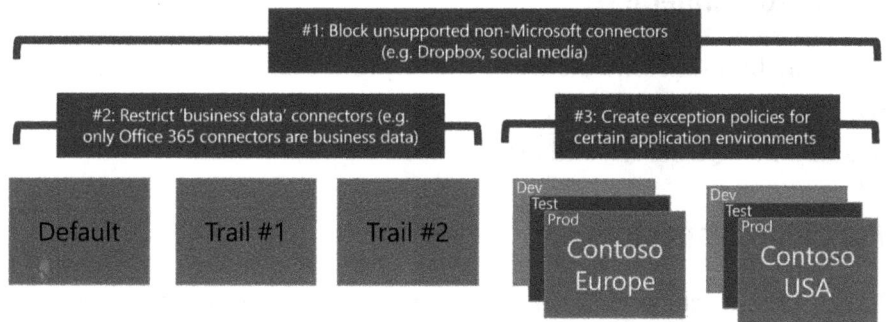

Figure 2-13. DLP grouping based on environment strategy

By grouping connectors and data sources into Business, Nonbusiness, or Blocked categories, organizations can enforce data protection policies effectively, reduce the risk of data loss or exposure, and maintain compliance with regulatory requirements. Additionally, administrators can configure DLP policies to specify which connectors can be used together based on their classification, ensuring secure data interactions within the Power Platform environment.

Overview of Connectors

Connectors in the Power Platform are essential elements that enable users to connect to a wide range of data sources, services, and systems, allowing them to build powerful apps, workflows, and automations. These connectors provide seamless integration between Power Apps, Power Automate, Power BI, and other Microsoft 365 services, as well as third-party applications and services. Here's an overview of connectors in the Power Platform.

Types of Connectors

Standard Connectors

These are built-in connectors provided by Microsoft that offer integration with various Microsoft services such as Office 365, Azure, Dynamics 365, SharePoint, SQL Server, and more.

Premium Connectors

Premium connectors offer integration with additional third-party services and systems beyond what is available with standard connectors. These connectors typically require a premium license to use and provide advanced capabilities for integrating with popular business applications, cloud services, and data sources.

Custom Connectors

Custom connectors allow users to create their own connectors to connect to custom data sources, internal systems, or third-party APIs that are not natively supported by standard or premium connectors. Users can build custom connectors using Power Platform's built-in tools or by leveraging Azure services.

Integration Capabilities

Data Integration: Connectors enable users to seamlessly integrate data from various sources into their Power Platform apps, workflows, and reports. This includes reading and writing data to databases, files, cloud storage, and other data repositories.

Service Integration

Connectors facilitate integration with a wide range of cloud services, APIs, and business applications, allowing users to automate business processes, trigger actions, and interact with external systems.

Event Triggers

Many connectors support event-based triggers, allowing users to automate workflows and processes based on events such as new emails, file uploads, data changes, or system alerts.

Authentication

Connectors support various authentication methods, including OAuth, API keys, and username/password authentication, ensuring secure access to data and services.

Connector Gallery

The Connector Gallery provides a comprehensive list of connectors available for use within the Power Platform ecosystem. Users can browse and search for connectors based on categories, popularity, or specific services.

The gallery includes connectors for Microsoft services, popular third-party applications, cloud services, social media platforms, databases, file storage services, and more.

Users can explore connector documentation, learn about connector capabilities, and install connectors directly from the gallery to start building apps and workflows.

Administration and Governance

Administrators can manage connectors and control access to external data sources through governance policies and Data Loss Prevention (DLP) rules.

Governance capabilities include monitoring connector usage, enforcing compliance with organizational policies, restricting access to sensitive data sources, and managing permissions for connector usage.

In summary, connectors in the Power Platform play a critical role in enabling users to integrate data, automate processes, and build applications that leverage a wide range of services and systems, both within the Microsoft ecosystem and across third-party platforms. With an extensive library of connectors and flexible integration capabilities, users can create sophisticated solutions to meet their business needs and drive digital transformation within their organizations.

CHAPTER 2   POWER PLATFORM ADMINISTRATION AND GOVERNANCE

Connector Action Control in DLP

You can utilize connector action control to manage individual actions within a specific connector. Refer Figure 2-14 to configure connectors in DLP within the Power Platform admin center.

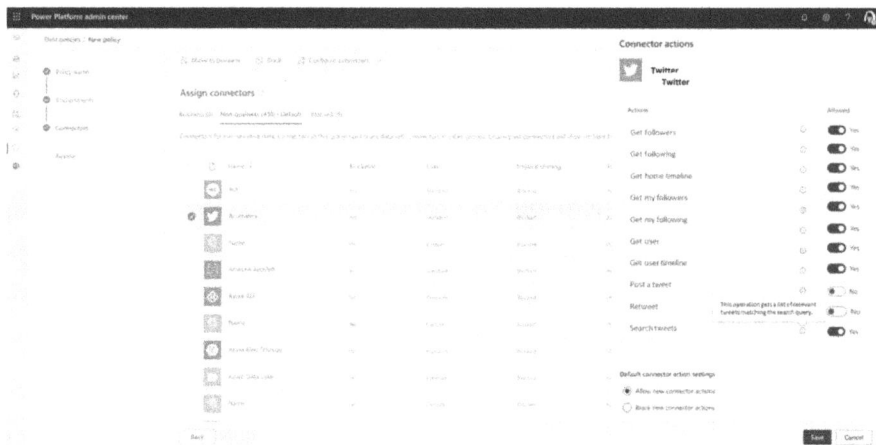

Figure 2-14. *Connector action-level DLP*

Here's how to do it:

1. Sign in to the Power Platform admin center as a system administrator.

2. Navigate to Policies ➤ Data policies in the left navigation pane.

3. Choose a policy and click "Edit Policy" in the command bar.

4. On the left side, select Prebuilt connectors.

5. Find your connector and click "More actions" next to it.

6. Then, select Configure connector ➤ Connector actions.

99

Connector Endpoint Filtering

Connector endpoint filtering enables administrators to control the specific endpoints that makers can connect to while building apps, flows, or chatbots. This feature is configured within a Data Loss Prevention (DLP) policy and is limited to six connectors. Refer Figure 2-15 that depicts how to configure endpoint filtering in DLP within the Power Platform admin center.

- HTTP
- HTTP with Microsoft Entra ID (AD)
- HTTP Webhook
- SQL Server (including access to Azure Synapse data warehouse via SQL Server Connector)
- Azure Blob Storage
- SMTP (SMTP stands for Simple Mail Transfer Protocol. It is a protocol used for sending email messages between servers.)

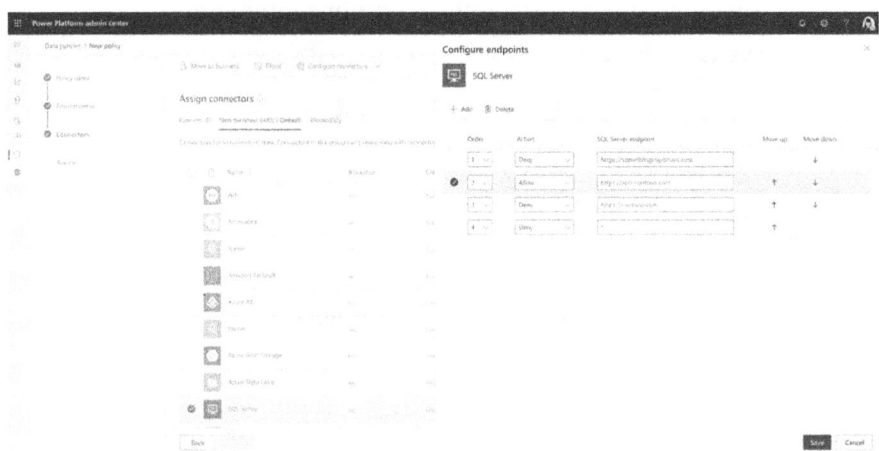

Figure 2-15. Connector endpoint filtering

When a maker attempts to connect their application, flow, or chatbot to a blocked endpoint, they will encounter a DLP error message.

Analytics and Auditing

Analytics for environment administrators are accessible through the Microsoft Power Platform admin center. These admin reports offer insights into usage, errors, and service performance at the environment level, enabling effective governance and change management services for users. It's important to note that these reports are specifically available for canvas apps and are not accessible for model-driven apps.

Admin insights in the Power Platform encompass various types of reports that provide valuable information for administrators:

> **Usage Reports**: These reports offer insights into the usage patterns of applications, including metrics such as active users, sessions, and usage trends over time.
>
> **Error Reports**: Error reports highlight any issues or errors encountered within applications, helping administrators identify and troubleshoot problems efficiently.
>
> **Service Performance Reports**: These reports provide visibility into the performance of the Power Platform services, including response times, latency, and availability metrics.
>
> **Capacity Reports**: Capacity reports offer details about resource utilization, including storage usage, API calls, and other resource consumption metrics.

CHAPTER 2   POWER PLATFORM ADMINISTRATION AND GOVERNANCE

User Reports: User reports provide information about user activity, such as logins, actions performed, and access privileges granted.

Location Reports: Location reports offer insights into the geographic distribution of users and their activity, helping administrators understand regional usage patterns.

Custom Reports: Administrators can create custom reports using Power BI to tailor insights into specific requirements and business needs.

Refer Figure 2-16 to learn about various reports within the Power Platform admin center.

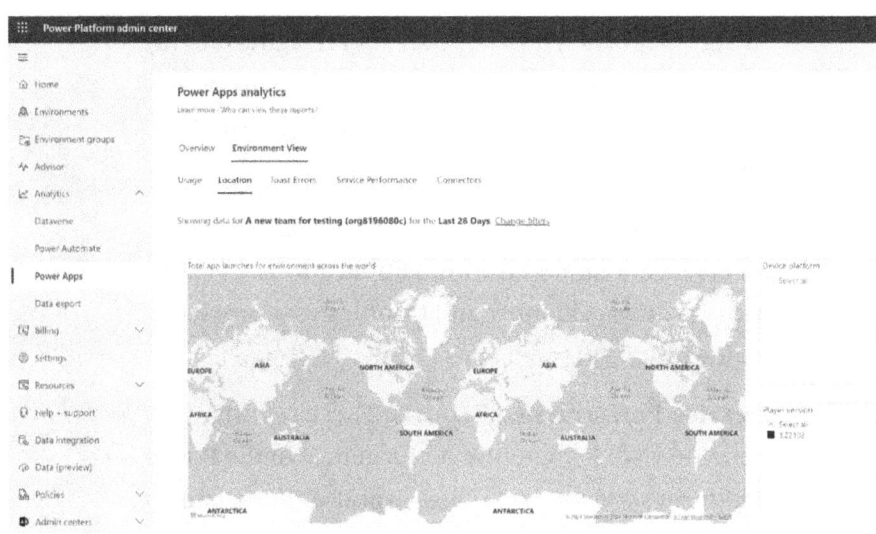

Figure 2-16. *Power Apps analytics*

Tenant-Level Analytics

The Power Platform offers administrators a comprehensive view of telemetry data across all environments and extensions within the tenant. Here's an overview of how it works:

> **Data Collection**: Power Platform resources periodically generate telemetry data for various operations and user activities. This data is collected and aggregated at the tenant level.
>
> **Aggregation Process**: Once enabled, tenant-level analytics aggregates data from all environments across different regions within the tenant. This aggregated data is then copied into the default environment region for tenant-level reporting.
>
> **Admin Consent**: To enable tenant-level analytics, a one-time operation is required to grant consent for data aggregation. This operation must be performed by an administrator with a tenant-level administrative role.
>
> **Accessing Reports**: After enabling tenant-level analytics, administrators can access the reports in the Power Platform admin center under Analytics ➤ Power Apps or Analytics ➤ Power Automate. Tenant-level reports are available in the Overview tab, while environment-level reports can be accessed in the Environment View tab.
>
> **Report Access**: The ability to view these reports is granted to administrators with specific roles and licenses: Refer Figure 2-17 to configure tenant-level analytics within the Power Platform admin center.

CHAPTER 2   POWER PLATFORM ADMINISTRATION AND GOVERNANCE

- **Environment Admin**: Can view reports for the environments where they have contributor or environment admin roles

- **Power Platform Admin**: Can view reports for all environments within the tenant

- **Dynamics 365 Admin**: Can view reports for all environments

Microsoft 365 Global Admin: Can view reports for all environments

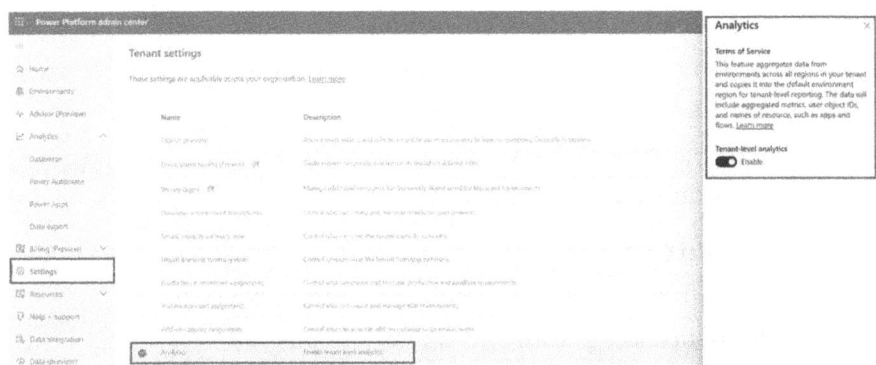

Figure 2-17. Power Platform admin center: Tenant-level analytics

These types of reports collectively enable administrators to monitor, analyze, and optimize the usage and performance of applications within the Power Platform environment.

In addition to these, Power Platform also offers Admin Analytics, providing insights at both environment and tenant levels. Here are some key points about Admin Analytics:

> **Access**: Admin Analytics can be accessed from the Power Platform admin center, providing administrators with visibility into usage, errors, and service performance.

Scope: Analytics is available at both the environment and tenant levels, allowing administrators to monitor specific environments or gain insights across the entire tenant.

Users: Access to Admin Analytics is granted to environment admins, Power Platform service admins, Dynamics 365 admins, and Global admins within the organization.

Data Retention: Data collected for Admin Analytics is stored for a period of 28 days, providing administrators with historical insights into usage patterns and trends.

Data Refresh: Analytics data is refreshed daily, ensuring that administrators have access to the most up-to-date information about environment and tenant-level activities.

Export Capability: Admin Analytics also offers the option to export data to Azure Data Lake, allowing administrators to perform further analysis or integrate with other data sources for advanced reporting and insights.

Analyze Telemetry with Application Insights

To set up data export from the Power Platform to Application Insights for monitoring and analytics purposes, follow these steps:

- **Ensure Permissions**: Make sure you have contributor, writer, or admin rights in the Application Insights environment where you want to export the data.

- **Unique Application Insights Environment**: Each Application Insights environment must be unique for an environment or tenant to ensure proper functioning of out-of-the-box reports.

- **Navigate to Data Export**: In the Power Platform admin center, go to the Data export section in the navigation pane.

- **Create Export Package**: Select the App Insights tab and click "New data export." Provide a friendly name for the export package and select the specific data type you want to export, such as Dataverse diagnostics and performance or Power Automate.

- **Select Data Source**: Choose the environment from which you want to export the data and specify any filters based on the environment type. Click "Next" to proceed.

- **Configure Destination**: Choose the Azure subscription, resource group, and Application Insights environment where you want to export the data. Ensure you have the necessary permissions for the Application Insights environment. Click "Next" to continue.

- **Review and Confirm**: Review the details of the new export package, including the data type, source environment, and destination. Once you're satisfied, click "Create" to set up the data export connection.

Once created, the data export connection will be established as demonstrated in Figure 2-18, and data will start being exported to your Application Insights environment within the next 24 hours.

CHAPTER 2 POWER PLATFORM ADMINISTRATION AND GOVERNANCE

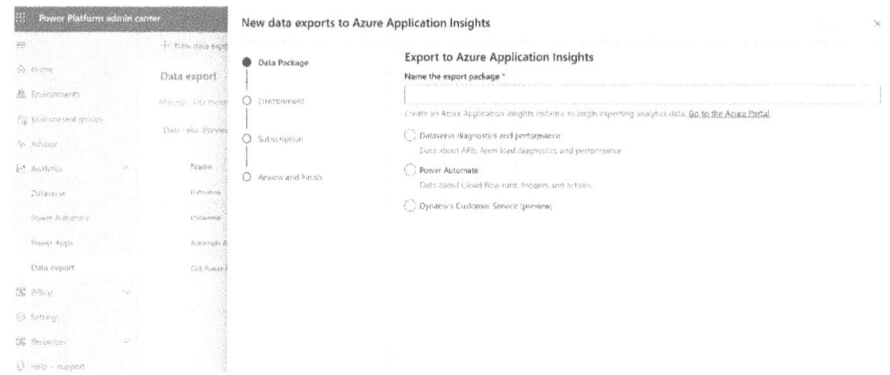

***Figure 2-18.** Power Platform admin center: Data export to Application Insights*

To delete an export package, follow these steps:

1. **Navigate to Data Export**: In the Power Platform admin center, go to the Data export section in the navigation pane.

2. **Select Export Package**: Switch to the App Insights tab and choose the export package you want to delete.

3. **Delete**: Click "Delete export" and confirm the deletion. You can set up a new connection at any time if you decide to restart the data export.

By following these steps, you can set up data export from the Power Platform to Application Insights and manage the export packages as needed for your monitoring and analytics requirements.

Data Export to Data Lake

With the Power Platform admin center, you can now export Power Platform inventory and usage data directly into Azure Data Lake Storage, providing flexibility for your organization's business needs.

Here's an overview of the key points to consider:

- **Data Retention Policies**: Exporting data into your organization's Azure Data Lake Storage allows you to store data according to your data retention policies, ensuring compliance and governance requirements are met.

- **Custom Reports with Power BI**: Having the data in your own data lake enables you to create custom reports using Power BI. You can generate reports at various levels, including business unit, tenant, and environment, providing insights into app usage and performance.

- **Integration with Azure Services**: Azure Data Lake Storage seamlessly integrates with other Azure services such as Azure Synapse Analytics, Power BI, and Azure Data Factory, providing a comprehensive cloud platform for handling large-scale data and advanced analytics.

- **Cost-Effective Solution**: Data Lake Storage is designed for cloud scale and performance, offering a cost-effective solution for running big data workloads. It allows your organization to analyze all its data in a single place without artificial constraints.

- **Licensing Requirements**: To enable data export, customers must have a paid, premium Microsoft Dataverse license for the tenant. Additional licensing requirements are outlined in the admin documentation and general availability release plans.

- **Capacity Requirements**: Minimum Dataverse capacity requirements for accessing data export features will be announced in advance of general availability, ensuring customers have the necessary resources to utilize the feature effectively.

Refer Figure 2-19 to configure tenant-level Data Export within the Power Platform admin center.

Figure 2-19. Power Platform admin center: Data export to Azure Data Lake

By leveraging the data export feature to Azure Data Lake Storage, organizations can gain valuable insights from Power Platform data while maintaining control over data retention and compliance.

Overview of Auditing

Auditing in the Power Platform provides organizations with a robust mechanism to track user activities, system events, and changes made within their environments. Here's an overview of auditing in the Power Platform:

> **Purpose**: The primary purpose of auditing is to maintain transparency, accountability, and compliance within the organization. It helps organizations understand who did what, when, and where within their Power Platform environments.

Audited Events: Auditing covers a wide range of events, including user logins, data access, record modifications, creation and deletion of resources (such as apps, flows, and connectors), security role changes, and administrative actions.

Types of Auditing: Auditing in the Power Platform consists of two main types:

Platform-Level Auditing

This type of auditing captures events related to the administration and management of the Power Platform itself, such as environment provisioning, user management, and licensing changes.

Data-Level Auditing

Data-level auditing focuses on tracking user interactions with data, including record changes, data access, and sharing activities.

Audit Logs

Audited events are recorded in audit logs, which can be accessed and analyzed by administrators through the Power Platform admin center. The audit logs provide detailed information about each audited event, including the user responsible, the action performed, the timestamp, and relevant details about the affected resources.

Retention Policies

Organizations can configure retention policies to determine how long audit logs are retained. This allows organizations to comply with regulatory requirements and internal policies regarding data retention.

Integration with Compliance Solutions

Audit logs from the Power Platform can be integrated with external compliance solutions and SIEM (Security Information and Event Management) systems for centralized monitoring, analysis, and reporting.

Granular Control

Administrators have granular control over auditing settings, allowing them to enable or disable auditing for specific environments and customize audit log retention policies based on organizational requirements.

Figure 2-20 demonstrates configuring audit for any environment within the Power Platform admin center.

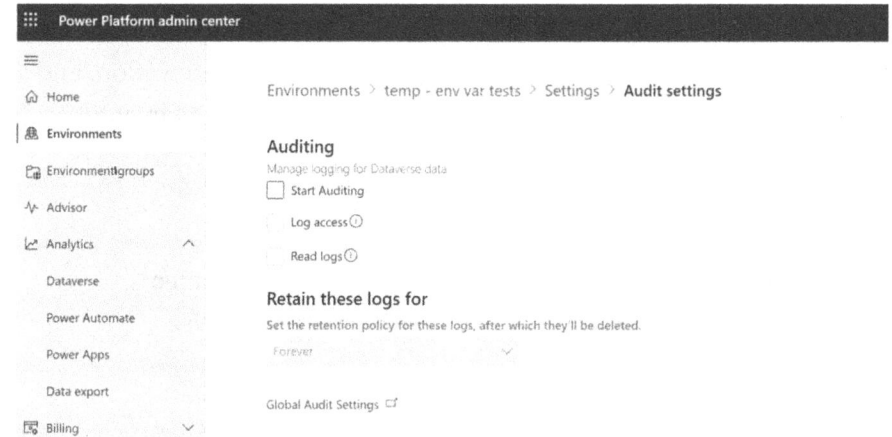

Figure 2-20. *Power platform admin center: Auditing*

Overall, auditing in the Power Platform plays a critical role in ensuring transparency, security, and compliance, empowering organizations to effectively manage their digital transformation initiatives while safeguarding their data and resources.

Best Practices and Tools

Implementing best practices and utilizing tools like COE (Center of Excellence) Kit, PowerShell scripts, and managed environments are essential for effectively managing and governing the Power Platform. Here's an overview of each.

Center of Excellence (COE) Kit

The Microsoft Power Platform CoE Starter Kit is a comprehensive collection of components and tools specifically designed to assist organizations in kick-starting their journey toward adopting and supporting the Microsoft Power Platform. With a primary focus on Power Apps, Power Automate, and Microsoft Copilot Studio, the CoE Starter Kit offers valuable resources to streamline processes, drive innovation, and maximize the potential of the Power Platform within the organization.

Key Components

> **Overview**: Define the goals and expected outcomes of your CoE to align with organizational objectives and drive success.
>
> **Admin**: Gain insights into your Microsoft Power Platform adoption by leveraging administrative tools and analytics to monitor progress and performance.
>
> **Govern**: Establish audit and compliance processes to ensure adherence to regulatory requirements and organizational standards.

Nurture: Accelerate adoption by fostering a vibrant community of makers, sharing best practices, and providing support and resources for continued learning and growth.

How to Use

Each component within the CoE Starter Kit offers a set-up guide to help organizations implement the tools and processes effectively.

Utilize the resources provided in each section to drive adoption, governance, and community engagement within your organization.

Dive deeper into each aspect of the CoE Starter Kit to explore additional features, best practices, and implementation strategies tailored to your organization's needs.

The most recently updated assets and resources related to the Microsoft Power Platform CoE Starter Kit can be accessed and downloaded from the official GitHub repository. `https://aka.ms/CoEStarterKitRepo`

PowerShell Scripts

PowerShell scripts automate administrative tasks and provide advanced capabilities for managing Power Platform environments, resources, and configurations.

Some common use cases are as follows:

Environment Provisioning: Automate the creation and configuration of Power Platform environments.

User Management: Automate user provisioning, role assignments, and license management.

Resource Monitoring: Retrieve usage metrics, audit logs, and health status information for monitoring and analysis.

Benefits: Increases efficiency, reduces manual errors, enables scalability, and supports custom automation workflows tailored to organizational requirements.

Managed Environments

Managed Environments offer premium capabilities for centralized management and control of the Power Platform at scale. They provide enhanced security, insights, and automation features within the Power Platform admin center as packaged offerings for admins .

Benefits: Provides centralized management, enhances security and compliance, improves insights and analytics, and enables automation of governance tasks.

In summary, leveraging best practices and tools such as COE Kit, PowerShell scripts, and Managed Environments empowers organizations to establish robust governance, streamline operations, ensure compliance, and maximize the value derived from the Power Platform. These resources and tools enable organizations to effectively manage their digital transformation initiatives and drive success across their Power Platform deployments.

CHAPTER 3

Dataverse Capabilities in Power Platform

Dataverse Overview

In today's ever-changing business world, organizations face the daunting task of managing and leveraging vast amounts of data to drive innovation, performance, and growth. To solve this challenge, Microsoft offers a powerful solution in the form of Microsoft Dataverse. This cloud-based data storage service is part of the Power Platform suite and serves to store and manage data that can be used by various Microsoft business applications and tools such as Dynamics 365, Power Apps, Power Automate, Copilot, Power BI, and more.

Dataverse provides organizations with a secure and scalable platform to store and manage business data. It enables the development of robust and efficient applications with capabilities such as data modeling, data integration, security, and compliance. One of the key benefits of Microsoft Dataverse is its integration with other Microsoft products and services. This leads to a seamless flow of information between applications and creates a unified information system for organizations. Users can create powerful business applications, automate processes, implement complex integrations, and more using the platform.

CHAPTER 3 DATAVERSE CAPABILITIES IN POWER PLATFORM

Brief History and Evolution of Microsoft Dataverse

Formerly known as Common Data Service for Apps (CDS), Dataverse has come a long way in providing a full suite of data services that enables organization to rapidly build scalable applications, automation, and analytical reports on their business data.

The history and evolution of Dataverse trace back to its roots when it was initially introduced by Microsoft in 2016 as part of the Dynamics 365 suite. Originally conceived as a platform to facilitate data integration and application development within Dynamics 365, Dataverse quickly garnered attention for its robust data modeling capabilities and seamless integration with other Microsoft products and services.

Over time, Microsoft expanded the scope and capabilities of the platform, rebranding it as Microsoft Dataverse in 2020 in order to reflect its broader applicability beyond Dynamics 365. With each iteration, Dataverse has continued to evolve, incorporating new features, enhancing performance, and embracing emerging trends such as low-code/no-code development. This rebranding marked a significant milestone in the evolution of the platform, signaling its transformation into a versatile data platform that underpins the entire Microsoft Power Platform. Today, Microsoft Dataverse stands as a cornerstone of the Power Platform, empowering organizations across industries to unlock the full potential of their data assets and drive innovation at scale.

Why Should Organizations Use Microsoft Dataverse?

Apart from leveraging the capabilities to manage, integrate, and analyze data effectively, here are some of the key reasons why organizations should start using Microsoft Dataverse for their business applications:

1. Unified Data Management

   Centralized Repository: Dataverse provides a single, centralized platform for storing and managing data from multiple sources, helping eliminate data silos, and ensuring data consistency across the organization.

   Standardized Data Model: The use of a common data model helps standardize how data is stored and accessed, making integration and data sharing across different systems and departments more seamless.

2. Integration with Microsoft Ecosystem

   Seamless Integration: Dataverse integrates smoothly with other Microsoft products like Power Apps, Power Automate, Power BI, Copilot, and Dynamics 365, allowing organizations to build comprehensive and interconnected solutions.

   Enhanced Productivity: By leveraging tools within the Microsoft ecosystem, organizations can enhance productivity through integrated workflows, automated processes, and unified data access.

3. Scalability and Performance

   High Scalability: Dataverse is designed to handle large volumes of data and high transaction rates, making it suitable for both small and large organizations.

CHAPTER 3　　DATAVERSE CAPABILITIES IN POWER PLATFORM

> **Reliable Performance**: The platform ensures fast and reliable access to data, which is crucial for applications requiring real-time data processing and analysis.

4. Security and Compliance

    Robust Security Features: Dataverse offers advanced security features such as role-based access control (RBAC), column-level security, and data encryption, ensuring that sensitive data is protected and accessible only to authorized users.

    Regulatory Compliance: Built-in compliance features help organizations adhere to various regulatory standards, including audit logs and data residency options, ensuring legal and regulatory requirements are met.

5. No-Code/Low-Code Development

    Empowering Citizen Developers: Dataverse supports no-code and low-code development environments, enabling business users to create custom applications, workflows, and reports without extensive coding knowledge.

    Power Apps: Users can quickly build applications using Power Apps that leverage Dataverse data, facilitating rapid innovation and adaptation to business needs.

6. Data Insights and Analytics

    Integration with Power BI: Dataverse's integration with Power BI allows organizations to create detailed, interactive reports and dashboards, providing valuable insights into their data.

Advanced Analytics: The platform supports data analytics and machine learning, helping organizations uncover trends, patterns, and insights that drive better decision-making.

7. Automation and Workflow Management
   Power Automate: Integration with Power Automate enables organizations to automate business processes and workflows, reducing manual tasks and improving operational efficiency.
   Business Rules: Dataverse allows the definition of business rules and logic to enforce data validation, trigger actions, and automate routine processes.

8. Customization and Extensibility
   Tailored Data Structures: Organizations can create custom tables and columns within Dataverse, ensuring that the data model aligns with their specific business needs.
   Developer Extensibility: For more advanced scenarios, developers can extend Dataverse functionality through custom plugins, workflows, and API integrations, providing the flexibility to meet unique business requirements.

9. Data Connectivity
   Wide Range of Connectors: Dataverse provides numerous connectors to integrate with external data sources and services, facilitating data import and export.
   Virtual Tables: Virtual tables allow real-time data access from external sources without duplicating data, enhancing data accessibility and integration.

10. Cost-Effectiveness
 Flexible Pricing Models: Dataverse offers various pricing options to cater to different organizational sizes and needs, making it a cost-effective solution for managing and leveraging data.

In summary, organizations can leverage Microsoft Dataverse for its robust data management, integration, and analysis capabilities. Its seamless integration with the Microsoft ecosystem, advanced security features, scalability, and support for no-code/low-code development environments make it a versatile and powerful platform. By adopting Dataverse, organizations can enhance productivity, drive innovation, ensure data security, and make informed decisions based on comprehensive data insights.

Overview of Dataverse Layers

Microsoft Dataverse is built on a multilayered architecture that ensures robustness, flexibility, scalability, and security. Understanding these layers helps users and developers leverage Dataverse more effectively for their data management and application development needs. Here is an overview of the key layers in Dataverse.

Presentation Layer

The Presentation Layer is the interface where users interact with Dataverse. This layer includes various tools and platforms that provide a user-friendly environment for accessing, visualizing, and manipulating data.

A. **Power Apps**: A platform for building custom applications that leverage Dataverse data. Users can create canvas apps, model-driven apps, and Power Pages applications without extensive coding knowledge. These applications use Dataverse tables for storing data, implementing security profiles based on roles assigned to users, and enable users to leverage the Dataverse features for data entry and visualization.

B. **Power Automate**: A tool for automating workflows and integrating Dataverse with other services. It enables users to create automated processes triggered by specific events. Power Automate cloud flows support over a thousand connectors to different Microsoft and non-Microsoft products and services.

C. **Power BI**: A business analytics tool that provides data visualization and reporting capabilities, allowing users to create insightful dashboards and reports using Dataverse data. Power BI also enables users to create relationships between the tables and other data sources with common elements based on specific business needs.

D. **Dynamics 365**: Microsoft's suite of enterprise applications, which utilize Dataverse for data storage and management. This includes applications for sales, customer service, marketing, and more.

Service Layer

The Service Layer provides the APIs and services necessary for data access and interaction. It facilitates communication between the Presentation Layer and the underlying data and business logic.

- A. **Web API**: A RESTful API that allows programmatic access to Dataverse data. It supports standard CRUD (Create, Read, Update, Delete) operations and enables integration with external systems. Processes can be created on tables, and the Web API can be leveraged to call these processes from external systems.

- B. **OData Service**: An Open Data Protocol (OData) service for querying and updating data, providing a standard way to interact with Dataverse.

- C. **SDK (Software Development Kit)**: A collection of tools and libraries for developing applications and customizations that interact with Dataverse. The SDK supports .NET and other development environments.

Business Logic Layer

The Business Logic Layer hosts the rules, processes, and custom logic that define how data is handled and manipulated. This layer ensures that business rules are consistently applied across all interactions with the data.

- A. **Business Rules**: Declarative rules that enforce data validation and business logic without requiring custom code. They run on the client side to provide immediate feedback to users.

B. **Business Process Flows**: Visual guides that lead users through a series of steps to complete a business process, ensuring consistency and compliance.

C. **Workflows**: Automated processes that perform actions based on specific triggers, such as row creation or modification. Workflows can be synchronous (real-time) or asynchronous (background).

D. **Plugins**: Custom codes that execute in response to specific events in Dataverse. Plugins provide the ability to implement complex business logic and integrate with external systems.

Data Layer

The Data Layer is responsible for the actual storage and management of data. It includes the database management system and data schema definitions.

A. **Tables**: Structured data storage units similar to database tables. Each table stores rows with specific attributes.

B. **Columns**: Attributes of the tables that define the data type (e.g., text, number, and date) and other properties such as required status and default values.

C. **Relationships**: Define how tables relate to each other, supporting complex data structures and hierarchical data models. Relationships include one-to-many, many-to-one, and many-to-many.

D. **Data Integrity and Constraints**: Mechanisms to ensure data consistency and integrity, including primary keys, foreign keys, and validation rules.

Security Layer

The Security Layer ensures that data is protected and accessible only to authorized users. It includes various mechanisms to enforce security at multiple levels.

　　A. **Role-Based Access Control (RBAC)**: Manages user permissions based on roles. Each role has a set of privileges that define what actions users can perform and what data they can access.

　　B. **Column-Level Security**: Controls access to individual columns within a table, ensuring that sensitive information is only accessible to authorized users.

　　C. **Row-Level Security**: Restricts access to specific rows within a table, allowing for granular control over data visibility.

　　D. **Data Encryption**: Protects data both at rest and in transit. Dataverse uses encryption to ensure data privacy and compliance with regulatory requirements.

　　E. **Audit Logs**: Tracks changes to data and user actions, providing a detailed record for security audits and compliance purposes.

In summary, the layered architecture of Microsoft Dataverse (as shown in Figure 3-1) ensures a comprehensive and flexible platform for data management and application development. By separating concerns into distinct layers—Presentation, Service, Business Logic, Data, and Security—Dataverse offers robust capabilities for handling complex data scenarios, enforcing business rules, integrating with external systems, and ensuring data security and compliance. This structured approach allows organizations to build scalable, efficient, and secure solutions tailored to their specific business needs.

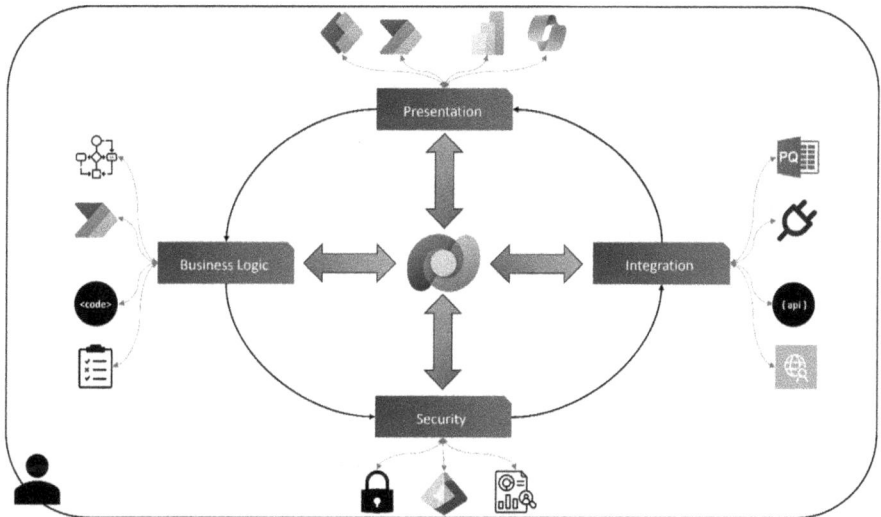

Figure 3-1. *Dataverse overview*

Key Components of Microsoft Dataverse

Microsoft Dataverse comprises several essential components, each playing a vital role in helping organizations store, manage, and utilize their data effectively. Let's explore these components in detail.

CHAPTER 3 DATAVERSE CAPABILITIES IN POWER PLATFORM

1. Tables

    Tables are the foundational building blocks of Dataverse. They represent distinct types of data, such as customers, products, accounts, users, opportunities, projects, orders, etc. Users can define custom tables tailored to their specific business needs, allowing for precise and granular data modeling. Each table consists of a set of attributes that define the structure and characteristics of the data it holds. Here are the types of tables that can be used/created in Dataverse:

    A. **Standard Tables**: These are predefined data tables provided by Microsoft as part of the Dataverse environment. Standard tables cover common business scenarios such as accounts, contacts, leads, opportunities, cases, products, and more.

    Standard tables come with predefined columns and relationships tailored to specific business processes, making them suitable for out-of-the-box use in Dynamics 365 applications and other solutions.

    B. **Custom Tables**: These are user-defined data tables created by administrators or developers to meet specific business requirements. Users can define custom tables to store data that is unique to their organization's processes, workflows, or industry-specific needs.

    Custom tables can be created from scratch, allowing users to define their own set of columns, relationships, and business logic tailored to their specific use cases. They provide flexibility and extensibility, enabling organizations to model complex data structures and accommodate evolving business needs.

C. **Activity Tables**: These tables represent various types of interactions or activities tracked within the system, such as emails, appointments, tasks, phone calls, and more. They are designed to capture communication and interaction data related to customers, contacts, or other tables within the system.

   Activity tables come with predefined columns and relationships optimized for tracking activity data, making them suitable for use in customer relationship management (CRM) scenarios.

D. **Intersect Tables**: These tables represent many-to-many relationships between other tables within Dataverse. They serve as junction tables that facilitate the mapping of relationships between rows in different tables.

   Intersect tables typically consist of two lookup columns that reference the related tables and additional attributes to capture metadata or additional information about the relationship.

E. **Metadata Tables**: These tables store configuration and metadata information about the Dataverse environment itself. They include tables such as Entity, Attribute, Relationship, Form, View, Plugin Type, Web Resource, Solution, and more.
   Metadata tables are used by administrators, developers, and system integrators to configure, customize, and extend the Dataverse environment.

F. **Virtual Tables**: These tables provide a mechanism for integrating and accessing data from external sources within the Dataverse environment without the need to physically store the data in Dataverse tables. Users can define the structure of the virtual table, including columns, relationships, and other metadata, to reflect the schema of the external data source.

Virtual tables provide a logical abstraction layer that allows users to interact with external data as if it were native Dataverse data, enabling seamless integration and access across the platform. They support integration with a variety of external data sources, including databases, web services, APIs, and custom connectors. Integration with external data sources can be achieved through a variety of protocols and standards, such as OData, REST API, SQL, and others, depending on the capabilities of the external system.

Once configured, virtual tables appear as native tables within the Dataverse environment, allowing users to query, create, update, and delete rows using standard Dataverse APIs and tools. Data access operations performed on virtual tables are transparently translated into the corresponding operations on the external data source, ensuring seamless integration and data consistency.

Virtual tables leverage caching and data retrieval optimization techniques to enhance performance and minimize latency when accessing external data. Furthermore, depending on the configuration and capabilities of the external system, virtual tables may support features such as incremental data loading, data filtering, and caching to improve query performance and responsiveness.

Virtual tables inherit security and access control settings from Dataverse, allowing administrators to define permissions and roles for accessing external data within the platform. Users can leverage Dataverse security features such as role-based access control (RBAC), row-level security, and column-level security to control access to virtual table data based on organizational policies and requirements.

G. **Elastic Tables**: These tables are designed to handle large volumes of data in real time. They provide users with extensibility to import, store, and analyze large volumes of data without scalability, latency, or performance issues.

Elastic tables are built on top of Azure Cosmos DB and come with unique capabilities for flexible schema, horizontal scaling, and automatic removal of data after a time period. They automatically scale to ingest tens of millions of rows every hour.

Users can leverage elastic tables to handle varying workloads, from routine operations to peak loads during events like end-of-quarter reporting or large-scale data imports.

In summary, by leveraging these different types of tables, users can effectively model their data, streamline business processes, and build custom applications tailored to their unique requirements within the Microsoft Dataverse environment.

2. Columns

   Columns represent the individual attributes or properties of a table, defining the data types and format of the information stored in each column. Dataverse supports various types of columns, including text, number, date/time, currency, option sets, lookup columns, auto-number, calculated, formula, and more. Users can configure properties such as column labels, data validation rules, and default values for each column. Here is an overview of columns in Dataverse:

   A. **Data Types:** Columns in Dataverse have specific data types that define the kind of data they can store, such as text, rich text, number, date/time, currency, Boolean, option set, lookup, etc. The choice of data type for a column depends on the nature of the data it will store and the operations that will be performed on it.

   B. **Column Properties:** Each column has various properties that can be configured to define its behavior, appearance, and validation rules. Properties such as column label, display name, description, maximum length, format, default value, and required status can be customized to suit the specific requirements of the data being stored. Dataverse ensures that no two columns in a table can have the same logical name to prevent schema validation issues, referencing the column while creating applications, etc.

C. **Validation Rules**: Columns can have validation rules defined to ensure data integrity and consistency. These validation rules can include conditions, patterns, or ranges that data must meet to be considered valid, such as required columns, data format validation, and range checks. Validation rules enable users to set up columns so that additional coding is not required for basic validation like input provided by the user should be in a specific range when configured as a number, a decimal, a whole number, a URL, specific number of characters, and so on.

D. **Choice Columns**: There are three types of choice columns supported by Dataverse. These choices serve similar purposes but have distinct characteristics and use cases.

   i. **Yes/No Choice**: These columns allow users to set up a Boolean data type on the column where users can provide a default value while configuration.

   ii. **Global Choices**: These are predefined sets of options that are defined at the organization level and can be reused across multiple tables and columns within the Dataverse environment. When creating global choices, administrators define the list of options and their corresponding values in a centralized location accessible to all users and applications.

   Global choices offer consistency and standardization across the organization, ensuring that the same set of options is available for selection wherever applicable. They are well-suited for scenarios where the same set of options needs to be used across multiple tables or where standardization of choices is essential for data consistency and reporting purposes.

iii. **Local Choices**: These are specific to individual tables or columns within Dataverse and are defined at the table level. When creating local choices, users define the list of options and their corresponding values directly within the column configuration. Local choices are scoped to the table or column in which they are defined, meaning they are only available for selection within that specific context.

Local choices provide flexibility for tailoring choices to the specific needs of individual tables or columns, allowing users to define unique sets of options based on the requirements of each table.

E. **Relationships**: Columns can establish relationships between tables, allowing data in one table to be linked or related to data in another table. Common types of relationships include one-to-many, many-to-one, and many-to-many relationships, which define how rows in one table are associated with rows in another table. For example, an account can be related to multiple contacts, multiple users can be related to multiple accounts, multiple accounts can be related to an organization, and so on.

F. **Lookup Columns**: These columns allow users to establish relationships between tables by referencing rows from another table. Lookup columns display a dropdown list of related rows from the referenced table, enabling users to select a row to associate with the current row. Dataverse lookup column enables users to reference the same table, thereby providing a parent child row relationship capability.

G. **Formula Columns**: These columns in Dataverse allow users to create calculated columns that perform real-time calculations based on other columns' values in the same table. This feature enhances data management by enabling the automation of complex calculations and business logic without requiring coding. Users can leverage Power Fx formulas to implement logic including logical mathematical calculations, string formatting, string manipulation, etc. Formula columns are a preview feature at this point and are soon expected to replace calculated columns in Dataverse.

The formula columns feature enhances data accuracy, efficiency, and adaptability, allowing users to manage data more effectively without requiring extensive custom development.

H. **Calculated Columns**: These columns allow users to define dynamic calculations based on the values of other columns within the same table. Calculated columns use formula expressions to calculate values based on predefined logic or mathematical operations, providing dynamic data based on other column values.

I. **Roll-Up Columns**: These columns enable users to perform aggregate calculations across related rows from another table and store the result in a single column. Roll-up columns calculate aggregate values such as sum, average, minimum, maximum, and count of related rows, providing summarized data for analysis and reporting.

J. **Autonumber**: This column feature is designed to automatically generate unique, sequential, or formatted identifiers for rows within a table. It is particularly useful for creating primary keys or other unique identifiers that follow a specific pattern.

Autonumber columns automatically generate unique values for each new row added to a table, ensuring that each row has a distinct identifier. Users can define the format of the autonumber values to meet specific business requirements. This includes setting prefixes, suffixes, and customizable numeric sequences. The most common use of autonumber columns is to create sequential numbers. For example, a product table might have a product ID column that increments with each new product (e.g., PRD-0001, PRD-0002, etc.).

By customizing the autonumber format to fit specific needs, organizations can ensure that their data is well-organized and easily manageable.

In summary, columns play a vital role in defining the structure, behavior, and relationships of data within tables in Microsoft Dataverse. By configuring columns effectively, users can ensure data consistency, integrity, and usability within their applications and business processes tailored to their specific business requirements.

3. Keys

In Dataverse, keys are special columns or combinations of columns within tables that uniquely identify each row in the table. Keys play a fundamental role in maintaining data integrity and establishing relationships between tables. There are two main types of keys in Dataverse tables:

A. **Primary Key**: This is a column or combination of columns that uniquely identifies each row in the table. Each Dataverse table must have a primary key, and it ensures that every row in the table has a unique identifier. By default, every table in Dataverse has a Globally Unique Identifier (GUID) primary key column called "Primary Key" or "EntityId," which is automatically generated for each new row added to the table.

   In addition to the default primary key, users can define custom primary key columns based on their specific requirements. These custom primary keys can be single columns or combinations of multiple columns.

B. **Foreign Key**: This is a column or set of columns in one table that references the primary key column(s) in another table. Foreign keys establish relationships between tables by defining dependencies or associations between related rows. When a foreign key column in one table references the primary key column(s) in another table, it ensures referential integrity, meaning that every value in the foreign key column must correspond to a valid value in the primary key column(s) of the referenced table.
   Foreign keys are used to enforce data integrity and maintain consistency between related rows in different tables.

In summary, keys in Dataverse tables play a crucial role in data modeling, relationship management, and data integrity enforcement. By defining appropriate primary and foreign keys, users can ensure that data is accurately identified, related, and maintained within their Dataverse environment.

4. Forms

   In Dataverse, there are several types of forms that users can create and customize to define the layout and behavior of data entry screens for tables.

   Each type of form serves a specific purpose and is designed to cater to different user scenarios and requirements. Forms can be utilized on model-driven apps, canvas Power Apps, and Power Pages with a basic layout and additional customizations with scripting and PowerFx formulas. Here are the different types of forms available in Dataverse:

   A. **Main Form**: This is the primary form used for viewing and editing rows within a table. Generally, it is also the default form that users interact with when accessing data in model-driven applications.

   Main forms can be customized and designed in specific ways catering to specific business requirements. They provide capabilities for the users to include or exclude specific columns on the table, rearrange layouts, configure properties and settings such as form navigation, tab display order, functions to run upon form load, etc.

   B. **Quick Create Forms**: These forms provide a simplified interface for quickly creating new rows without navigating away from the current view. They are particularly handy and improve user experience when dependent data needs to be added for related tables.

   Quick create forms typically include a subset of columns relevant for creating new rows and are designed for rapid data entry. They are accessed via the "Quick Create" button or link in Dataverse applications and can be customized to tailor the data entry experience for specific use cases.

C. **Quick View Forms**: These forms allow users to display related information from another table directly on the form of the primary table. They provide a read-only view of selected columns from the related table, enabling users to access key information without navigating to separate forms or rows.

Quick View Forms are commonly used to surface contextual information or related data points within the context of a primary row.

D. **Card Forms**: These are compact forms designed to display key information about a row in a condensed format. They are often used in views, grids, or dashboards to provide an overview of multiple rows at a glance.

Card Forms typically include a limited number of columns and are optimized for displaying on smaller screens or in situations where space is limited.

E. **Mobile Forms**: These forms are optimized for use on mobile devices, providing a responsive and touch-friendly user interface. They are designed to adapt to different screen sizes and orientations, ensuring a consistent user experience across mobile devices.

Mobile Forms can be customized to prioritize essential columns, optimize layout for touch input, and enhance performance for mobile users.

F. **Main Forms (Tablet)**: These forms are optimized for tablet devices and provide a user interface tailored for larger screens and touch input. They offer similar customization options as standard Main Forms but are optimized for tablet-based experiences.

Main Forms for tablets can accommodate additional columns, utilize larger form layouts, and leverage touch gestures for navigation and interaction.

In summary, each type of form in Dataverse serves a specific purpose and can be customized to meet the unique needs of different user scenarios, devices, and applications. By leveraging the flexibility and customization capabilities of forms, users can design intuitive and efficient data entry experiences tailored to their specific requirements.

5. Views

    In Dataverse, views are predefined queries that specify how data should be displayed in lists and grids within applications. Views allow users to filter, sort, and group data based on specific criteria, providing a customized and organized view of data. There are several types of views available in Dataverse, each serving different purposes and catering to various user needs. Here are the main types of views:

    A. **System Views**: These are predefined views provided by Microsoft that cover common scenarios and use cases. They are available out-of-the-box and cannot be modified directly. However, users can clone system views to create custom versions as per requirements.

Some examples of system views include "All Accounts," "My Active Contacts," "Active Cases," "All Opportunities," and more.

B. **Personal Views**: These are custom views created by individual users to personalize their data-viewing experience. Users can define filters, sorting criteria, and column layouts tailored to their specific preferences and requirements.

Personal views are private to the user who created them and can only be accessed by that user.

C. **System Chart Views**: These views are predefined visual representations of data in the form of charts or graphs. They provide graphical insights into data and are often used for data visualization and analysis.

System chart views are available out-of-the-box and can be added to dashboards or accessed directly from table rows.

D. **System Dashboard Views**: These views are predefined collections of visual components, including charts, lists, and web resources, arranged on a single page. They provide a consolidated view of key metrics, trends, and data summaries, allowing users to monitor performance and track progress at a glance.

System dashboard views are available out-of-the-box and can be customized by administrators to include additional components or rearrange existing ones. They also support data drill down providing further visibility of key metrics on data visualizations.

E. **Lookup Views:** These views are used when selecting related rows from a lookup column within a form or when configuring relationship mappings between tables. They provide a searchable list of rows from the related table, allowing users to select a row to associate with the current row.

Further capabilities of lookup views include filtering on related rows based on parent relationship between the tables, search, and filter in the case of large data sets.

F. **Custom Views:** These views are user-defined views created by administrators or developers to meet specific business requirements. Users can define custom filters, sorting criteria, column layouts, and other display options to tailor the view to their needs.

Custom views also support adding columns referencing related tables and provide a holistic view of data. They can be shared with other users or made available to specific teams or security roles within the organization.

In summary, by leveraging different types of views, users can effectively organize, analyze, and visualize data within Microsoft Dataverse applications, providing a customized and intuitive user experience designed to deliver specific needs and preferences.

6. Business Rules

   In Dataverse, business rules provide a powerful mechanism for implementing client-side logic and automating business processes without the need for custom code. Business rules allow users to define conditions and actions that are executed in response to user interactions or data changes within forms. This feature enables users to apply logic on specific forms or the entire table seamlessly. Here are the main components of business rules in Dataverse:

   A. **Conditions**: Business rules consist of one or more conditions that define when the rule should be triggered. Conditions are based on column values, data comparisons, or logical expressions. The first step of a business rule is always a condition that defines the path of how the logic will proceed further based on the criteria defined on the condition.

   B. **Actions**: Actions specify the logic to be performed when the conditions of the business rule are met. Actions include setting column values, showing/hiding columns, enabling/disabling columns, setting column requirements, and displaying error messages. Actions enable users to set column values based on a calculation, string manipulations, column values from the current table, and clearing out the value of a column.

   C. **Scope**: Business rules can be applied at the table level or form level within Dataverse. Table-level business rules apply to all forms associated with the table, while form-level business rules apply only to a specific form.

Users can define multiple business rules for a table or form to implement complex business logic and workflows.

D. **Triggers**: Business rules are triggered by specific events or actions, such as when a form is loaded, saved, or data in a column is changed. Triggering events include form events (e.g., OnLoad and OnSave), column events (e.g., OnChange), and form navigation events (e.g., OnTabChange).

Users can specify multiple triggering events for a single business rule to handle different scenarios and user interactions.

In summary, business rules in Microsoft Dataverse provide a user-friendly and code-free way to implement client-side logic and automate business processes within forms. By defining conditions and actions, users can customize form behavior, enforce data validation rules, and improve the user experience within Dataverse applications. Business rules work seamlessly and integrate with other Dataverse features as well. They can be combined with other customization options, such as JavaScript, workflows, and plugins, to implement more complex business logic and workflows.

7. Business Process Flows
   Business Process Flows (BPFs) in Dataverse are a powerful feature designed to guide users through a defined set of steps or stages to achieve a specific outcome or complete a business

CHAPTER 3   DATAVERSE CAPABILITIES IN POWER PLATFORM

process. These flows help ensure that business processes are followed consistently and efficiently, enhancing productivity and compliance within the organization. Here are some integral components and an overview of business process flows in Dataverse:

i. A business process flow breaks down processes into distinct stages where each stage represents a phase in the overall workflow. These stages guide users through the steps required to complete the process.

ii. Each stage contains specific steps that need to be completed. Steps can include data entry, decision points, and actions that must be taken before moving to the next stage. Users can also call Power Automate cloud flows from a stage in business process flows.

iii. When a business process flow is created for a table, a separate table with relationship mapping is created. This enables developers to setup stand-alone processes like Power Automate cloud flows that can be triggered on events such as start of a specific stage or completion of a specific stage, etc.

iv. Business process flows can include conditional logic to branch the process flow based on specific criteria or data values, allowing for more complex and dynamic process management. Actions taken in a stage can route users to a specific process based on the criteria provided. This allows the flexibility of implementing multiple processes based on different criteria that can be implemented through conditions.

v. The entire flow is presented in a visual format that provides a guided experience for users, making it easy for them to understand and follow the required steps. The visual representation enhances user experience and process adherence.

In summary, business process flows in Microsoft Dataverse provide a structured and visual way to manage and automate business processes. By breaking down processes into stages and steps, integrating with Dataverse data, and allowing for conditional branching and automation, BPFs enhance consistency, efficiency, and compliance in organizational workflows. This feature empowers users to follow best practices and ensures that critical business processes are executed correctly and efficiently.

8. Workflows

    Workflows in Dataverse are automated processes that can perform a variety of tasks within the Dataverse environment. They help streamline business processes by automating repetitive tasks, enforcing business rules, and ensuring data consistency and accuracy. Workflows can be triggered by specific events or run on-demand, making them a versatile tool for enhancing productivity and operational efficiency. Here is an overview of workflows in Dataverse:

    A. **Automation of Business Processes**: Workflows automate routine and repetitive tasks, reducing manual effort and minimizing the risk of human error. They can be configured for tables to run on specific events and perform actions based on the business needs.

Workflows can be triggered by specific events such as row creation, update, or deletion. They can also be run manually or on a scheduled basis. Users can leverage data from related tables also to facilitate the completion of the process tailored to specific business needs.

Workflows support conditional logic, allowing for complex branching and decision-making based on specific criteria or data values. They can interact with Dataverse tables to create, update, delete, or retrieve rows, providing seamless integration with the underlying data. Each workflow consists of a series of steps, which can include actions such as sending emails, creating tasks, calling power automate cloud flows, updating columns, or executing custom code.

B. **Types of Workflows**: Generally, workflows can be categorized into two types.

   i. **Synchronous Workflows**: These workflows execute immediately when triggered, allowing for real-time processing and immediate feedback. They are often used for tasks that need to be completed before a row is saved.

   ii. **Asynchronous Workflows**: These workflows run in the background after the triggering event, suitable for processes that do not need to be completed immediately. They are ideal for tasks that can be processed later, without impacting the user experience.

In summary, workflows in Dataverse are a powerful tool for automating business processes, enhancing efficiency, and ensuring consistency across the organization. By leveraging trigger-based execution, conditional logic, and seamless integration with Dataverse tables, workflows enable users to automate complex tasks and enforce business rules effectively. This capability not only improves productivity but also enhances data integrity, compliance, and overall operational efficiency. According to Microsoft documentation, workflows are soon to be replaced with Power Automate cloud flows. However, until Power Automate cloud flows provide with capabilities to synchronously run processes, workflows are highly reliable for synchronous processes.

9. Plugins

    i. Plugins in Dataverse are custom business logic implementations that run in response to specific events on Dataverse tables. They provide a way to extend Dataverse's functionality by allowing developers to write .NET code that executes when particular operations, such as create, update, or delete, occur. Here is an overview of plugins in Dataverse.

    ii. Plugins are triggered by events on Dataverse tables, such as row creation, update, deletion, or retrieval. These events can be synchronous (real-time) or asynchronous (background).

    iii. Developers can write custom .NET code to implement specific business rules, validations, or actions that need to occur in response to the triggering events. Plugins enable advanced customization and extension of Dataverse, allowing organizations to tailor the platform to their unique business requirements.

iv. Plugins can be registered at different stages of the execution pipeline, including prevalidation, preoperation, and postoperation stages. This flexibility allows for precise control over when the custom logic is executed. They run within the Dataverse framework, benefiting from built-in security and managed execution, which ensures reliability and performance.

In summary, plugins in Microsoft Dataverse are a powerful tool for extending the platform's functionality through custom business logic. By enabling real-time, event-driven processing and integration with external systems, plugins help organizations automate complex processes, enforce business rules, and ensure data integrity. With their ability to handle both synchronous and asynchronous operations, plugins offer flexibility and efficiency in managing data and workflows within Dataverse.

10. Security Roles

    Role-based access control (RBAC) is a fundamental aspect of security in Microsoft Dataverse, enabling organizations to control access to data and functionality based on users' roles and permissions. RBAC in Dataverse is a flexible and granular security model that allows administrators to define roles, assign permissions, and manage access to tables, columns, and other resources within the environment. Here are more details on how RBAC works in Dataverse:

A. **Roles**: Sets of permissions that define what actions users assigned to the role can perform within Dataverse are represented by roles. Dataverse provides several built-in roles, such as System Administrator, System Customizer, and various predefined roles for specific applications (e.g., Sales Manager, Customer Service Representative).

   Administrators can create custom roles tailored to the organization's specific security requirements. This includes granting access to certain tables with certain privileges. Dataverse follows the least restrictive permission policy where users assigned the highest roles are made effective at first.

B. **Privileges**: These are individual permissions that define specific actions or operations that users can perform within Dataverse. They include Create, Read, Write, Delete, Append, Append To, Assign, Share, and more, each corresponding to a specific action or operation on the specified table.

   Roles are composed of a combination of privileges, allowing administrators to tailor permissions to meet the needs of different user roles.

C. **Access Levels**: These define the level of access users have to individual rows within tables. Dataverse provides several built-in access levels, such as None, User, Business Unit, Parent Child Business Unit, Organization, and more.

   Access levels control whether users can read, write, delete, or share rows based on their role and the security hierarchy within the organization.

D. **Table- and Column-Level Security**: Administrators can configure table- and column-level security to control access to specific tables and columns within Dataverse. Table-level security allows administrators to restrict access to entire table based on user roles or teams.

   Column-level security enables administrators to hide or restrict access to individual columns within tables based on user roles or teams.

E. **Hierarchical Security**: Dataverse supports hierarchical security, allowing organizations to model complex organizational structures and enforce security policies based on hierarchical relationships. This enables permissions to be inherited based on the user's position in the organizational hierarchy, ensuring that users only have access to the data they are authorized to view or modify.

F. **Sharing and Team Security**: Dataverse allows users to share rows with other users or teams, granting them additional access to specific rows. Administrators can create teams and define team-based security roles to control access to rows based on team membership.

   Sharing and team-based security provide additional flexibility for granting temporary or ad-hoc access to rows as needed.

In summary, by leveraging role-based access control (RBAC) in Microsoft Dataverse, organizations can ensure that sensitive data is protected, regulatory compliance requirements are met, and users have appropriate access to the data and functionality they need to perform their roles effectively. RBAC provides a flexible and scalable security model that adapts to the organization's evolving needs and requirements.

11. Dataverse Security

    Security in Microsoft Dataverse is a comprehensive framework designed to protect data, enforce access controls, and ensure compliance with organizational policies and regulations. The security model in Dataverse encompasses various components and features to safeguard data at different levels of granularity. Here is an overview of Dataverse security:

    A. **Data Encryption**: Dataverse provides data encryption capabilities to protect sensitive data both at rest and in transit. Encryption ensures that data is securely stored and transmitted, mitigating the risk of unauthorized access or data breaches.

    B. **Audit and Compliance**: Dataverse includes audit capabilities to track and log user actions and system events within the environment. Audit logs capture information such as who accessed data, what changes were made, and when they occurred, providing a comprehensive trail of data access and modifications.

    Audit logs help organizations demonstrate compliance with regulatory requirements and internal security policies. Dataverse provides organizations with customizable audit log retention policies, enabling them to plan better on saving logs for time periods best suited for the application.

    C. **Integration with Entra ID**: Dataverse integrates seamlessly with Azure Entra ID for user authentication and identity management. Entra ID integration allows organizations

CHAPTER 3 DATAVERSE CAPABILITIES IN POWER PLATFORM

to leverage security features such as conditional access, multifactor authentication (MFA), and identity protection to enhance security in Dataverse. Dataverse data can also be accessed using Service Principal and Application User setup leveraging Entra ID to integrate with other applications.

In summary, by leveraging these security features and capabilities, organizations can establish a robust security posture in Microsoft Dataverse, ensuring the confidentiality, integrity, and availability of their data assets while meeting compliance requirements and mitigating security risks.

12. Import and Export Data (with Excel)

    In Microsoft Dataverse, users can import and export data using Excel, providing a convenient and familiar way to manage data in bulk. Importing data from Excel allows users to quickly add or update rows, while exporting data to Excel enables users to analyze, manipulate, and share data outside of the Dataverse environment. Here are more details on how import and export data capabilities work in Dataverse using Excel:

    A. **Importing Data from Excel**: Users can prepare the data they want to import into Dataverse in an Excel spreadsheet. Each column in the Excel spreadsheet corresponds to a column in the Dataverse table they are importing into. The process of importing data can be initiated by accessing the data import wizard in Dataverse.

    The import wizard enables users to select the tables in which they want to import the data and further eases the process of data mapping between the Excel and the Dataverse table by providing an interactive user experience for mapping columns. The import capabilities also provide with features such as duplicate detection rules, data validation, and error handling rules.

To view the results of the data import, Dataverse also provides feedback with details of successfully imported data, failures, errors, and warnings encountered during the data import.

B. **Exporting Data to Excel**: Users can select the data they want to export from Dataverse. This could be rows from a specific table or a filtered subset of rows based on specific criteria. The export process can be initiated from the Dataverse interface, typically from the command bar or ribbon.

Users may have the option to specify additional export options, such as including related rows, selecting specific columns to export, or applying data filters for the data to be exported. Once the data for export is ready, Dataverse exports a downloadable Excel file with the data that can be further used for analysis, reporting, or sharing.

C. **Benefits of Importing and Exporting Data with Excel**: Users can leverage their existing knowledge of Excel to manage data in Dataverse, reducing the learning curve and improving user adoption. Importing data from Excel allows users to quickly add or update large volumes of data in Dataverse, saving time and effort. Exporting data to Excel provides users with the flexibility to analyze, manipulate, and visualize data using Excel's powerful features and tools.

In summary, the import and export data capabilities in Dataverse using Excel provide users with a seamless and efficient way to manage data, facilitating data integration, analysis, and collaboration within the organization.

Summarizing the key components in Microsoft Dataverse, we have learnt that it encompasses a comprehensive set of components designed to facilitate efficient data management and application development. From data storage and management to business logic, automation, security, and integration, these components provide the necessary tools to build scalable, secure, and flexible solutions tailored to organizational needs.

Use Cases and Applications of Dataverse

Microsoft Dataverse is a versatile data platform that supports a wide range of use cases and applications across various industries and business scenarios. Its flexibility and integration capabilities make it a valuable tool for organizations looking to streamline operations, improve data management, and enhance decision-making processes. Here is an overview of the primary use cases and applications of Dataverse:

  A. Customer Relationship Management (CRM)
  Dataverse is often used as the backend for CRM systems, providing a unified data model for managing customer information, interactions, and transactions.
  Applications: Below are some examples:
   i. **Sales Management**: Track leads, opportunities, and sales activities. Automate sales processes and workflows to enhance efficiency.

ii. **Customer Service**: Manage customer inquiries, service requests, and support tickets. Implement automated routing and escalation processes.

iii. **Marketing Automation**: Manage marketing campaigns, track customer engagement, and analyze campaign performance.

B. Enterprise Resource Planning (ERP)
Dataverse supports ERP systems by providing a robust data infrastructure for managing core business processes.
Applications: Below are some examples:

i. **Inventory Management**: Track inventory levels, manage stock, and automate reordering processes.

ii. **Finance and Accounting**: Manage financial transactions, automate billing, and generate financial reports.

iii. **Human Resources**: Track employee records, manage payroll, and automate HR workflows.

C. Custom Business Applications
Dataverse enables the creation of custom applications tailored to specific business needs without extensive coding.
Applications: Below are some examples:

i. **Project Management**: Create applications to track project tasks, milestones, and resources. Automate project workflows and reporting.

ii. **Field Service Management**: Develop applications to manage field service operations, schedule service calls, and track technician activities.

CHAPTER 3 DATAVERSE CAPABILITIES IN POWER PLATFORM

    iii. **Compliance Management**: Build applications to track compliance with industry regulations, manage audit trails, and automate compliance reporting.

D. Data Integration and Consolidation
Dataverse acts as a central data hub, integrating data from various sources to provide a unified view.
Applications: Below are some examples:

    i. **Data Warehousing**: Consolidate data from multiple systems into Dataverse for centralized reporting and analytics.

    ii. **System Integration**: Integrate Dataverse with other enterprise systems (e.g., ERP, CRM, and HR systems) to ensure data consistency and real-time updates.

    iii. **Master Data Management**: Maintain a single source of truth for critical business data, ensuring data accuracy and consistency across the organization.

E. Analytics and Reporting
Dataverse provides a structured data environment for advanced analytics and reporting.
Applications: Below are some examples:

    i. **Business Intelligence (BI)**: Use Power BI to create interactive dashboards and reports that provide insights into business performance.

    ii. **Data Analytics**: Perform advanced data analysis to uncover trends, patterns, and anomalies that inform strategic decisions.

    iii. **KPI Tracking**: Monitor key performance indicators (KPIs) and generate real-time reports to track business performance against goals.

F. **Automation and Workflow Management**
   Dataverse supports the automation of business processes through Power Automate and built-in workflow capabilities.
   Applications: Below are some examples:
   i. **Process Automation**: Automate routine tasks such as approvals, notifications, and data updates to improve efficiency and reduce manual effort.
   ii. **Workflow Orchestration**: Create complex workflows that span multiple systems and processes, ensuring seamless coordination and execution.
   iii. **Event-Driven Actions**: Trigger automated actions based on specific events or conditions, such as data changes or time-based triggers.

G. Healthcare Applications
   Dataverse can be used to manage patient data, medical records, and healthcare workflows.
   Applications: Below are some examples:
   i. **Patient Management**: Track patient records, appointments, and medical history. Automate patient communication and reminders.
   ii. **Clinical Workflows**: Streamline clinical workflows, from patient intake to discharge, ensuring efficient and coordinated care.
   iii. **Regulatory Compliance**: Ensure compliance with healthcare regulations (e.g., HIPAA) through secure data management and audit trails.

In summary, Microsoft Dataverse is a versatile data platform that supports a wide range of use cases and applications across various industries. Its ability to integrate with other Microsoft services, automate business processes, and provide a secure and scalable data environment makes it an essential tool for organizations looking to optimize their data management and application development efforts. By leveraging Dataverse, organizations can enhance operational efficiency, improve decision-making, and drive innovation.

Summary

Microsoft Dataverse is a robust data platform providing a unified and flexible environment for managing and leveraging data across a wide range of applications. It is designed to optimize data management, enhance operational efficiency, and foster innovation within organizations.

Dataverse's architecture supports scalability, ensuring it can handle large volumes of data and high transaction rates efficiently. It integrates seamlessly with Microsoft services such as Power Apps, Power Automate, Power BI, and Dynamics 365, enabling comprehensive data solutions and facilitating automation, analytics, and application development.

Security is a cornerstone of Dataverse, offering role-based access control, data encryption, column-level security, and detailed audit logs. These features ensure that data is protected, compliant with regulations, and accessible only to authorized users.

Dataverse also provides a versatile set of tools for data integration, allowing organizations to consolidate data from various sources into a single platform. This centralization enables more accurate reporting and better decision-making.

Furthermore, the platform supports custom business logic and process automation through business rules, workflows, plugins, and business process flows. This flexibility allows businesses to tailor Dataverse to their specific needs, automating routine tasks and ensuring consistency in data handling and business processes.

In summary, Microsoft Dataverse is an essential tool for organizations looking to streamline their data management processes, integrate various data sources seamlessly, and harness the power of automation and advanced analytics. Its comprehensive features and secure environment make it a valuable asset for driving operational efficiency and innovation.

CHAPTER 4

Data Integration, Data Export, and Analytics in Dataverse

The main goal of this chapter is to empower readers with the knowledge and skills to master data integration, streamline data export processes, and create compelling visualizations within the Power Platform ecosystem. By the end of this chapter, readers should be proficient in handling data seamlessly across various sources, exporting it efficiently, and presenting meaningful insights through powerful visualizations.

Introduction to Dataflows

Dataflows are a Power Platform component that allow users to extract, transform, and load (ETL) data from a wide variety of sources into the Dataverse or other storage locations. Dataflows provide a robust and scalable way to prepare data, ensuring that it is clean, consistent, and ready for use across multiple applications.

As data volumes continue to increase, the challenge of transforming that data into well-structured, actionable information grows accordingly. Dataflows are a cloud-based, self-service data preparation technology that allow users to ingest, transform, and load data into Microsoft Dataverse environments, Power BI workspaces, or their organization's Azure Data Lake Storage account. Utilizing Power Query—a unified data connectivity and preparation tool already integrated into various Microsoft products like Excel and Power BI—dataflows provide a streamlined data preparation experience. Users can run dataflows either on demand or automatically on a set schedule, ensuring that the data always remains current.

Dataflows are integrated into multiple Microsoft products and do not require a specific license to create or run. They are available in Power Apps, Power BI, and Dynamics 365 Customer Insights, with the capability to create and run dataflows included in the licenses for these products. While the core features of dataflows are consistent across all these platforms, there may be some product-specific features unique to dataflows created within each product.

Key Features

> **Source Connectivity**: Dataflows can connect to numerous data sources, including databases, online services, and files.
>
> **Transformations**: They offer extensive data transformation capabilities, allowing users to clean and shape data as needed.
>
> **Scheduled Refresh**: Dataflows can be scheduled to refresh automatically, ensuring that the data remains up to date.

Dataflows are integrated with other Power Platform services like Power BI, Power Apps, and Power Automate, making them an essential tool for businesses looking to leverage data-driven insights.

Purpose and Benefits of Dataflows

Dataflows are designed to support the following scenarios.

Reusable Transformation Logic

Dataflows enable the creation of reusable transformation logic that can be shared across multiple semantic models and reports within Power BI. This promotes reusability of data elements and eliminates the need for separate connections to cloud or on-premises data sources.

Persist Data in Azure Data Lake Gen 2

Dataflows allow you to store data in your own Azure Data Lake Gen 2 storage. This enables you to make the data accessible to other Azure services beyond Power BI.

Single Source of Truth

By curating raw data into a single source of truth using industry-standard definitions, dataflows ensure consistency and reliability. This curated data can be used by other services and products within the Power Platform, facilitating widespread adoption by restricting analysts' access to the underlying data sources.

Enhanced Security

Dataflows enhance security by exposing data to report creators within the dataflows themselves, limiting access to the underlying data sources. This reduces the load on source systems and allows administrators to have finer control over data refresh operations.

Scalability with Large Data Volumes

For handling large data volumes and performing ETL at scale, dataflows with Power BI Premium provide more efficient scaling and greater flexibility. Dataflows support a wide range of cloud and on-premises data sources, making them suitable for diverse data environments.

Integration with Power BI Desktop and Service

Dataflows can be used with Power BI Desktop and the Power BI service to create semantic models, reports, dashboards, and apps utilizing the Common Data Model. These resources offer deep insights into business activities. Additionally, dataflow refresh scheduling is managed directly from the workspace where the dataflow was created, similar to managing semantic models.

Benefits of Dataflows

Dataflow has applications ranging from data integration to data validation. Following are some of the key benefits.

Data Migration

Many businesses are enhancing or migrating their legacy applications to Power Apps due to its well-recognized potential. Often, these applications have large data sizes. The extracted data must go through a series of preparation functions before being loaded into Dataverse. Dataflows handle this process seamlessly by mapping the columns of the destination Dataverse table, ensuring smooth and efficient data migration.

Decouples Data Transformation from Modeling and Visualization

Dataflows separate the data transformation layer from the modeling and visualization layers in Power BI solutions. This decoupling streamlines the workflow and improves manageability.

Centralized Data Transformation

By storing data transformation code in a central location (the dataflow), rather than distributing it across multiple artifacts, dataflows enhance consistency and maintainability in your data management processes.

Simplified Skill Requirements

Creating dataflows requires only Power Query skills. This allows a dataflow creator to be part of a collaborative team that builds the entire BI solution or operational application, even in environments with multiple creators.

Product-Agnostic Design

Dataflows are not limited to Power BI. They are product-agnostic, meaning their data can be accessed and utilized by other tools and services, providing flexibility and broader applicability.

Leverages Power Query

Dataflows take advantage of Power Query, a robust, graphical, self-service data transformation tool. This allows users to perform complex data transformations easily and efficiently.

Cloud-Based Operation

Running entirely in the cloud, dataflows require no additional infrastructure. This simplifies deployment and management, reducing overhead costs and complexity.

Flexible Licensing Options

Users can start working with dataflows through licenses for Power Apps, Power BI, and Customer Insights, offering multiple entry points and flexibility in how dataflows are integrated into existing workflows.

Self-Service Data Preparation

Designed for self-service scenarios, dataflows support advanced transformations while being accessible to users without an IT or developer background. This democratizes data preparation and empowers a wider range of users to contribute to data projects.

While Power Apps dataflows offer many advantages for integrating and transforming data within the Microsoft Power Platform, they also come with certain disadvantages. Here are some potential drawbacks.

Disadvantages of Power Apps Dataflows

Complexity

> **Steep Learning Curve:** For users who are not familiar with data integration tools, the initial setup and configuration can be complex and time-consuming.

> **Advanced Configuration:** Advanced data transformations and mappings might require a deeper understanding of dataflow mechanics, which can be challenging for nontechnical users.

Performance

Processing Time: Dataflows can sometimes take a significant amount of time to process large volumes of data, which can affect performance, especially for real-time data requirements.

Resource-Intensive: Dataflows can be resource-intensive, potentially impacting the performance of other services within the Power Platform or the underlying data source systems.

Limitations in Functionality

Data Transformation Limits: There are certain limitations in the types of data transformations and manipulations that can be performed directly within Power Apps dataflows compared to more robust ETL (Extract, Transform, Load) tools.

Connector Limitations: While Power Apps supports numerous connectors, there may be some specific connectors or data sources that are not supported or have limited functionality.

Data Refresh and Sync Issues

Scheduling Constraints: The frequency and timing of data refreshes might not meet all business requirements, particularly for scenarios requiring near real-time data updates.

Sync Errors: Data synchronization errors can occur, requiring manual intervention to resolve, which can be cumbersome and time-consuming.

CHAPTER 4   DATA INTEGRATION, DATA EXPORT, AND ANALYTICS IN DATAVERSE

Use-Case Scenarios for Dataflows

Dataflows in the Power Platform play a crucial role in connecting, transforming, and preparing data for use across these applications. They allow users to extract data from a variety of sources, clean and transform it, and then load it into a target destination for reporting and analysis. This chapter explores several use-case scenarios demonstrating the practical applications and benefits of dataflows within the Power Platform ecosystem.

Scenario 1: Enhanced Sales Reporting

Background

A mid-sized enterprise with a growing sales team needs a comprehensive reporting solution to track performance metrics, sales targets, and pipeline status. The sales data is scattered across multiple systems including CRM, ERP, and a legacy database.

Step 1: Data Collection

Using Power BI dataflows, the enterprise can connect to various data sources. Power BI offers connectors for CRM systems like Dynamics 365, ERP systems, and databases. Dataflows allow the integration of these disparate data sources into a unified dataset.

Step 2: Data Cleansing

The raw sales data often contains inconsistencies and errors. Dataflows provide powerful data transformation capabilities, including

- Removing duplicates
- Handling missing values
- Standardizing data formats

Step 3: Data Transformation

Transforming data is crucial for meaningful analysis. Dataflows can

- Aggregate sales data by region, product, and sales representative
- Calculate key performance indicators (KPIs) such as monthly sales growth, target achievement rate, and average deal size
- Create custom columns and measures for deeper insights

Step 4: Loading Data

Once the data is prepared, it can be loaded into Power BI datasets. These datasets serve as the foundation for creating interactive and insightful reports and dashboards. The data is refreshed automatically, ensuring that the sales team always has access to up-to-date information.

Benefits

- **Centralized Reporting**: Consolidates data from multiple sources into a single, cohesive view
- **Real-Time Insights**: Provides timely and accurate sales performance metrics
- **Decision Support**: Empowers sales managers with actionable insights to drive strategy and performance

Creating and Configuring Dataflows

Dataflows in Power Apps allow you to connect, clean, transform, and load data into Microsoft Dataverse or Azure Data Lake Gen2. The process involves authoring a dataflow by defining data connections, shaping data with Power Query, mapping data to the Common Data Model, setting

CHAPTER 4   DATA INTEGRATION, DATA EXPORT, AND ANALYTICS IN DATAVERSE

up refresh schedules, and troubleshooting any issues. Dataflows support integrating data from multiple sources to enhance data management and analytics.

A dataflow in Power Apps is a collection of tables managed within Power Apps environments. You can add, edit tables, and manage data refresh schedules directly from this environment. Figure 4-1 demonstrates the dataflow architecture diagram.

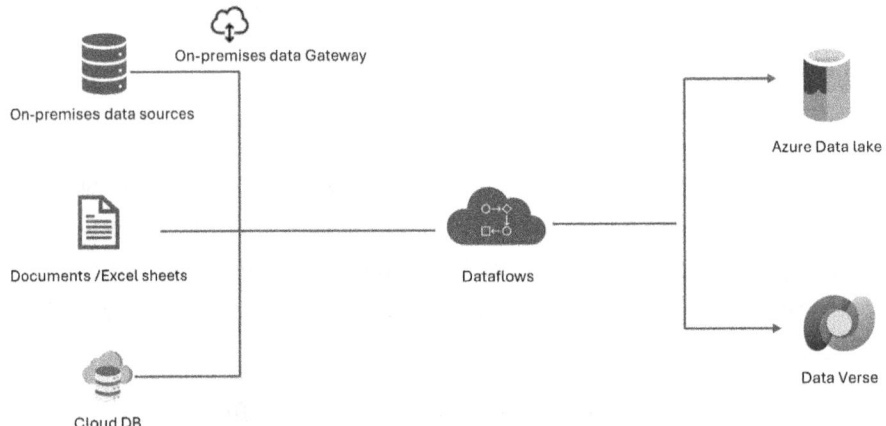

Figure 4-1. *Dataflow diagram*

To use a dataflow

- **Authoring**: In the Power Apps portal, select the data source, destination, and use Power Query to transform data.

- **Scheduling**: Set the frequency for data refreshes.

- **Using the Data**: Build apps, flows, reports, and dashboards, or connect to the data using Azure services.

Each step is designed to streamline data management and integration.

CHAPTER 4 DATA INTEGRATION, DATA EXPORT, AND ANALYTICS IN DATAVERSE

Create a Dataflow

To create a dataflow in Power Apps

1. **Sign In and Verify Environment**: Sign in to Power Apps and use the environment switcher on the right side of the command bar to select the appropriate environment.

2. **Access Dataflows**: On the left navigation pane, select **Dataflows**. If not visible, choose ...More and then **Dataflows**.

3. **Create New Dataflow**: Click "New dataflow" and select Start from blank. Enter a name, choose where to store tables (Dataverse or Azure Data Lake), and select **Create**. *Refer to Figure 4-2.*

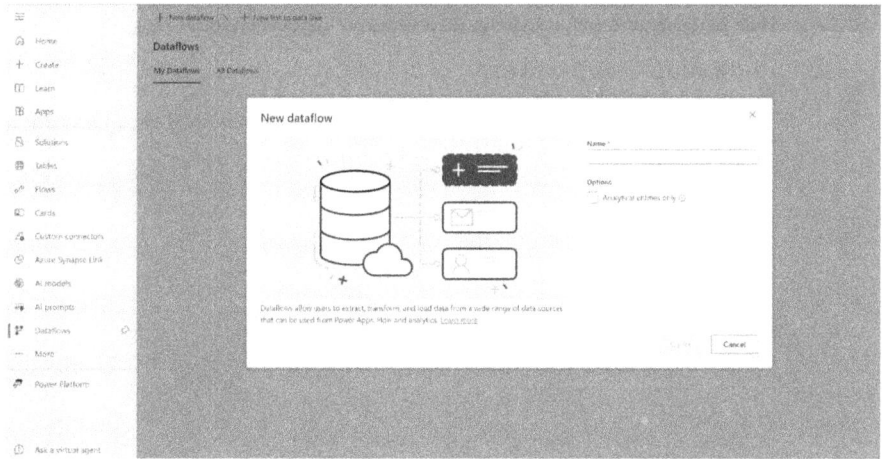

Figure 4-2. *Create dataflows*

4. **Choose Data Source**: On the Choose data source page, select the source where the tables are stored.

CHAPTER 4   DATA INTEGRATION, DATA EXPORT, AND ANALYTICS IN DATAVERSE

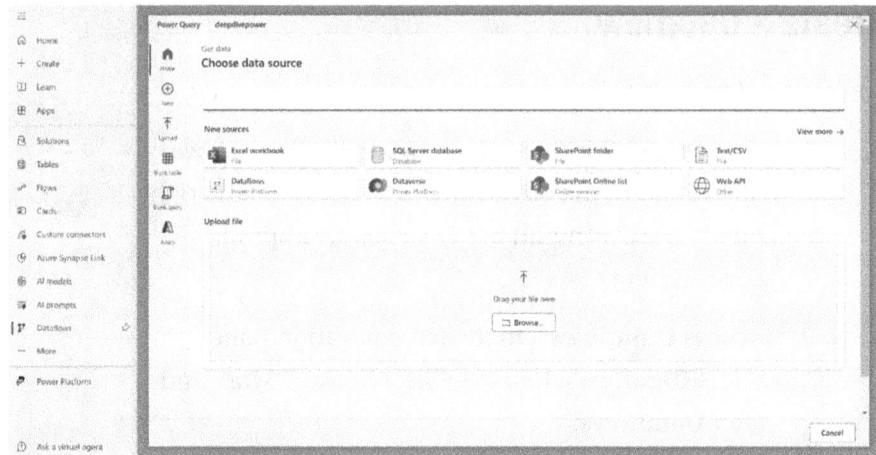

Figure 4-3. Choose data source

5. **Connection Settings**: After you select a data source, you're prompted to provide the connection settings, including the account to use when connecting to the data source. Select **Next**.

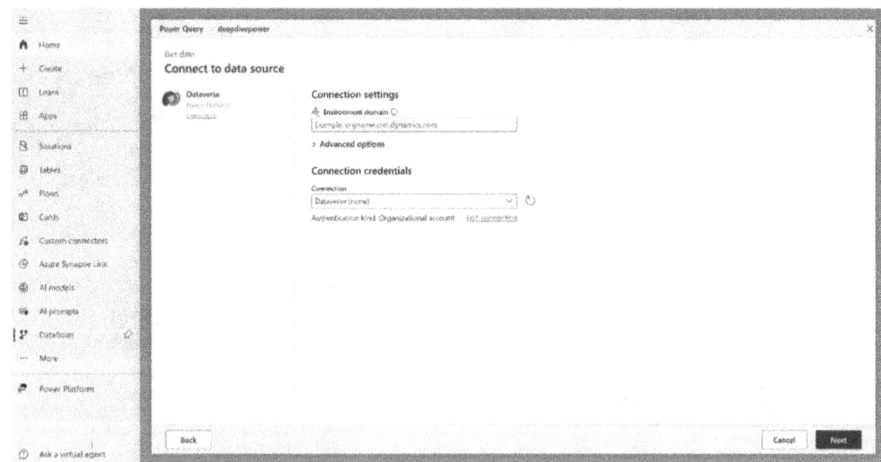

Figure 4-4. Connect to data source

Once you connect to a data source, you select the data for your table. The Power Platform dataflow service will then automatically reconnect to this source to refresh the data at the frequency you set during the setup process.

Transformations and Data Preparation

In the world of data management, transforming and preparing data is a crucial step in ensuring that the data is ready for analysis, reporting, and decision-making. Power Platform dataflows provide robust tools for these processes, leveraging Power Query to enable users to connect, clean, and transform data from various sources.

Dataflows and Power Query

Dataflows in Power Apps and Power BI allow users to integrate data from multiple sources into a unified, standardized format. Power Query, the data connection and transformation tool integrated within these platforms, offers a user-friendly interface for data preparation. It supports a wide range of transformations, enabling users to clean and shape data as needed.

Connecting to Data Sources

The first step in using dataflows is connecting to the desired data sources. Power Platform dataflows support a variety of sources including databases, cloud services, and on-premises systems. Once connected, users can select the specific data they need for their tables. The dataflow service will then maintain this connection, automatically refreshing the data at scheduled intervals to ensure that it remains up-to-date.

Data Transformations

Transforming data involves modifying it to meet specific requirements or to improve its quality. In Power Query, transformations can include operations such as filtering rows, removing duplicates, pivoting and unpivoting columns, merging tables, and performing mathematical or statistical calculations. These transformations help in cleaning the data, ensuring its consistency, and preparing it for further analysis.

Filtering and Sorting

Filtering allows users to remove unnecessary data, focusing only on the relevant subsets. This can be done based on specific criteria, such as removing records with null values or filtering rows based on date ranges. Sorting, on the other hand, helps in organizing data in a particular order, which can be crucial for analysis.

Data Cleaning

Data cleaning is an essential transformation step to remove errors and inconsistencies. This can include removing duplicates, correcting data entry errors, standardizing data formats, and handling missing values. Clean data is vital for accurate analysis and reporting.

Aggregation and Grouping

Aggregation involves summarizing data, such as calculating averages, sums, or counts. Grouping allows users to organize data into categories based on specific fields. These operations are useful for generating summary reports and insights.

Advanced Transformations

Power Query also supports advanced transformations for more complex data preparation needs.

These can include

> **Pivot and Unpivot**: Pivoting transforms row data into columns, while unpivoting does the reverse. These operations are useful for reshaping data to fit specific analytical needs.
>
> **Merging and Appending**: Merging tables combines data from different sources into a single table based on a common field, while appending adds rows from one table to another. These operations are essential for integrating disparate data sources.
>
> **Custom Calculations**: Users can create custom calculations using Power Query's formula language, M. This allows for the creation of calculated columns, custom metrics, and other complex transformations.

Data Preparation for Analysis

The ultimate goal of data transformations is to prepare data for analysis. This involves ensuring that the data is structured correctly and that it meets the specific requirements of the analysis tools being used. Power Platform Dataflows make it easy to load transformed data into destinations such as Microsoft Dataverse, Azure Data Lake Storage, or Power BI for further analysis and reporting.

Data Refresh and Scheduling

Once the data is transformed and loaded, it is essential to keep it updated. Power Platform Dataflows allow users to schedule data refreshes at regular intervals. This ensures that the data remains current, reflecting any changes in the source systems. Users can set refresh frequencies based on their specific needs, ranging from hourly to daily updates.

Integration with Other Tools

Power Platform Dataflows integrate seamlessly with other tools in the Microsoft ecosystem, such as Power BI and Azure services. This integration allows users to leverage the full capabilities of these tools for further data analysis, reporting, and visualization. For example, data loaded into Power BI can be used to create interactive dashboards and reports, providing valuable insights into business operations.

Best Practices for Data Transformations

To make the most of data transformations and preparation, it is important to follow best practices:

> **Plan Ahead**: Understand the data sources and the specific transformation requirements before starting.
>
> **Document Transformations**: Keep a record of the transformations applied to maintain transparency and reproducibility.
>
> **Test Incrementally**: Apply and test transformations incrementally to ensure accuracy at each step.

CHAPTER 4   DATA INTEGRATION, DATA EXPORT, AND ANALYTICS IN DATAVERSE

Optimize Performance: Consider the performance impact of complex transformations and optimize where necessary.

Monitor Data Quality: Continuously monitor the quality of the transformed data to ensure it meets the required standards.

Conclusion

Transformations and data preparation are fundamental processes in the data management life cycle. Power Platform Dataflows provide powerful tools for these tasks, enabling users to connect, clean, transform, and prepare data efficiently. By leveraging the capabilities of Power Query and integrating with other Microsoft tools, users can ensure that their data is ready for analysis, leading to better insights and informed decision-making. Following best practices ensures that the data preparation process is effective, accurate, and efficient.

Integration with Power Query

Power Query is a powerful data connection and transformation tool integrated within Power Platform Dataflows. It enables users to connect to various data sources, clean, and transform data using a user-friendly, intuitive interface. Power Query provides a range of transformation options, from basic data cleaning to complex data shaping, ensuring that data is ready for analysis and reporting.

In Dataflows, Power Query is leveraged to author dataflows, allowing users to connect to different data sources, define the data extraction process, and apply transformations. This process involves selecting and filtering data, performing aggregations, and ensuring the data is in the desired format. Power Query's ability to handle various data

CHAPTER 4   DATA INTEGRATION, DATA EXPORT, AND ANALYTICS IN DATAVERSE

transformations makes it an essential tool for preparing data efficiently and accurately. Refer Figure 4-5 to see how to use advanced editor for Power Query.

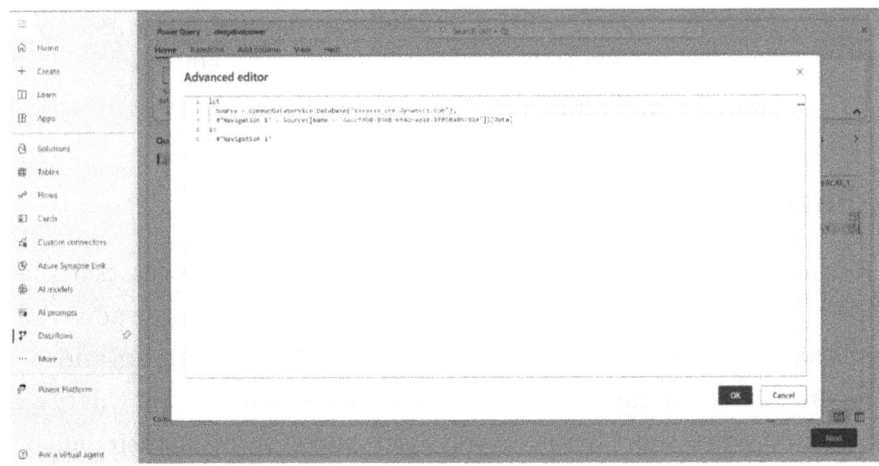

Figure 4-5. *Power query*

Data Transformation and Cleansing

Data transformation and cleansing are critical steps in preparing data for analysis. These processes involve removing duplicates, correcting data inconsistencies, standardizing data formats, and handling missing values. Power Query offers a suite of tools to perform these tasks, including filtering, sorting, merging, and splitting columns, ensuring the data is clean, consistent, and ready for use.

Advanced Dataflow Scenarios

Advanced dataflow scenarios include complex transformations and integration with other services. Examples include creating computed tables for in-storage transformations using the M language, performing incremental refreshes to update only changed data, and linking tables across different dataflows. These advanced features enable users to manage large datasets efficiently and integrate seamlessly with services like Azure Data Lake Storage and Power BI, enhancing the overall data management and analytics capabilities.

Advanced dataflow scenarios involve leveraging complex transformations and integrations to enhance data management capabilities. Here are some key features:

- **Computed Tables**: Use the M language for in-storage transformations, enabling complex calculations and reshaping within Azure Data Lake Storage.

- **Incremental Refresh**: Update only changed data since the last refresh to improve efficiency. This feature is available in Power Apps Plan 2 and Power BI Premium.

- **Linked Tables**: Create dataflows linking tables across different dataflows, enabling dynamic, interconnected data management.

- **Integration with Azure Services**: Utilize services like Azure Data Factory and Azure Databricks for comprehensive data processing and management.

These advanced features help manage large datasets efficiently, optimize data processing, and seamlessly integrate with a broader data ecosystem, enhancing overall analytics and reporting capabilities.

Dataflow Scheduling and Automation

Dataflow scheduling and automation within the Power Platform are essential features for maintaining the freshness and reliability of data used in Power BI reports and other downstream applications. These capabilities ensure that dataflows are refreshed regularly and efficiently, enabling users to make informed decisions based on up-to-date information.

Dataflow Scheduling

Dataflow scheduling allows users to define when dataflows should be refreshed automatically. This process ensures that data is always current and reflects the latest changes from the underlying data sources. Key aspects of dataflow scheduling include

> **Frequency**: Users can set the frequency of dataflow refreshes, such as daily, weekly, or at custom intervals. This flexibility enables organizations to align data refreshes with their business needs and data update cycles.
>
> **Time Zone Support**: Dataflow scheduling supports time zone configurations, ensuring that refreshes occur at appropriate times, regardless of the geographical location of the data sources or users.
>
> **Multiple Schedules**: For dataflows with different update requirements, users can define multiple refresh schedules. This capability enables fine-grained control over when and how often dataflows are refreshed.
>
> **Dependencies**: Users can specify dependencies between dataflows to ensure that they refresh in the correct order. This feature is particularly useful when dataflows rely on each other or when there are dependencies on external data sources.

Dataflow Automation

Dataflow automation extends beyond scheduling and encompasses a range of capabilities aimed at streamlining dataflow management and execution. These automation features enhance efficiency, reliability, and scalability in data preparation processes. Key aspects of dataflow automation include:

> **Error Handling**: Automation mechanisms can handle errors that occur during dataflow refreshes. This includes logging errors, retrying failed refreshes, and sending notifications to administrators or users when issues arise.

> **Notifications**: Users can configure notifications to receive alerts when dataflow refreshes encounter errors or when specific conditions are met. Notifications help ensure that stakeholders are informed of any issues affecting data availability or quality.

> **Integration with Workflow Tools**: Dataflow automation can be integrated with workflow automation tools like Power Automate. This enables users to trigger actions or workflows based on dataflow refresh events, such as sending emails, updating records in other systems, or generating reports.

> **Monitoring and Insights**: Automation features provide visibility into dataflow performance and health. Administrators can monitor refresh history, track execution times, and analyze refresh logs to identify bottlenecks or issues that may require optimization.

Benefits of Dataflow Scheduling and Automation

- **Data Freshness**: Scheduled refreshes ensure that data in Power BI reports is always up-to-date, providing users with accurate insights for decision-making.

- **Efficiency**: Automation streamlines dataflow management tasks, reducing manual effort and minimizing the risk of errors or delays in data preparation processes.

- **Reliability**: Automation features include error handling and notifications, improving the reliability of dataflows and enabling proactive issue resolution.

- **Scalability**: Automated processes can scale to handle large volumes of data and complex data transformation requirements, supporting the evolving needs of organizations as they grow.

- **Productivity**: By automating routine tasks, users can focus on higher-value activities such as data analysis, visualization, and deriving insights from data.

Monitoring and Managing Dataflow Execution

Monitoring and managing dataflow execution are essential tasks for ensuring the reliability, performance, and accuracy of dataflows within the Power Platform. These activities involve tracking dataflow refreshes, diagnosing issues, optimizing performance, and ensuring data quality. Here's how to effectively monitor and manage dataflow execution.

Dataflow Monitoring Tools

Refresh History: Power Platform provides a refresh history log that tracks the execution history of dataflows. This log includes details such as refresh start time, duration, status (success/failure), and error messages.

Execution Metrics: Metrics such as data refresh duration, data volume processed, and refresh frequency provide insights into the performance and efficiency of dataflows.

Dataflow Health: Monitoring tools may include health indicators or dashboards that display the overall health status of dataflows, highlighting any issues or anomalies.

Here are some key actions recommended to take:

Regularly review the refresh history log to identify patterns, trends, or abnormalities in dataflow execution.

Monitor key performance metrics to assess dataflow efficiency and identify areas for optimization.

Use health indicators to quickly identify dataflows that require attention or troubleshooting.

Troubleshooting and Diagnostics

Error Diagnostics: When dataflow refreshes fail, diagnostic tools help identify the root cause of the failure by providing detailed error messages, stack traces, and debugging information.

Data Profiling: Data profiling tools analyze the quality and structure of data within dataflows, identifying anomalies, inconsistencies, or data quality issues.

Dependency Analysis: Trace dependencies between dataflows and their underlying data sources to troubleshoot issues related to data availability, connectivity, or schema changes.

Actions

Use error diagnostics to analyze failed dataflow refreshes, identify the underlying cause of errors, and take corrective actions.

Leverage data profiling tools to assess data quality, identify outliers or anomalies, and implement data cleansing or transformation measures as needed.

Conduct dependency analysis to understand the impact of changes in underlying data sources on dataflow execution and ensure dataflow consistency and reliability.

Performance Optimization

Query Performance Tuning: Analyze dataflow execution plans and query performance to identify bottlenecks, optimize query execution, and improve dataflow refresh performance.

Incremental Refresh: Implement incremental refresh strategies to minimize data processing and optimize dataflow refresh times, especially for large datasets.

Resource Allocation: Allocate sufficient resources (e.g., CPU, memory) to dataflows to ensure optimal performance and scalability.

Actions

Fine-tune dataflow queries and transformations to optimize query performance and reduce data processing times.

Implement incremental refresh strategies to refresh only the data that has changed since the last refresh, reducing overall refresh duration and resource consumption.

Monitor resource utilization and allocate additional resources as needed to accommodate growing data volumes or complex data transformation requirements.

Governance and Compliance

Data Access Controls: Enforce access controls and permissions to govern who can create, modify, or refresh dataflows, ensuring data security and compliance with regulatory requirements.

Audit Logs: Maintain audit logs of dataflow activities, including refreshes, modifications, and access attempts, to track data lineage and comply with audit and compliance mandates.

Data Retention Policies: Define data retention policies to manage the life cycle of dataflow execution logs and audit trails, ensuring compliance with data retention requirements.

Actions

> Configure role-based access controls (RBAC) to restrict access to dataflows and enforce segregation of duties (SoD) to prevent unauthorized modifications or refreshes.
>
> Enable audit logging for dataflow activities and periodically review audit logs to monitor compliance with governance policies and detect any unauthorized or suspicious activities.
>
> Define data retention policies and archive or delete dataflow execution logs and audit trails according to regulatory requirements and organizational policies.

Effective monitoring and management of dataflow execution are essential for ensuring the reliability, performance, and integrity of dataflows within the Power Platform. By leveraging monitoring tools, setting up alerts and notifications, troubleshooting and diagnostics, performance optimization strategies, and governance and compliance measures, organizations can maintain dataflow health, mitigate risks, and drive better business outcomes through accurate and timely data insights.

Azure Synapse Link for Dataverse

Azure Synapse Link for Dataverse provides a seamless integration between Azure Synapse Analytics and Microsoft Dataverse, enabling organizations to derive near-real-time insights from their data. This integration empowers businesses to unlock the full potential of their data by leveraging advanced analytics and machine learning capabilities offered by Azure Synapse Analytics while keeping their data synchronized and up-to-date with Dataverse.

Here are some of the key benefits of using Azure Synapse Link in Dataverse:

1. **Real-Time Data Synchronization**: Azure Synapse Link ensures that data changes made in Dataverse are automatically synchronized with Azure Synapse Analytics in near-real-time. This means that as data is added, updated, or deleted in Dataverse, the changes are immediately reflected in Azure Synapse Analytics, providing users with access to the latest data for analysis.

2. **Direct Query Access**: Azure Synapse Link establishes a direct query access mechanism between Azure Synapse Analytics and Dataverse. This eliminates the need for data duplication or staging, as users can query the data in Dataverse directly from Azure Synapse Analytics without any data movement.

3. **Unified Analytics Platform**: By integrating Dataverse with Azure Synapse Analytics, organizations can leverage the powerful analytics and machine learning capabilities of Azure Synapse Analytics to derive insights from their Dataverse data. This includes advanced analytics features such as predictive modeling, machine learning, and big data processing.

4. **Scalability and Performance**: Azure Synapse Analytics is built for scalability and high-performance analytics. With Azure Synapse Link for Dataverse, organizations can analyze large volumes of data stored in Dataverse with ease, taking advantage of the distributed processing capabilities of Azure Synapse Analytics.

5. **Security and Compliance**: Azure Synapse Link ensures that data security and compliance requirements are met by providing built-in security features such as encryption, access control, and compliance certifications. This enables organizations to analyze their Dataverse data in a secure and compliant manner.

6. **Integration with Power Platform**: Azure Synapse Link seamlessly integrates with Microsoft Power Platform, allowing organizations to build end-to-end analytics solutions that leverage both Dataverse and Azure Synapse Analytics. This enables users to visualize insights, create reports and dashboards, and automate business processes using Power BI, Power Apps, and Power Automate.

In summary, Azure Synapse Link for Dataverse enables organizations to harness the power of Azure Synapse Analytics for advanced analytics and near-real-time insights while seamlessly integrating with their existing Dataverse environments. It simplifies the analytics process, improves data accessibility and agility, and empowers organizations to make data-driven decisions more effectively.

Introduction to Azure Synapse Link

Azure Synapse Link is a cutting-edge service provided by Microsoft Azure, designed to seamlessly integrate data between Azure Synapse Analytics and various operational databases and data stores. It enables organizations to unlock the full potential of their data by facilitating real-time analytics, eliminating the need for complex data movement processes.

With Azure Synapse Link, businesses can establish a direct connection between Azure Synapse Analytics and their operational databases, such as Azure SQL Database, Azure Cosmos DB, and now, Microsoft Dataverse (formerly known as Common Data Service). This direct connection enables near-real-time data synchronization, allowing organizations to analyze the latest data without delays.

One of the key advantages of Azure Synapse Link is its ability to enable analytics directly on operational data, without the need for ETL (Extract, Transform, Load) processes or data replication. This eliminates the latency associated with traditional data warehousing solutions, enabling organizations to derive insights from their data faster and make informed decisions in real time.

Azure Synapse Link leverages the capabilities of Azure Synapse Analytics, a powerful analytics platform that integrates data warehousing, big data analytics, and data integration services into a single, unified experience. This allows organizations to perform advanced analytics, including machine learning, artificial intelligence, and predictive analytics, on their operational data, further enhancing their ability to derive valuable insights and drive business outcomes.

In summary, Azure Synapse Link revolutionizes the way organizations access and analyze their data by providing a seamless integration between Azure Synapse Analytics and operational databases. By enabling near-real-time analytics directly on operational data, Azure Synapse Link empowers organizations to make faster, data-driven decisions and unlock new opportunities for innovation and growth.

Overview of Near-Real-Time Insights

Imagine a world where data is not just a static resource but a dynamic force, constantly in motion, evolving with each passing moment. Azure Synapse Link, in tandem with Dataverse, transforms this vision into reality, offering organizations the ability to tap into the pulse of their data in real time.

With Azure Synapse Link, the barriers between data sources and analytics tools crumble away, replaced by a seamless connection that enables data to flow freely, unencumbered by the constraints of traditional ETL processes. This direct link between Azure Synapse Analytics and Dataverse allows for near-instantaneous synchronization of data, ensuring that insights are always based on the most fresh and most up-to-date information.

But the true magic of Azure Synapse Link lies not just in its ability to synchronize data in real time but in its capacity to unlock the full potential of that data through advanced analytics. Within the powerful analytics platform of Azure Synapse Analytics, organizations gain access to a vast array of analytical tools and techniques, from machine learning algorithms to predictive modeling capabilities.

When combined with the rich and diverse data stored within Dataverse, these analytical tools become catalysts for innovation, empowering organizations to uncover hidden patterns, identify emerging trends, and make informed decisions with unprecedented speed and accuracy.

Whether it's detecting anomalies in real-time sensor data, predicting customer behavior based on historical interactions, or optimizing business processes on the fly, the possibilities with Azure Synapse Link and Dataverse are truly limitless.

Enabling Near-Real-Time Analytics

You can utilize Azure Synapse Link to establish a connection between your Microsoft Dataverse data and Azure Synapse Analytics, thereby accelerating your journey to insights. This guide illustrates the steps to:

CHAPTER 4   DATA INTEGRATION, DATA EXPORT, AND ANALYTICS IN DATAVERSE

Connect your Dataverse data to your Azure Synapse Analytics workspace using the Azure Synapse Link service:

- Manage Dataverse tables integrated with Azure Synapse Link.
- Monitor the status of your Azure Synapse Link.
- Unlink and relink your Azure Synapse Link as needed.
- View and analyze your data within Azure Synapse Analytics.

Prerequisites

Dataverse: You must possess the Dataverse system administrator security role. Additionally, tables intended for export via Azure Synapse Link must have the "Track changes" property enabled.

Azure Data Lake Storage Gen2: An Azure Data Lake Storage Gen2 account is required, with Owner and Storage Blob Data Contributor role access. Hierarchical namespace must be enabled for both initial setup and delta sync. "Allow storage account key access" is necessary only for the initial setup.

Synapse workspace: You need a Synapse workspace with Synapse Administrator role access within Synapse Studio. The workspace must reside in the same region as your Azure Data Lake Storage Gen2 account. The storage account must be added as a linked service within Synapse Studio.

Figure 4-6 depicts how to configure Azure Synapse Link within the Power Platform.

Configuring and Activating Azure Synapse Link

1. Sign in to Power Apps and navigate to your preferred environment.

2. On the left navigation pane, locate Azure Synapse Link. If it's not visible, expand the options by selecting "…More" and choose "Discover all." Then, select Azure Synapse Link under the Data Management section.

3. On the command bar, click "+ New link."

4. Opt for the "Connect to your Azure Synapse workspace" option.

5. Choose the Subscription, Resource group, Workspace name, and Storage account. Ensure that the Synapse workspace and storage account fulfill the prerequisites outlined earlier. Proceed by selecting "Next."

CHAPTER 4   DATA INTEGRATION, DATA EXPORT, AND ANALYTICS IN DATAVERSE

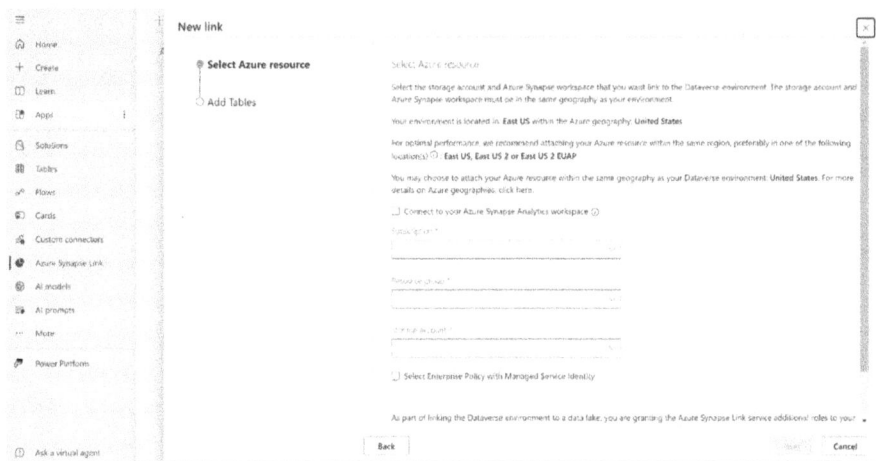

Figure 4-6. *Configuration of Azure Synapse Link*

6. Add the tables you want to export, and then select "Save". Only tables with change tracking enabled can be exported.

Enable Change Tracking to Control Data Synchronization

For large organizations managing data synchronization with external sources, enabling change tracking for specific tables (entities) can streamline the process and optimize resource utilization. This allows selective export or retrieval of data, ensuring efficient synchronization with external data warehouses.

Figure 4-7 shows a screenshot of how to configure Advanced settings of Managed Data Lake through Azure Synapse link.

191

To enable change tracking using PowerApps settings

1. Sign in to Power Apps.
2. Navigate to the Dataverse section and select "Tables."
3. Choose the desired table from the list and then access its properties by selecting "Properties."
4. In the Edit Table page, locate the "Advanced options" section.
5. Within the "For this table" section, enable the "Track Changes" checkbox.
6. Confirm the selection by checking the checkbox to enable Track Changes.
7. Save the changes to ensure that the selected table now tracks changes for synchronization purposes.

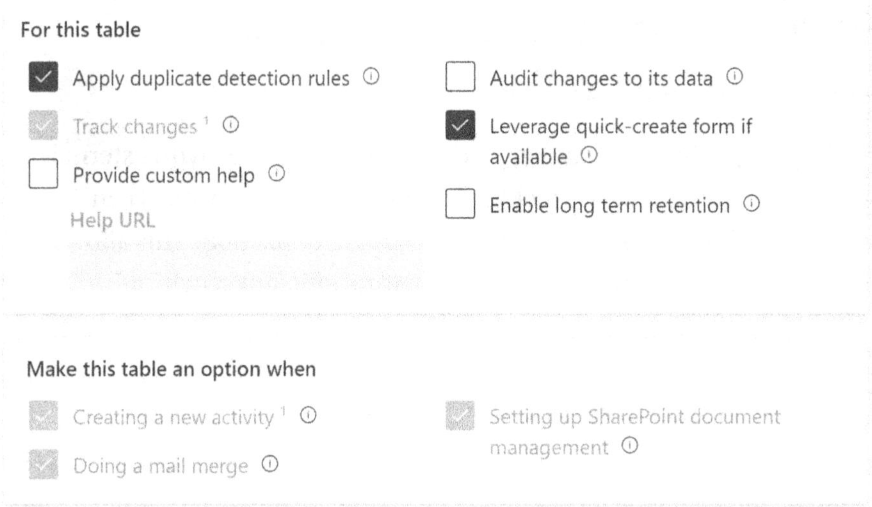

For this table

- [x] Apply duplicate detection rules
- [x] Track changes [1]
- [ ] Provide custom help

    Help URL

- [ ] Audit changes to its data
- [x] Leverage quick-create form if available
- [ ] Enable long term retention

Make this table an option when

- [x] Creating a new activity [1]
- [x] Doing a mail merge
- [ ] Setting up SharePoint document management

Figure 4-7. Enable track changes for the table

By following these steps, organizations can efficiently manage data synchronization processes, reduce server resource loads, and save processing time, ultimately enhancing the effectiveness of data management strategies.

Azure Synapse Link with Delta Lake

Delta Lake is an open-source project designed to enable the construction of a lakehouse architecture atop data lakes. It offers ACID (atomicity, consistency, isolation, and durability) transactions, scalable metadata handling, and unifies both streaming and batch data processing on existing data lakes. Azure Synapse Analytics is compatible with the Linux Foundation Delta Lake. The current version of Delta Lake available with Azure Synapse supports languages such as Scala, PySpark, and .NET.

Apache Parquet serves as the baseline format for Delta Lake, allowing you to benefit from efficient compression and encoding schemes inherent to the format. Parquet uses column-wise compression, which is efficient and saves storage space. Queries fetching specific column values don't need to read the entire row data, thus improving performance. Consequently, serverless SQL pools require less time and fewer storage requests to read the data.

Benefits of Delta Lake

- **Scalability**: Delta Lake, built on the open-source Apache license, is designed to handle large-scale data-processing workloads, meeting industry standards.

- **Reliability**: Delta Lake ensures data consistency and reliability through ACID transactions, even during failures or concurrent access.

- **Performance**: Utilizing Parquet's columnar storage format, Delta Lake offers better compression and encoding techniques, enhancing query performance compared to CSV files.

- **Cost-Effectiveness**: Delta Lake's highly compressed data storage format can significantly reduce storage costs and optimize data processing, potentially decreasing the total processing time and computing costs.

- **Data Protection Compliance**: With features like soft-delete and hard-delete, Delta Lake helps comply with data privacy regulations, including GDPR.

How Delta Lake Works with Azure Synapse Link for Dataverse

When configuring an Azure Synapse Link for Dataverse, you can enable the export to Delta Lake feature and connect it to a Synapse workspace and Spark pool. Azure Synapse Link exports selected Dataverse tables in CSV format at specified intervals, which are then processed through a Delta Lake conversion Spark job. After conversion, the CSV data is cleaned up to save storage space. Additionally, daily maintenance jobs are scheduled to perform compaction and vacuuming processes, merging and cleaning up data files to optimize storage and enhance query performance.

Prerequisites

- **Dataverse**: You must have the Dataverse system administrator security role. Tables intended for export via Azure Synapse Link must have the "Track changes" property enabled.

- **Azure Data Lake Storage Gen2**: You need an Azure Data Lake Storage Gen2 account with Owner and Storage Blob Data Contributor role access. The account must enable hierarchical namespace and public network access for both initial setup and delta sync. "Allow storage account key access" is required only for the initial setup.

- **Synapse Workspace**: You must have a Synapse workspace with Owner role access control (IAM) and Synapse Administrator role access within Synapse Studio. The Synapse workspace and Azure Data Lake Storage Gen2 account must be in the same region, and the storage account must be added as a linked service within Synapse Studio.

- **Spark Pool**: A Spark Pool in the connected Azure Synapse workspace is with Apache Spark Version 3.3 and recommended configurations.

- **Microsoft Dynamics 365**: Minimum version 9.2.22082 is required.

Connecting Dataverse to Synapse Workspace and Exporting Data in Delta Lake Format

1. Sign in to Power Apps and select your preferred environment.

2. In the left navigation pane, choose Azure Synapse Link. If it's not visible, select "...More" and find the item.

3. On the command bar, select "+ New link."

CHAPTER 4   DATA INTEGRATION, DATA EXPORT, AND ANALYTICS IN DATAVERSE

4. Select "Connect to your Azure Synapse Analytics workspace" and then choose the Subscription, Resource group, and Workspace name.

5. Select "Use Spark pool for processing" and then choose the precreated Spark pool and Storage account.

By following these steps, you can effectively integrate and manage your Dataverse data with Azure Synapse Analytics using Delta Lake, optimizing performance and ensuring data reliability.

Below is a description of the end-to-end flow for connecting Dataverse data to Azure Synapse Link with Delta Lake.

Figure 4-8 demonstrates the high-level architecture of managed data lake using Synapse Link and Dataverse.

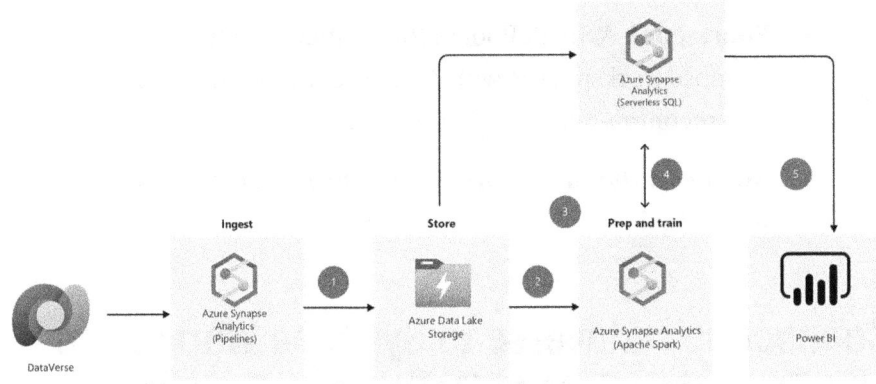

Figure 4-8. *Dataverse and Synapse with Delta Lake*

Monitor Azure Synapse Link

After setting up Azure Synapse Link, you'll have two versions of table data synchronized by default in Azure Synapse Analytics and/or Azure Data Lake Storage Gen2. These ensure you always have access to updated data:

1. **Near-Real-Time Data**: This version provides efficiently synchronized data from Dataverse via Azure Synapse Link. It captures changes since the last synchronization, ensuring you have the latest data available for analysis.

2. **Snapshot Data**: Snapshot data offers a read-only copy of near-real-time data, updated at regular intervals, typically every hour. This static view provides a point-in-time snapshot for historical analysis.

To access and analyze the synchronized tables

- Navigate to your Azure Synapse Analytics workspace.
- Expand "Lake Databases" in the left panel and select the relevant database associated with your Dataverse environment.
- Within the database, navigate to the "Tables" section to find both Near-Real-Time Data Tables (prefixed with "DataverseTableName") and Snapshot Data Tables (prefixed with "DataverseTableName_partitioned").

Once you've explored your synchronized data, consider leveraging Discover Hub in Power Apps to further analyze and consume it effectively:

1. Go to Power Apps and select Azure Synapse Link.
2. Choose your linked service and navigate to the Discover Hub tab.
3. Here, you'll find recommended tools and curated documentation to maximize the value of your data.

CHAPTER 4   DATA INTEGRATION, DATA EXPORT, AND ANALYTICS IN DATAVERSE

With these resources at your disposal, you can unlock valuable insights and drive informed decision-making using your synchronized Dataverse data within Azure Synapse Analytics.

View Your Data from Synapse Workspace

1. Select the Azure Synapse Link and then select Go to Azure Synapse Analytics workspace on the command bar.

2. Expand Lake Databases on the left pane, select dataverse-environmentNameorganizationUniqueName, and then expand Tables. All Parquet tables are listed and available for analysis with the naming convention DataverseTableName. (Non_partitioned Table).

Real-Time Data Sync Mechanisms Using Microsoft Fabric

Microsoft Dataverse's direct link to Microsoft Fabric allows organizations to extend their Power Apps and Dynamics 365 applications and processes into Fabric seamlessly. The Link to Microsoft Fabric feature in Power Apps enables direct access to all Dynamics 365 and Power Apps data within Microsoft OneLake, the integrated data lake for Microsoft Fabric.

Key Benefits

- No need for exporting data, building ETL pipelines, or using partner integration tools.
- Shortcuts allow data to stay in Dataverse, while authorized users access and work with it in Fabric.

- Link data from all Dynamics 365 apps, including Finance and Operations.

- Create Power Apps and automations to act on insights from OneLake.

Microsoft OneLake helps eliminate data silos by combining data from various sources such as applications, devices, websites, mobile apps, sensors, and signals with business process data from Dynamics 365. This integration allows for better prediction and management of potential delays or shortages, ensuring customer satisfaction. Dataverse's shortcuts to OneLake enable working with data without creating multiple copies.

Linking to Fabric from Power Apps

1. In Power Apps (make.powerapps.com), navigate to the Tables area.

2. Select Analyze ➤ Link to Microsoft Fabric on the command bar.

3. Follow the wizard to link your Dataverse environment to a Fabric workspace.

4. A Synapse lakehouse, SQL endpoint, and Power BI dataset are created.

5. Dataverse tables are linked to the lakehouse via shortcuts.

6. Grant access to other users for working with Dataverse data in Fabric. Data updates in Dataverse will reflect in the lakehouse, SQL endpoint, and Power BI dataset automatically.

Direct Access to Your Data in Microsoft OneLake

1. The Link to Fabric feature provides a direct, secure connection between Dataverse data and a Fabric workspace.

2. An optimized data replica in delta parquet format is created, governed, and secured by Dataverse.

3. Admins manage linked tables via the Azure Synapse Link for Dataverse page and monitor storage consumption in the Power Platform admin center.

Note By linking to Microsoft Fabric, all nonsystem Dataverse tables with the Track changes property enabled are added by default.

Existing tables selected during public preview can continue to be used. Linking to new environments will add all tables, possibly increasing Dataverse storage consumption.

Comparing Link to Fabric with Azure Synapse Link for Dataverse

Link to Fabric	Azure Synapse Link
No copy, direct integration with Microsoft Fabric.	Export data to your own storage and integrate with Synapse, Microsoft Fabric, and other tools.
Data stays in Dataverse with secure access in Microsoft Fabric.	Data stays in your own storage, and you manage user access.
All tables are chosen by default.	System administrators can select required tables.
Consumes additional Dataverse storage.	Consumes your own storage, plus other compute and integration tools.

Existing Azure Synapse Links can connect to Microsoft Fabric to leverage innovations like Power BI DirectLake mode reports and integrated Spark and data pipelines.

Dataverse Plugins and Custom APIs

Microsoft Dataverse, a versatile data platform part of the Power Platform suite, provides a robust framework for extending the functionality of Dynamics 365 and Power Apps. Two critical components of this extensibility are Dataverse Plugins and Custom APIs. These tools allow developers to create sophisticated customizations, automate business processes, and integrate Dataverse with external systems. This article delves into the details of Dataverse Plugins and Custom APIs, highlighting their functionalities, use cases, and implementation.

Plugins

Plugins in Dataverse are custom business logic handlers triggered by specific events within the platform. They are essential for automating and extending business processes by executing custom code in response to data operations such as create, update, delete, and retrieve. Plugins run on the server side, ensuring that custom business logic is applied consistently regardless of how data changes are initiated (through the web, mobile, or integrations).

Key Features

> **Event-Driven Execution:** Plugins can be registered to respond to specific events within Dataverse, such as the creation of a new record, updates to existing records, deletions, or even custom events. This event-driven model allows for granular control over business logic execution.

Synchronous and Asynchronous Execution: Plugins can run either synchronously or asynchronously. Synchronous plugins execute immediately as part of the transaction, making them suitable for real-time validation and immediate feedback. Asynchronous plugins, on the other hand, execute in the background, which is ideal for tasks that do not need to block the main transaction, such as long-running operations or integrations with external systems.

Pre- and Post-Operation Stages: Plugins can be configured to run at different stages of the event pipeline. The pre-operation stage allows for the validation or modification of data before the main operation, while the post-operation stage is useful for operations that depend on the main operation's results.

Extensibility and Reusability: Plugins are developed in .NET, allowing developers to use familiar tools and libraries. They can be packaged and reused across different Dataverse instances, promoting modularity and maintainability.

Use Cases

1. **Data Validation and Enforcement of Business Rules**: For example, a plugin can ensure that a customer's email address is unique before a new customer record is created.

2. **Automated Workflows**: Plugins can trigger additional actions automatically, such as sending notifications, updating related records, or logging changes.

3. **Integration with External Systems**: Plugins can call external APIs or services to synchronize data between Dataverse and other systems, ensuring data consistency across platforms.

4. **Complex Calculations and Data Transformations**: Plugins can perform complex computations that go beyond what is possible with out-of-the-box workflows and business rules.

Implementation Steps

Develop the Plugin: Write the plugin in C# using Visual Studio. The plugin must implement the IPlugin interface.

Register the Plugin: Use the Plugin Registration Tool provided by Microsoft to register the plugin assembly and specify the events that will trigger the plugin.

Deploy and Test: Deploy the plugin to the Dataverse environment and thoroughly test to ensure it behaves as expected in all scenarios.

CHAPTER 4   DATA INTEGRATION, DATA EXPORT, AND ANALYTICS IN DATAVERSE

Custom APIs

Custom APIs in Dataverse allow developers to expose their custom business logic as API endpoints. These APIs can be consumed by various clients, including Power Apps, Power Automate, and external applications, providing a flexible way to interact with Dataverse data and execute custom operations.

Key Features

> **Custom Operations**: Unlike OData APIs, which are primarily CRUD-based, Custom APIs can encapsulate complex business logic and operations that involve multiple steps or transactions.
>
> **Security and Authentication**: Custom APIs leverage Dataverse's built-in security model, ensuring that only authorized users and applications can access the API. This ensures compliance with the security and data access policies defined in Dataverse.
>
> **Flexible Input and Output Parameters**: Custom APIs support a wide range of input and output parameter types, allowing for complex data structures to be passed to and from the API.
>
> **Integration with Power Platform**: Custom APIs can be called directly from Power Apps and Power Automate, enabling seamless integration into low-code/no-code solutions.

Use Cases

1. **Advanced Business Logic**: Custom APIs can encapsulate complex business logic that involves multiple data operations or external service calls, providing a single endpoint for these operations.

2. **Data Aggregation and Reporting**: Custom APIs can be used to aggregate data from multiple entities and return it in a single response, simplifying data retrieval for reporting purposes.

3. **External System Integration**: Custom APIs can act as intermediaries between Dataverse and external systems, facilitating data exchange and synchronization.

4. **Custom Actions and Workflows**: Define operations that go beyond standard CRUD operations, such as initiating a specific workflow or performing batch updates.

Implementation Steps

Define the API: Use the Power Platform admin center or the solution explorer in Power Apps to define the custom API. Specify the name, bound entity (if applicable), and input/output parameters.

Develop the Logic: Write the logic for the API in a plugin or a workflow extension that will be called when the API is invoked.

Register and Publish: Register the custom API and associate it with the plugin or workflow extension. Publish the API to make it available for use.

Consume the API: Use the Dataverse Web API, Power Apps, or Power Automate to call the custom API and perform the defined operations.

Conclusion

Dataverse Plugins and Custom APIs are powerful tools for extending the capabilities of Microsoft Dataverse. Plugins provide a way to execute custom business logic in response to data events, ensuring that complex rules and processes are consistently enforced. Custom APIs, on the other hand, offer a flexible way to expose this logic as reusable services that can be consumed by a variety of clients.

Together, these extensibility features enable organizations to tailor Dataverse to their specific business needs, automate intricate processes, and integrate seamlessly with other systems, all while maintaining a secure and manageable environment. Whether you are enforcing business rules, automating workflows, or integrating with external systems, Dataverse Plugins and Custom APIs provide the essential tools needed to create a robust and scalable solution.

Integration with External Services

Integrating the Power Platform with external services can significantly enhance the capabilities of your applications, workflows, and analytics. This integration allows you to leverage data and functionalities from a variety of sources, creating a more robust and versatile digital environment.

CHAPTER 4 DATA INTEGRATION, DATA EXPORT, AND ANALYTICS IN DATAVERSE

Here's how to approach integration and some common scenarios and solutions.

Learn How to Integrate Power Platform with External Services for Enhanced Data Capabilities

The Power Platform, comprising Power Apps, Power Automate, Power BI, and Power Virtual Agents, offers a broad range of integration capabilities with external services. These integrations can be achieved using built-in connectors, custom connectors, APIs, and gateways:

> **Built-in Connectors**: The Power Platform provides a vast library of built-in connectors that facilitate easy integration with various third-party services like Microsoft 365, Azure services, Salesforce, Google services, and more. These connectors allow you to pull data into your applications, automate workflows, and create insightful reports without needing extensive coding knowledge.
>
> **Custom Connectors**: When a built-in connector isn't available for a specific service, custom connectors can be created. Custom connectors use REST APIs to connect to external services. You define the API's endpoint, authentication methods, and the actions and triggers you need to integrate with your Power Platform solution.
>
> **APIs and Webhooks**: APIs (Application Programming Interfaces) and webhooks are essential for more advanced integrations. APIs allow your Power Platform applications to interact

with external services programmatically. Webhooks enable real-time communication by sending automated messages or data updates from one app to another when an event occurs.

Data Gateways: On-premises data gateways enable secure data transfer between on-premises data sources and the Power Platform. This is crucial for businesses that need to integrate legacy systems or databases that reside on-premises with their cloud-based Power Platform applications.

Steps for Integration

1. **Identify Requirements**: Determine the specific external services you need to integrate with and define the integration requirements.

2. **Choose the Integration Method**: Decide whether to use built-in connectors, custom connectors, APIs, or data gateways based on your requirements.

3. **Set Up the Integration**: Configure the chosen integration method by following the necessary steps to connect the external service with your Power Platform application.

4. **Test the Integration**: Ensure that the integration works correctly by testing it thoroughly. Validate data flows and functionality to confirm that the integration meets your needs.

5. **Monitor and Maintain**: Regularly monitor the integration to ensure it continues to function as expected. Make necessary updates and maintenance to handle any changes in the external services or Power Platform.

CHAPTER 4 DATA INTEGRATION, DATA EXPORT, AND ANALYTICS IN DATAVERSE

Common Integration Scenarios and Solutions

1. **Data Synchronization Between Systems**: Many organizations need to keep data synchronized between various systems, such as a CRM and an ERP system. Using Power Automate, you can create workflows that automatically update records in one system when changes are made in another. For example, when a new customer is added in Dynamics 365 (CRM), a corresponding record can be created in SAP (ERP).

   Solution: Use Power Automate with built-in connectors for Dynamics 365 and SAP. Define a trigger for the creation of a new customer and an action to create a record in SAP.

2. **Automated Notifications and Alerts**: Integrating with communication tools like Microsoft Teams or Slack can improve team collaboration and responsiveness. For instance, you might want to send a notification to a team channel when a high-priority support ticket is created.

   Solution: Create a Power Automate flow that triggers on the creation of a high-priority ticket in a support system like ServiceNow. Use the connector for Microsoft Teams or Slack to send a notification message to the appropriate channel.

3. **Enhancing Customer Engagement**: Chatbots created with Power Virtual Agents can be integrated with various customer service platforms to provide

better support. For instance, integrating a chatbot with Zendesk can help answer common customer queries and create tickets for more complex issues.

Solution: Use the Power Virtual Agents and the Zendesk connector to create a chatbot that interacts with customers, providing instant responses and escalating issues to human agents when needed.

4. **Data Analytics and Reporting**: Combining data from different sources for comprehensive reporting and analytics is a common requirement. For example, you may want to combine sales data from Salesforce with financial data from an on-premises SQL Server for comprehensive financial analysis.

    Solution: Use Power BI with connectors for Salesforce and an on-premises data gateway to connect to the SQL Server. Create data models and reports that combine and analyze data from both sources.

5. **Event-Driven Workflows**: Automating processes based on events can improve efficiency. For instance, integrating IoT devices with the Power Platform can automate maintenance requests when a machine reports a malfunction.

    Solution: Use Power Automate with IoT connectors to trigger workflows based on IoT device data. When a device reports an issue, the flow can create a maintenance ticket in a system like Dynamics 365 Field Service.

Integrating the Power Platform with external services significantly extends its capabilities, allowing organizations to create powerful, data-driven applications and workflows. By leveraging built-in connectors, custom connectors, APIs, and data gateways, businesses can enhance their operational efficiency, improve customer engagement, and gain deeper insights into their data. These integrations facilitate seamless data flow between systems, automated processes, and comprehensive analytics, driving better decision-making and business outcomes.

Power BI Integration with Microsoft Dataverse

Microsoft Dataverse and Power BI are integral components of Microsoft's Power Platform, providing a seamless ecosystem for data management, analytics, and business intelligence.

Microsoft Dataverse is a scalable data platform that supports the storage and management of data used by business applications. It offers a secure and organized environment for data, facilitating its use across Dynamics 365 applications, Power Apps, Power Automate, and other services. Dataverse allows users to define entities and relationships, enforce business rules, and ensure data integrity and security.

Power BI, on the other hand, is a powerful business analytics tool designed to visualize and analyze data. It enables users to create interactive reports and dashboards, providing deep insights into business operations. Power BI can connect to various data sources, including Dataverse, and transform raw data into meaningful visualizations.

Significance of Visualizing Microsoft Dataverse Data

Visualizing data stored in Dataverse using Power BI offers numerous advantages for organizations, enhancing decision-making, operational efficiency, and strategic planning:

> **Enhanced Data Comprehension**: Visualizing data makes complex datasets more understandable. Graphs, charts, and dashboards created in Power BI help users quickly grasp trends, patterns, and anomalies in Dataverse data.
>
> **Real-Time Insights**: Power BI allows for the creation of real-time dashboards that update automatically as the data in Dataverse changes. This real-time capability is crucial for timely decision-making and responding to business dynamics promptly.
>
> **Improved Data Accessibility**: By integrating Dataverse with Power BI, data becomes more accessible to nontechnical users. They can interact with intuitive reports and dashboards without needing deep technical knowledge, democratizing data insights across the organization.
>
> **Actionable Insights**: Power BI enables the creation of actionable insights from Dataverse data. Users can drill down into details, identify root causes, and predict future outcomes using advanced analytics and machine learning capabilities built into Power BI.

Enhanced Collaboration: Power BI facilitates better collaboration within teams by allowing users to share reports and dashboards. This shared understanding of data fosters coordinated efforts and aligned strategies across departments.

Customizable and Extensible: The integration allows for highly customizable and extensible solutions. Power BI's flexibility in creating tailored visuals and integrating with other Microsoft services enhances the overall data strategy of an organization.

Integrating Power BI with Microsoft Dataverse

Connecting Power BI to Dataverse: Power BI provides direct connectors to Dataverse. Users can connect to Dataverse by selecting it as a data source within Power BI, authenticating using their Microsoft credentials, and importing the necessary data tables.

Data Transformation and Modeling: Once connected, Power BI's Power Query Editor allows users to transform and clean the data as needed. This step involves shaping the data, such as removing unnecessary columns, creating new calculated columns, and establishing relationships between tables to reflect the underlying data model of Dataverse accurately.

Creating Visualizations: With the data modeled, users can start creating visualizations. Power BI offers a rich set of visualization options, including bar charts, line charts, pie charts, maps, and more. Users can drag and drop fields to create these visuals and configure them to represent data effectively.

Building Dashboards: Visuals can be combined into dashboards, providing a holistic view of business metrics. Dashboards in Power BI are interactive, allowing users to filter data, drill down into details, and view data from different perspectives.

Publishing and Sharing Reports: Once reports and dashboards are created, they can be published to the Power BI service. This makes the reports accessible to other users within the organization. Power BI's sharing capabilities ensure that relevant stakeholders have access to up-to-date insights.

Embedding Power BI in Applications: Power BI reports and dashboards can be embedded into applications built on Power Apps or Dynamics 365. This integration ensures that users have access to critical insights within the context of their workflows, enhancing productivity and decision-making.

Use Cases

Sales Performance Analysis: Organizations can integrate sales data from Dynamics 365 Sales into Power BI to analyze sales performance.

Visualizations can show trends over time, compare sales targets with actuals, and highlight top-performing products and salespeople.

Customer Service Insights: By visualizing data from Dynamics 365 Customer Service, businesses can track customer service metrics such as case resolution times, customer satisfaction scores, and agent performance. This helps in identifying areas for improvement and enhancing customer experiences.

Inventory Management: Integrating Power BI with inventory data in Dataverse helps in monitoring stock levels, tracking inventory turnover rates, and forecasting demand. This ensures optimal inventory management and reduces the risk of stockouts or overstocking.

Financial Reporting: Financial data stored in Dataverse can be visualized in Power BI to create comprehensive financial reports. This includes tracking revenue, expenses, profit margins, and financial KPIs, enabling better financial planning and management.

Project Management: Data from project management applications built on Power Apps can be visualized to monitor project progress, resource allocation, and budget adherence. This ensures projects stay on track and stakeholders are informed about project status.

Best Practices

Data Governance: Ensure that data governance policies are in place. This includes setting up proper permissions, data classification, and compliance with regulatory requirements to secure sensitive data.

Performance Optimization: Optimize data models and reports for performance. This includes minimizing the number of visuals on a report page, using import mode for large datasets, and leveraging aggregations and incremental refresh capabilities.

User Training and Adoption: Provide training to users to ensure they can effectively use Power BI. This includes understanding how to interact with reports, create personal dashboards, and use advanced features like drill-through and bookmarks.

Continuous Improvement: Regularly review and update reports and dashboards to reflect changing business needs. Gather feedback from users to enhance the relevance and usability of the insights provided.

Integration with Other Tools: Leverage Power BI's integration capabilities with other Microsoft tools such as Azure Synapse Analytics for advanced analytics and Microsoft Teams for collaborative discussions around data insights.

Dataverse Connectors in Power BI

Dataverse connectors in Power BI enable seamless integration between Dataverse and Power BI, allowing users to visualize and analyze Dataverse data effortlessly. These connectors provide a direct link to Dataverse, making it easy to bring data into Power BI for reporting and analytics.

Key Features

Direct Integration: Dataverse connectors provide a direct integration pathway, ensuring that data can be imported into Power BI without the need for complex ETL processes.

Real-Time Data Access: By connecting Power BI directly to Dataverse, users can access up-to-date data in real time, enabling timely insights and decision-making.

Simplified Data Modeling: The connectors support importing Dataverse tables and relationships, making it easier to build data models in Power BI that reflect the structure of the data in Dataverse.

Security and Compliance: The integration respects the security and compliance settings in Dataverse, ensuring that data access is controlled and compliant with organizational policies.

CHAPTER 4   DATA INTEGRATION, DATA EXPORT, AND ANALYTICS IN DATAVERSE

How to Use Dataverse Connectors in Power BI

Connecting to Dataverse

Open Power BI Desktop.

Select "Get Data" and choose "Dataverse" from the list of available connectors.

Authenticate using your Microsoft credentials to access your Dataverse environment.

Importing Data

Select the tables you want to import into Power BI.

Use Power Query Editor to transform and clean the data as needed before loading it into the Power BI model.

Creating Reports

Build visualizations using the imported data.

Use Power BI's robust visualization tools to create interactive and insightful reports.

Publishing to Power BI Service

Publish the reports to the Power BI service to share them with other users within your organization.

Embedding Power BI Reports

Embedding Power BI reports allows users to integrate Power BI's interactive analytics into other applications, such as Power Apps, Dynamics 365, or custom web applications. This enables users to access powerful insights within the context of their daily workflows.

Key Features

> **Seamless Integration**: Power BI reports can be embedded into various applications, providing a unified experience for users who can view and interact with reports without leaving their primary work environment.

Customization: Embedded reports can be customized to fit the look and feel of the host application, ensuring a consistent user experience.

Interactivity: Embedded reports retain all the interactive capabilities of Power BI, including filtering, drilling down, and exploring data.

Security: Embedding respects the security settings of Power BI, ensuring that users can only access the data they are authorized to view.

How to Embed Power BI Reports

Generate Embed Link

In the Power BI service, navigate to the report you want to embed.

Use the "Embed" option to generate an embed link or obtain the embed code.

Integrate into Application

For Power Apps or Dynamics 365, use the Power BI tile control to add the report.

For custom web applications, use the Power BI JavaScript API to embed the report. This involves adding the embed code to your web page and configuring the API to handle authentication and report interactions.

Configure Permissions

Ensure that the appropriate permissions are set up so that users can view and interact with the embedded reports based on their roles and access levels.

Tabular Data Stream (TDS) Endpoint

The Tabular Data Stream (TDS) endpoint provides a SQL-based interface to Dataverse, allowing tools and applications that support TDS to connect to Dataverse data. This enables a broader range of SQL-based integrations and data access methods.

Key Features

SQL Connectivity: TDS endpoint allows users to connect to Dataverse using SQL Server Management Studio (SSMS) or other SQL-based tools, providing familiar SQL querying capabilities.

Real-Time Data Access: Users can execute real-time queries against Dataverse data, which is especially useful for ad hoc analysis and reporting.

Integration with SQL-Based Tools: The TDS endpoint extends the reach of Dataverse data to a variety of SQL-based applications and services, enhancing data accessibility and integration possibilities.

Security and Compliance: Access through the TDS endpoint respects Dataverse security roles and permissions, ensuring that data access is controlled and compliant with organizational policies.

How to Use the TDS Endpoint

Enable TDS Endpoint

Ensure that the TDS endpoint is enabled for your Dataverse environment. This can typically be done through the Power Platform admin center.

Connect Using SQL Tools

Open SQL Server Management Studio (SSMS) or another SQL tool that supports TDS.

Connect to the Dataverse instance using the TDS endpoint URL. The connection string usually includes the organization URL and appropriate authentication credentials.

Query Dataverse Data

Use standard SQL queries to interact with Dataverse tables and data.

Perform data operations such as SELECT, JOIN, and WHERE clauses to retrieve and analyze data.

Integrate with Applications

Use the TDS endpoint to integrate Dataverse data with other SQL-based applications and services, enhancing the overall data strategy and accessibility.

Integrating Power BI with Microsoft Dataverse unlocks a powerful synergy, transforming raw data into actionable insights. This integration not only enhances the visibility and accessibility of data but also drives informed decision-making across the organization. By leveraging the strengths of both platforms, businesses can create a data-driven culture that fosters agility, innovation, and competitive advantage. Whether it's through real-time dashboards, in-depth analytics, or collaborative reports, the integration of Power BI and Dataverse stands as a cornerstone for modern data strategy and business intelligence.

Tools

The Dataverse Accelerator is a powerful tool designed to enhance and streamline the development and management of applications within the Microsoft Dataverse environment. It provides early access to experimental and preview features, allowing developers to leverage cutting-edge capabilities and optimize their workflows.

Key Features of Dataverse Accelerator

Low-Code Plugins

> **Reusable Workflows:** Create server-side synchronous business logic workflows that execute in real time.
>
> **Power Fx Integration:** Use Power Fx expressions to define event handlers and integrate with Dataverse business data and external data sources.
>
> **Instant Plugins:** Triggered manually by users through buttons, unbound actions in Power Automate flows, or canvas apps.
>
> **Automated Plugins:** Triggered by specific data events like Create, Update, or Delete, with options to run before or after the event.

Plugin Monitor

> **Trace Log Interface:** Surface the existing plugin trace log table in Dataverse environments.

Development and Debugging: Designed to aid in developing and debugging Dataverse plugins and custom APIs.

API Playground

Preauthenticated Testing Tool: Allows makers to quickly and conveniently interact with the Dataverse Web API

Experimentation and Learning: Ideal for testing and learning how to use the API effectively

Benefits of Using Dataverse Accelerator

Enhanced Productivity: Streamlines development processes, allowing for faster and more efficient application creation.

Competitive Edge: Early access to new features helps maintain a competitive edge by staying ahead of the curve.

Improved Development Experience: Tools like the Plugin Monitor and API Playground enhance the overall development and debugging experience.

Community Feedback: Provides a platform for users to share feedback and contribute to the development of new features.

Installation and Access

Automatic Availability: Available in all new Microsoft Dataverse environments

Security Roles: Requires specific privileges such as the System Customizer role to access and use the accelerator

Update the Dataverse accelerator

If the Dataverse accelerator is already installed and you want to install the latest version, follow these steps:

1. In the Power Platform admin center, select Environments.

2. Open the environment-level view of apps

3. Locate the Dataverse Accelerator app.

4. When there's an update available, select Update available next to the app.

5. Follow the instructions on your screen to apply the update.

The Dataverse Accelerator is a valuable tool for developers working within the Microsoft Dataverse environment. By providing early access to experimental features and powerful development tools, it enhances productivity, optimizes workflows, and ensures that users are well-prepared for upcoming platform updates. Whether you're creating low-code plugins or experimenting with new APIs, the Dataverse Accelerator offers a robust set of capabilities to support your development needs.

CHAPTER 5

Dataverse Connectors and Gateway

Introduction to Dataverse Connectors

Microsoft Dataverse is a robust and scalable data platform that lies at the heart of the Microsoft Power Platform. It provides a secure and reliable means to store and manage data used by business applications. One of the key features that amplify the utility of Dataverse is its connectors.

Dataverse connectors refer to integrations that allow Dataverse, a part of the Microsoft Power Platform, to interact and communicate with other systems, applications, and data sources. They play a pivotal role in the Microsoft Power Platform, enabling seamless integration between Microsoft Dataverse and a multitude of other systems, applications, and data sources. This integration capability is critical for organizations aiming to harness the full potential of their data, automate workflows, and develop sophisticated applications with ease.

By providing ready-to-use connectors, Dataverse simplifies the process of building applications. Users can integrate complex data sources and services with minimal coding, allowing even nondevelopers to create powerful applications. As business needs grow, the ability to connect to additional data sources and systems without extensive redevelopment is crucial. Dataverse connectors provide the scalability required to handle increasing data volumes and complexity.

Dataverse connectors offer a broad range of functionalities to ensure robust and efficient data integration and management. These functionalities include data integration and synchronization, data transformation, automation, workflow management, security, and compliance.

In a nutshell, Dataverse connectors basically are integration tools that enable Dataverse to communicate and interact with other external data sources, applications, and services. These connectors facilitate the flow of data between Dataverse and various endpoints, enabling businesses to build integrated solutions without extensive custom development.

Types of Connectors

Types of connectors in Dataverse can be broadly categorized into standard connectors and custom connectors, each serving different purposes and use cases. Here is a detailed overview of the types of Dataverse connectors:

   A. **Standard Connectors**: These are prebuilt connectors provided by Microsoft for services like Microsoft 365, Dynamics 365, Azure services, SQL Server, SharePoint, etc. These connectors are regularly updated and maintained by Microsoft to ensure compatibility and performance. Here are some of the most commonly used standard connectors:

1. SharePoint

    - **Document Management**: Sync document metadata between SharePoint document libraries and Dataverse tables. This also facilitates document collaboration, secure storage leveraging role-based access, and version control of critical business documents.

    - **Lists Integration**: Sync data between SharePoint Lists and Dataverse tables. This is applicable on a wide variety of use cases including task management, document metadata automation and integration, handling legacy SharePoint applications, etc.

2. Dynamics 365

    - **Dynamics 365 Applications**: Sync data between various Dynamics 365 applications (sales, finance and operations, business centers, etc.) for comprehensive data overview and advanced analytics.

3. Azure Services

    - **File Management**: Manage and store large files (blobs) with Azure Blob Storage for cost minimization and additional security layers for critical files. Additional configuration can be implemented for automated backup and restore processes for Dataverse data.

    - **Analytics**: Azure analytics can be leveraged for data analysis, log analysis, application insights on applications, etc.

- **Azure SQL**: Sync data between Dataverse tables and Azure SQL tables for advanced analytics, storage of large data sets, etc.
- **Cognitive Services**: Enhance applications with AI tools, ML processes, etc. for implementing OCR, document analysis, text services, etc.

4. Microsoft 365

    - **Emails**: Integrate with Outlook to receive and send emails directly from Dataverse. This can be leveraged to optimize communication in cases like sales, order management, healthcare applications, etc.
    - **Excel**: Automate data import and export between Dataverse tables and Excel spread sheets. Excel integration with Dataverse can also be used for advanced data analysis and reporting on Dataverse data.
    - **Microsoft Teams**: Automate workflows involving Microsoft Teams for better collaboration and enablement among teams. Workflows can also be set up for automated notifications and alerts to Teams channels.

5. Google Services

    - Managing emails by integrating with Gmail. Connectors can also be used to set up workflows to sync data between Dataverse tables and Google Sheets, sync files, and documents with Google Drive.

CHAPTER 5 DATAVERSE CONNECTORS AND GATEWAY

6. e-Signature services

    - Multiple third-party services like DocuSign, Adobe, Here Sign, etc. can be integrated for automating management of invoices, contracts, and document generation requirements.

7. Content Generation Services

    - Content generation services like generating word documents, pdf documents from templates, Excel sheets based on data manipulation, etc. enable users to set up solutions that require output files based on the requirements. Power Automate and Power Apps can integrate with services like Encodian, PlumSail, custom functions, etc. to achieve these requirements.

There are several other services and systems that can directly be leveraged for implementing various use cases following high-security authentication protocols ensuring data protection and simplified development using standard connectors in Dataverse.

B. **Custom Connectors**: While many connectors are provided out of the box by Microsoft, sometimes organizations need to connect to unique or proprietary services that aren't covered by the prebuilt connectors. In such cases, custom connectors come into play. These are user-defined connectors tailored to specific business requirements or external systems not covered by standard connectors. These connectors can be created to connect with virtually any external system, API, or service that exposes a RESTful

API. Custom connectors allow you to define your own set of actions and triggers based on an API. Apart from third-party systems and services, custom connectors are often widely used for

1. **Legacy System Integrations**: Many organizations still rely on legacy systems that do not have modern APIs or prebuilt connectors. Custom connectors enable integration with these systems by defining a connection to their APIs or web services. This allows organizations to modernize their workflows and data management practices without completely overhauling their existing infrastructure.

2. **Internal APIs**: Organizations often develop their own internal APIs to expose business logic and data services. Custom connectors allow these internal APIs to be consumed within the Power Platform, facilitating the creation of custom applications, automations, and analytics solutions that leverage internal data and processes.

Creating and using custom connectors effectively require adherence to best practices. Here are some recommended practices:

1. **Authentication**: Always use secure authentication methods such as OAuth 2.0, API keys, or other industry-standard protocols. Avoid using basic authentication or exposing sensitive information in URLs. Once the authentication section is configured for the custom connector, all platforms (Power Apps or Power Automate) using the custom connector will have to be authenticated by the users.

2. **Encryption**: Ensure that data transmitted between Dataverse and the external service is encrypted. Use HTTPS for all API calls to protect data in transit. Although custom connectors also support HTTP protocol, for best practices, it is advised to use the HTTPS protocol.

3. **Access Control**: Implement granular access control to restrict who can create, modify, or use the custom connector. Use role-based access control (RBAC) to manage permissions. Security settings can be configured on custom connectors, and they can be shared with users within the organization with permissions to read or edit the custom connector.

4. **Documentation**: It is important to provide comprehensive documentation for the API endpoints, including request and response formats, required parameters, authentication methods, and examples. Alongside API documentation, it is also recommended to document the custom connector itself, detailing the actions, triggers, and configuration steps. This helps users understand how to use the connector and what functionality it provides.

5. **Error Handling**: Defining meaningful error messages that help users understand what went wrong and how to fix it helps users and developers debug appropriately in case of errors while using the triggers and actions of the custom connector. It is recommended to avoid generic error messages and instead use appropriate HTTP status codes to

indicate success, client errors, and server errors. For example, 200 for success, 400 for bad requests, and 500 for server errors. When deploying to production or implementing solutions for business-critical applications, it is recommended to implement retry logic for handling transient errors, such as network issues or temporary service outages. This can improve the reliability of the connector.

6. **Versioning**: Maintaining version control for the custom connector to ensure backward compatibility allows users to continue using older versions while new features or changes are introduced in newer versions. This also supports and provides a window to clearly communicate the deprecation policy for old versions of the connector and also helps users to migrate to newer versions with negligible downtime of applications.

7. **Performance**: As a best practice, it is recommended to configure the custom connector to optimize the number of API calls being made to the service. Capabilities like pagination, filtering, and querying provided by the API can be used to limit the amount of data retrieved. Wherever possible, batch processing can be leveraged to handle multiple operations in a single API call that can reduce the overhead and improve overall performance.

Custom connectors in Microsoft Dataverse are a powerful tool for extending the capabilities of the Power Platform. They enable users to connect to virtually any web-based service or API, allowing for seamless integration and automation of business processes. By following

CHAPTER 5   DATAVERSE CONNECTORS AND GATEWAY

best practices and understanding the core concepts, users can create robust, secure, and efficient custom connectors to meet their unique business needs.

In summary, Dataverse connectors, both standard and custom, are essential for integrating Dataverse with a wide range of external systems, applications, and data sources. They enable seamless data integration, automation, and workflow management, making it easier to build robust and efficient low-code applications. By leveraging these connectors, organizations can enhance productivity, improve decision-making, and drive innovation while ensuring data security and compliance.

Connecting to Cloud-Based Data Sources

Another key feature of Dataverse is its ability to connect to a wide variety of cloud-based data sources (e.g., Excel, SharePoint, SQL, etc.). This allows organizations to unify data from different systems, providing a single source of truth and enabling powerful insights and automation. In the previous section, we covered standard and custom connectors in Dataverse. In this section, we will cover more methods of connecting to cloud-based data sources from Microsoft Dataverse.

A. **Dataflows**: Dataflows enable users to connect to, transform, and load data from a wide variety of cloud-based data sources into Dataverse. Dataflows use Power Query, a powerful data transformation and preparation tool, to shape data before loading it into Dataverse. Here are some key features of Dataflows in Microsoft Dataverse:

1. **Connectors**: Support for a wide range of data sources, including SQL databases, web APIs, and online services.

2. **Transformation**: A rich set of data transformation capabilities, including filtering, merging, and aggregating data.

3. **Scheduling**: The ability to schedule data refreshes to ensure that Dataverse always contains up-to-date data.

B. **Virtual Tables**: Virtual tables in Dataverse allow users to create tables that connect to data stored in external systems. Unlike regular tables, virtual tables do not store data in Dataverse but instead retrieve data in real time from the external source. This allows for seamless integration without duplicating data. Here are some key features of virtual tables in Microsoft Dataverse:

1. **Real-Time Data Access**: Virtual tables allow Dataverse users to access and interact with data stored in external systems in real time. This means that any updates made in the external system are immediately reflected in Dataverse without the need for data synchronization or replication.

2. **Security and Access Control**: Virtual tables leverage Dataverse's security model, allowing administrators to define role-based access controls and permissions. This ensures that only authorized users can access and interact with the data in virtual tables.

CHAPTER 5   DATAVERSE CONNECTORS AND GATEWAY

3. **Composite Data Model**: By using virtual tables, organizations can create a composite data model that combines data from multiple sources. This enables a unified view of data across systems, facilitating better decision-making and insights.

4. **Ease of Use**: Virtual tables are designed to be user-friendly, allowing nondevelopers to configure and use them without extensive coding knowledge. The configuration process is typically done through the Dataverse UI or Power Platform admin center.

Capabilities to connect to cloud-based data sources using Microsoft Dataverse open up immense opportunities and use cases for a wide variety of solutions. Here are some high-level use cases of Microsoft Dataverse connecting to cloud-based data sources:

A. **Unified Customer View**: By connecting Dataverse to various cloud-based data sources, organizations can create a unified view of their customers. This enables better customer relationship management and more personalized interactions. For example, Dataverse can connect with CRM systems like Dynamics 365 or Salesforce-centralized customer data, track customer interactions and marketing campaigns, view past history with the customer, etc.

B. **Business Process Automation**: Integrating cloud-based data sources with Dataverse enables automation of complex business processes, improving efficiency and reducing manual effort.

For example, Dataverse can connect with various e-commerce platforms, HR systems, financial systems, etc. to handle and automate various processes.

C. **Data-Driven Decision-Making**: By consolidating data from various cloud-based sources into Dataverse, organizations can gain valuable insights and make data-driven decisions. For example, Dataverse can integrate with various tools and ERP systems to analyze sales performance, optimize marketing strategies, forecast revenue, etc.

While connecting Microsoft Dataverse with cloud-based data sources enables immense scope for building robust and scalable solutions, here are some limitations users generally come across:

A. **Data Latency**: Real-time data integration can be challenging due to network latency and the time it takes to retrieve data from cloud-based sources. This can impact the performance of applications that rely on up-to-date data.

B. **Data Volume**: Handling large volumes of data from cloud-based sources can be resource-intensive and may require significant storage and processing power. This can lead to increased costs and complexity.

C. **Security and Compliance**: Integrating with cloud-based data sources can introduce security and compliance challenges, especially when dealing with sensitive data. Organizations must ensure that data is handled securely and in compliance with relevant regulations.

D. **API Rate Limits**: Many cloud-based services impose rate limits on their APIs, restricting the number of requests that can be made within a given time period. This can affect the performance and reliability of integrations, especially in high-demand scenarios.

E. **Complexity of Custom Connectors**: Creating and maintaining custom connectors can be complex and require specialized knowledge of APIs and web services. This can be a barrier for organizations without dedicated development resources.

Figure 5-1 shows an overview of how Dataverse connects with cloud-based services to enable developers in building applications, automation, and analytical reports using data from the cloud.

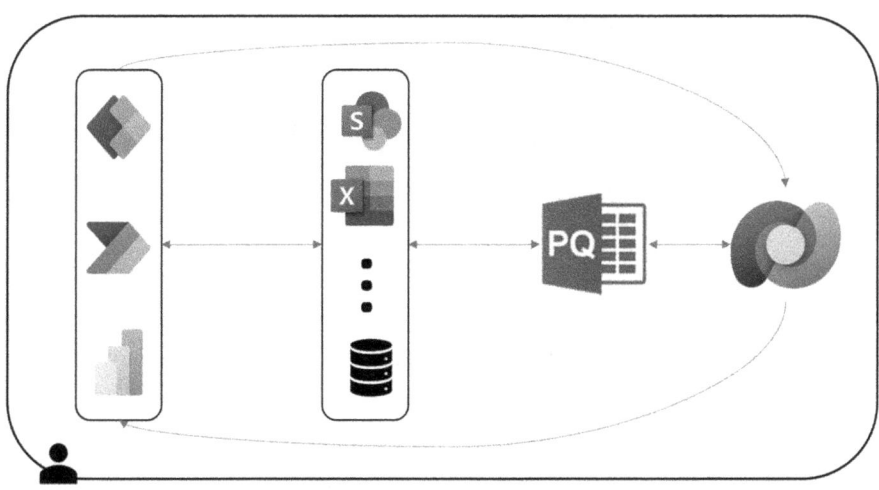

Figure 5-1. *Connecting to cloud-based services from Dataverse*

In summary, connecting to cloud-based data sources in Microsoft Dataverse unlocks a wide range of possibilities for organizations looking to unify their data, automate business processes, and gain valuable insights. By leveraging built-in connectors, custom connectors, dataflows, and virtual tables, organizations can integrate data from various sources seamlessly.

Adhering to best practices ensures secure, efficient, and reliable data integration, while understanding the limitations helps organizations plan and mitigate potential challenges. As technology continues to evolve, the future scope of Dataverse integrations promises even more powerful capabilities, enabling organizations to harness the full potential of their data.

By embracing these methods and best practices, organizations can create a robust data foundation that drives innovation, improves decision-making, and enhances operational efficiency. Microsoft Dataverse, with its extensive integration capabilities, stands as a key enabler in the journey toward data-driven transformation.

On-Premises Data Connectivity with Gateway Clusters

In today's digital landscape, organizations often operate with a hybrid data environment, where some data resides in on-premises systems while other data is hosted in the cloud. Microsoft Dataverse provides robust capabilities to connect to both cloud and on-premises data sources, ensuring seamless data integration and management. One of the key features enabling on-premises data connectivity is the use of gateway clusters. Dataverse supports both cloud-based and on-premises data sources, enabling comprehensive data management and integration

CHAPTER 5   DATAVERSE CONNECTORS AND GATEWAY

capabilities. In this section, we will explore the concepts, methods, best practices, use cases, limitations, and future scope of on-premises data connectivity with gateway clusters in Microsoft Dataverse in detail.

A gateway cluster in Microsoft Dataverse is a collection of on-premises data gateways that work together to ensure high availability, load balancing, and fault tolerance for connecting to on-premises data sources. Gateways act as a bridge, securely transmitting data between on-premises systems and cloud services like Dataverse, Power BI, Power Apps, and Power Automate. Here are the key components involved with gateway clusters:

A. **On-Premises Data Gateway**: This software is installed on a local server to facilitate secure data transfer between on-premises data sources and cloud services. It handles encryption, decryption, and data-routing tasks.

B. **Gateway Cluster**: A logical grouping of multiple on-premises data gateways to provide redundancy, load balancing, and high availability. If one gateway in the cluster fails, another gateway can take over, ensuring continuous data connectivity.

C. **Gateway Configuration**: The setup process involves configuring the gateways, defining data source connections, and setting up authentication and authorization protocols.

Setting up the on-premises data gateway requires installation of the data gateway software, and then the user needs to sign in and allow required access in order to leverage the setup in Power Platform solutions. Below is the step-by-step process for setting up the on-premises data gateway.

A. **Installation**: Download and install the on-premises data gateway software on a local server that has access to the on-premises data sources.

B. **Configuration**: During the installation, configure the gateway by providing a Microsoft Entra ID (previously Azure Active Directory or AAD) account for authentication. Once done, register the gateway with the Power Platform environment.

C. **Cluster Formation**: To create a gateway cluster, install additional gateways and register them under the same gateway cluster name. This process ensures that multiple gateways work together to handle data traffic.

D. **Data Source Definition**: Define the on-premises data sources that the gateway will connect to, such as SQL Server, Oracle, SharePoint, or file shares.

E. **Connection Setup**: Configure the connection settings for each data source, including server names, database names, authentication methods, and connection strings.

F. **Security Configuration**: Set up authentication and authorization protocols to ensure secure access to the data sources. Use Windows authentication, OAuth, or other secure methods as appropriate.

CHAPTER 5 DATAVERSE CONNECTORS AND GATEWAY

G. **Creating Connections**: In the Dataverse environment, create connections to the on-premises data sources using the configured gateways. While creating the connection, you can specify the gateway cluster to be used for each connection.

H. **Testing Connectivity**: Test the connections to ensure that Dataverse can successfully communicate with the on-premises data sources through the gateway cluster.

I. **Using Data in Dataverse**: Once connections are established, use the data from on-premises sources within Dataverse. This data can be used in Power Apps, Power Automate flows, Power BI reports, and other applications.

Figure 5-2 shows an overview of how Dataverse connects with on-premises data and enables users to leverage that for Power Apps, Power Automate, and Power BI.

CHAPTER 5 DATAVERSE CONNECTORS AND GATEWAY

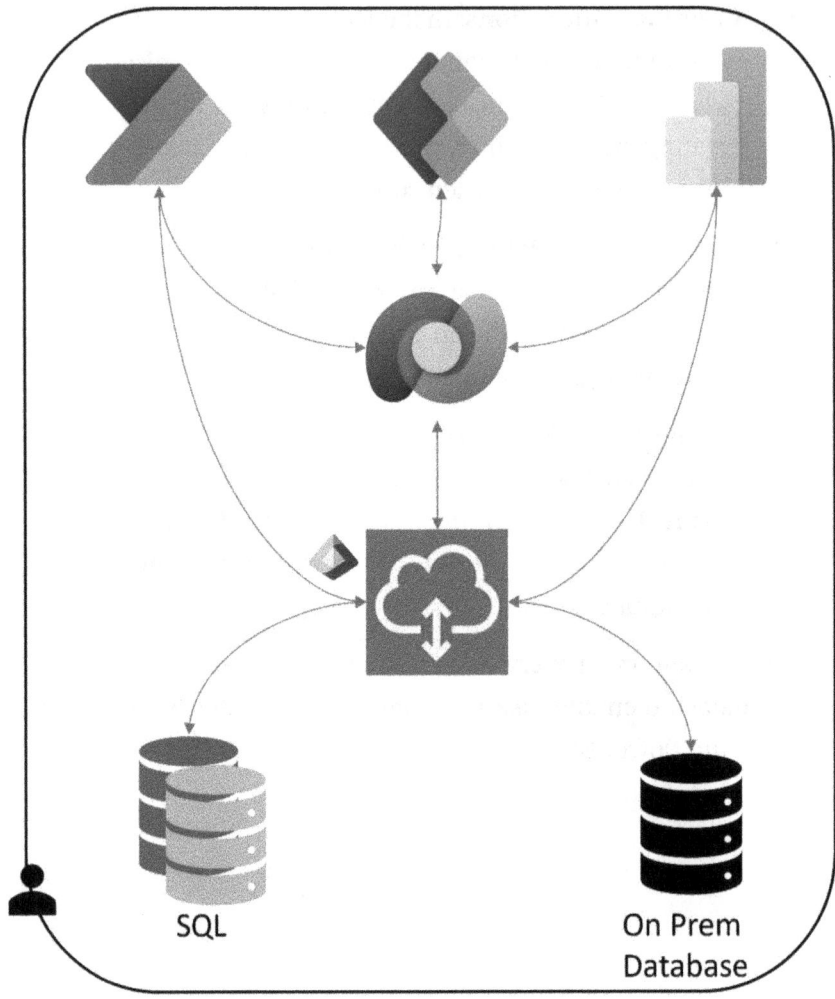

Figure 5-2. On-premises data gateway connection to Dataverse

Once the on-premises data gateway configuration is set up, connections can be created from Dataverse to build applications, automation, or reports based on the requirements. This setup can be leveraged across multiple applications spanning across multiple teams. Due to the critical nature of this setup and the dependency, it is advised to follow certain best practices for setting up the configuration. Here are some general best practices that can be followed for optimal use of the on-premises data gateway configuration:

A. **Cluster Configuration**: Using multiple gateways in a cluster ensures high availability and further provides redundancy, so if one gateway fails, another can take over without interrupting data connectivity.

B. **Regular Monitoring**: Continuous monitoring of the health and performance of the gateways in the cluster can help identify issues if any early on and provide a window to fix them with appropriate notice to the users and developers leveraging the setup. Using monitoring tools and alerts can also help detect and address issues promptly.

C. **Load Balancing**: Ensuring that data traffic is evenly distributed across the gateways in the cluster to prevent overloading any single gateway.

D. **Encryption**: Gateways support HTTPS for secure communication, and using encryption to secure data in transit between the on-premises data sources and the cloud is generally recommended as a best practice.

E. **Access Control**: In order to centralize and control the configuration setup, strict access control policies can be implemented to restrict who can configure and use the gateways. Role-based access control (RBAC) and least privilege principles can be leveraged for this.

F. **Performance Optimization**: Optimizing network settings to reduce latency and improve data transfer speeds and using direct network paths to minimize the number of network hops are good ways to optimize the overall performance. Apart from network optimization, users should also consider allocating sufficient resources and implementing data caching strategies to further improve the performance of the gateway setup.

Connecting to on-premises data gateway can solve a lot of problems when working with large data sets, legacy applications, following security, compliance, etc. Here are some use cases where this setup can be leveraged along with Dataverse to build scalable modern solutions:

A. **Hybrid Data Integration**: Organizations often have a mix of on-premises and cloud-based systems as the technology has been evolving. A lot of organizations still use on-premises servers for multiple reasons including but not limited to dependency on legacy applications, security and compliance of the data, and poor planning on upgrading to cloud-based services. Gateway clusters enable seamless integration of on-premises data with cloud-based applications, allowing for a unified data view and streamlined operations.

B. **Business Process Automation**: Most legacy applications and software are difficult to automate directly given the nature of the applications, the platforms they were built on, or the level of effort required to automate them. However, integrating with the on-premises data gateway and Power Automate (cloud and desktop flows) business

CHAPTER 5   DATAVERSE CONNECTORS AND GATEWAY

processes that involve on-premises data can be easily automated. Gateway clusters enable secure and reliable data transfer between on-premises systems and cloud-based automation workflows.

C. **Legacy System Integration**: As mentioned in the previous sections, many organizations rely on legacy systems that are critical to their operations. In order to build reporting, automation, or extending these applications, the on-premises data gateway along with Power Automate, Power Apps, Power BI, and Dataverse can be leveraged. Alongside, gateway clusters provide a way to integrate these legacy systems with modern cloud-based applications without the need for extensive re-engineering.

While connecting Microsoft Dataverse with on-premises data gateway enables immense scope for building robust and scalable solutions, here are some limitations users generally come across:

A. **Network Latency**: Data transfer between on-premises systems and the cloud can be affected by network latency. This can impact the performance of applications that rely on real-time data access. Apart from network latency issues, gateway clusters rely on Internet connectivity to function. Any disruption in Internet service can affect data connectivity between on-premises systems and the cloud.

B. **Complexity**: Setting up and managing gateway clusters can be complex, especially in large organizations with multiple data sources and stringent security requirements. It requires careful planning and ongoing maintenance.

C. **Licensing and Costs**: Using premium features and connectors in Dataverse may require additional licensing. Organizations need to consider the cost implications of using gateway clusters and plan their budgets accordingly. For planning efficient use of licenses on accounts utilizing the service, organizations should thoroughly refer to the official licensing documentation in order to best manage the expectations. Even with premium licensing, there could be areas where defined usage of connectors in terms of throttling limits may come into picture based on the requirements of the solution.

D. **Resource Consumption**: Gateway clusters require adequate resources on the local servers where the gateways are installed. This includes CPU, memory, and network bandwidth to handle data transfer operations. Having limited resource allocation might affect the free flow of data in real time, thereby affecting the cloud-based applications built on it.

Given the rapid growth of Microsoft Dataverse capabilities, here are some key features to expect in the future releases:

A. **Serverless Data Integration**: Serverless architectures are becoming more popular for data integration features regarding on-premises databases and legacy applications. Future enhancements with respect to Dataverse capabilities to integrate with on-premises systems may include serverless gateway clusters, providing scalable and cost-effective data connectivity.

B. **Improved Security Features**: With more organizations adopting Power Platform, one of the key areas to look out for development at scale is security features. Enhancements in security features, such as advanced encryption, multifactor authentication, and automated compliance checks, can further secure on-premises data connectivity.

C. **Simplified Management and Monitoring**: Future developments may also focus on simplifying the management and monitoring of gateway clusters. This includes enhanced user interfaces, automated alerts, and integration with centralized IT management tools that would essentially help users to simplify their effort when dealing with large data sets with the dependent critical line of business applications.

D. **Enhanced AI and ML Integrations**: Alongside computing, security, and monitoring, future developments may focus on integrating AI and ML capabilities with on-premises data accessed through gateway clusters. This can enable advanced analytics and predictive insights without moving data to the cloud.

In summary, on-premises data connectivity with gateway clusters in Microsoft Dataverse provides a powerful and flexible solution for integrating hybrid data environments. By leveraging gateway clusters, organizations can securely and efficiently connect their on-premises data sources to cloud-based applications, enabling real-time data access, comprehensive analytics, and streamlined business processes.

CHAPTER 5   DATAVERSE CONNECTORS AND GATEWAY

Adhering to best practices ensures that gateway clusters are configured for high availability, security, and performance. While there are limitations and challenges to consider, the benefits of using gateway clusters far outweigh the drawbacks, making them a valuable tool for modern data integration.

As technology continues to evolve, the future scope of on-premises data connectivity with gateway clusters promises even more advanced capabilities, enabling organizations to harness the full potential of their hybrid data environments. By embracing these methods and best practices, organizations can create a robust data foundation that drives innovation, improves decision-making, and enhances operational efficiency.

Troubleshooting Data Source Connectivity Issues

Connecting to various data sources in Microsoft Dataverse can sometimes pose challenges. In order to maintain SLAs, ensure least downtime on applications, and achieve seamless data integration, it is important to understand how to troubleshoot these issues. Here are some tips, steps, and explanations on how to troubleshoot data source connectivity issues in Microsoft Dataverse.

Connectivity issues can happen due to multiple reasons. Some of the most common issues users encounter are

   A. **Network Connectivity Issues**: When connecting with on-premises data or to data sources from other services, network connectivity issues might arise in case the data source connection is not functional or broken.

B. **Authentication and Authorization Problems**:
    Different services use different mechanisms for
    authentication configuration. Inappropriate roles
    or permissions on the accounts trying to access
    the data source might lead to authentication and
    authorization problems. Improper configuration
    for retrieving refresh tokens and changes on the
    authentication mechanism of the service might also
    cause this issue.

C. **Gateway Configuration Errors**: Gateway
    configuration needs to be followed step by step
    and should be accurate on each step. For example,
    configuring the gateway on a region that is different
    from the region where the Dataverse environment
    is hosted will result in inability to integrate data
    between the systems.

D. **Data Source Configuration Issues**: Data source
    connections are generally configured through
    standard connectors, custom connectors, Power
    Query, etc. Change in definition of the operations
    would require re-creating the connection and
    sometimes may also require changes to the setup.
    It is important to monitor the services for such
    changes in order to update the solution setup and
    avoid outage on the applications.

E. **Resource Limitations**: Many services enforce
    limits on the number of API calls, byte size on data
    transfer, number of operations, etc. on their API
    plans. These limitations need to be considered while
    designing the solution.

CHAPTER 5   DATAVERSE CONNECTORS AND GATEWAY

    F. **Service Outages**: Third-party services define their SLAs on the services they enable for access. Sometimes a general maintenance or technical issues might lead to service outage, which in turn could affect the applications utilizing these services. It is important to review the service outage on the service in case of unexpected errors.

Alongside best practices to monitor and set up connections from Dataverse to different services, here are some generic troubleshooting steps that can help users to quickly triage general connectivity issues:

    A. Verify Network Connectivity:

- Ensure that the Internet connection is stable and other Internet resources are accessible on the same connection.

- To verify that the connection is stable and there is no packet loss from or to the service, you can also ping the on-premises data source or cloud endpoint to ensure it is reachable. [cmd – ping <data_source_address>, cmd – tracert <data_source_address>]

- Verify that the firewall or proxy settings are not blocking access to the data source. Ensure that all required ports are open and configuring proxy settings is necessary.

    B. Validate Gateway Configuration:

- Ensure that the on-premises data gateway is correctly installed on the server. Also ensure that the gateway software is up to date. You can update the gateway software in case the current installed version is not the latest one.

CHAPTER 5   DATAVERSE CONNECTORS AND GATEWAY

- Check and verify the gateway status. You can check the status on the Power Platform admin center. Note that if the status is healthy, the gateway is connected and is functioning properly. If the status is disconnected, the gateway is not reachable, and you can restart the gateway service and then verify the status again.

C. Confirm Data Source Configuration:

- Check and validate the data source settings configured in the Dataverse environment. If the connection is configured through a connection string, ensure that the connection string is accurate. Also verify that the correct authentication method supported by the service is selected to ensure there are no configuration errors.

- Use the data source's native tools to test the connection. For example, if connecting to SQL server, you can test using SQL Server Management Studio. You can also use tools like Postman to verify the connection and test the operation by making a demo API call.

- Ensure that the user account used for the connection is properly configured on the data source and the necessary roles or permissions are provided to access the data.

CHAPTER 5 DATAVERSE CONNECTORS AND GATEWAY

D. Monitor Resource Utilization:

- Monitor the server resources wherever applicable. For example, if connecting to an on-premises data source using the on-premises data gateway, monitor the CPU, memory, disk space, etc. where the data source is hosted.

- If the resource utilization is high, you can consider scaling up the server resources or utilize load balancing across multiple servers.

E. Identify Service Outages:

- Visit the Microsoft Service Health Dashboard to check for any reported outage or issues with Dataverse or related services.

- Most services also provide dashboards to check the service status, and you can do so by also subscribing to service alerts and stay informed about any disruptions.

F. Resolve Authentication and Authorization Issues:

- Verify that the credentials used for the data source connection are correct. It is important to ensure that the appropriate authentication method is selected (e.g., Windows Authentication, SQL Authentication).

- If using OAuth or other token-based authentication, ensure that the access tokens are valid and have not expired. While setting up custom connectors, ensure that correct URLs are provided for getting refresh tokens.

CHAPTER 5   DATAVERSE CONNECTORS AND GATEWAY

G. Analyze Gateway Logs:

- Ensure that logging is enabled on the gateway. This can be configured in the gateway settings. This enables users to look for error messages or warnings that can provide insights into connectivity issues.

- Correlating gateway logs with data source logs can help identify any discrepancies or issues.

H. Use Network Tracing Tools:

- Network tracing tools can help identify issues with connections or errors when accessing the data source. Tools like Wireshark and Fiddler can help capture network traces.

- Analyze the captured traffic between Dataverse and the data source during the connection attempt to identify anomalies like dropped packets or failed handshakes.

I. Leverage Dataverse Diagnostic Tools:

- Leverage Dataverse diagnostic tools available in the Power Platform admin center to identify and troubleshoot issues. You can run diagnostics to check the health of the Dataverse environment and identify any potential connectivity issues.

- Reviewing the diagnostic reports can help understand the root cause of the issue and take corrective actions.

In summary, troubleshooting data source connectivity issues in Microsoft Dataverse involves a systematic approach to identify and resolve problems. By following the steps outlined in this section, you can effectively troubleshoot and resolve connectivity issues, ensuring seamless integration and data flow between on-premises and cloud environments.

Maintaining best practices and leveraging advanced troubleshooting techniques can help prevent issues and minimize downtime. As organizations increasingly rely on hybrid data environments, understanding how to manage and troubleshoot data source connectivity in Dataverse becomes critical for operational efficiency and business continuity.

Scaling and Growth Considerations

As organizations grow and their data needs expand, the ability to scale data integration solutions becomes increasingly important. Microsoft Dataverse, along with its connectors and gateways, provides a robust framework for integrating diverse data sources. However, scaling these integrations to meet growing demands requires careful planning and consideration. Here are some factors that explore scaling and growth considerations for Dataverse connectors and gateways.

From the previous sections of this chapter, we now have a good understanding of Dataverse connectors and connecting to data sources using on-premises data gateways. Below is an outline focusing individually on both methods of connecting to data from Dataverse.

CHAPTER 5   DATAVERSE CONNECTORS AND GATEWAY

Scaling Dataverse Connectors

A. Connector Capacity Planning

- Different data sources might have different capacity plans with regard to data transfer, operations, etc. For better estimating the connector capacity required, it is essential to evaluate the current volume of data being processed through the connectors. Identifying peak usage times and data loads is also recommended for efficiently estimating the connector capacity.

- While designing the solution and during UAT phases, it is difficult to determine the usage of the connector. However, the usage can be projected based on future data growth, further data integration, additional users, etc. Considering factors like increased user adoption, additional data sources, new business processes, etc. based on historical trends and business forecasts is a recommended plan of action to identify and incorporate a scaling plan.

- The capacity or consumption of the connector can vary based on requirements and the components in the solution for which it will be used for. Determining the capacity requirements for the connectors, including throughput, latency, and concurrency needs will help understand the challenges that the solution will face while scaling. It is advised to plan accordingly for scaling the subscription to the service or additional licenses or further optimization of design in order to accommodate project data growth and usage of the connector.

B. Optimizing Connector Performance

- Most data sources provide options for batch processing of data, advanced filtering, sorting, etc. on the API actions. Optimizing queries to minimize data transfer and processing time, using filters and selecting only necessary data to reduce the load is considered to be a general best practice, especially when planning for scaling the solution.

- Using data caching mechanisms to store frequently accessed data locally and thereby reducing the need for repeated data retrievals is another way of optimizing the connector performance. Appropriate cache expiration policies can be implemented to ensure that the data is up to date.

- Users can implement incremental data loads to transfer only changed data instead of loading full datasets. Most data sources provide capabilities for tracking changed data, and incremental data loads can be leveraged for efficiently processing large data sets.

- Continuous monitoring of the data and connectors is essential while considering the growth and scale of solutions. Dataverse monitoring tools can be leveraged to identify bottlenecks and optimize configuration based on performance metrics.

CHAPTER 5   DATAVERSE CONNECTORS AND GATEWAY

C. Ensuring High Availability and Reliability

- In order to improve user experience and the overall performance of the solution, implement redundancy by configuring multiple connectors for critical data sources. Users can set up failover mechanisms to switch to backup connectors in case of primary connector failures.

- Load balancing is an important factor to consider for scaling applications. Organizations can plan to distribute data loads evenly across multiple connectors to prevent overloading any single connector. Efficient load balancing strategies improve the overall performance and reliability of solutions.

- Most services keep updating the APIs for matching industry standards and provide maximum SLAs. Teams can plan for regularly updating connectors to the latest versions to benefit from performance improvements and bug fixes.

Scaling On-Premises Data Gateways

A. Gateway Cluster Configuration

- Redundancy is an important factor while considering scaling and growth of applications. A single gateway sometimes cannot handle large data sets, high availability, and efficient data transfer. Installing multiple gateways and configuring them as a cluster can ensure high availability and load balancing. Registering the gateways under the same gateway cluster name during installation is considered as a best practice.

- It is also critical to continuously monitor the gateway health. Use the Power Platform admin center to monitor the health and status of each gateway in the cluster and also set up alerts to notify administrators of any issues or failures.

- For large data sets considering user adoption while scaling solutions, it is essential to allocate sufficient CPU, memory, and network resources to the servers hosting the gateways. Users can regularly review and adjust resource allocation based on usage patterns and performance metrics.

B. Performance Optimization for Gateways

- Optimizing network configuration plays a key role for scaling and growth consideration of applications involving on-premises data. Ensure that the network paths between the gateways, on-premises data sources, and cloud services are optimized. Network latency can be minimized by using direct network paths and reducing the number of hops.

- Users can also implement data compression techniques to reduce the amount of data transferred between on-premises systems and the cloud. Gateways can be configured to use compression where supported.

CHAPTER 5   DATAVERSE CONNECTORS AND GATEWAY

- Continuously monitoring gateway performance metrics such as data transfer rates, latency, and error rates is considered to be a general best practice. These metrics can help identify performance bottlenecks and optimize configurations.

C. Enhancing Security and Compliance

- Data security and role-based access are critical factors for scaling applications. In order to ensure industry-best standards are being practiced, implement strong authentication methods and encryption to secure data transferred through gateways. It is generally recommended to configure gateways to use HTTPS for secure communication.

- Users can define and enforce access controls to restrict who can configure and use the gateways. Implementing user role-based access control (RBAC) can ensure that only authorized users have access.

- There can be critical organization and customer data involved in applications. Ensure that the data transfer process complies with relevant data protection regulations, such as GDPR, HIPAA, or industry-specific standards. It is generally considered to be a best practice to regularly review and update compliance policies and procedures.

CHAPTER 5   DATAVERSE CONNECTORS AND GATEWAY

Scaling Dataverse connectors and gateways is essential for organizations that need to integrate data from multiple sources, handle increasing data volumes, and ensure high availability and performance. Here are some use cases where scaling Dataverse connectors and gateways plays a crucial role:

A. **Real-Time Analytics and Reporting**: Businesses often require real-time data analytics to make informed decisions. Optimized connectors and high-performance gateways enable real-time data access for analytics and reporting tools like Power BI that further provide a holistic view of the data to relevant stakeholders.

B. **Enterprise Data Integration**: Organizations often need to integrate data from multiple on-premises and cloud-based systems. Scaling connectors and gateways ensures seamless integration and high performance for enterprise-wide data access.

C. **Customer Data Management**: Managing customer data across multiple systems is critical for customer relationship management (CRM). Therefore, ensuring reliable and high-performance data connectivity helps maintain up-to-date and accurate customer information.

D. **Business Process Automation**: Automating business processes often involves integrating data from various sources that can either be cloud-based or on-premises or both. Based on the nature of the solution, scalable connectors and gateways facilitate the automation of complex workflows using tools like Power Automate.

In summary, scaling Dataverse connectors and gateways is crucial for organizations looking to manage growing data integration needs effectively. By planning for capacity, optimizing performance, ensuring high availability, and maintaining security and compliance, organizations can scale their data connectivity solutions to meet increasing demands. Understanding the challenges and leveraging future innovations can further enhance the scalability and efficiency of Dataverse connectors and gateways. This comprehensive approach ensures that data remains accessible, reliable, and secure as organizations grow and evolve.

Real-World Use Cases

Microsoft Dataverse connectors and gateways are integral to modern data integration strategies, enabling seamless and secure connectivity between diverse data sources and Dataverse. This section explores real-world use cases across various industries, demonstrating how these tools facilitate efficient data aggregation, real-time analytics, business process automation, and more. Here are a few real-world use cases that organizations can leverage using Dataverse connectors and gateways:

A. **Enterprise Data Integration**: Large organizations often need to aggregate data from multiple on-premises and cloud-based systems into a centralized database or platform. This integration helps provide a unified view of operations, facilitate decision-making, and streamline business processes.

- For example, if a multinational financial services company needs to integrate data from various departments, such as banking, insurance, and investment services, to provide a comprehensive view of customer accounts and transactions, Dataverse connectors can be used to integrate data from SQL databases, legacy systems, and third-party financial applications. If the data is on an on-premises server, a gateway can be deployed to securely connect on-premises databases with Dataverse, ensuring real-time data access and updates.

B. **Real-Time Analytics and Reporting**: Organizations require up-to-date data for analytics and reporting to make timely and informed decisions. Integrating various data sources into a single platform like Dataverse allows for real-time data access and analysis.

- For example, if a retail chain with hundreds of stores across the country needs to monitor sales, inventory, and customer preferences in real time to optimize stock levels and improve customer experience, Dataverse connectors can be used to connect to POS systems, inventory management databases, and e-commerce platforms to gather real-time data. If the data is on an on-premises server, gateways can be leveraged to integrate on-premises inventory databases with Dataverse for centralized data management.

C. **Business Automation**: Automating business processes often involves integrating data from various sources to streamline operations, reduce manual effort, and improve accuracy. There can be many use cases including but not limited to sending notifications, requesting approvals, generating template-based documents, performing actions, etc.

- For example, if a manufacturing company wants to automate its order-processing workflow, which involves data from CRM systems, ERP systems, and logistics providers, Dataverse connectors can be used to integrate CRM data for customer orders, ERP data for production schedules, and logistics data for shipment tracking. If the system involves data from on-premises servers, gateways can be used to connect on-premises ERP systems with Dataverse to ensure seamless data flow and real-time updates.

D. **Customer Data Management**: Managing customer data across multiple systems is critical for providing personalized and consistent customer experiences. Integrating data sources into Dataverse helps create a comprehensive view of customer interactions.

- For example, if telecommunications company needs to integrate customer data from billing systems, CRM, support tickets, and social media interactions to provide a holistic view of customer engagement, Dataverse connectors can be used to connect billing databases, CRM platforms, and social media monitoring tools. In case the system requires data from on-premises servers, gateways can be used to securely integrate on-premises billing systems with Dataverse for a complete customer profile.

E. **Supply Chain Management**: Integrating data from various parts of the supply chain is essential for efficient operations, inventory management, and decision-making.

- For example, if a pharmaceutical company needs to manage its supply chain effectively, including raw material procurement, production, warehousing, and distribution, Dataverse connectors can be used to integrate data from procurement systems, production databases, warehouse management systems, and logistics providers. If the system involves data from on-premises servers, gateways can be leveraged to connect on-premises production databases and warehouse management systems with Dataverse.

F. **Financial Data Consolidation**: Consolidating financial data from multiple systems is crucial for accurate financial reporting, compliance, and strategic planning.

- For example, if a multinational corporation needs to consolidate financial data from various subsidiaries and business units across different countries for corporate financial reporting and compliance, Dataverse connectors can be used to connect to various financial systems, including accounting software, ERP systems, and banking platforms. If the solutions depend on data from on-premises data servers, gateways can be used to securely integrate on-premises financial systems with Dataverse for centralized data consolidation.

G. **Healthcare Data Integration:** Integrating healthcare data from various sources is essential for providing comprehensive patient care, improving operational efficiency, and supporting research initiatives.

- For example, if a network of hospitals needs to integrate patient data from different EHR systems, laboratory information systems, and imaging systems to provide a unified patient record and support clinical decision-making, Dataverse connectors can be used to connect to various EHR systems, lab databases, and imaging systems. In case of legacy applications that need to be modernized and also have dependency on on-premises databases, gateways can be leveraged to securely connect on-premises healthcare systems with Dataverse.

H. **Human Resources Management:** Integrating data from various HR systems helps streamline employee management, payroll processing, and compliance reporting.

- For example, if a global corporation needs to integrate data from different HR systems across its subsidiaries for centralized employee management and reporting, Dataverse connectors can be used to connect to HR management systems, payroll software, and benefits administration platforms. When data from on-premises servers is involved, gateways can be used to securely integrate on-premises HR systems with Dataverse for centralized data access.

I. **Marketing Campaign Management**: Integrating data from various marketing platforms and customer interactions helps optimize marketing campaigns and improve ROI.

- For example, if an e-commerce company needs to integrate data from its email marketing platform, social media channels, and website analytics to optimize its marketing campaigns, Dataverse connectors can be used to connect to email marketing platforms, social media APIs, and web analytics tools. In the case of data dependency on on-premises servers, gateways can be leveraged to integrate on-premises CRM and sales systems with Dataverse.

J. **IoT Data Management**: Managing and analyzing data from IoT devices requires robust data integration solutions to handle large volumes of real-time data.

- For example, if a city government implements a smart city initiative involving data from various IoT devices, including traffic sensors, environmental monitors, and public safety cameras, Dataverse connectors can be used to integrate data from IoT platforms and devices. If there are dependencies on on-premises data servers, gateways can be used to securely transfer data from on-premises IoT hubs to Dataverse.

In summary, real-world use cases for Dataverse connectors and gateways demonstrate their versatility and importance in integrating diverse data sources to support various business needs. From enterprise

CHAPTER 5　DATAVERSE CONNECTORS AND GATEWAY

data integration and real-time analytics to healthcare data management and IoT data integration, scalable and reliable connectors and gateways are critical for ensuring seamless data flow, improving operational efficiency, and enabling informed decision-making. By understanding and implementing these use cases, organizations can leverage Dataverse to drive growth and innovation across different industries.

Summary

Dataverse connectors and gateways serve as the backbone of modern data integration strategies, enabling seamless connectivity between a multitude of data sources and Microsoft Dataverse. These powerful tools provide organizations with the ability to aggregate, manage, and analyze data from both on-premises systems and cloud-based applications, facilitating more informed decision-making and streamlined operations.

Dataverse connectors simplify the integration process by offering prebuilt and custom options, ensuring compatibility with a wide range of data sources. This flexibility allows businesses to connect disparate systems, unify their data, and maintain data consistency across platforms. Whether it's integrating CRM, ERP, or custom applications, connectors play a critical role in building a cohesive data ecosystem.

On-premises data gateways are indispensable for organizations that need to bridge the gap between local data sources and cloud services securely. With features like high availability, load balancing, and secure data transmission, gateways ensure that critical business data is always accessible and protected. This reliability is crucial for maintaining business continuity and operational efficiency.

While the benefits are substantial, deploying and managing connectors and gateways come with challenges such as network latency, resource constraints, and complex configurations. However, advancements in technology promise to address these issues. The future holds exciting prospects, including AI integration for predictive analytics, serverless architectures for scalability, enhanced monitoring tools, and edge computing for real-time data processing.

The strategic implementation of Dataverse connectors and gateways enables a myriad of use cases across industries. From real-time analytics and enterprise data integration to customer data management and supply chain optimization, these tools empower businesses to harness the full potential of their data. By integrating data from various sources, organizations can achieve a unified view of their operations, improve decision-making, and drive innovation.

In summary, Dataverse connectors and gateways are foundational components for any organization aiming to thrive in today's data-driven landscape. They provide the necessary infrastructure to integrate, secure, and scale data solutions effectively. As businesses continue to grow and evolve, these tools will remain critical in enabling seamless data connectivity, ensuring data integrity, and fostering innovation. By leveraging the capabilities of Dataverse connectors and gateways, organizations can transform their data management practices, optimize their operations, and achieve their strategic objectives.

CHAPTER 6

Modern App Design with Power Apps

Introduction to Modern App Design

In today's fast-paced digital landscape, app design has evolved from basic functionality to a user-centric approach that prioritizes engagement and satisfaction. The Microsoft Power Platform stands at the forefront of this evolution, offering a comprehensive suite of tools that empower developers and nondevelopers alike to create modern, responsive, and intuitive applications. In this chapter, let's delve into how app design principles have evolved within the Power Platform and understand the significance of modern app design in enhancing user engagement and satisfaction.

    A.   Evolution of App Design Principles

- Initially, app design focused primarily on functionality that ensured that apps performed their intended tasks efficiently without much focus on user journeys within the scope of the application. However, as users' expectations grew, the emphasis shifted toward user experience alongside capabilities to perform the intended functionality. Modern app design within the Power Platform now incorporates user-centric principles, ensuring that applications are not only functional but also intuitive and enjoyable to use.

- With the rise of mobile devices, responsive design became crucial. The Power Platform supports responsive design, allowing apps to adapt seamlessly to different screen sizes and devices. This ensures a consistent and optimized user experience across desktops, tablets, and smartphones.

- Accessibility has become a cornerstone of modern app design. The Power Platform provides tools and guidelines to help developers create applications that are accessible to all users, including users who are differently abled. This inclusive approach ensures that apps can reach a broader audience and comply with regulatory standards.

- Modern app design leverages AI and automation to enhance functionality and user engagement. Power Platform's integration with AI Builder and Power Automate enables the creation of intelligent applications that can perform complex tasks, predict user needs, and streamline workflows.

B. Significance of Modern App Design in Enhancing User Engagement and Satisfaction

- Modern app design prioritizes intuitive user interfaces (UIs) that are easy to navigate and understand. The in-app experience is a guided user journey for the application users to use the application efficiently. The Power Platform offers a range of customizable templates and drag-and-drop features, enabling the creation of visually appealing and user-friendly UIs without extensive coding.

- Personalization is key to user engagement. By leveraging Power Platform's capabilities, developers can create apps that offer personalized experiences based on user data and preferences. This can significantly enhance user adoption and scaling applications across multiple streams with varied user profiles.

- Interactive elements, such as dynamic forms, real-time data updates, and responsive buttons, are integral to modern app design. Power Platform's tools, such as Power Apps and Power BI, enable the creation of highly interactive applications that keep users engaged and invested in their tasks.

- Modern app design aims to streamline workflows and improve productivity. Power Platform's integration capabilities allow for seamless data flow between different systems and applications, reducing the need for manual data entry and minimizing errors. This leads to more efficient processes and a better user experience.

- Security and compliance are critical aspects of modern app design. The Power Platform provides robust security features, including data encryption, role-based access control, and compliance with industry standards. This ensures that applications are secure and trustworthy, which is essential for user confidence and satisfaction.

In summary, the evolution of app design principles within the Microsoft Power Platform highlights a shift toward creating user-centric, responsive, and intelligent applications. By embracing modern app design, organizations can enhance user engagement and satisfaction, resulting in more successful and impactful applications. Whether you're a seasoned developer or a business professional with minimal coding experience, the Power Platform provides the tools and capabilities to bring your app ideas to life, meeting the demands of today's tech-savvy users. Dive into the world of modern app design with the Power Platform and unlock new possibilities for innovation and growth.

Responsive Design Essentials

Responsive design is an essential aspect of modern application development, ensuring that applications provide an optimal user experience across a wide range of devices and screen sizes. With the Microsoft Power Platform, developers can create applications that are not only functional but also visually appealing and accessible on desktops, tablets, and smartphones. In this section, we will discuss more about the fundamentals of responsive design within the Power Platform, offering detailed insights and practical guidance for creating versatile and user-friendly applications.

Responsive design refers to the practice of creating applications that automatically adjust their layout and functionality to suit different screen sizes and devices. The primary goal is to ensure that users have a seamless experience, whether they are accessing the app on a large desktop monitor or a small smartphone screen. Key principles of responsive design include flexible grid layouts, scalable images, and media queries that adapt the application's styling based on the device's characteristics.

A. Core Principles of Responsive Design in the Power Platform

- **Flexible Grid Layouts**: A flexible grid layout is the foundation of responsive design. It involves creating a grid system that can adjust its columns and rows to fit different screen sizes. In the Power Platform, Power Apps provides tools for defining flexible grid layouts, allowing developers to design interfaces that can adapt dynamically.

  How to implement flexible grid layouts?

  - Power Apps supports three types of applications that users can select from when building applications. Developers can select from either canvas Power Apps, model-driven apps, or Power Pages to build their applications based on the use case they are developing.

  - Power Apps offers container controls that can be leveraged to wrap around other controls such as the gallery, text labels, text inputs, date input, checkbox, etc., which can automatically adjust their size and layout based on the screen dimensions.

  - Instead of using fixed pixel values, developers can define sizes and positions in relative units (e.g., percentages with reference to the container or the screen) to ensure elements scale proportionally with the screen size.

- To maintain usability, developers can set minimum and maximum sizes for key elements. This prevents them from becoming too small or too large on different devices.

- **Scalable Images and Media**: Scalable images and media ensure that visual content looks good on all devices without compromising performance. This involves using vector graphics, responsive image techniques, and adaptive media handling.

    How to implement scalable images and media?

    - Developers can leverage Scalable Vector Graphics (SVGs) as they are ideal for icons and simple graphics and can scale without losing the quality.

    - Instead of using fixed images, developers can use media queries to serve different image sizes based on the device resolution. This reduces load times and improves performance.

    - Implement lazy loading for images and media to ensure that only the necessary content is loaded initially, improving the application's speed and responsiveness.

- **Media Queries**: Media queries are a cornerstone of responsive design, allowing developers to apply different styles based on the device's characteristics, such as screen width, height, resolution, and orientation.

How to implement media queries?

- In order to adjust the layout according to the device screen size, developers can define breakpoints that correspond to common device screen sizes.

- Media queries can be used to handle changes in device orientation (portrait vs. landscape), ensuring the application remains user-friendly in both modes.

- Developers can leverage conditional styling to elements based on the screen size to enhance readability and usability.

B. Responsive Design Tools in the Power Platform

The Power Platform, particularly Power Apps, offers several built-in features and tools that facilitate responsive design. Understanding and leveraging these tools is crucial for creating modern, responsive applications.

- **Power Apps Screen Size and Orientation Properties**: Power Apps provides properties to detect and respond to the screen size and orientation. These properties enable developers to dynamically adjust the layout and elements of the application.

  Key Properties

  - **App.Width and App.Height**: These properties return the width and height of the screen, allowing developers to create responsive layouts.

- **App.MinScreenWidth and App. MinScreenHeight**: Define minimum screen dimensions for the application to ensure usability.

- **App.Orientation**: Detects the device orientation, enabling developers to adjust the layout for portrait or landscape modes.

• **Container Controls**: Container controls in Power Apps, such as the Gallery, Data Table, and Forms, are designed to adapt to different screen sizes automatically. These controls are essential for creating responsive layouts.

Key Features

- **Flexible Containers**: Developers can implement flexible containers that can resize and rearrange their content based on the available space with reference to the app properties.

- **Nested Containers**: Canvas apps support horizontal, vertical, and block-type containers. These containers can be nested into one another for creating a dynamic UI. Developers can use nested containers within each other to create complex, adaptive layouts that respond to various screen sizes.

- **Component Libraries**: Component libraries in Power Apps allow developers to create reusable components that can be easily adapted for different screen sizes. This promotes consistency and efficiency in the development process.

  Key Features

  - **Responsive Components**: Developers can design components with responsiveness in mind, ensuring they can adapt to various screen sizes and orientations. Components can be used across applications and can reduce workload when developing multiple applications for the same organization following a specific design pattern.

  - **Component Parameters**: Components allow passing parameters from the app to control their behavior and appearance based on the device characteristics. Developers can leverage this and design dynamic applications compatible for various screen sizes.

Best Practices for Responsive Design in Power Platform

To ensure the success of your responsive design efforts, it's important to follow best practices that enhance usability, performance, and maintainability. Here are some generally recommended best practices that developers can follow to build responsive apps with Power Apps:

CHAPTER 6   MODERN APP DESIGN WITH POWER APPS

- A. Prioritize Content
  - It is important to focus on delivering the most critical and relevant content first, ensuring that users can access required information and functionality regardless of the device they are using.
  - A clear content hierarchy should be established that prioritizes essential elements making them easily accessible on smaller screens. Developers can start with a basic design that works on all devices and then enhance it with additional features and styles for larger screens.
- B. Optimize Performance
  - Responsive design should not compromise the performance of applications. Developers must ensure that the app loads quickly and runs smoothly across all devices.
  - Developers can focus on optimizing images, scripts, and other resources to reduce load times and improve the performance of the app. Using efficient data handling techniques, such as pagination and filtering, can help manage large datasets without slowing down the application.
  - Regularly testing and profiling the application on various devices help in identifying and addressing performance bottlenecks.
- C. Maintain Consistency
  - Consistency in design and functionality is crucial for providing a seamless user experience. Developers must ensure that the application behaves predictably across different devices.

CHAPTER 6   MODERN APP DESIGN WITH POWER APPS

- Consistent styling and design patterns can be leveraged to maintain a cohesive look and feel across the application.

- Developers must ensure that the application is tested on a variety of devices and screen sizes to verify consistency and identify any issues.

- Gathering user feedback to understand how the application performs in real-world scenarios helps in identifying user issues, and developers can make necessary adjustments accordingly to implement the user feedback.

D. Leverage Power Platform Features

- Developers should take full advantage of the features and capabilities offered by the Power Platform to enhance the responsive design efforts.

- Power Automate is a powerful tool that can help with loading large data sets quickly, operate under service account context, streamline workflows, and automate processes. Developers can leverage Power Automate to integrate with Power Apps and deliver a smooth and efficient user experience.

- AI Builder is another feature that can be used to add intelligent features to applications. Developers can leverage features such as predictive analytics and natural language processing, enhancing functionality and user engagement.

- Most applications also require analytical capabilities to provide a holistic view of the data to the application users. Developers can leverage Power BI to embed Power BI reports and dashboards in order to provide rich, interactive data visualizations that adapt to different screen sizes.

- The out-of-the-box controls in Power Apps may sometimes be restrictive, and therefore, developers can leverage custom components that can be built using Power Apps Component Framework (PCF). Developers can design and develop responsive controls leveraging PCF that can be used in the applications, thereby enhancing overall user experience.

In summary, responsive design is a critical aspect of modern application development, ensuring that applications provide an optimal user experience across a wide range of devices and screen sizes. The Microsoft Power Platform offers a comprehensive suite of tools and features that enable developers to create responsive, user-friendly applications with ease. By understanding and implementing the core principles of responsive design, leveraging the capabilities of the Power Platform, and following best practices, developers can create versatile applications that meet the needs of today's tech-savvy users.

Whether you're building a sales dashboard, a customer relationship management (CRM) system, or any other type of application, embracing responsive design within the Power Platform will help you deliver a superior user experience, enhance user engagement, and drive business success.

Introduction to App Development in Power Platform

Microsoft Power Platform is a suite of powerful tools designed to ease app development, enabling both professional developers and nondevelopers to create robust applications with minimal coding. Comprising four key components—Power Apps, Power Automate, Power BI, and Power Virtual Agents—the Power Platform offers a comprehensive solution for developing, automating, analyzing, and engaging through applications. This section provides a high-level overview of the app development process within the Power Platform, setting the stage for more detailed exploration in subsequent sections.

Power Apps is a low-code/no-code development environment that empowers users to create custom applications tailored to their specific needs. It supports the creation of canvas apps, model-driven apps, and Power Pages (formerly known as Power Apps Portals), each offering unique capabilities:

- **Canvas Apps**: Allow users to design applications by dragging and dropping elements onto a canvas, providing full control over the app's appearance and behavior. Similar to Excel formulas, canvas apps use a formula language for adding logic and controlling the behavior of the app components.

- **Model-Driven Apps**: Focus on data and processes, leveraging the Microsoft Dataverse (formerly known as Common Data Service) to create apps with complex business logic and workflows. Users can quickly create applications by defining data models, forms, views, and business processes.

- **Power Pages**: Enable the creation of external-facing websites that allow users outside the organization to interact with Dataverse data. Power Pages can be customized to fit the organization's branding and functional requirements. Developers can leverage various authentication methods, including Azure AD, LinkedIn, and Google, to provide secure access to external users.

Key Concepts in Power Platform App Development

Power Platform enables developers to integrate multiple tools and build robust and scalable applications for a variety of user personas. Based on the use case being developed, developers can design the solution with various components supported by the platform. Here are some key concepts and components that developers can leverage when designing their solutions using Power Platform:

A. Dataverse

- Microsoft Dataverse is the underlying data platform that supports all components of the Power Platform. It provides a secure and scalable environment for storing and managing data, enabling users to build applications that leverage shared data models and business logic.

- Canvas apps, model-driven apps, and Power Pages can all connect to Dataverse and leverage the Dataverse APIs in the form of connectors, web API, or forms and views to interact with Dataverse data.

CHAPTER 6   MODERN APP DESIGN WITH POWER APPS

B. Connectors

- Connectors enable Power Platform applications to interact with external data sources and services. With hundreds of prebuilt connectors and the ability to create custom connectors, users can integrate their apps with a wide range of systems, including Microsoft 365, Azure, Dynamics 365, and third-party services.

- Canvas apps can directly utilize connectors for performing actions on the data source. However, model-driven apps and Power Pages are tightly coupled with Dataverse and therefore can leverage connectors using Power Automate flows.

C. AI Builder

- AI Builder brings artificial intelligence capabilities to the Power Platform, allowing users to add AI models to their applications without requiring extensive data science knowledge.

- AI Builder supports features like form processing, object detection, prediction, and text recognition, enhancing the functionality of Power Apps and Power Automate flows.

- While canvas apps can directly leverage AI builder models, model-driven apps and Power Pages can interface with AI builder through custom pages or Power Automate Cloud Flows.

D. Common Data Model

- The Common Data Model provides a standardized data schema that allows applications to share and understand data more easily.

- By using CDM, developers can ensure consistency and interoperability between different applications and services within the Power Platform.

- For example, CDM can be leveraged to create canvas apps, model-driven apps, and Power Pages on the same tables and packaged into solutions depending on the use case being built.

E. Power BI

- Developers can use Power BI to create reports and dashboards based on data from Dataverse and various other data sources.

- Depending on the use case, these reports and dashboards can be embedded on to canvas apps, model-driven apps, and Power Pages, thereby providing analytical capabilities within the applications itself.

F. SharePoint Integration

- Microsoft Dataverse supports integration with SharePoint document libraries as an out-of-the-box functionalities.

- SharePoint document libraries can be directly accessed via connectors in canvas apps. When the integration is enabled at table levels and enabled on the forms, model-driven apps and Power Pages allow users to directly access the SharePoint file upload and download functionalities from the app itself.

Application Development Lifecycle in Power Platform

Like developing every other application, developers can follow a strategic path to successfully scale and drive user adoption for solutions built using the Power Platform. Here are some key aspects of application development lifecycle for solutions built using the Microsoft Power Platform:

A. Planning and Design

- The app development process begins with planning and design.
- This involves identifying the business problem, defining requirements, and designing the user interface and experience.
- Tools like Power Apps Studio allow users to prototype and iterate on their designs quickly.

B. Development

- During the development phase, users create the application by configuring data sources, designing forms and screens, and adding business logic.

- Power Apps provides a rich set of controls and functions that enable users to create interactive and dynamic applications.

C. Testing

- Testing is a crucial step in the app development lifecycle. Users should thoroughly test their applications to identify and fix any issues before deployment.
- Power Apps allows for easy testing and debugging within the development environment. These test results can be leveraged to fix issues and provide a seamless user experience to the end users.

D. Deployment

- Once the application is tested and ready, it can be deployed for the end users. Power Platform provides various deployment options, including publishing the app to a specific environment, sharing it with individual users or groups, and embedding it within other applications or websites.

E. Maintenance and Updates

- After deployment, ongoing maintenance and updates are necessary to ensure the application remains functional and meets evolving business needs.
- Power Platform's integrated development environment makes it easy to update and manage applications post-deployment.

Benefits of Using Power Platform for App Development

Compared to other platforms for application development, Power Platform provides with a set of tools that if put together can produce great results for organizations. Apart from the available Microsoft tools, Power Platform also supports a number of connectors that can help leverage other tools and services to build integrated applications. Here are some benefits of using Power Platform for app development:

A. Rapid Development

- The low-code/no-code nature of Power Platform enables rapid development and iteration, allowing users to quickly create and deploy applications that address immediate business needs.

B. Integration and Extensibility

- Power Platform's extensive library of connectors and integration capabilities ensures that applications can easily interact with other systems and services, providing a unified and cohesive solution.

C. Scalability and Security

- Built on Microsoft's robust cloud infrastructure, the Power Platform ensures that applications are scalable and secure, meeting enterprise-grade requirements for performance and compliance.

D. Collaboration and Citizen Development

- Power Platform fosters collaboration between professional developers and business users (citizen developers), enabling organizations to leverage the expertise of both groups and drive innovation. Organizations can implement tenant-wide Power Platform policies for environments and connectors to govern the overall adoption effort at the tenant level.

E. Analytics and Insights

- By integrating Power BI with Power Apps and Power Automate, users can gain valuable insights from their data, enabling data-driven decision-making and continuous improvement.

In summary, the Microsoft Power Platform represents a paradigm shift in how applications are developed, democratizing the process and empowering a broader range of users to contribute to digital transformation initiatives. Alongside, Power Apps is a transformative tool that empowers organizations to develop custom business applications rapidly and efficiently. With its low-code/no-code approach, seamless integration with the Microsoft ecosystem, and robust features, Power Apps is revolutionizing how businesses approach application development. By enabling both professional developers and citizen developers to create and share applications, Power Apps fosters innovation, enhances collaboration, and drives business success.

The subsequent sections of this chapter will delve deeper into each aspect, offering detailed guidance and best practices to help you harness the full potential of the Power Platform in your app development journey. Whether you are a seasoned developer or a business professional looking to build your first app, the Power Platform offers the tools and capabilities to bring your ideas to life and drive meaningful business outcomes.

Building Canvas Apps

Canvas apps are one of the most versatile and powerful features of Microsoft Power Platform, enabling users to design and build custom applications with a high degree of control over the apps' appearance and functionality.

They allow users to design apps by dragging and dropping controls onto a blank canvas. This visual approach to app development provides flexibility and creativity, enabling users to create highly customized user interfaces. Unlike model-driven apps, which are data-centric and follow a predefined structure, canvas apps start with a blank slate, giving developers the freedom to shape the app according to specific business needs.

This section will walk you through the process of building canvas apps, covering the essential steps and best practices.

Key Features of Canvas Apps

A. Drag-and-Drop Interface

- Users can easily add and arrange controls, such as buttons, text boxes, and galleries, using a drag-and-drop interface.

- Control properties and formulas can be leveraged for aesthetically positioning the controls on the canvas apps.

- Developers can also use containers configured based on the app screen configuration, and then all controls placed in the container will follow the container configuration for positioning the controls.

B. Customizable Layout

- Developers have full control over the layout and design, allowing for the creation of unique and tailored user experiences.

- Canvas app layouts can also be configured to automatically adjust based on screen orientation and screen sizes, as discussed in the previous sections of this chapter.

C. Formula-Based Logic

- Canvas apps use Power Fx-based formulas to drive the logic on the controls. Each control has a specific set of properties that can be configured using Power Fx to build the business process associated to the control and thereby achieve the intended functionality.

- Power Fx is very similar to Excel formulas, and it makes easier for both professional and citizen developers to build applications.

D. Integration with Data Sources

- Canvas apps have the ability to connect to multiple data sources, including Microsoft Dataverse, SharePoint, SQL Server, and third-party services.

- For connectors that are not available, developers can create custom connectors and leverage them with canvas apps.

CHAPTER 6   MODERN APP DESIGN WITH POWER APPS

E. Integration with Power Automate

- Canvas apps provide with the ability to integrate with Power Automate cloud flows that can be directly called from a control in the canvas app.

- Developers can build Power Automate flows to run processes based on actions in the app and create workflows to perform defined actions based on specific events.

F. Integration with Power BI

- Canvas apps provide with the ability to embed Power BI reports on the app screens following the appropriate access control of the user using the app.

- Developers can set row-level security on the Power BI reports and securely embed them in the app for the users to have a holistic view of the data along with insights based on the requirements.

G. Code Components

- Canvas apps support a lot of controls out of the box. These controls can be utilized for displaying data, capturing data, and requesting inputs from the users. In certain use cases, there may be requirements for additional functionality from these controls.

- Developers can leverage custom components by using multiple canvas app controls and create the custom component to suit the requirement.

- Apart from custom components using canvas controls, developers can also create code components using PCF and leverage that for successful user adoption.

H. Temporary Data Storage

- A lot of use cases might require temporary storage of data within the app before actually sending anything to the data source.
- Canvas apps provide this capability through collections. Developers can use collections to temporarily store and manipulate data based on the requirements of the app.

I. Integration with SharePoint

- Canvas apps can be used to design SharePoint List and Library forms. The out-of-the-box SharePoint forms do not provide a lot of flexibility in terms of customization and branding.
- Developers can customize SharePoint forms with canvas Power Apps and provide a smoother user experience for the end users utilizing the service.

Getting Started with Canvas Apps

A. Access Power Apps

- Navigate to the Power Apps maker portal (`https://make.powerapps.com`) and sign in with your Microsoft account. Note that to create an app, a Microsoft business or school account is required.

- Select the appropriate environment where you want to create your canvas app. Environments help segregate data and apps based on different business needs or departments. If unsure about which environment to select, contact your Power Platform Administrator or IT department to get more information.

- Developers can also set up developer environments (if allowed in the organization) to develop apps and then later export the app as a package or a solution and deploy to the intended target environment.

B. Create a New Canvas App

- There are multiple options users can select from when creating a new canvas app. These options include creating an app from data, template, page design, etc. On the Power Apps home page, click "Create" and choose the option suited to the use case you are building.

- Provide a name for the app and select the format (tablet or phone) based on the intended device usage.

- Click on the gear icon to check the settings for the app. You can change the screen size, set configuration that defines the layout of the app, and enable any preview features as applicable.

CHAPTER 6　MODERN APP DESIGN WITH POWER APPS

C. Design the User Interface

- Start by adding screens to your app. Screens act as different pages or views in your application. You can add screens for different functionalities, such as Home, Details, and Form screens. Review the screen properties to set any commands that run when a user navigates to or away from the screen.

- Review on the app properties such as App. OnStart and add any formulas to set variables or load data when the app is launched based on the requirements.

- Use the Insert menu to add controls. You can select controls based on data types or function of the data such as requesting user for an input, displaying a single record in the form of a card, displaying a filtered list of data in a table form, etc.

- Some of the commonly used controls are

  - **Text Input**: To capture input from the user in the form of text. This control supports both single line and multiple lines of text.

  - **Checkbox, Toggle, and Radio Buttons**: To capture Yes/No choice-type inputs.

  - **Gallery**: To display a list of items. Galleries can be configured to filter a data source based on other controls to show most relevant data.

  - **Form**: To facilitate data entry and display based on requirement. Form controls enable users to directly add fields as data cards without much requirement of customization.

CHAPTER 6   MODERN APP DESIGN WITH POWER APPS

- **Button**: To initiate actions based on user interaction.
- **Media**: To add images, audio, and video.
- **Dropdown, Combo-box**: To capture choice, lookup type inputs.
- Customize properties of the controls based on the requirements. Different controls have different properties that you can customize. Some basic properties applicable to most controls are size, position, color, font, display mode, visibility, etc.

D. Connect Data Source

- Click the Data icon in the left pane and choose "Add data." Select the data source you want to connect to, such as Microsoft Dataverse, SharePoint, or an Excel file.
- Follow the prompts to configure the connection. For example, if connecting to a SharePoint list, you'll need to provide the URL of the SharePoint site and select the specific list. Similarly, if connecting to Dataverse, you will have to select the tables that you need to use in the app.
- Bind the data from your sources to the controls in your app. For instance, set the Items property of a Gallery control to the name of your data source to display records. Use formulas to filter or select nested properties from the data.

CHAPTER 6   MODERN APP DESIGN WITH POWER APPS

E. Implement Logic

- Use the formula bar to add logic and functionality to your controls. Formulas in Power Apps are similar to Excel formulas and can be used to manipulate data, perform calculations, and control the behavior of controls. Here are some basic examples:

    - **TextInput1.Value**: Retrieves the text entered in a modern Text Input control.

    - **Checkbox1.Checked**: Returns true or false based on whether the check box is checked or not.

    - **Datepicker1.SelectedDate**: Returns the selected date from the date picker control.

- Use formulas to dynamically set properties of controls based on user interactions or data changes:

    - For example, you can change the color of a label based on a condition.

    - You can also configure visibility of a control based on formulas. For example, to make the Datepicker1 visible only if the Checkbox1 is checked, navigate to the visible property of the Datepicker1 control and use the formula Checkbox1.Checked.

    - To set the mode of Datepicker1 as disabled or enabled based on the Checkbox1 control, you can use the formula if(Checkbox1.Checked, DisplayMode.Edit, DisplayMode.Disabled) on the Display Mode property of the Datepicker1 control.

- Implement navigation between screens using the Navigate function. For example, Navigate(Screen2, ScreenTransition.Fade) transitions from the current screen to Screen 2 with a fade effect.

F. Test and Debug

- Use the Preview button (play icon) to run your app and test its functionality. This allows you to interact with the app as a user would.

- Use the debugging tools provided by Power Apps to troubleshoot issues. Check the formulas for errors and use the OnError property to handle exceptions gracefully.

- You can also use the monitor tool that opens the app in play mode and monitors the actions performed. The monitor tool helps analyze errors, issues, and delays on the app in detail based on user interaction with the app.

G. Publish App

- Click the File menu and select Save. Provide a version comment to keep track of changes.

- After saving, select Publish to make the app available to other users. You can also share the app with specific users or groups within your organization.

H. Share and Collaborate

- Click the Share button and specify the users or groups you want to share the app with. You can assign different roles, such as user or co-owner.

- A user with co-owner permission on the application has access to make edits to the app and also share with other users.

- Power Apps supports collaboration, allowing multiple users to work on the same app. Use the Version history feature to manage changes and revert to previous versions if needed.

Best Practices for Building Canvas Apps

A. Design and Use Case

- It is important to clearly define the purpose of the app and the business problems it aims to solve. Having clear requirements helps manage expectations and also analyze if the tool is the best fit to solve the problem at hand.

- Identifying the primary users and defining the different personas that will be using the app help developers to build functionalities according to the specific needs of these users.

- It is always recommended to design an intuitive and user-friendly interface. Avoiding clutter and keeping navigation straightforward improve the overall user experience. A lot can be achieved using the technology, but it is recommended to follow minimal design practices and prioritize essential functionalities in order to avoid unnecessary confusion and clutter in the app.

CHAPTER 6 MODERN APP DESIGN WITH POWER APPS

- Creating a detailed functional design document that highlights the use cases and functionality built in the app plays a vital role in collaboration. It is considered to be a best practice to incorporate the documentation process stagewise so that all steps and important information are accurately documented.

B. Responsive Design

- As a best practice, developers should prioritize user journey and easiness of use when designing the app. Relative positioning and sizing can be leveraged to create a responsive layout that adapts to different screen sizes.

- It is recommended to test the app on various devices to ensure a consistent user experience. Having a seamless experience, no matter the device being used, drives user adoption in the right direction.

C. Optimize Performance

- Canvas apps can be restrictive in terms of amount of data being loaded into the app. Having all the data load during app load itself can make the app extremely slow.

- It is recommended to use delegation to optimize data loading for large datasets. Delegation allows canvas apps to process data on the server side, reducing load times.

- As a best practice, images and media files can be compressed to improve the overall app performance.

CHAPTER 6   MODERN APP DESIGN WITH POWER APPS

- In the case of batch processing or bulk queries, developers can leverage Power Automate cloud flows to run the processes in the backend to avoid overloading the app with multiple operations at the same instance.

D. Security and Compliance

- It is important to ensure that sensitive data is protected and complies with organizational security policies.

- Canvas apps work on user context, and developers can leverage this to implement role-based access to perform CRUD operations on sensitive data.

E. Error Handling

- To improvise user experience, it is important to clearly communicate to the user about any error occurring in the app.

- Incorporating clear error messages with appropriate error codes is considered as a general best practice as it enables users to share relevant information.

- With appropriate information about the issues and errors users are facing, developers can reduce time and effort on triaging and fixing those issues.

F. Monitor and Improve

- For business-critical applications, it is recommended to continuously collect feedback from users and improve the app based on their recommendations.

- Based on the nature of engagement and use case of the application, developers can regularly update the app to add new features, fix bugs, and enhance performance.

- It is recommended to log all the issues users raise and clearly define requirements in order to manage expectations and avoid technical debt when developing applications.

Use Cases for Canvas Apps

A. **Employee Onboarding**: Organizations can set up an app to guide new employees through the onboarding process, providing them with necessary resources, tasks, and contacts.

B. **Time Card**: Power Platform can be leveraged to set up a time card solution for organizations. Developers can leverage Canvas Apps as a front-end interface for users to log their time and then integrate with Power Automate and Power BI to send notifications and visualize data, respectively.

C. **Inventory Management**: Organizations can set up a canvas app to track inventory levels, manage stock, and generate purchase orders. Power Automate can be used to automate associated business processes and notify key stakeholders based on preset triggers.

D. **Expense Request**: Teams can leverage canvas apps to create an expense request and approval application. Users can log their expenses on the canvas app forms, and a workflow can be set up providing the functionality for multistep approvals, log history, etc. The expense request app can further be modernized using AI builder capabilities that can help with the receipt and invoice scanning, thereby auto-populating the expense data to be submitted for approval.

E. **Visitor Tracking**: Canvas apps can also be leveraged for visitor tracking at facilities of the organization. Developers can utilize the camera control to capture an image or scan a QR code sent to the visitors, allowing them to go through a seamless entry and exit process.

In summary, building canvas apps with Microsoft Power Platform is a powerful way to create custom business applications tailored to specific needs. By leveraging the low-code/no-code capabilities, intuitive design tools, and seamless integration with various data sources, users can develop functional and aesthetically pleasing apps rapidly. Canvas apps can integrate with Power Automate and Power BI that enables developers to better design solutions and deliver success. As you delve deeper into Power Apps, you will discover endless possibilities for transforming business processes and enhancing productivity.

Model-Driven App Development

Model-driven apps in Microsoft Power Platform provide a data-centric approach to app development, emphasizing the structure and relationships of data. Unlike canvas apps, which start with a blank canvas allowing for full-design flexibility, model-driven apps rely on the underlying data model to drive the user interface and user experience.

Model-driven apps depend on Dataverse table configurations and security roles assigned to users to display forms, views, dashboards, etc. on the app. As they have high dependency on a data model, one of the core requirements is Dataverse. Without Dataverse, model-driven apps cannot be created.

In this section, we will walk through the process of building model-driven apps, covering essential steps, best practices, and use cases.

Key Features of Model-Driven Apps

A. Data-Centric Design

- Built on Microsoft Dataverse (formerly Common Data Service), model-driven apps are designed around the data and its relationships.

- Users can add tables to the sitemap that brings along all components including forms and views for those tables to the app. No additional logic configuration is required to save the data or create related data to complete a process flow.

B. Component Reusability

- Developers can leverage reusable components like forms, views, and dashboards.

- Essentially if there are multiple model-driven apps being built that would use one or more same tables, the forms, views, and dashboards created for one app can be used directly across all applications based on the requirement.

CHAPTER 6   MODERN APP DESIGN WITH POWER APPS

- Another added advantage of Dataverse table forms and views is that they can also be directly used in canvas apps.

C. Code Components

- Model-driven apps support a lot of controls out of the box based on the data type of fields. These controls can be utilized for displaying data, capturing data, and requesting inputs from the users. In certain use cases, there may be requirements for additional functionalities from these controls.

- Developers can leverage PCF components for adding any additional functionality around these fields. For example, if the data type of a field is a whole number and it is being used to capture the service rating on a scale of 1–5 from the end user, a PCF control can be created that displays a radial knob or a linear scale or emojis to capture this information and enhance the user experience.

D. Predefined Layouts

- The platform provides a consistent and responsive user interface across different devices. As long as there is no custom development implemented, model-driven apps are accessible across all devices and responsive toward various screen sizes.

- In case there are any custom components implemented through PCF or scripting, it is recommended to design the controls in a way that they are responsive.

CHAPTER 6 MODERN APP DESIGN WITH POWER APPS

E. Built-in Business Logic

- Easily implement business processes, rules, and workflows to ensure data integrity and automate tasks.

- Business rules set up on tables are directly applied to the forms on model-driven apps. This allows developers to automate simple tasks like setting fields based on other fields, set field as required or visible, etc.

F. Advanced Scripting

- Model-driven apps can further be extended by implementing code that can be called as functions on specific events.

- For example, dropdowns and lookup fields can be filtered based on inputs provided in another field or any other related data that can be used to filter the rows.

- Developers can create custom commands and customize the command bars on forms and views to implement advanced functionality. Earlier, this was supported only via code, but now, command bar can be customized with Power Fx also.

G. Security and Compliance

- Model-driven apps endure a robust security model with role-based access control ensuring data protection and compliance with organizational policies.

- Developers or system administrators can set up security roles and map them to users. These security roles can then be used to govern the access a user has on data. Security roles can be used to secure row-level data, forms, views, etc.

H. Integration Capabilities

- Model-driven apps can leverage Power Automate cloud flows to implement complex workflows and process automation based on the business requirements.

- Developers can leverage the custom pages feature of model-driven apps to enhance and customize the look and feel and add any additional functionality as required by simply using the canvas controls on these custom pages. Custom pages can be added to the navigation bar on the model-driven app and do support formula-based navigation to other pages.

- In case required, developers can add links to external HTML pages or websites or Power BI reports to the navigation bar on the model-driven app to directly launch other applications.

Getting Started with Model-Driven Apps

A. Access Model-Driven Apps

- Navigate to the Power Apps maker portal (https://make.powerapps.com) and sign in with your Microsoft account. Note that to create an app, a Microsoft business or school account is required.

CHAPTER 6   MODERN APP DESIGN WITH POWER APPS

- Select the appropriate environment where you want to create your model-driven app. Environments help segregate data and apps based on different business needs or departments. If unsure about which environment to select, contact your Power Platform Administrator or IT department to get more information.

- Developers can also set up developer environments (if allowed in the organization) to develop apps and then later export the app as a package or a solution and deploy to the intended target environment.

B. Define Data Model

- Start by clicking on the Solutions option in the navigation bar to view all the exiting solutions in the environment. Create a new solution if required for the model-driven app.

- This solution will act as a container for all the components required for the model-driven app. Note that a model-driven app can utilize components from other solutions in the same environment too.

- With this setup, you will have to ensure that all the dependencies are transported to the intended target environment before deploying the solution containing the model-driven app.

- Solutions allow users to provide a publisher for the solution. If unsure about the publisher for the solution, contact the Power Platform administrator to get more details. Once the publisher is added and the solution is created, the publisher for that solution cannot be changed.

- Once the solution is created, start adding or creating tables as required by the application. These tables will store all the data related to the app. Ensure all data types of the columns are properly verified before creating the table.

- After creating the tables, establish the relationships between the tables to correctly model the data. Developers can set up many-to-one, one-to-many, and many-to-many relationship types between the tables as required.

C. Design Forms, Views, and Charts

- Forms are the front-end components required to view and edit rows in the table. Create forms as required for the tables. Dataverse tables support multiple types of forms including main form, card form, quick create form, etc. Set up the forms as required by the app.

- When adding the attributes to the form, developers can customize certain properties like sections, tabs, appearance of the control, labels, visibility, etc. Set up the entire configuration of the table forms as required by the application.

CHAPTER 6   MODERN APP DESIGN WITH POWER APPS

- Views define how the rows in the table are listed. Multiple filters can be added to a view along with sorting on various columns based on the use case. Developers can also add role-based security here to display rows relevant to the logged in user only.

- Dashboards provide with an overview of key metrics and data. Developers can set up new dashboards for tables by adding various components like charts, lists, and web resources to better visualize the data and provide actionable insights.

- Charts help visualize data within views and dashboards. Developers can set up different types of charts like a pie chart, line graph, or bar charts, etc. to graphically represent the data. Chart properties such as series, categories, and aggregation types need to be accurately set up for properly visualizing the data.

D. Implement Workflows and Business Logic

- Business rules can be leveraged to apply logic directly on forms without writing code. Developers can add new rules to tables for setting field values, validations, marking fields required, etc. using business rules.

- Business process flows help guiding users through a preset process for ensuring data quality. Developers can leverage business process flows to implement a series of steps that would enforce the users to enter the required data. Based on the changes of the state of the business process flow, further automation can be set up to streamline processes.

- Workflows and Power Automate flows can be used for automating processes such as creating records, sending email notifications, generating documents, etc. Developers can leverage this feature to enhance the overall user experience of the application.

E. Test and Publish

- Before publishing the app, ensure that it is thoroughly tested by following each user persona. This method will allow testing of various security roles involved as well.

- Testers can leverage the preview mode of the app and test the functionality. They can also verify the responsiveness and ensure a smooth user experience by performing an end-to-end test.

- Once the app is tested, it can be published or deployed to target production environments. Developers need to ensure that all required components and dependencies are either packaged in the same solution or available already in the target environment.

- Once deployed, the app can be shared with other users. Organizations can leverage security groups also to share the app at once with multiple users in a group and then manage the group instead of individually operating on user accounts when trying to share the app or removing a user's access.

CHAPTER 6   MODERN APP DESIGN WITH POWER APPS

Best Practices for Building Model-Driven Apps

A. Optimized Data Model

- It is important to clearly define the purpose of the app and the business problems it aims to solve. During the design phase, it is critical to categorize the primary users of the app and the business processes that they will be following.

- An integrated data model with appropriate relationship mapping enables developers to repurpose the tables, and therefore, it is recommended to normalize the data and associated requirements to reduce redundancy and ensure data integrity.

- As a general best practice, it is recommended to document the data model in the form of an entity relationship diagram and update all changes regularly in order to keep track of how the system is functioning and identify the key tables being used in the solution. This also helps other developers and key stakeholders to better understand the solution and devise optimal strategies for driving growth and scaling the application.

B. Reusable Components

- It is recommended as a best practice to use standard components and templates to ensure a consistent user experience across all forms and dashboards of the app.

- Developers can leverage controls built using PCF that can be reused across multiple fields, views, etc. ensuring a smoother user experience.

- Components built using PCF can also be packaged into solutions for enabling other teams within the organization or outside of the organization to implement solutions using these controls. It is a standard best practice to package controls into solutions so that they can be extended for larger groups of users in various solutions.

- As PCF components depend on creating the control using code, it is recommended to add appropriate error handling and notify users with accurate error messages for a smoother user experience.

C. Optimize Performance

- For large datasets, it is recommended to leverage views with appropriate filtering and paging of data so that users can access most relevant data based on their requirements. Enabling search on key columns enables users to directly search from the data set and quickly get to the rows that they need to access. This optimizes the overall performance of the application and also helps in driving user adoption.

- Although using code components can help improvising the user interface, it is recommended to follow minimalistic design patterns and focus on essential functionalities in order to avoid unnecessary delay that can slow down the application.

CHAPTER 6   MODERN APP DESIGN WITH POWER APPS

D. Security and Compliance

- Model-driven apps should function based on security roles on the Dataverse tables. As a standard best practice, developers must implement appropriate security roles based on the user personas so that the end users only interact with the data they should.

- Using column security also enables masking of sensitive column-level data, and it is recommended to implement this for further securing the application.

E. Error Handling

- Model-driven apps already have basic error control logic implemented to efficiently navigate the users. In case of custom development with any additional logic, it is recommended to have appropriate error handling in place. Clearly communicating the error to the end users enables developers to quickly identify the root cause and resolve any associated issues.

- There can be multiple components associated to the app. For example, a workflow, a plugin, a business rule, or a custom component might be the root cause of an error, and forming the error messages based on the component makes it easier to track and resolve issues.

CHAPTER 6   MODERN APP DESIGN WITH POWER APPS

F. Monitoring and Improvements

- Collecting user feedback and strategizing to improve the application based on that is considered as a general best practice. Depending on the nature of the application and its business importance, teams can strategize task boards in order to prioritize enhancements for the application.

- Components such as controls created with PCF, flows created with Power Automate, etc. may depend on versions, and release of newer versions may result in some of the core functionalities not working as expected. It is recommended to ensure that the components being used are of the latest version and thoroughly tested to avoid any user inconvenience in production.

- Developers can also add training guides and tutorials on the intended usage on how to's of the application as links in the navigation bar. This helps as a self-service feature to guide users on how to effectively make use of the application.

Use Cases for Model-Driven Apps

A. **Project Management**: Based on the defined data model, organizations can build project management apps or use the project operations solution to enable ease of project management across the organization. Users can track project tasks, milestones, resources, etc. Dashboards and charts can also be leveraged to monitor the project progress and identify any issues.

B. **Customer Relationship Management**: Most CRM systems require integrated data models. Using Dataverse capabilities with model-driven apps, organizations can set up systems track and manage customer interactions, sales opportunities, and service requests. Users can use system charts and set up their own to gain insights into customer behavior and sales performance.

C. **Compliance and Audit Management**: Organizations can leverage model-driven apps for tracking compliance activities, managing audit findings, and ensuring that regulatory requirements are met. Developers can implement processes with the help of business rules and workflows to enforce compliance policies and automate audit processes.

D. **Field Service Management**: Model-driven apps can be used to manage work orders, schedule and dispatch field technicians, and track service activities. As model-driven apps also support offline capabilities for certain specifications, these features can be leveraged to build integrated field service management systems that allow users to use the application in remote areas also.

E. **Human Resources Management**: Another use case for model-driven apps is to manage employee records, track leave requests, and automate onboarding processes. Integrating with canvas apps, Power Automate flows, SharePoint, etc., this enables organizations to streamline HR processes and ensure compliance with organizational policies.

F. **Admin App:** In solutions where Dataverse is being used to store all the data and different sets of users interact with the data through different media like canvas apps, Power Pages, Power Automate, or Power BI, model-driven apps can serve as admin applications where users with the required roles and security permissions can access and perform CRUD operations on the entire dataset.

In summary, building model-driven apps with Microsoft Power Platform offers a powerful way to create data-centric applications that are scalable, secure, and easy to manage. By leveraging the capabilities of Dataverse, reusable components, and built-in business logic, users can develop robust applications that meet specific business needs.

Whether you are managing customer relationships, optimizing field service operations, or ensuring regulatory compliance, model-driven apps can help you achieve your goals and drive business success.

Customizing Themes and Branding

Customizing themes and branding in Power Platform apps are essential for creating a consistent user experience that aligns with an organization's brand identity. Both canvas apps and model-driven apps offer various customization options, but the methods and capabilities differ between the two.

In this section, we will walk through in detail on the steps and best practices for customizing themes and branding in both canvas apps and model-driven apps.

Customizing Themes and Branding in Canvas Apps

Canvas apps offer extensive flexibility in terms of design and customization. They are most flexible with capabilities to customize branding on control-level components of the app. Here's how you can customize themes and branding in canvas apps:

A. Define a Color Scheme

- Choose the primary colors that represent your brand. These colors can be used for key elements such as headers, buttons, banners, navigation bars, etc.

- Set up a secondary color palette matching your brand that can be used for backgrounds, borders, and comparatively less prominent elements (e.g., hover colors, selected colors, etc.)

- Once the primary and secondary colors are finalized, define text colors for various levels of text like heading, title, subtitle, body, etc. Ensure that text colors contrast well with background colors to maintain readability.

B. Set up a Theme

- Creating a theme involves defining the color and style settings that will be applied consistently across your app.

- Developers can leverage Power Apps variables for storing color values. This allows for easy changes and consistency across the app. For example:

- Set(colorPrimary, RGBA(10,120,225,1)) will set the variable "colourPrimary" with the color value as mentioned in the formula.
- Set(colorSecondary, Color.Blue) will set the variable "colorSecondary" as Blue.

- To ease the process of setting branding on individual controls, developers can set up custom components and create a component library that can be used across all apps.
- A single hidden screen with all the controls like text labels, inputs, date picker controls, dropdowns, etc. with appropriate branding can be set up, and a simple copy paste functionality can also be used.

C. Apply Styles to Controls

- Developers can leverage rectangles or containers for headers and footers. The primary color variable can be used to set the Fill property of these controls on the app. Once done, add text labels for titles and navigation links, setting their color property to contrast appropriately.
- For controls like buttons, set the Fill property to colorPrimary and the HoverFill property to a darker shade of the primary color.
- For text inputs and forms, apply consistent styles for border colors, background colors, and text colors and ensure that the form controls like text inputs, combo boxes, and dropdowns are styled to match the theme.

D. Use Media and Images

- Upload your organization's logo and custom icons. The logo can be placed in a prominent position, such as the header or a dedicated splash screen.

- Use background images sparingly to avoid clutter and ensure they don't interfere with readability. Overlapping controls may cause issues while interacting with the control, and therefore, layering these components properly is critical for the app to function as expected.

- Try to use high-definition images or SVG's to ensure that the images do not loose quality and provide a consistent user experience across different screen sizes and devices.

E. Responsive Design

- Use relative positioning and sizing to ensure controls adapt to different screen sizes and devices. Using containers and grouping enable developers to manage layouts effectively.

- It is best to test the app on various devices and screen sizes (e.g., phones, tablets, and desktops) to ensure consistent appearance and functionality.

Customizing Themes and Branding in Model-Driven Apps

Model-driven apps offer a more structured approach to customization, with predefined layouts and components. Customizing themes and branding involves configuring the out-of-the-box options and leveraging custom themes.

A. Define a Color Scheme

- Choose primary and accent colors that align with your brand. These will be used for elements like navigation, headers, and buttons. Ensure that the text colors have sufficient contrast with background colors for readability.

B. Configure Basic Customizations

- For managing theme settings on model-driven apps, it can be done by accessing the theme customizations of the environment from the Power Platform admin center.

  Create a new theme or modify an existing one. Properties such as Logo, Navigation Bar Color, Header Color, and Global Link Color can be customized in the theme settings.

- Upload your organization's logo to be displayed in the app header. You can also add a favicon to customize the browser tab icon.

C. Apply Advanced Customizations

- Developers can leverage custom CSS to apply more advanced styles and achieve specific branding requirements. This can be done by injecting CSS through web resources and applying it using JavaScript on the form load.

- Form customization plays a major role in usability, and developers can lay out the attributes on the form based on the organization guidelines. Custom branding can be added to the form headers and footers.

- Styling charts to match the color scheme makes them visually appealing and aligned with the organization branding.

D. Enhanced Visuals

- Power BI reports can be embedded onto the model-driven app pages and can be accessed from the navigation bar.

- Developers can create the reports with visuals that are consistently styled based on the organization's branding guidelines. Similarly, Power BI tiles can be branded accordingly and added to the dashboards to present a unified branding scheme for the end users.

E. Custom Icons and Images

- Icons on elements like tables can be replaced with custom icons matching the branding guidelines for developing the application.

- Developers can leverage web resources to store custom graphics and use them as icons wherever required (e.g., table icons, command bar button icons, etc.)

- Background images can be added to forms and dashboards. It is good to ensure that images are optimized for performance and don't hinder usability.

CHAPTER 6　MODERN APP DESIGN WITH POWER APPS

Best Practices for Branding and Custom Themes

A. Consistency

- As a general best practice, it is recommended to maintain consistency in colors, fonts, and styles across all screens and components.

- Developers can leverage global variables and styles to ensure uniformity, thereby providing a consistent look and feel on the apps.

B. Readability

- It is critical to ensure that there is sufficient contrast between text and background colors.

- There are multiple font options supported, and as a best practice, it is advised to choose fonts that are legible and appropriate for the app's purpose.

C. Performance

- One of the major components that can be optimized is the use of images and media in apps. It is recommended to use high-resolution media as applicable but not overdo as it can heavily affect the app performance.

- As a best practice, developers should ensure that they use minimalist styling and avoid overcomplicated styling that could affect the app load and in turn affect the app performance.

CHAPTER 6 MODERN APP DESIGN WITH POWER APPS

D. User Experience

- Developers should properly understand the business requirements and formulate a user journey for processes to be built on the app. It is important to design with the user in mind, ensuring the app is intuitive and easy to navigate.

- As a general best practice, it is recommended to collect feedback from users and iterate on the design based on their input.

E. Accessibility

- At times, the direct users of the app can include a group of differently abled users. In order to drive user adoption, it is recommended to follow accessibility guidelines and ensure that the app is usable by everyone.

- Power Apps tools provide features like accessibility checker, and developers can leverage these features to enhance the user experience. Some key areas of focus for accessibility include colors, keyboard navigation, etc.

In summary, customizing themes and branding in Power Platform apps allows you to create a cohesive and professional user experience that reflects your organization's identity. Whether you're building canvas apps with their extensive design flexibility or model-driven apps with their structured approach, both offer powerful customization options. By following the detailed steps and best practices outlined in this section, you can ensure your apps are not only functional but also visually appealing and aligned with your brand.

Accessibility Considerations

Ensuring accessibility in applications built with Microsoft Power Platform is essential to provide a seamless and inclusive user experience for all users, including those with disabilities. Accessibility involves making sure that everyone, regardless of their physical or cognitive abilities, can use the application effectively.

In this section, we will cover the principles of accessibility, specific considerations for canvas and model-driven apps, tools for testing and validating accessibility, and best practices to follow.

Accessibility is founded on several principles, which guide the design and development of inclusive applications. Here are some key design principles that developers should keep in mind when developing apps using Microsoft Power Apps:

A. Perceivable

- Information and user interface components must be presented in ways that users can perceive and act upon. This includes providing text alternatives for non-text content and ensuring content can be presented in different ways without losing the actual meaning and intended usage of the application.

- Users should be able to interact with the controls, and developers should ensure that there is no overlap on the display and all controls are easily accessible.

B. Operable

- User interface components and navigation must be operable. Users should be able to navigate and interact with the application using various input methods, such as keyboard, mouse, and touch.

- The controls should be easy to use across devices and support all applicable methods of action like operating with a mouse-controlled device vs. operating with a touch-enabled device.

C. Understandable

- Information and the operation of the user interface must be understandable. This involves making text readable and comprehensible, ensuring predictable behavior, and providing assistance for users to avoid and correct mistakes.

- Developers should leverage features like recommendations and tool tips to guide users through a process or help them understand what specific controls would do.

D. Robust

- Content must be robust enough to be interpreted reliably by a wide variety of user agents, including assistive technologies.

- This means adhering to standards and ensuring compatibility with current and future technologies.

Accessibility Considerations for Canvas Apps

Canvas apps in the Power Platform allow for significant design flexibility, which means developers need to be proactive in ensuring accessibility. Here are a few considerations that developers can adhere to when designing canvas apps:

CHAPTER 6   MODERN APP DESIGN WITH POWER APPS

A. Accessible Controls

- Ensure every interactive control, like buttons and input fields, has an associated label. Use the built-in Label control to provide text labels. Developers can also leverage hover properties to pop any long descriptions required for the controls.

- Provide descriptive alternative text for media controls, i.e., images and icons using the "AccessibleLabel" property.

- Set the tab order for interactive elements using the TabIndex property to ensure logical navigation with a keyboard. If using containers, this is automatically handled by Power Apps based on the position of the control.

B. Colors and Contrast

- It is important to ensure that there is sufficient contrast between text and background colors. It is recommended to use tools like the Web Content Accessibility Guidelines (WCAG) contrast checker to validate contrast ratios.

- Developers must avoid using color alone to convey information. Supplementing with text or patterns to ensure that information is perceivable by users with color blindness helps drive user adoption.

C. Text and Font

- Use clear and readable fonts. Developers may follow the company logo fonts, but sometimes that can make the app difficult to use, and therefore avoid overly decorative fonts that may cause inconvenience to the end users.

- It is critical to ensure that text is large enough to be readable without zoom. If possible, add functionality that allows users to resize text without losing the functionality or content.

D. Navigation

- Ensure that all interactive elements can be navigated using the keyboard. It is better to test the tab order and ensure that it follows a logical sequence.

- Developers should also focus on providing visible focus indicators for interactive elements to help users understand where they are within the application.

E. Screen Reader Compatibility

- Developers can leverage ARIA (Accessible Rich Internet Applications) attributes to enhance screen reader compatibility. For example, use ARIA label to provide context for buttons and other controls.

- It is advised to define roles for controls using ARIA roles to help screen readers identify the purpose of elements.

Accessibility Considerations for Model-Driven Apps

Model-driven apps are more structured and data-driven, which simplify some aspects of accessibility but still require careful attention. Here are a few considerations that developers can adhere to when building model-driven apps:

CHAPTER 6   MODERN APP DESIGN WITH POWER APPS

A. Form Design

- Ensure all fields have clear and descriptive labels. Use the built-in mechanisms for associating labels with fields. Developers can also add field descriptions that can provide more details on what data is being captured to clearly communicate the requirement to the end users.

- Use section headings to organize content logically. This helps users navigate forms more easily and improves the overall user experience.

B. Views and Grids

- Ensure that views and grids have descriptive column headers. Currently, views do not support adding more description or changing the column headers on the views. Therefore, developers must ensure that these headers provide meaningful context to the end users.

- Verify that users can navigate through rows and columns using the keyboard and users are able to tab through the page.

C. Dashboards and Charts

- Provide text descriptions for charts and visualizations. Use the chart title, legends, and labels to convey the meaning of the data.

- It is important to ensure that dashboards are organized logically and are navigable using both keyboard and screen readers.

Tools for Testing and Validating Accessibility

Microsoft Power Platform and other tools offer several features to help test and validate accessibility. Here are a few tools that developers can leverage for testing and validating accessibility:

A. **Accessibility Checker**: Power Apps includes an Accessibility Checker that scans for common accessibility issues and provides guidance on how to fix them. Developers can leverage these insights and improve the overall user experience of the application.

B. **Screen Reader Testing**: Developers can test applications and verify that text controls are easy to read by using popular screen readers such as NVDA (Non-Visual Desktop Access) or JAWS (Job Access With Speech).

C. **Keyboard Testing**: Developers can test the keyboard navigation on the app by using only the keyboard to ensure all interactive elements are accessible and the tab order is logical. Canvas app controls support properties like tab index or focus to enable tabbing through the form screens. Using containers automatically sets the tab order.

D. **Color Contrast Analyzers**: Tools like the WCAG Color Contrast Checker can be leveraged to validate color contrast ratios and ensure that there are no issues with the choice of colors.

E. **Browser Developer Tools**: Most modern browsers include developer tools that can help test for accessibility, such as Lighthouse in Google Chrome. Developers can leverage this to identify and fix issues in the testing phase itself.

Best Practices for Accessibility in Power Platform Apps

A. Plan for Accessibility from the Start

- It is a recommended best practice to incorporate accessibility in the early phases of app development rather than it being an afterthought.
- Involving differently abled user groups in the research and testing phases itself will help developers to identify any issues and build the app in a more user-friendly way.

B. Training and Awareness

- Providing the development, testing, and design teams with training on accessibility principles and guidelines can be quite beneficial in the overall planning for app development.
- It is recommended to stay ahead and keep up with the latest accessibility standards and best practices for building applications.
- Once the app is ready, it is also beneficial to test end-to-end process along with different sets of users to identify and fix any potential issues early on.

CHAPTER 6   MODERN APP DESIGN WITH POWER APPS

C. Consistent Testing

- As a best practice, organizations can designate dedicated testing teams to conduct regular accessibility testing throughout the development lifecycle to identify and address any issues.

- As discussed in the previous sections, it is important to gather feedback from the app users regarding the user experience, and the same is applicable for accessibility as well. Based on the feedback, teams can prioritize and resolve any accessibility-related issues to further drive user adoption across the organization.

D. Built-in Features

- It is recommended to use the standard Power Platform controls and components as much as possible as they are already designed with accessibility in mind.

- Developers can refer to Microsoft's accessibility guidelines and resources for Power Platform to ensure compliance with best practices.

E. Documentation and Support

- Along with trainings, tutorials, and how to's, organizations can direct teams to offer clear documentation and support resources for differently abled users to help them navigate and use the app.

- As a best practice, it is recommended to include an accessibility statement that outlines commitment to accessibility and provides contact information for support to the end users.

331

In summary, building accessible applications using Microsoft Power Platform is not just a legal or regulatory requirement but a moral imperative to ensure inclusivity. By adhering to the principles of accessibility and leveraging the tools and features provided by the Power Platform, you can create applications that are usable by everyone, regardless of their abilities.

Whether you are developing canvas apps with their high degree of customization or model-driven apps with their structured data-centric approach, following best practices and conducting thorough testing will help you deliver accessible and user-friendly applications.

Integration with Power Automate and Copilots

Integrating Power Apps with Power Automate and AI Copilots can significantly enhance the capabilities of your applications, enabling automation of complex workflows and incorporation of intelligent assistance. In this section, we will explore the integration process, benefits, use cases, and best practices for leveraging these powerful tools together.

Integrating Power Apps with Power Automate

Power Automate flows can be integrated with Power Apps where a cloud flow can be triggered from a control in the canvas app or from a selected row in model-driven apps. Here are a few steps on how to get started:

A. Identify the Use Case

- Identify the need for automating a process or an action that a user would perform in the app. It is better to start with simpler processes like using flows to send out an email notification, request for an approval, or update a row in a related table.

CHAPTER 6   MODERN APP DESIGN WITH POWER APPS

- Ensure that the use case is a right fit to be automated using Power Automate. It is essential to keep the app performance in mind so as to not deteriorate user experience.

B. Power Apps Trigger in Power Automate

- To call a Power Automate cloud flow from a canvas app, use the Power Apps trigger for the flow. The trigger allows you to pass a text, number, email, Boolean, file, etc. as an input. Once the input is configured, add the steps to the flow to perform the required actions.

- For example, if automating a process to send an email, you can configure the trigger to request for the email address, subject and content of the email from the app, and add an action to send an email using the service provider of choice. All inputs from the app configured on the trigger are available to select from the dynamic selector.

- To call a Power Automate cloud from a model-driven app, use the "When a row is selected" trigger from Dataverse. Currently, to directly call a flow on demand from model-driven apps, it can be done through custom code and using the "When an HTTP request is received" trigger. Once the trigger is configured, add the steps to the flow to perform the required actions.

- For example, if automating a process where if a user selects a row and triggers the flow, it should request for an approval from the supervisor of the user, you can use the data from the trigger and map to the approval action using the dynamic selector. After the approval action, you can add an "Update a row" action or "Send an Email" action to either update the row or send the response via email.

C. Connect Power Apps to Power Automate

- To connect a Power Automate cloud flow with a canvas app, you can add it by clicking the Power Automate icon and selecting the flow in the Power Apps maker portal.
- For model-driven apps, the "When a row is selected" trigger automatically adds the flow as an option on the selected table.

D. Test and Publish

- Once the setup is ready, you can test in the preview mode and publish the app. Once published and the app is live, you can run more tests to verify the outcome.
- To verify all the steps in the Power Automate flow have been executed, you can verify that in the run history of the flow.

CHAPTER 6 MODERN APP DESIGN WITH POWER APPS

Integrating Power Apps with AI Copilots

AI Copilots can be integrated into Power Apps to enhance the functionality with intelligent features. Here are few steps on how to get started:

- A. Identify the Use Case

  - Identify where AI assistance can add value to the app, such as automating responses, providing insights, or aiding data entry.

  - Based on the use case, choose the relevant AI capabilities, such as natural language processing (NLP), machine learning, or prebuilt AI models in AI Builder.

- B. AI Builder in Power Apps

  - AI Builder is a Microsoft Power Platform capability that provides AI models designed to optimize your business processes.

  - In Power Apps, navigate to AI Builder, and you can either create a model from scratch or select one from the already available models based on the requirement.

  - Train your model using your data and publish it for use in your app.

- C. Integrate AI Models

  - AI models can be integrated with Power Apps in multiple ways. For canvas apps, you can add the AI model to your app by inserting it as a control. You can also leverage Power Automate cloud flows to process the data through an AI model.

CHAPTER 6 MODERN APP DESIGN WITH POWER APPS

- Once the model is added to an app, set up the inputs for the AI model (e.g., images, text) and configure how the outputs will be displayed in your app.

D. Test and Refine

- Test the integration by running your app and ensuring the AI model works as expected. For example, if the model reads data from PDF files, you can upload a file and verify if the correct data was extracted.

- Based on the testing and the user experience of end users, continuously refine the AI model based to improve accuracy and relevance.

Use Cases of Integrating Power Apps with Power Automate and AI Copilots

A. Automate Business Processes

- Developers can set up Power Automate flows to automate business processes. These processes include performing CRUD operations on data, sending email notifications, requesting approvals, generating documents, etc.

- Using Copilots, organizations can enable users to get details and summarize data by chatting with a virtual chatbot.

- To further enhance the solution, AI models can be leveraged to extract and analyze data and ease the process of data entry for the end users, thereby driving user adoption.

- For example, organizations may have expense solutions set up and Power Apps being used by the users to log their expenses. Power Automate cloud flows can be set up to request approvals on the expense and send out email notifications to relevant stakeholders. Copilots can be set up to enable users to get a summary of their expense data and categorize it as needed. Furthermore, AI models can be used to process receipts and extract data from uploaded files for the users to directly verify and submit their expense reports.

B. Data Collection and Analysis

- Organizations can set up solutions built using Power Apps, Power Automate, AI models, and Copilots to collect data, process it, and provide insights and analysis on the data.

- For example, developers can build Power Apps to collect survey data for a service or a product. Power Automate can be used to send out automated email notifications to relevant stakeholders with a link to the survey. AI models and Copilots can be integrated into this solution to utilize sentiment analysis models and gain more insights from the data and devise appropriate strategies to act on the data.

C. Sales and Marketing

- Organizations can leverage the Power Platform to build integrated sales and marketing apps to enhance user experience and drive user adoption.

- For example, developers can leverage Power Apps to build apps to manage the customer data, leads, opportunities, etc. Power Automate can be leveraged to update rows, send email notifications, create files, reports, etc. AI and Copilots can be used to further enhance the solution by integrating with the AI capabilities to score leads, predict conversions, analyze performance, etc.

Best Practices for Integrating Power Apps with Power Automate and AI Copilots

A. Define Objectives

- As a standard best practice, it is recommended to clearly define the requirements and objectives that need to be achieved with the integration to ensure all components work toward a common goal.

B. Performance

- Developers must ensure that the integration does not compromise the overall performance of the app. It is recommended to optimize the Power Automate flows and AI models for efficiency.

C. Security

- Security is one of the major aspects of developing and integrating applications. Integrating with services like Power Automate and AI Copilots may have certain security concerns.

- Developers must ensure data privacy and security by adhering to best practices for data handling and access controls in all the integration components.

- Power Automate flows triggered from canvas apps use the manual trigger. This trigger allows the flow owner to configure the connection settings in a way that the flow either uses the flow owner's connection or the connection of the user triggering the flow. It is critical to configure this appropriately in order to follow compliance and not share connections with users who are not supposed to access it.

D. User Training

- It is best to ensure that there is adequate training provided to the end users regarding interaction with the integrated solution to maximize adoption and effectiveness.

- For developers and testing teams maintaining the application, it is a recommended best practice to document the design, any changes to the functionality, changes in the business process, etc. to maintain a track of the changes and development.

E. Monitor and Iterate

- To enhance the end user experience, it is recommended to continuously monitor the performance of the integrations and iterate based on user feedback and performance metrics.

- Monitoring also allows developers to identify any intermittent issues or bugs and fix them to avoid any errors for the end users.

In summary, integrating Power Apps with Power Automate and AI Copilots offers a powerful combination to automate workflows, enhance user experience, and provide intelligent assistance. By leveraging the capabilities of each tool and following best practices, you can build robust and scalable solutions that drive efficiency and innovation in your organization.

This integrated approach enables you to automate complex processes, make data-driven decisions, and provide personalized experiences, ultimately enhancing productivity and business outcomes.

Data Visualization Techniques

Data visualization is an essential aspect of any modern application, as it helps transform complex data sets into understandable and actionable insights. Power Apps, as part of the Microsoft Power Platform, provides various tools and techniques to create compelling data visualizations.

In this section, we will explore the different methods and best practices for visualizing data using Power Apps.

Power Apps allows users to create custom business applications that can connect to a wide range of data sources, including Microsoft Dataverse, SharePoint, SQL Server, and other third-party services. Data visualization within Power Apps can be achieved using built-in controls, integration with Power BI, and custom visualizations using JavaScript libraries.

Built-in Visualization Controls in Canvas Apps

Canvas Apps provide several built-in controls that can be used to visualize data effectively. These controls are easy to use and can be customized to suit specific requirements.

A. Gallery

- The gallery control is a versatile tool for displaying a collection of items, such as records from a data source. It can be customized to show data in various layouts, including lists, grids, and cards.

- Galleries can be used to display lists of items like products, customers, or orders. Developers can customize the layout, style, and formatting of items. Data source fields can be bound to specific controls within the gallery.

- To make the user experience smoother, filters and sorting can be added to the data displayed in the gallery using formulas and controls.

B. Data Table

- The data table control provides a tabular view of data, similar to a traditional spreadsheet. It allows users to display and interact with data in a structured format.

- Data tables can be leveraged to display tabular data with multiple columns. The control enables developers to customize column widths, headers, and row styles.

- Additional functionalities like sorting, filtering, and selecting of rows can be added to the data table controls.

C. Chart

- Power Apps includes several chart controls for visualizing data trends and patterns, such as bar charts, line charts, and pie charts.

- Developers can leverage charts to display numerical data that show trends, distributions, and comparisons. Canvas apps support configuring chart types, data bindings, labels, and formatting.

- Charts can be dynamically updated based on user interactions and data changes.

D. Form

- The form control is used for displaying and editing records from a data source. While primarily for data entry, forms can include visual elements to enhance the user experience.

- Forms can be used to display and edit individual records with detailed information. Developers can add input controls, labels, and custom formatting. Data cards can be used to display and edit fields.

- To improve the data quality, data validation rules and conditional formatting can also be implemented.

Bulit-In Visualization Controls in Model-Driven Apps

Model-driven apps provide several built-in controls that can be used to visualize data effectively. These controls are easy to use and can be customized to suit specific requirements.

CHAPTER 6 MODERN APP DESIGN WITH POWER APPS

A. Views

- A view is used to display rows from a table. There are different types of views that can be created for a table in Dataverse.

- Developers can configure views to display data based on filters on various columns of the table and also define sorting orders as required.

B. Form

- The form control is used for displaying and editing rows from the Dataverse tables. While primarily for data entry, forms can include visual elements to enhance the user experience.

- Forms can be used to display and edit individual rows with detailed information. Developers can add input controls, labels, and custom formatting. Subgrids can be added to forms to display data from related tables.

- To improve the data quality, data validation rules and conditional formatting can also be implemented.

C. Dashboards

- Dashboards and charts in model-driven apps can be leveraged to display data in a graphical way. There are different types of charts that can be created and added to a dashboard.

- Based on the role-based security access, end users will only see the data that they have access to.

Integration with Power BI

- Power BI is a powerful business analytics tool that can be integrated with Power Apps to provide advanced data visualization capabilities. Power BI offers a wide range of visualizations and allows for interactive data exploration.

- Power Apps allows you to embed Power BI reports and dashboards directly into your apps, providing users with rich, interactive visualizations.

- Developers can create Power BI reports and then add visuals as tiles in canvas apps or just use the published link of the report in model-driven apps.

Custom Visualizations Using JavaScript Libraries

- For advanced and highly customized visualizations, Power Apps allows for the integration of JavaScript libraries. This approach provides maximum flexibility and can be used to create unique data visualizations.

- For example, in canvas apps, HTML text control can be leveraged to render HTML and JavaScript code. It can be used to embed custom visualizations created with JavaScript libraries such as D3.js, Chart.js, or Plotly.

- For model-driven apps, published reports or custom integration can be added as links in the navigation bar.

Use Cases for Data Visualization in Power Apps

A. Customer Relationship Management

- Organizations can set up customer relationship management systems using Power Apps. The customer data can be filtered upon in the apps using galleries or data tables in canvas apps and using views and forms in model-driven apps.

- For analytics and insights on the customer reviews, performance, sales summaries, etc., Power BI reports or charts and dashboards can be set up to provide the users with most relevant data and visuals.

B. Human Resource Management

- Organizations can set up human resource management solutions using Power Apps. Visualizing data is a critical piece that can help managers to view records of their teams and also gain actionable insights from key metrics.

- Capabilities to filter records based on area, expertise, location, experience, etc. are added advantages that enable users to follow-through processes in an efficient way.

CHAPTER 6   MODERN APP DESIGN WITH POWER APPS

Best Practices for Data Visualization in Power Apps

A. Understand Data and Audience

- As a general best practice, it is important to first understand the data and the related data associated to the data that needs to be visualized. This would help developers understand the challenges and devise a strategy to select the controls most appropriate to visualize the key attributes of the dataset.

- Alongside, it is best to tailor visualizations to the needs and preferences of the end users of the solution. This would help in easily communicating the usage and also drive user adoption.

- To set up useful data visualizations that would make easier for the end users to follow through, it is recommended to consider the level of detail, complexity, and interactivity required.

B. Consistent Design Patterns

- To make the solutions more user friendly, it is recommended to ensure that visualizations are easy to understand. Developers should focus on using clear labels, legends, and colors to enhance readability and avoid any clutter.

- As a best practice, developers should follow a design pattern and keep it minimalistic. It is recommended to maintain a consistent design language across all visualizations to provide a cohesive user experience. This includes colors, fonts, styles, etc.

CHAPTER 6 MODERN APP DESIGN WITH POWER APPS

C. Optimized Performance

- For the app to perform optimally and enhance user experience, it is recommended to ensure that visualizations load quickly and perform well, even with large data sets.

- Developers can leverage data aggregation and filtering techniques to reduce the amount of data processed.

D. Testing and Feedback

- As a best practice, it is recommended to verify that visualizations work correctly on different devices and screen sizes.

- It is important to ensure that interactive elements are accessible on touchscreens and smaller displays alike.

- It is recommended to include context and explanations for visualizations to help users understand the data. Developers can leverage using titles, subtitles, and annotations to convey insights.

In summary, data visualization is a critical component of modern applications, enabling users to gain insights and make informed decisions. Power Apps, as part of the Microsoft Power Platform, offers a variety of tools and techniques for creating compelling data visualizations. By leveraging built-in controls, integrating with Power BI, and using custom JavaScript visualizations, you can create powerful and interactive visual experiences.

Following best practices for data visualization ensures that your applications are not only functional but also user-friendly and accessible. Whether you are building simple dashboards or complex analytical tools, Power Apps provides the flexibility and capabilities needed to meet your data visualization needs.

Testing and Debugging Modern Apps

Testing and debugging are crucial steps in the development process to ensure that applications built using Microsoft Power Platform are functional, reliable, and user-friendly.

In this section, we will walk through a comprehensive overview of testing and debugging techniques for both canvas apps and model-driven apps within the Power Platform.

Testing Canvas Apps

Canvas apps provide a flexible environment to design and build custom applications with a drag-and-drop interface. Due to their customizable nature, thorough testing is essential to ensure that all functionalities work as expected.

Types of Testing in Canvas Apps

A. Unit Testing

- Unit testing is the first phase in testing applications. It focuses on testing individual functions, controls, and formulas and helps ensure that each component works correctly in isolation.

B. Integration Testing

- In the integration testing phase, the interaction between different components and services is tested.

- Developers must ensure that data flows correctly between the app and external systems like Dataverse, SharePoint, or SQL Server.

CHAPTER 6   MODERN APP DESIGN WITH POWER APPS

C. User Acceptance Testing (UAT)

- This phase involves end-users to verify that the app meets their requirements and performs as expected in real-world scenarios.

D. Performance Testing

- It is critical to test the performance of the application. It helps developers to assess the app's responsiveness and speed under various conditions.

- Through performance testing, developers can also identify performance bottlenecks and ensure that the app can handle expected load.

Tools and Techniques for Testing Canvas Apps

A. Power Apps Studio

- Developers can use the preview mode to run the app in the development environment and test its functionality.

- The monitor tool can be used to trace events, actions, and data operations within the app. It helps in identifying issues related to data flow, formula execution, and performance.

- While building the application, developers can utilize the formula checker to check and validate formulas used in controls and ensure that they produce the correct results.

B. Test Cases and Scripts

- The testing team can create detailed test cases and scripts for different scenarios, including edge cases.
- It is important to document expected outcomes for each test case to compare with actual results.
- This allows developers to easily understand and fix issues without much rework.

C. Debugging Techniques

- Developers can implement error handling within the app to catch and display meaningful error messages.
- Labels or text controls can be used to display intermediate values and states for debugging purposes.
- Developers should ensure to maintain the versions of the app to easily revert to a previous state if issues arise.

D. Power Apps Checker

- Developers can utilize Power Apps Checker to analyze the app's code for common issues, performance tips, and best practices.
- This tool helps in identifying and fixing potential problems early in the development process.

E. Automated Testing Tools

- The Power Apps test framework can be used for automated UI testing of canvas apps.
- Testing teams can create test scripts that simulate user interactions and validate app behavior.

CHAPTER 6   MODERN APP DESIGN WITH POWER APPS

- Tools like Selenium can also be used with a custom setup to automate the testing of canvas apps in a web browser.

Testing Model-Driven Apps

Model-driven Apps are more structured and data-centric, built on top of Dataverse. They leverage predefined components and business logic, which necessitates a different approach to testing.

Types of Testing for Model-Driven Apps

A. Unit Testing

- Unit testing is the first phase in testing applications. It focuses on testing individual components like forms, views, business rules, and workflows and helps ensure that each component works correctly in isolation.

B. Integration Testing

- In the integration testing phase, the interaction between different components, external systems, and services is tested.

- Developers must ensure that data is correctly processed and displayed across various parts of the app.

C. User Acceptance Testing (UAT)

- This phase involves end-users to verify that the app meets their requirements and performs as expected in real-world scenarios.

CHAPTER 6 MODERN APP DESIGN WITH POWER APPS

  D. Performance Testing

  - This phase involves end-users to verify that the app meets their requirements and performs as expected in real-world scenarios.

Tools and Techniques for Testing Model-Driven Apps

  A. Power Apps Studio

  - Developers can utilize the associated designers to configure and test forms, views, and dashboards.

  - The app can be run in the development environment to test its functionality and user experience.

  - The business process flow debugger tool can be used to test and debug business process flows within the app.

  B. Test Cases and Scripts

  - The testing team can create detailed test cases and scripts for different scenarios, including edge cases.

  - It is important to document expected outcomes for each test case to compare with actual results. This allows developers to easily understand and fix issues without much rework.

C. Debugging Techniques

- For components built using custom code or any custom logic implementation in model-driven apps, developers can implement error handling to catch and display meaningful error messages.

- Auditing features in Dataverse can be leveraged to log changes and operations for debugging purposes.

- Advanced Find can be used to query and validate data within Dataverse.

D. Power Platform Admin Center

- Developers can utilize the Power Platform admin center to monitor app performance, track usage, and identify issues related to environment configuration and resources.

E. Automated Testing Tools

- Microsoft's EasyRepro (https://github.com/microsoft/EasyRepro) framework can be used for automated UI testing of model-driven apps.

- Testing teams can create test scripts that simulate user interactions and validate app behavior.

- Tools like Selenium can be used with a custom setup to automate the testing of model-driven apps in a web browser.

Common Debugging Scenarios and Solutions

A. Data Connectivity Issues

- For data connectivity issues in canvas apps, ensure that data sources are correctly configured and accessible.

- Developers can use the Monitor tool to trace data operations and identify connectivity issues.

- While dealing with data connectivity issues in model-driven apps, verify that in case there are any virtual tables used, the connections are properly configured, and if there are any associated gateways, they are functioning as expected.

B. Performance Issues

- As canvas apps provide with more flexible customization capabilities, they improve app performance, optimize formulas, reduce the number of controls on each screen, and minimize the use of OnStart actions that load large datasets.

- To resolve performance issues in model-driven apps, optimize views and queries, use indexed fields, and ensure that custom plugins and workflows are efficient.

C. User Interface Issues

- For resolving user interface issues in canvas apps, ensure that controls are correctly bound to data sources and that visibility, size, and position properties are set correctly. Also ensure that controls are not overlapping, and if there are overlapping controls, they are appropriately layered so that the intended functionality is not affected.

- In model-driven apps, the UI issues could occur due to custom code or improper data binding to controls. To resolve such issues, verify that forms and views are configured correctly and that any custom JavaScript code is functioning as expected.

D. Business Logic Errors

- To resolve business logic errors in canvas apps, developers can leverage the formula checker and verify all the formulas are error-free. Logic implemented on individual controls also needs to be verified in order to ensure that the app functions as expected.

- In model-driven apps, test all the business rules, workflows, plugins, etc. to ensure they execute correctly under different conditions.

Best Practices for Debugging and Testing

A. Plan and Document Tests

- As a recommended best practice, it is advised to develop a comprehensive testing plan that includes all types of testing: unit, integration, UAT, and performance.

- Testing teams can document test cases, scripts, and expected outcomes for reference and future testing.

B. Automate Tests

- Automated testing tools can be leveraged to reduce manual effort and ensure consistent test coverage.
- Testing teams can set up scheduled automated tests to catch regressions early.

C. Segregate Environments

- It is a standard best practice to segregate environments for development, testing, and production.
- Developers can use the development environments to develop and customize any changes and perform unit testing.
- Testing teams can then use the test environments to complete end-to-end test cases.
- Once the solution is processed through these two stages, it can be moved to the production environment for end users.

D. Engage End Users

- To reduce the deployment timelines, it is recommended to involve end-users in testing to gather feedback and identify usability issues.
- Developers and testing teams can conduct UAT sessions to ensure the app meets user requirements and expectations.

E. Monitor and Iterate

- As a general best practice, developers can continuously monitor app performance and usage to identify and address issues.

- It is recommended to iterate on feedback and testing results to improve the app's functionality and user experience.

In summary, testing and debugging are critical components of the app development lifecycle in Microsoft Power Platform. By thoroughly testing canvas apps and model-driven apps, you can ensure that your applications are reliable and performant and meet user expectations.

Utilizing the tools and techniques provided by Power Apps and Power Automate, along with automated testing frameworks, will help you streamline the testing process and maintain high-quality standards in your applications.

Summary

The journey through modern app design with Power Apps has revealed a powerful, versatile platform that empowers both professional developers and citizen developers to create innovative, user-centric applications. As we explored the evolution of app design principles within the Power Platform, it became evident that the core strength of Power Apps lies in its ability to democratize app development, making it accessible to a wider audience without compromising on functionality or sophistication.

One of the most significant aspects of modern app design with Power Apps is its inclusive approach. The platform's low-code/no-code environment allows individuals with minimal coding experience to build robust applications, while still providing advanced capabilities for

CHAPTER 6   MODERN APP DESIGN WITH POWER APPS

seasoned developers. This blend of simplicity and power is what sets Power Apps apart, enabling organizations to leverage their existing talent pool effectively.

Another cornerstone of Power Apps is its seamless integration with other Microsoft services and third-party applications. This connectivity allows for the creation of comprehensive solutions that can pull data from various sources, automate workflows, and provide insights through powerful analytics. By bridging the gap between different systems, Power Apps facilitates a more cohesive and efficient digital environment.

The future of app design with Power Apps looks promising as Microsoft continues to enhance the platform with new features and capabilities. With ongoing advancements in AI, machine learning, and data integration, Power Apps is poised to remain at the forefront of modern app development. The introduction of Copilots and advanced automation tools promises to further streamline development processes and enable even more sophisticated applications.

In conclusion, modern app design with Power Apps represents a paradigm shift in how applications are conceived, developed, and deployed. By embracing a user-centric approach, leveraging low-code/no-code tools, and ensuring seamless integration with other systems, Power Apps empowers organizations to innovate rapidly and efficiently. As we move forward, the principles and practices discussed in this chapter will serve as a foundation for creating applications that not only meet but exceed user expectations, driving digital transformation and business success.

PART II

Power Platform Components and Real-world Use cases

CHAPTER 7

Microsoft Copilot Studio

This chapter provides a detailed overview of Microsoft Copilot Studio, empowering users to leverage its capabilities effectively in various AI-driven projects. By delving into Copilot Studio's functionalities and features, readers will gain insights into how to create, configure, and optimize AI Copilots for diverse applications.

Introduction to Microsoft Copilot Studio

Microsoft Copilot Studio is a graphical low-code tool for creating and maintaining Copilots. A Copilot is an AI-powered conversational interface based on large language models (LLMs) and additional sources of knowledge. It's a powerful AI companion that can handle a range of requests, from providing simple responses to common questions to resolving issues requiring complex conversations.

Copilots can engage with customers and employees in multiple languages across websites, mobile apps, Facebook, Microsoft Teams, or any channel supported by the Azure Bot Service.

CHAPTER 7   MICROSOFT COPILOT STUDIO

Key Features

Create Custom Copilots: Design conversational applications using generative AI and large language models tailored to specific needs and workflows.

Customize Copilot for Microsoft 365: Build Copilot extensions to serve your business process needs within Microsoft 365, enhancing productivity and streamlining operations.

Collaboration: Copilot Studio enhances collaboration by integrating with Microsoft Teams, allowing for seamless communication and task management within teams. It can summarize conversations, suggest follow-ups, and integrate with other tools for a cohesive workflow.

Use One Connected Platform: Built on a foundation of top conversational AI technologies, Copilot Studio is interoperable with Azure AI Studio and other apps, ensuring seamless integration and expanded capabilities.

Building Custom Copilots with Copilot Studio
Getting Started

To create a custom Copilot, begin by logging into Copilot Studio. The platform will automatically configure the necessary services, allowing you to start building in minutes.

Imagine you want to create a custom Copilot for your website to assist customers with product information and order management.

CHAPTER 7 MICROSOFT COPILOT STUDIO

If you create a Copilot with the Copilot Studio app in Microsoft Teams, you won't see the Copilot in the web app of Copilot Studio. New Copilots created in the web app and in Teams are configured with Only for Teams and Power Apps authentication.

Create a Copilot

- Go to the Copilot Studio home page. https://copilotstudio.microsoft.com/
- Select + New Copilot from the Copilots page, or select Home, then choose + Create a Copilot.
- For Copilot name, enter a name for your Copilot.
- Select Create.

Refer to Figure 7-1, which shows the create screen where you can create your own Copilot or choose one from the template.

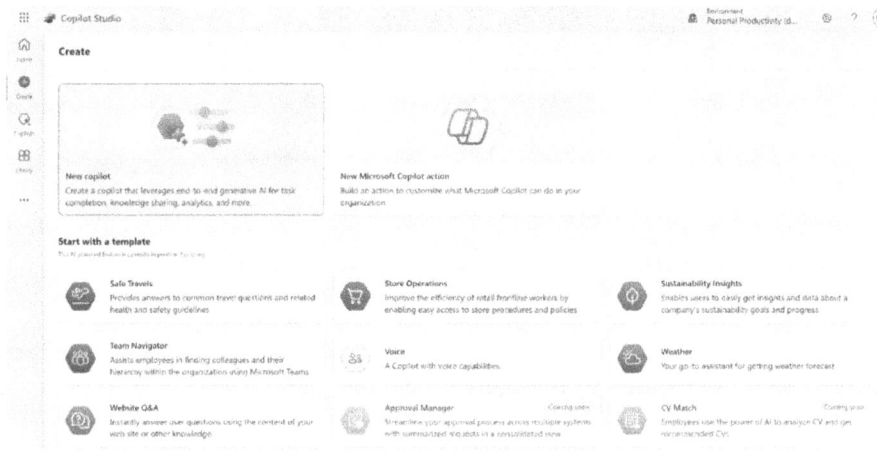

Figure 7-1. *Copilot studio: Create Copilot*

CHAPTER 7 MICROSOFT COPILOT STUDIO

Delete a Copilot

- You can delete Copilots to remove them from your environment.
- Go to the Copilot Studio home page.
- In the navigation menu, select Copilots.
- Select the Copilot you want to delete; then, select… at the top.
- Confirm the deletion of the Copilot by typing Copilot's name. Once you confirm, all Copilot content will be deleted after a few minutes.

Refer to Figure 7-2, which shows the delete screen.

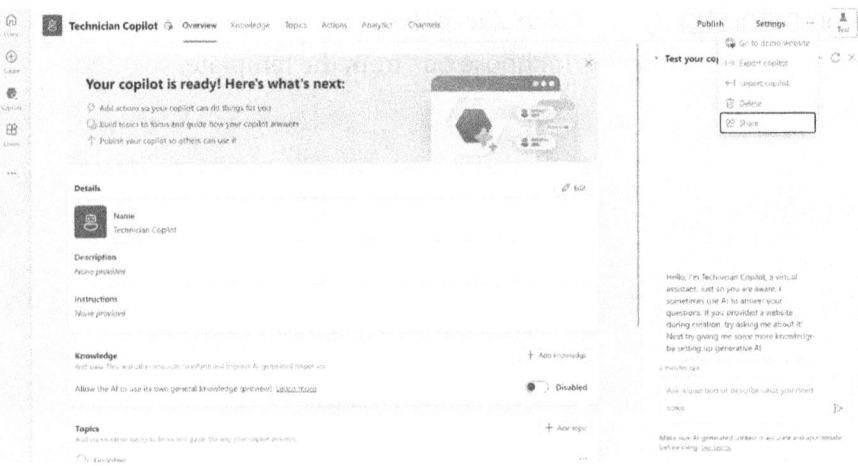

Figure 7-2. Copilot Studio: Delete Copilot

Grounding Your Copilot in Data

Use generative answers to enable multiturn chat over your organization's real-time data, from local files to SharePoint sites, public websites, and custom backends. This setup allows your Copilot to cover a wide range of topics within minutes using your public website's product information.

For critical topics like account management, design specific conversational flows that Copilot will follow. You can use visual authoring or natural language to create these prioritized topics before moving to generative AI. For example, create a topic that collects user details, authenticates the user, and interacts with your order management systems in a specific sequence. Another example is discounting, where responses must comply with legal and compliance requirements, so you provide managed responses.

Generative Actions

With generative actions, you can provide a list of plugins to the Copilot, selecting from over 1200 data connectors like SAP, Workday, Salesforce, etc. These connectors enable the Copilot to dynamically execute actions, handling complex queries effortlessly.

Custom Development and Integration

For more custom development, use Azure models and services with Copilot Studio. This hybrid approach of low-code and custom pro-code integration allows you to bring custom language models, Azure OpenAI on your data, knowledge bases, image generation with DALL-E, telemetry, and more into your Copilot Studio Copilot.

CHAPTER 7　MICROSOFT COPILOT STUDIO

Publishing Your Copilot

When ready, publish your Copilot to multiple channels, whether internal or external, to interact with users across different platforms such as websites, Microsoft Teams, social apps, mobile apps, Azure Bot Service channels, and more. Escalate conversations to first-party Dynamics 365 and third-party tools like Genesys, LivePerson, Salesforce, and ServiceNow when human assistance is needed.

Performance Monitoring and Management

Review Copilot performance with the built-in analytics dashboard to monitor key metrics, evaluate performance, and identify new Copilot topics. Secure and manage your Copilot with governance and control features in the central admin center, ensuring data protection with data loss prevention policies, role-based access control, environment management, and more.

Use Cases

Copilot Studio provides a platform to build Copilots for specific needs, industries, and departments using your data. These custom Copilots can serve Business-to-Employee (B2E), Business-to-Business (B2B), and Business-to-Consumer (B2C) scenarios.

　　For example:

- **IT Support Copilot**: Assists with technical issues and troubleshooting
- **Customer Service Copilot**: Helps customers choose the right product and manage orders
- **Supplier Management Copilot**: Tracks the status of orders for suppliers

Microsoft Copilot Studio represents a significant advancement in integrating AI into everyday applications. By providing intelligent assistance, enhancing productivity, and making AI accessible to a broader audience, it is poised to revolutionize how we interact with technology and perform daily tasks. As AI continues to evolve, platforms like Copilot Studio will play a crucial role in shaping the future of work and productivity.

Security and Governance

The security and governance of the Copilot Studio service are essential to ensuring the safe and compliant use of AI capabilities within your organization. Copilot Studio is governed by your commercial license agreements, including the Microsoft Product Terms and the Data Protection Addendum.

Compliance and Trust

The Microsoft Trust Center is the primary resource for Power Platform compliance information. You can learn more about Copilot Studio's compliance offerings and data protection measures by visiting the Microsoft Trust Center. Power Platform also includes an extensive set of Data Loss Prevention (DLP) features to help manage and secure your data.

Configuring Data Loss Prevention Policies

To protect your organization's data, you can configure Data Loss Prevention policies for Copilots within your environment. These policies ensure that data is handled securely and that the risk of data exfiltration is minimized:

- Go to the Power Platform admin center.
- Navigate to the Data Loss Prevention policies section.
- Create or modify a DLP policy to include Copilot Studio connectors.

Copilot Studio connectors can be classified within a DLP policy under the following data groups:

- Business
- Nonbusiness
- Blocked

Connector Configuration Examples

Application Insights: Block Copilot makers from connecting Copilots with Application Insights.

Chat without Microsoft Entra ID Authentication: Block Copilot makers from publishing Copilots that are not configured for authentication, ensuring Copilot users require authentication to chat.

Direct Line Channels: Block Copilot makers from enabling or using Direct Line channels (e.g., Demo website, Custom website, and Mobile app).

Facebook Channel: Block Copilot makers from enabling or using the Facebook channel.

Knowledge Source with SharePoint and OneDrive: Block Copilots configured with SharePoint and OneDrive as knowledge sources, supporting DLP connector endpoint filtering.

Knowledge Source with Public Websites and Data: Block Copilots configured with public websites as knowledge sources, supporting endpoint filtering.

Knowledge Source with Documents: Block Copilots configured with documents as knowledge sources.

Microsoft Teams Channel: Block Copilot makers from enabling or using the Teams channel.

Omnichannel: Block Copilot makers from enabling or using the Omnichannel.

Skills with Copilot Studio: Block Copilot makers from using skills in Copilot Studio.

Example: Data Loss Prevention for Skills in Copilot Studio

Bot makers can extend their bots with skills, but you may want to restrict their use to prevent data exfiltration. Use the skills with Microsoft Copilot Studio connector in Power Platform DLP policies to stop bot makers from adding skills to their bots. You can configure these policies to block skills or HTTP requests from Copilot Studio Copilots.

Publishing Controls

Admins can disable the publishing of Copilots to manage and secure the deployment of AI capabilities:

Disable Copilot Publishing: Use the Power Platform admin center to turn off the ability to publish Copilots with generative answers and actions for your tenant.

Disable Data Movement Across Geographic Locations: Prevent data movement for Copilot Studio-generative AI features outside the United States.

Enable Copilot Studio Conversational Plugins: Securely manage the use of conversational plugins within your organization.

Customer Lockbox: Copilot Studio supports securely accessing customer data using Customer Lockbox.

Example: Blocking Channels in Copilot Studio

Copilot Studio supports four channels: Direct Line, Teams, Omnichannel, and Facebook. Admins can block these channels using a DLP policy to prevent Copilots from being published to these platforms:

- Go to the Power Platform admin center.
- Navigate to the DLP policy settings.
- Block all channels to disable Copilot publishing.
- Default authentication settings

When creating a new copilot, the Authenticate with Microsoft authentication option is turned on by default. The Copilot automatically uses Microsoft Entra ID authentication, restricting chat interactions to Teams. However, Copilot makers can select the No authentication option to allow anyone with the link to chat with the Copilot.

Audit Logs

All logging in Copilot Studio is done at the SDK layer, so a single action can trigger multiple logged events. Here's a list of events that you can audit.

CHAPTER 7 MICROSOFT COPILOT STUDIO

Event Categories and Descriptions

Category	Event	Description
Copilots	BotCreate	The creation of a new Copilot in Copilot Studio
Copilots	BotDelete	The deletion of a Copilot in Copilot Studio
Copilots	BotAuthUpdate	Updating the authentication settings of a Copilot in Copilot Studio
Copilots	BotIconUpdate	Updating the Copilot icon in Copilot Studio
Copilots	BotPublish	Publishing of a Copilot in Copilot Studio
Copilots	BotShare	Sharing of a Copilot to other users in Copilot Studio
Copilots	BotAppInsightsUpdate	Updating the App Insights logging configuration of a Copilot
Copilot Component	BotComponentCreate	The creation of a component (such as a topic or skill)
Copilot Component	BotComponentUpdate	The update of a component (e.g., topic, skill, etc.)
Copilot Component	BotComponentDelete	The deletion of a component (e.g., topic, skill, etc.)
AI Plugin	AIPluginOperationCreate	Creating an AI plugin
AI Plugin	AIPluginOperationUpdate	Updating an AI plugin
AI Plugin	AIPluginOperationDelete	Removing an AI plugin
Environment Variable	EnvironmentVariableCreate	Creating an environment variable
Environment Variable	EnvironmentVariableUpdate	Updating an environment variable
Environment Variable	EnvironmentVariableDelete	Deleting an environment variable

CHAPTER 7   MICROSOFT COPILOT STUDIO

By implementing these security and governance measures, you can ensure that your organization's data is protected while leveraging the powerful capabilities of Copilot Studio. For more detailed information, see section "Configuring Data Loss Prevention Policies" for Microsoft Copilot Studio chatbots.

Getting Started with Generative AI

Generative AI is a subset of artificial intelligence focused on creating content from data, including text, images, and code. In Copilot Studio, generative AI plays a crucial role by leveraging large language models (LLMs) to provide advanced conversational capabilities and intelligent responses, enabling the creation of highly effective AI Copilots. These Copilots can assist with a variety of tasks, from answering simple questions to managing complex workflows, thereby enhancing productivity and user experiences across multiple platforms.

Figure 7-3 depicts a comprehensive overview of AI and Generative AI.

CHAPTER 7 MICROSOFT COPILOT STUDIO

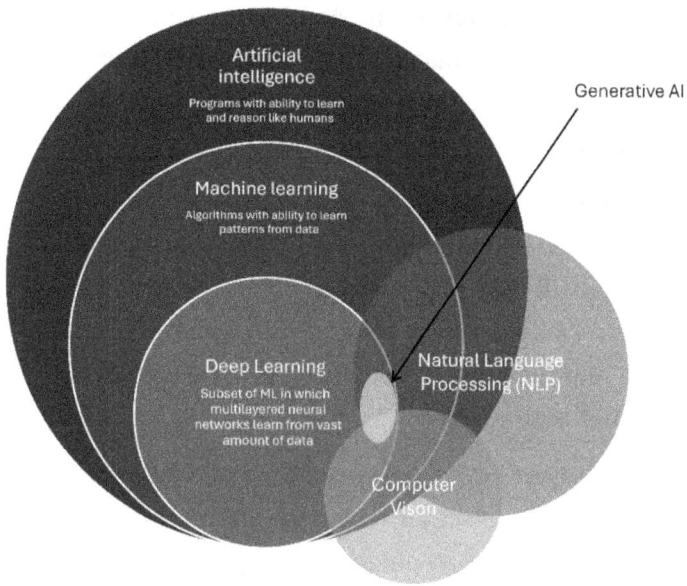

Figure 7-3. overview of AI

Overview of Generative AI in Copilot Studio

Generative AI is an artificial intelligence technology that uses large language models (LLMs) to generate original content and provide natural language understanding and responses. In Copilot Studio, you can use the following generative AI features to retrieve and create content, either individually or altogether.

- **Create a Copilot Instantly**: Without the need for manual topic authoring, a blank Copilot can generate responses based on specified knowledge sources, such as websites and files.

CHAPTER 7   MICROSOFT COPILOT STUDIO

- **Harness AI General Knowledge**: By enabling this option, the Copilot can respond to general inquiries that are not specific to your knowledge sources or topics.

- **Author Topics Using Natural Language**: Simply describe the functionality you want, and Copilot Studio will create the topic for you. This includes conversational responses and various types of nodes. Use the suggested default topic as a foundation for further customization.

- **Enable Generative Actions**: Allow the Copilot to dynamically select the most relevant topics and actions (formerly known as plugins) during runtime: AI-based Copilot authoring.

Figure 7-4 shows how to enable Generative AI in the Copilot Studio.

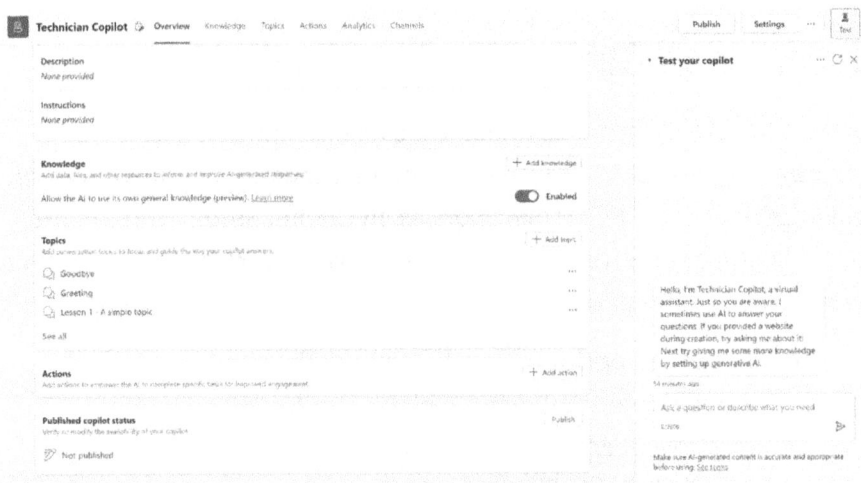

Figure 7-4. Generative AI option in the Copilot Studio

Generative Answers

Generative answers in Microsoft Copilot Studio allow your Copilot to find and present information from multiple sources, internal or external, without precreated topics. These generative answers can be used as primary information sources or as fallback options when authored topics can't address a user's query. This capability enables the rapid creation and deployment of functional Copilots without the need to manually author multiple topics that might not cover all customer questions.

Key Features of Generative Answers

Primary or Fallback Information Source: Generative answers can serve as the main source of information or act as a backup when pre-authored topics fail to address user queries. This ensures a comprehensive coverage of potential questions.

Enhanced User Interaction: Traditionally, if a Copilot couldn't determine a user's intent, it would ask the user to rephrase their question. If it still couldn't understand after two prompts, it would escalate to a live agent using the system Escalate topic. With generative answers, the Copilot now uses advanced Natural Language Processing (NLP) to parse user input and generate relevant responses before escalating to a live agent.

Multiturn Conversations: Generative answers enable the Copilot to maintain context over multiple exchanges, resulting in more natural and engaging interactions. This allows the Copilot to follow up on previous questions and provide more accurate responses.

Organizational Data Utilization: Generative answers can access and use real-time data from a variety of sources, including local files, SharePoint sites, public websites, and custom backends. This ensures that the Copilot provides accurate and up-to-date information.

Handling Complex Queries: The Copilot can address complex user queries by dynamically executing actions through plugins and connectors. This allows for sophisticated interactions and provides users with comprehensive solutions to their inquiries.

Summarization and Delivery: After parsing and collating relevant information from specified sources, generative answers summarize the search results into plain language that is easily understood by the user. This makes the information more accessible and user-friendly.

Examples of Generative Answers in Action

Customer Support: A Copilot can access product information from a company's website and provide detailed answers to customer inquiries, reducing the need for live agent intervention.

Internal Knowledge Base: For employees seeking information on company policies or procedures, a Copilot can pull data from internal sources like SharePoint and deliver concise, accurate answers.

Order Management: A Copilot can assist customers in tracking orders by accessing data from multiple systems, providing real-time updates without manual topic creation.

Getting Started with Generative Answers

To implement generative answers as a fallback topic when a user's intent cannot be addressed by existing Copilot topics, follow these steps:

Specify Knowledge Sources: Identify and configure the internal and external sources from which the Copilot will retrieve information.

Enable NLP Capabilities: Ensure that the Copilot is set up to use NLP (Natural Language Processing is a field of artificial intelligence that focuses on enabling computers to understand, interpret, and generate human language) to parse user inputs and generate relevant responses.

Test and Refine: Conduct thorough testing to verify that the generative answers are accurate and meet user needs. Make adjustments as necessary to improve the response quality.

Figure 7-5 depicts how to specify knowledge sources.

CHAPTER 7   MICROSOFT COPILOT STUDIO

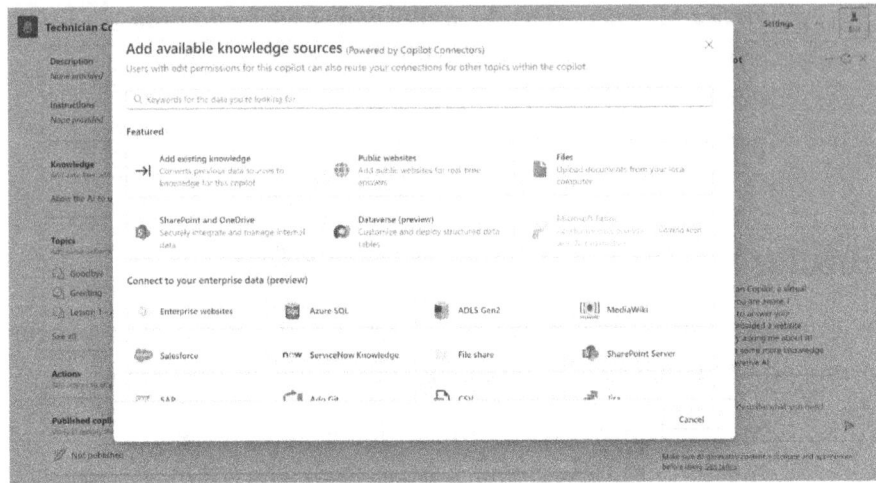

Figure 7-5. *Add knowledge sources to the Copilot*

Generative answers significantly enhance the functionality and efficiency of Copilots, enabling them to handle a broader range of inquiries with minimal manual intervention. By leveraging the power of generative AI, organizations can provide users with quick, accurate, and contextually relevant information, improving overall user satisfaction and reducing the workload on human agents.

Prompting in Copilot Studio

Prompting is a critical aspect of training and guiding LLMs to produce desired responses. In Copilot Studio, prompting involves

1. **Designing Prompts**: Creating specific prompts that guide the Copilot to respond appropriately to different types of queries. Prompts can be structured to handle various scenarios, ensuring the Copilot provides accurate and relevant information.

2. **Custom Prompts**: Users can define custom prompts for specific workflows or topics, tailoring Copilot's responses to meet organizational needs. This includes setting up managed topics that follow specific conversational flows. These custom prompts can be created in AI builder.

3. **Continuous Improvement**: By monitoring Copilot interactions and analyzing performance metrics, users can refine and improve prompts over time, enhancing Copilot's effectiveness.

Use of Custom Data sources

Copilot Studio allows for the integration of custom data sources, expanding the range of information that Copilots can access and utilize. This includes

1. **Data Connectors**: With over 1200 data connectors available, Copilots can connect to various lines of business applications, such as SAP, Workday, Salesforce, and more. These connectors enable the Copilot to pull data dynamically and provide informed responses.

2. **Knowledge Sources**: Copilots can be configured to use different knowledge sources, such as SharePoint, OneDrive, public websites, and custom databases. This allows the Copilot to provide accurate and up-to-date information based on the latest available data.

3. **Custom Backends**: Organizations can integrate their own custom backends, ensuring that the Copilot can access proprietary data and systems to deliver tailored responses that align with internal processes and workflows.

Generative AI in Copilot Studio empowers organizations to create sophisticated AI Copilots that enhance user experiences and operational efficiency. By leveraging LLMs, low-code development, and integration with custom data sources, Copilot Studio enables the creation of intelligent, responsive, and adaptable Copilots that can serve a wide range of functions across various platforms and channels.

Enhancing Copilot with Connectors

Connectors are integral to extending the functionality of your Copilots in Microsoft Copilot Studio. They enable the Copilot to interact with various external systems, databases, and services, providing enriched and dynamic responses based on real-time data.

Here's how connectors can enhance your Copilot.

Key Features of Connectors

Wide Range of Integrations: Connectors in Copilot Studio allow integration with over 1200 services, including popular enterprise systems like SAP, Workday, Salesforce, and many others. This extensive range of integrations ensures that your Copilot can access and utilize data from multiple sources.

- **Seamless Data Retrieval**: Connectors facilitate seamless data retrieval from various sources, including cloud storage services (e.g., SharePoint, OneDrive), databases, APIs, and custom backends. This enables your Copilot to provide accurate and up-to-date information to users.

- **Actionable Insights**: By leveraging connectors, Copilots can perform actions based on retrieved data. For example, a Copilot can update a CRM record, process an order, or fetch real-time analytics, providing actionable insights and automating workflows.

- **Security and Compliance**: Connectors in Copilot Studio are designed with security and compliance in mind. They ensure secure data transmission and adhere to organizational policies, including data loss prevention (DLP) and regulatory compliance standards.

Benefits of Using Connectors

Enhanced Functionality: Connectors significantly enhance the functionality of your Copilot by enabling it to interact with a wide variety of systems and services. This makes the Copilot more versatile and capable of handling complex queries.

Real-Time Data Access: With connectors, your Copilot can access real-time data, providing users with the most current information. This is particularly beneficial for scenarios like customer support, where timely and accurate information is crucial.

Improved Efficiency: Connectors streamline workflows by automating data retrieval and actions. This reduces the need for manual intervention, improving operational efficiency and freeing up resources for more strategic tasks.

Customization and Flexibility: Connectors allow you to customize Copilot's capabilities to meet specific organizational needs. Whether it's integrating with a proprietary system or accessing specialized data, connectors provide the flexibility to tailor Copilot's functionality.

Implementing Connectors in Copilot Studio

Selecting the Right Connectors

Identify Needs: Determine the systems and services your Copilot needs to interact with based on user requirements and organizational processes.

Choose Connectors: Select the appropriate connectors from Copilot Studio's extensive library. Consider factors like data source compatibility, security, and compliance requirements.

Configuring Connectors

Authentication: Configure authentication settings to ensure secure access to the connected systems. This may involve setting up API keys, OAuth tokens, or other authentication mechanisms.

Data Mapping: Map the data fields between the Copilot and the external systems to ensure accurate data retrieval and action execution.

Integrating Connectors into Cloud Flows

Define Actions: Specify the actions the Copilot should perform using the connectors. This could include data queries, updates, or triggering workflows based on user input.

Test and Validate: Thoroughly test the integration to ensure that the Copilot interacts correctly with the connected systems. Validate the data accuracy and action execution.

Monitoring and Maintenance

Performance Monitoring: Continuously monitor the performance of the connectors to ensure they are functioning correctly and efficiently.

Regular Updates: Keep the connectors and related configurations up to date to accommodate any changes in the external systems or organizational requirements.

Figure 7-6 depicts how to configure connectors within Copilot Studio.

CHAPTER 7   MICROSOFT COPILOT STUDIO

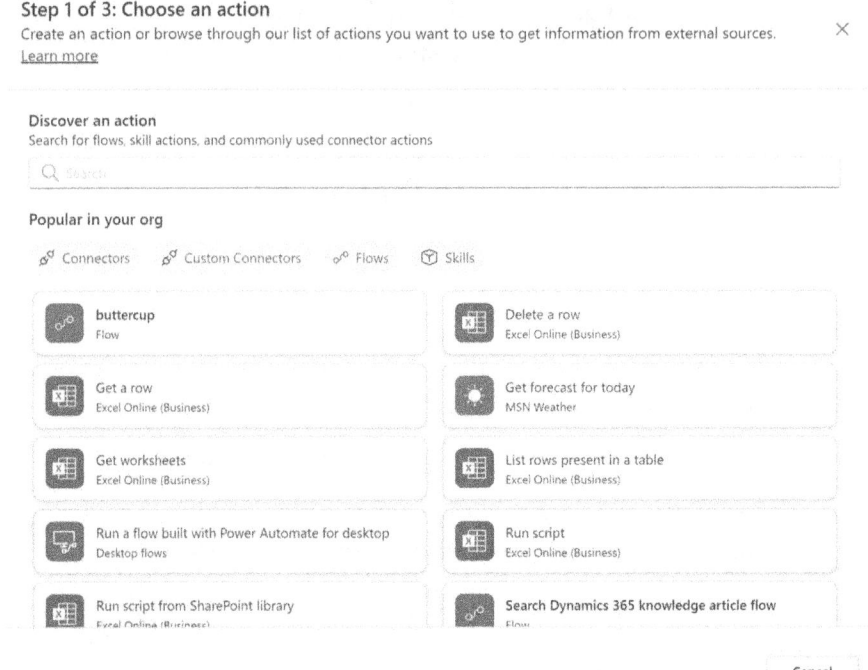

Figure 7-6.   Add connectors through action

Examples of Connectors in Action

Customer Relationship Management (CRM)

Use Case: A sales Copilot retrieves customer information from Salesforce to provide sales reps with real-time updates on customer interactions and opportunities.

Action: The Copilot can update customer records, log interactions, and provide insights based on CRM data.

Human Resources (HR)

Use Case: An HR Copilot accesses employee data from Workday to answer queries about leave balances, benefits, and payroll.

Action: The Copilot can initiate leave requests, update personal information, and provide payroll details.

Technical Support

Use Case: A support Copilot integrates with a ticketing system like ServiceNow to fetch and update support tickets.

Action: The Copilot can create new tickets, update ticket statuses, and provide solutions based on knowledge base articles.

Financial Services

Use Case: A financial advisory Copilot retrieves market data and portfolio information from financial databases to provide investment advice.

Action: The Copilot can generate reports, perform risk assessments, and suggest investment strategies.

Enhancing Security and Governance with Connectors

Connectors in Copilot Studio are equipped with robust security features to protect data integrity and ensure compliance with organizational policies. Key aspects include

> **Data Encryption**: All data transmitted through connectors is encrypted to prevent unauthorized access.
>
> **Access Controls**: Fine-grained access controls ensure that only authorized users and systems can interact with the connected data.
>
> **Audit Logs**: Comprehensive audit logs track all interactions and actions performed by the Copilot, aiding in compliance and security monitoring.

Conclusion

Connectors are a vital component of Microsoft Copilot Studio, enhancing Copilot's capabilities by enabling seamless interaction with various external systems and services. By leveraging connectors, organizations can create more powerful, efficient, and versatile Copilots that provide valuable insights, automate workflows, and improve user experiences. Whether it's accessing real-time data, automating complex tasks, or ensuring compliance, connectors play a crucial role in maximizing the potential of your AI-powered Copilot.

Generative Actions in Copilot Studio

Generative Actions are a powerful feature in Microsoft Copilot Studio that allow Copilots to dynamically select and execute the most appropriate topics and actions at runtime. This capability leverages advanced AI to enhance Copilot's ability to handle complex and unforeseen queries, providing users with seamless and efficient interactions.

Key Features of Generative Actions

1. **Dynamic Topic and Action Selection**: Instead of relying solely on pre-authored topics, generative actions enable the Copilot to dynamically choose the best topics and actions based on the user's input. This ensures that the Copilot can respond accurately even to unexpected questions.

2. **Action Execution Through Plugins**: Generative actions utilize a wide range of plugins and connectors, allowing the Copilot to perform specific tasks or retrieve information from various systems. This includes integration with over 1200 data connectors such as SAP, Workday, and Salesforce, enabling the Copilot to handle complex workflows and data retrievals.

3. **Dynamically Chaining Plugins**: Generative actions can dynamically chain multiple plugins together to produce actionable customer responses. This enables the Copilot to handle complex tasks that require information from various sources and processes.

4. **Automatic Slot-Filling**: Generative actions can automatically slot-fill further details to obtain the necessary information for completing tasks. This reduces the need for user input by intelligently gathering required data.

5. **Handling Multi-Intent Queries**: Generative actions are capable of handling multi-intent queries that were not anticipated or built by the user. This enhances Copilot's flexibility and ability to manage diverse and complex user requests.

6. **Powered by Azure OpenAI Service with LangChain Concepts**: Generative actions leverage the Azure OpenAI Service and incorporate "LangChain" concepts, enabling advanced natural language processing and understanding. This provides robust AI capabilities for generating relevant and accurate responses.

7. **Enhanced Flexibility and Scalability**: By leveraging generative actions, Copilots can be more flexible and scalable. They can adapt to a wide range of scenarios without the need for extensive manual configuration, making it easier to deploy and maintain advanced conversational experiences.

8. **Improved User Experience**: Generative actions improve the user experience by providing more accurate and contextually relevant responses. This reduces the need for users to repeat or rephrase their questions, leading to more efficient and satisfying interactions.

Implementing Generative Actions
Configuration and Setup

Select Plugins: Choose from a variety of available plugins that your Copilot can use to perform actions. This can include connectors to enterprise systems, APIs, and other data sources.

Define Triggers: Set up triggers that determine when generative actions should be invoked. This can be based on specific keywords, user intent, or other contextual cues.

Creating and Managing Actions

Visual Authoring: Use Copilot Studio's low-code visual authoring tools to create and manage actions. This allows you to define the logic and flow of actions without needing extensive programming skills.

Natural Language Description: Describe the desired actions in natural language, and Copilot Studio will generate the corresponding workflow. This simplifies the process of creating complex actions.

CHAPTER 7   MICROSOFT COPILOT STUDIO

Testing and Optimization

Simulate Interactions: Test the generative actions in simulated interactions to ensure they perform as expected. This helps identify and resolve any issues before deploying the Copilot.

Optimize Performance: Continuously monitor the performance of generative actions and make necessary adjustments to improve accuracy and efficiency. Use analytics to understand how users interact with the Copilot and refine the actions accordingly.

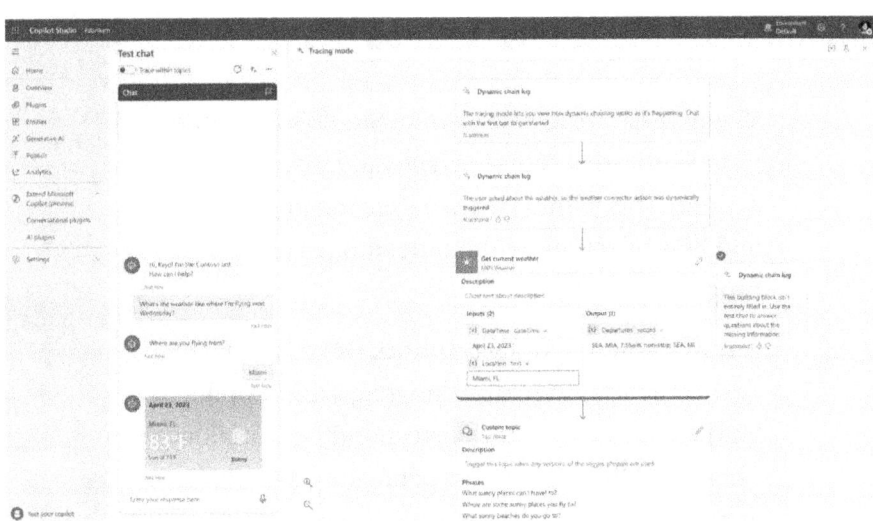

Figure 7-7. Generative Actions: Dynamics chain

Examples of Generative Actions

Order Processing: A customer asks about the status of an order. The Copilot dynamically selects the appropriate action to retrieve order details from the backend system and provides the user with real-time updates.

HR Assistance: An employee inquiries about their remaining vacation days. The Copilot uses a plugin to access HR data from Workday and presents the information to the employee.

Technical Support: A user reports an issue with a software application. The Copilot dynamically selects troubleshooting steps and guides the user through resolving the problem, pulling information from internal knowledge bases and external resources.

Benefits of Generative Actions

- **Reduced Manual Effort**: By automating the selection and execution of actions, generative actions reduce the need for manual topic creation and maintenance.
- **Increased Efficiency**: Users receive faster and more accurate responses, enhancing their overall experience and satisfaction.
- **Enhanced Adaptability**: Copilots can adapt to a wide range of scenarios, making them more versatile and capable of handling diverse user needs.

- **Improved Resource Utilization**: Organizations can leverage generative actions to optimize the use of their data and systems, ensuring that the Copilot can access and utilize information effectively.

Figure 7-7 demonstrates a screenshot of Generative Actions, dynamic chain within Copilot Studio.

Generative Actions in Copilot Studio represent a significant advancement in AI-driven conversational interfaces, providing the capability to handle complex queries and tasks with ease. By integrating this feature, organizations can create more intelligent, responsive, and efficient Copilots that deliver superior user experiences.

Copilot Studio Architecture

The architecture of Microsoft Copilot Studio integrates various components and services to create a robust environment for developing and managing AI-powered Copilots.

Below is a brief overview of the architecture based on Figure 7-8.

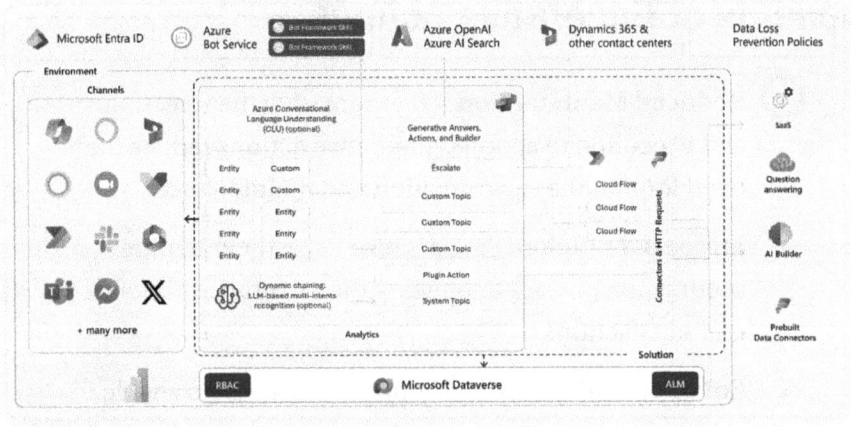

Figure 7-8. Copilot Studio architecture

CHAPTER 7   MICROSOFT COPILOT STUDIO

Overview of Copilot Studio Architecture
Environment and Authentication

Microsoft Entra ID: Provides identity and access management services, ensuring secure authentication and authorization for users interacting with Copilots.

Azure Bot Service: Hosts and manages bots, providing a scalable platform for deploying Copilots.

Channels: Copilots can interact with users across multiple channels, including Microsoft Teams, Dynamics 365, and other platforms. Additional channels supported include Facebook, Slack, and custom applications.

Core AI Services

Azure Conversational Language Understanding (CLU): Optional service for enhancing natural language understanding, allowing Copilots to comprehend and process user input effectively.

Azure OpenAI and Azure AI Search: These services power the generative AI capabilities, enabling the Copilot to generate responses, perform actions, and access information from various sources.

Generative AI Components

Generative Answers, Actions, and Builder: This component leverages large language models (LLMs) to provide dynamic and contextually relevant responses. It includes

Generative Answers: Automatically generates answers based on specified knowledge sources.

Generative Actions: Dynamically selects appropriate topics and actions to execute at runtime.

Builder: Facilitates the creation and management of custom topics and actions.

Custom Topics and Plugin Actions: Allows the creation of specific conversational topics and actions to tailor Copilot's behavior to specific use cases.

Data Integration and Management

Microsoft Dataverse: Acts as the central data repository, storing and managing data used by the Copilot.

Connectors and HTTP Requests: Enables integration with external data sources and services, allowing the Copilot to access and use real-time data.

Dynamics 365 and Other Contact Centers: Integrates with CRM and other contact center solutions to provide comprehensive support and interaction capabilities.

Analytics and Management

Dynamic Chaining with LLM-Based Multi-intents Recognition: Allows the Copilot to handle multiple user intents within a single conversation, dynamically chaining responses and actions to provide coherent and comprehensive support.

Role-Based Access Control (RBAC): Ensures that only authorized users have access to specific functions and data, enhancing security and compliance.

Security and Compliance

Data Loss Prevention (DLP) Policies: Implements policies to prevent data exfiltration and ensure compliance with organizational and regulatory standards.

Prebuilt Data Connectors and AI Builder: Provides preconfigured connectors and AI models to streamline the integration and deployment of Copilots.

CHAPTER 7 MICROSOFT COPILOT STUDIO

Solution Lifecycle Management

Application Lifecycle Management (ALM):
Manages the development, testing, and deployment lifecycle of Copilots, ensuring efficient and effective updates and maintenance.

The Copilot Studio architecture is designed to provide a comprehensive and secure platform for developing, deploying, and managing AI-powered Copilots. By integrating advanced AI services, robust data management, and flexible deployment options, Copilot Studio enables organizations to create highly functional and responsive conversational agents tailored to their specific needs.

Monitoring and Diagnosing

Effective monitoring and diagnosing are crucial for ensuring the smooth operation and performance of Copilots created in Microsoft Copilot Studio. Here is a detailed overview of how you can monitor and diagnose Copilots in Copilot Studio.

Monitoring Tools and Capabilities

Azure Monitor: Utilize Azure Monitor to track the performance, availability, and overall health of your Copilots. Azure Monitor provides metrics, logs, and alerts that can help you understand how your Copilot is performing in real-time.

Metrics: Track key performance indicators such as response times, error rates, and throughput.

Logs: Collect and analyze logs to troubleshoot issues and understand usage patterns.

Alerts: Set up alerts to notify you of critical issues, such as high error rates or service downtime.

Application Insights: Integrated with Copilot Studio to provide deep insights into your Copilot's performance.

Telemetry: Collects detailed telemetry data on user interactions, system performance, and anomalies.

Dashboards: Use customizable dashboards to visualize data and monitor key metrics.

Error Tracking: Identifies and tracks errors, providing detailed diagnostics to help resolve issues.

Diagnostic Capabilities

Log Analytics: Use Log Analytics to aggregate and analyze log data from various sources. It helps in identifying trends, anomalies, and potential issues.

Query Language: Use Kusto Query Language (KQL) to query and analyze logs.

Insights: Generate insights into user behavior, system performance, and error patterns.

Health Checks: Regular health checks can help ensure that all components of your Copilot are functioning correctly.

Automated Tests: Implement automated tests to check the functionality of critical components.

Manual Reviews: Conduct regular manual reviews of logs and metrics to identify potential issues.

Diagnostic Events and Auditing

Auditing: Keep track of important events and changes within Copilot Studio to maintain security and compliance.

BotCreate: Tracks the creation of new Copilots.

BotDelete: Logs the deletion of Copilots.

BotAuthUpdate: Monitors changes to authentication settings.

BotPublish: Records the publishing of Copilots.

BotShare: Tracks when Copilots are shared with other users.

Component Events: Monitors the creation, update, and deletion of components (topics, skills, etc.).

AI Plugin Events: Tracks the creation, update, and deletion of AI plugins.

Environment Variable Events: Monitors changes to environment variables.

Comprehensive Analytics

- **Performance Issues**: Monitor response times and identify bottlenecks using Application Insights and Azure Monitor.

- **Scaling**: Ensure that your Copilot is properly scaled to handle the expected load.

- **Optimization**: Optimize Copilot's logic and reduce unnecessary complexity.

- **Error Handling**: Use detailed error logs to identify and resolve issues.

- **Retry Logic**: Implement retry logic for transient errors.

- **Fallback Mechanisms**: Ensure there are fallback mechanisms in place for critical failures.

- **User Experience Issues**: Analyze user interaction data to identify and address issues impacting the user experience.

- **Feedback**: Collect user feedback to understand pain points and areas for improvement.

- **Testing**: Regularly test the Copilot to ensure it meets user expectations.

Reporting and Analytics

Analytics sessions track user engagement with your Copilot and capture how well your Copilot handles user tasks. A single conversation can contain one or more analytics sessions, each associated with a specific topic. The last nonsystem topic triggered—or the first system topic triggered, if no nonsystem topics were triggered—is associated with the analytics session.

Figure 7-9 depicts all measured KPIs tracked in the out-of-the-box analytics.

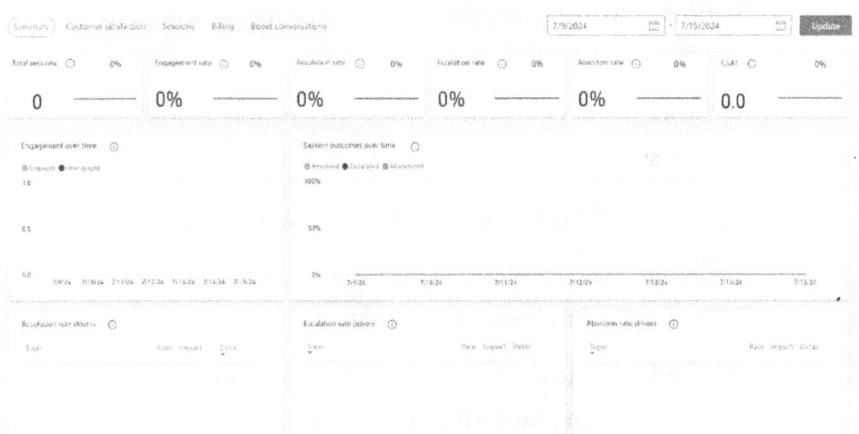

Figure 7-9. *Analytics: Copilot Studio*

Summary Charts

The summary charts measure how well your Copilot is doing and help identify the topics with the most impact on your Copilot's performance. A session will time out after 30 minutes of inactivity.

Figure 7-9 demonstrates a Copilot reporting a screenshot of a Copilot within Copilot studio.

Key Performance Indicators: The summary tab includes various charts with graphical views of your Copilot's key performance indicators. These charts provide insights into:

- **Engagement Levels**: Tracks how often sessions become engaged

- **Resolution Rates**: Monitors the percentage of sessions that are resolved

- **Escalation Rates**: Tracks how often sessions are escalated

- **Abandonment Rates**: Monitors the percentage of sessions that are abandoned

- **Topic Performance**: Identifies the most and least effective topics based on session outcomes

Customer Satisfaction

The Customer Satisfaction (CSAT) tab of the Analytics page provides a detailed view of customer satisfaction survey data. It includes the average CSAT score, primary user query themes, and actionable insights on drivers of satisfaction or dissatisfaction with your Copilot's responses.

- Key Features

- **Average CSAT Score**: Displays the average customer satisfaction score over the selected period

- **Primary User Query Themes**: Highlights the main themes of user queries, helping you understand common user concerns or interests

- **Actionable Insights**: Provides insights into the factors driving satisfaction or dissatisfaction, allowing you to make targeted improvements

By default, the page shows key performance indicators for the last seven days. To change the time period, use the date pickers at the top of the page. You can retrieve data for any period within the last 45 days.

Topic Summary Charts

The topic summary charts in Copilot Studio provide a comprehensive overview of a topic's performance indicators over a specified time period, highlighting any changes in performance metrics. Here's a breakdown of what each chart measures.

Description and Details

Total Sessions

> **Description**: The total number of sessions that involved the topic within the specified time period.
>
> **Details**: This metric helps in understanding the frequency of interactions users have with a particular topic, indicating its relevance and usage rate.

Average CSAT

> **Description**: The average customer satisfaction (CSAT) survey score for the specified time period.
>
> **Details**: The CSAT score provides insights into user satisfaction with the responses provided by the Copilot for a specific topic. A higher score indicates better user satisfaction.

Resolution Rate

Description: The percentage of engaged sessions that are resolved.

Details: This metric shows the efficiency of a topic in resolving user queries. A higher resolution rate suggests that the topic effectively addresses user needs and contributes to successful interactions.

Escalation Rate

Description: The percentage of engaged sessions that are escalated.

Details: This rate measures how often sessions involving a particular topic require escalation to a live agent or another form of higher-level support. A lower escalation rate is typically desirable, indicating that the topic adequately handles user inquiries without needing additional intervention.

Abandon Rate

Description: The percentage of engaged sessions that are abandoned.

Details: The abandon rate indicates the frequency with which users leave sessions without achieving resolution or requiring escalation. A lower abandon rate is preferable, suggesting that users are generally finding the help they need without giving up.

Monitoring and diagnosing Copilots in Copilot Studio involve a combination of tools and practices aimed at ensuring high performance, reliability, and user satisfaction. By leveraging Azure Monitor, Application

CHAPTER 7 MICROSOFT COPILOT STUDIO

Insights, and robust logging and auditing mechanisms, you can maintain the health of your Copilots, quickly identify and resolve issues, and continuously improve the user experience.

Publish and Integrate Copilots

To publish and integrate Copilots into various platforms, you can follow these general guidelines for each scenario:

1. Add a Copilot to a Live Website

    Create and Configure the Copilot:

    Use Copilot Studio to design and configure Copilot's functionalities.

    Customize Copilot's responses and behavior according to your website's needs.

    Generate the Embed Code:

    Once the Copilot is ready, generate the embed code provided by Copilot Studio.

    Integrate into Website:

    Insert the embed code into the HTML of your website.

    Ensure the script is placed within the <body> tag where you want the Copilot to appear.

    Test and Monitor:

    Test the copilot on your live site to ensure it functions correctly.

Use monitoring tools like Azure Monitor and Application Insights for performance tracking and issue diagnostics.

2. Add a Copilot to Power Pages

    Create and Configure the Copilot:

    Design and configure the Copilot using Copilot Studio.

    Obtain the Embed Code:

    Generate Copilot's embed code.

    Integrate with Power Pages:

    Access Power Pages, navigate to the desired page, and use the HTML editor to embed the Copilot code.

    Test and Monitor:

    Validate Copilot's integration and performance.

    Use Azure Monitor and Application Insights for ongoing monitoring.

3. Add Chatbots to Microsoft Teams

    Create the Chatbot:

    Use Microsoft Power Virtual Agents to create and configure the chatbot.

    Publish the Chatbot:

    Publish the chatbot within the Copilot Studio portal.

    Integrate with Teams:

Use the Microsoft Teams admin center to add the chatbot to Teams.

Configure the chatbot's settings and permissions.

Test and Monitor:

Ensure the chatbot is functional in Teams.

Utilize Microsoft's monitoring tools for performance and diagnostics.

4. Add a Copilot to Facebook

   Create and Configure the Copilot:

   Design and configure the Copilot using Copilot Studio.

   Set Up Facebook Integration:

   Create a Facebook Page or use an existing one.

   Set up a Facebook App and configure it for Messenger Follow `https://developers.facebook.com/` to learn more on how to set up a Facebook App.

   Connect Copilot with Facebook:

   Use the Facebook Messenger API to connect your Copilot to the Facebook page.

   Obtain App access tokens and credentials from Facebook Developer portal.

   Test and Monitor:

   Test Copilot's functionality within Facebook Messenger.

   Monitor Copilot's performance using Facebook's analytics tools.

5. Add a Copilot to Mobile or Custom Apps

    Create and Configure the Copilot:

    Use Copilot Studio to design and configure the Copilot.

    Generate API or SDK:

    Obtain the necessary API or SDK provided by Copilot Studio for mobile integration.

    Integrate into Mobile App:

    Use API/SDK to integrate the Copilot into your mobile or custom app's codebase.

    Test and Monitor:

    Test the Copilot within the mobile app.

    Utilize monitoring tools like Azure Monitor for performance tracking.

6. Add a Copilot to Azure Bot Service Channels

    Create the Bot:

    Use Azure Bot Service to create and configure the bot.

    Configure Channels:

    Use the Azure portal to configure and add channels like Skype, Slack, Telegram, etc.

    Integrate Copilot Features:

    Incorporate Copilot functionalities into the bot's code and configuration.

    Test and Monitor

Test the bot across different channels.

Use Azure Monitor and Application Insights for performance monitoring and diagnostics.

Tools for Monitoring and Diagnosing

Azure Monitor: Helps track performance, detect issues, and set up alerts for your Copilot integrations.

Application Insights: Provides detailed analytics and diagnostics for real-time monitoring and troubleshooting.

Auditing and Troubleshooting Practices

- Regularly review logs and metrics to identify and resolve issues.
- Implement robust error handling and logging mechanisms within Copilot's code.
- Conduct regular performance testing to ensure optimal user experience.
- Utilize detailed auditing to track interactions and user feedback for continuous improvement.

These guidelines provide a general framework for integrating Copilots across various platforms. For more specific instructions, refer to the respective platform's documentation and resources.

Tools—Power CAT Copilot Studio Kit

The Power CAT Copilot Studio Kit is a comprehensive set of capabilities designed to augment Microsoft Copilot Studio. The kit helps makers test custom Copilots, use large language models to validate AI-generated content, and track aggregated key performance indicators. This tool can be downloaded from https://github.com/microsoft/Power-CAT-Copilot-Studio-Kit

Testing Capabilities

The Power CAT Copilot Studio Kit is a user-friendly application that empowers makers to configure Copilots and test sets. It has native capabilities such as Excel export or import for bulk creation and updates.

By running individual tests against the Copilot Studio APIs (Direct Line), the Copilot responses are evaluated against expected results. To further enrich results, additional data points can be retrieved from Azure Application Insights and from Dataverse by analyzing Conversation Transcript records (to get the exact triggered topic name, intent recognition scores, etc.). For AI-generated answers, which are by nature nondeterministic, AI Builder prompts are used to compare the generated answer with a sample answer or with validation instructions.

Supported Test Types

- Response Exact Match
- Attachments Match
- Topic Match (requires Dataverse enrichment)
- Generative Answers (requires AI Builder for response analysis and Azure Application Insights for details on why an answer was or was not generated)

CHAPTER 7   MICROSOFT COPILOT STUDIO

Copilot KPIs

Aggregate and retain key performance indicators from your custom Copilots without having to parse complex conversation transcripts.

By integrating these tools and practices, administrators can ensure that their Copilots in Copilot Studio are performing optimally, meeting user expectations, and adhering to organizational policies and compliance requirements.

Summary

This chapter provides a comprehensive overview of Copilot Studio, detailing its capabilities and applications within the Microsoft Power Platform. Starting with an introduction to Copilot Studio, readers are guided through the initial setup and configuration, enabling them to create their first projects with ease. The chapters cover essential topics such as building and training AI models, integrating these models into Power Apps, and leveraging various tools for monitoring and diagnosing performance.

Additionally, the chapter addresses critical aspects of security and compliance, offering best practices to ensure data privacy and adherence to industry standards. Advanced features and customizations are explored, empowering users to build bespoke AI solutions tailored to their specific needs. Through real-world case studies and insights from experts, readers gain practical knowledge and learn from successful implementations.

Finally, a wealth of resources and tools is presented, ensuring readers have the tools and knowledge to fully leverage Copilot Studio in their projects.

CHAPTER 8

Workflow Automation Using Power Automate

Getting Started with Power Automate

Microsoft Power Automate, formerly known as Microsoft Flow, is a powerful automation tool that allows users to create automated workflows between applications and services to synchronize files, get notifications, collect data, and more. It is part of the Microsoft Power Platform, which also includes Power Apps, Power BI, and Power Virtual Agents.

Power Automate enables both technical and nontechnical users to automate tasks and processes efficiently, enhancing productivity and reducing manual effort.

Power Automate Overview

Power Automate (`https://www.microsoft.com/en-us/power-platform/products/power-automate`) provides a user-friendly interface and a variety of connectors to integrate with numerous Microsoft and third-party services. Here are a few key features of Power Automate:

CHAPTER 8   WORKFLOW AUTOMATION USING POWER AUTOMATE

A. Automate Workflows

- Users can leverage Power Automate flows that automate repetitive tasks and processes. Flows in Power Automate can be triggered by an event, a manual button, or on a schedule.

- Based on the requirement, user can configure a trigger and drop action that the flow needs to perform in a logical sequence.

B. Triggers

- Triggers are basically the first step in a Power Automate flow. They define the condition or event on which the flow needs to be triggered.

- Power Automate provides with the capability to configure triggers with multiple options including filters, specific metadata changes, schedule, request input in case of manual triggers, etc.

- To integrate with other applications, Power Automate flows can be created to perform as a service, and using the "when an HTTP request is received" trigger, these flows can be consumed as an API call.

C. Actions

- Actions are the steps executed in a workflow created using Power Automate flows. These actions can be arranged sequentially or parallelly based on the requirement.

- Power Automate supports actions that act as API calls to the services that need to be used. Apart from services, there are also actions like initializing variables, adding conditional checks, using loops, etc. that help in logically building the automation pieces.

D. Cloud Flows

- Cloud flows are processes configured to run in the cloud. They do not need additional configuration and do not require additional resources to be set up.

- Connectors play a vital role in creating automation workflows using cloud flows. Services that have APIs can be automated using connectors and custom connectors in cloud flows.

E. Desktop Flows

- Desktop flows in Power Automate enable developers to automate processes and services that do not directly have APIs configured. For example, if the requirement is to extract data from a web page, it can either be done using an API call to the service, and if there is no API configured, desktop flows can be leveraged to scrape the data using UI automation.

- Desktop flows run on physical machines and need to be configured for the automation processes to run appropriately.

- Desktop flow runs can be orchestrated using cloud flows. Developers can assign machines to bots and ensure high availability in case of bulk processes.

F. Connectors

- Connectors help developers to utilize other services securely in Power Automate flows. Using connectors, actions can be added to the flow in a logical way to build an automation process.

- Currently, Power Automate supports over 1000 connectors to various products and services from Microsoft and other third parties. In case a service does not have a connector, developers can leverage custom connectors to create their own connector and utilize it.

G. Templates

- To get started with Power Automate cloud flows, users can leverage the template library that houses a lot of predefined flows based on specific use cases.

- These templates can further be customized based on the business requirements.

H. AI Builder

- The AI Builder capability of the Power Platform enables developers to add intelligence to workflows.

- Features such as text recognition, sentiment analysis, and prediction models can be utilized in the automation by adding the respective actions to the Power Automate flow.

CHAPTER 8 WORKFLOW AUTOMATION USING POWER AUTOMATE

I. Approval Workflows

- Developers can leverage the Approvals functionality in Power Automate cloud flows to easily set up approval processes for documents, requests, and more, ensuring proper authorization and accountability.

- Approvals use Outlook emails and Teams-actionable messages for notifying users and automatically update the process flow based on user responses.

Different Types of Flows in Power Automate

Power Automate offers various types of flows to cater to different automation needs. Here are the different types of flows developers can create to automate business processes:

A. Automated Flows

- These flows trigger based on an event specified on the service. For example, when a file is created in SharePoint, when a row is modified in Dataverse, when a new email arrives in Outlook, etc.

- Automated flows can be used in multiple scenarios, and developers can leverage multiple connectors to create a comprehensive process.

- A few common scenarios for automated flows are

    ◦ Send an email notification to a group of users when a new file is uploaded to a document library in SharePoint.

- Request for an approval from a set of users when a new row is added to a table in Dataverse. Once all approvers have responded, update the Dataverse row to display the latest status.

- Automated flows run in the context of the flow owner. This means all the connectors use the flow owner's connections by default unless there are new connections or connection references added and the flow configuration is pointed to use the other connections.

B. Scheduled Flows

- Scheduled flows, as the name suggests run on a schedule. Developers can configure the flow to run on a scheduled recurrence like once every day, twice a month, etc. Scheduled triggers also support a specific time stamp and time zone configuration to accurately match business requirements.

- Some common scenarios for scheduled flows are

  - Get a list of active planner tasks assigned to the members of a team and send a consolidated report to their manager on a weekly basis.

  - Archive files in SharePoint on a daily basis by using predefined logic based on attributes of the SharePoint document library.

- Scheduled flows also run in the context of the flow owner by default. Developers can share the flow with other users as co-owners and allow the co-owner to add their connection and map all actions to use those connections based on the requirements.

C. Manual Flows

- Manual flows are also known as button flows. As the name suggests, these flows are triggered manually by a user.

- Cloud flows support various platforms from where manual flows can be triggered. Some of these platforms include

    ○ Trigger a flow using a button from a canvas power app.

    ○ Trigger a flow from a Dataverse table row by using the 'For a selected row' trigger.

    ○ Trigger a flow from SharePoint lists by using the 'For a selected item' trigger.

    ○ A button can also be added to the Power Automate app for mobile devices, and a manual flow can be configured to trigger when a user clicks that button.

- Some common scenarios that leverage manual flows are

    ○ Trigger a process flow with inputs provided by the user triggering the flow.

    ○ Send a predefined email to a set of users based on the inputs provided by the user triggering the flow.

    ○ Perform a set of actions based on the inputs provided by the user in a canvas power app.

- Generate a report of all orders placed by the customer when the flow is triggered from a model-driven power app.

• Manual flows again run based on the flow owner's connection by default. However, they can be shared with other users as run-only users, and the connection settings can be configured in a way that they use the connection of the user that is triggering the flow.

D. Business Process Flows

• A business process flow is a guided multistage process that helps users to follow a predefined logical path to complete a business process. Developers can add multiple stages to a business process flow and set up the configuration to trigger cloud flows when a user completes a stage and starts a new stage.

• Business process flows are generally added to Dataverse tables and used on model-driven Power Apps to guide users and help ensure data consistency and accuracy across complex workflows.

• A few common use cases of business process flows are

- Standardizing the process for handling customer support cases.

- Standardize process for data entry while creating a new opportunity. This helps ensure that the users provide all required data and validate each step of the process.

CHAPTER 8 WORKFLOW AUTOMATION USING POWER AUTOMATE

E. Desktop Flows

- Desktop flows combined with cloud flows help in automating complex processes from end to end. They enable the Robotic Process Automation (RPA) capability for users to automate APIs and also UI-based actions.

- Desktop flows can be leveraged to automate repetitive tasks on the desktop or web applications by recording and replaying user actions.

- They allow users to record and automate actions performed on their desktops or web applications. These flows are crucial for tasks that involve interacting with user interfaces, such as data entry, form-filling, and navigating through application menus.

- While cloud flows focus more on modern applications, desktop flows support automating legacy applications also.

- A few common use cases of desktop flows include

    ○ Automating data entry into legacy systems where there is no API support. For example, organizations using legacy accounting systems that have high dependency on other critical processes can leverage desktop flows to automate data entry by mimicking a manual user process, thereby reducing time and effort.

- Desktop flows can also be used for scraping data from web apps where there is no API support. Developers can feed the desktop flow by recording the manual steps like login to the application, navigate to the appropriate tab, open the form, fill out the data, and submit. Desktop flows can recognize the UI elements and follow the process based on the business requirements.

- Desktop flows can be triggered from cloud flows. They can run in two modes:

  - Attended

    - Attended RPA involves automation that requires human intervention or supervision.

    - These bots are typically used to assist human workers by automating parts of their workflows while they perform other tasks.

    - Attended RPA is often used in scenarios where decision-making or human judgment is needed during the process.

  - Unattended

    - Unattended RPA, on the other hand, involves automation that runs without human intervention.

    - These bots operate in the background, executing predefined tasks and workflows autonomously.

CHAPTER 8 WORKFLOW AUTOMATION USING POWER AUTOMATE

- Unattended RPA is suited for tasks that are repetitive, do not require human judgment, and can be scheduled or triggered automatically.

Advanced Features in Power Automate

- Power Automate integrates with AI Builder, allowing users to incorporate AI capabilities into their workflows without needing data science expertise. Examples include extracting text from images, performing sentiment analysis on text, and predicting future outcomes based on historical data.

- Power Automate provides robust features for creating approval workflows. These workflows can be customized to include multiple approvers, conditional steps, and automated reminders. Approval processes ensure that critical actions are properly authorized and documented.

- The Power Automate portal provides tools to monitor the performance and health of flows. Users can view run history, track performance metrics, and troubleshoot issues. Setting up alerts and notifications for failed flows helps in proactive management.

- Establishing governance policies is essential for controlling who can create and run flows within an organization. Power Automate supports data loss prevention (DLP) policies to restrict the use of specific connectors and ensure compliance with organizational security standards.

- Implementing error handling in workflows is crucial for ensuring reliability and resilience. Power Automate allows users to configure run-after settings to handle errors gracefully. For example, if a step fails, users can define alternative actions or notifications to manage the error.

- Power Automate flows can be integrated with other third-party applications also. The manual button-triggered flows directly support Microsoft services by default. However, organizations can leverage "when an HTTP request is received" trigger and set up cloud flows that can be called as APIs from other applications by using simple HTTP requests.

Use Cases for Power Automate

Power Automate helps teams better function by automating simple repetitive tasks. Integrating with day-to-day Microsoft 365 services, teams can leverage simple cloud flows to automate sending notifications, requesting approvals, generating reports, etc.

While there are abundant use cases for Power Automate, here are a few use cases that can help users get started:

A. Automate Document Approvals

- Users can streamline the document approval process by creating automated workflows that route documents to the right approvers and track the status.

- SharePoint document libraries and lists can be leveraged to manage the documents and approval metadata, respectively, and users can create an audit log for any future reference purposes.

B. Automate Notifications

- Users can set up cloud flows to automatically send notifications to customers about order statuses, appointment reminders, and support ticket updates.

- Teams can set up cloud flows to automatically notify team members about their pending active tasks, deadlines, etc.

- Organizations can leverage cloud flows to send automated notifications on company updates, holiday calendars, important announcements, etc.

C. Automate Data Collection

- Users can leverage Power Automate to collect data from various sources (e.g., forms and emails) and store it in a centralized repository like SharePoint or Dataverse.

- Further processes like approvals can be set up on the collected data, and users can streamline business processes by reducing to-and-fro email exchanges, paper trails, etc.

D. Social Media Monitoring

- Organizations can set up flows to monitor social media for specific keywords or hashtags and send notifications or store the data for analysis.

- Cloud flows can also be leveraged to post updates on social media based on a scheduled or a manual trigger based on the requirements.

E. Employee Onboarding

- Organizations can leverage Power Automate flows to automate the onboarding process for new employees by creating workflows that assign tasks, send welcome emails, and provision access to systems.

- Cloud flows can be set up to send reminder notifications to newly onboarded employees for any pending processes that need their attention in order to complete the onboarding process.

In summary, Microsoft Power Automate is a versatile and powerful tool that can transform how organizations handle routine tasks and processes. By enabling both technical and nontechnical users to create automated workflows, Power Automate helps improve efficiency, reduce errors, and free up valuable time for more strategic activities.

Whether you're looking to automate simple notifications or complex business processes, Power Automate provides the tools and capabilities to help you achieve your goals.

Create Flows Using Power Automate

Power Automate enables users to create automated processes using actions, triggers, and controls. In this section, we will walkthrough the process of setting up cloud flows and desktop flows to automate simple processes using Power Automate.

CHAPTER 8   WORKFLOW AUTOMATION USING POWER AUTOMATE

Creating Cloud Flows in Power Automate

Creating an automated flow in Power Automate is straightforward. Here's a step-by-step guide to creating a simple flow that sends an email notification when a new item is added to a SharePoint list.

- A. Sign-In to Power Automate

    - Navigate to make.powerautomate.com (Power Automate maker portal) to login and start creating a flow.

    - It is mandatory to have a work or a school Microsoft account to create Power Automate flows.

    - Ensure that you are in the right environment while creating the flow.

- B. Create a New Flow

    - Click Create in the left-hand navigation pane to start creating a new cloud flow. You will see options for the type of flow you want to create.

    - Select Automated Cloud Flow option as we are creating a flow that will trigger when a new item is added to a SharePoint list.

- C. Define the Trigger

    - In the Build an automated flow pane, name your flow (e.g., "Send an email when a new item is added to <SharePoint List Name>").

    - Search for the trigger when an item is created and select it from the list of SharePoint triggers and click Create.

CHAPTER 8   WORKFLOW AUTOMATION USING POWER AUTOMATE

D. Configure the Trigger

- Enter the SharePoint site address and the name of the list where the new item will be added. Frequently used SharePoint sites automatically appear in the dropdown option where you need to provide the site details. Once the site is selected, it will automatically show available lists in the lists dropdown.

- For building advanced flows where the trigger should only function based on a specific condition, you can add a trigger condition based on the requirements.

E. Add an Action

- Click New step to define what happens next.

- In the Choose an action pane, search for Send an email (V2) and select it from the Office 365 Outlook connector.

- Configure the email action:
  - To: Enter the recipient's email address.
  - Subject: Enter the subject of the email (e.g., "<Item Title> added to <SharePoint List Name>").
  - Body: Customize the email body, using dynamic content from the SharePoint list item (e.g., Title, Created By, Link to Item, etc,).
  - You can configure more options like Bcc, Cc, importance of the email, add attachments, etc.

F. Save and Test the Flow

- Click Save to save your flow. If you are using the new designer of Power Automate, you will have to save the flow and publish it so that the flow can then be tested.

- To test the flow, add a new item to your specified SharePoint list.

- Verify that the email notification is sent to the configured recipient with the correct details.

- Based on the license type, it may take some delay for the flow to trigger and send out the email notification.

Creating Desktop Flows in Power Automate

Here's a step-by-step guide to creating a simple desktop flow that utilizes the recording feature to record the actions performed by the user.

A. Install Power Automate Desktop

- Download and install Power Automate Desktop from the Power Automate website. Ensure that you have the latest version installed.

- Open the Power Automate Desktop application and sign in with your Microsoft account.

- It is mandatory to have a work or a school Microsoft account to create Power Automate flows.

- Ensure that you are in the right environment while creating the flow.

B. Create a New Desktop Flow

- In Power Automate Desktop, click New flow to create a new desktop flow.
- Name your flow and click Create.

C. Record Actions

- Click Recorder to start recording your actions.
- Perform the tasks you want to automate, such as opening applications, entering data, and navigating through menus.
- Stop the recorder once you have completed the actions.

D. Edit and Customize the Flow

- Use the flow designer to edit and customize the recorded actions. You can add conditions, loops, and error handling to make the flow more robust.
- Test the flow to ensure it performs the desired actions correctly. You can add break points to debug and fix any issues.

E. Save and Run the Flow

- Save your flow and run it to see the automation in action.
- For attended RPA, you can trigger the flow manually when needed. You can also trigger this flow from a cloud flow and set the mode to attended. Configure the desktop flow in a way that it waits for the user actions wherever required.

CHAPTER 8   WORKFLOW AUTOMATION USING POWER AUTOMATE

- For unattended RPA, schedule the flow or set up triggers to run it automatically. You can set up the cloud flow to trigger the desktop flow after a set of actions have been performed or add actions after the desktop flow action and configure input/output variables to handle data exchange.

In summary, creating flows in Microsoft Power Automate empowers users to automate a wide range of tasks and processes, enhancing productivity and operational efficiency. With its intuitive interface, extensive library of connectors, and robust capabilities, Power Automate makes it easy for both technical and nontechnical users to build workflows that integrate seamlessly with various applications and services.

Whether designing simple automated notifications, complex approval workflows, or leveraging AI capabilities, Power Automate offers the tools needed to streamline business operations. By understanding the different types of flows—such as automated, button, scheduled, business process, and Desktop flows—users can select the appropriate flow type for their specific needs.

Incorporating best practices, such as proper error handling, governance, and monitoring, ensures reliable and secure automation. Overall, Power Automate's versatile and user-friendly platform enables organizations to reduce manual effort, improve accuracy, and focus on higher-value activities, driving innovation and growth.

Advanced Flow Design Using Copilots

Microsoft Power Automate is a powerful platform for automating workflows across applications and services, enabling both technical and nontechnical users to streamline their processes. With the introduction of Copilots, Power Automate has taken automation to the next level by providing intelligent guidance and suggestions for creating more sophisticated flows.

This feature leverages AI to assist users in designing complex workflows efficiently, ensuring best practices and optimizing performance.

Overview of Copilots in Power Automate

Copilots in Power Automate are AI-driven assistants that help users create, refine, and optimize their automated workflows. They provide contextual recommendations, suggest improvements, and offer real-time assistance throughout the flow creation process.

By harnessing the power of AI, Copilots enable users to build advanced flows with greater confidence and efficiency.

Key Features of Copilots in Power Automate

A. Intelligent Recommendations

- Copilots analyze the user's workflow and suggest actions, triggers, and conditions that align with the intended automation.
- Users can leverage these suggestions and further customize based on the requirements.

B. Real-Time Assistance

- As users build their flows, Copilots provide on-the-spot guidance to ensure the workflow is constructed correctly.

- Users can leverage the information provided by Copilots and implement that in their workflows. Copilot suggestions also point users to the appropriate documentation, and users can refer to that in case needed.

C. Best Practice Guidance

- Copilots recommend best practices for designing robust and efficient flows, helping users avoid common pitfalls.

D. Optimization Suggestions

- Copilots analyze the flow for potential optimizations, suggesting ways to improve performance and reduce execution time.

- These suggestions also help beginners understand the core principles and standard practices for building flows using Power Automate.

E. Error Detection and Resolution

- Copilots help identify and resolve errors in the flow, providing troubleshooting tips and solutions.

- The Copilot summary for failed actions also helps users compare with similar issues and refer to similar posts raised on the Microsoft Power Automate community forums.

CHAPTER 8   WORKFLOW AUTOMATION USING POWER AUTOMATE

Designing Advanced Flows with Copilots

A. Define the Flow Objective

- Clearly define the business process or task you want to automate. It is important to understand the input, output, and key steps involved.

- It is also recommended to determine the end objectives of the flow, such as reducing manual effort, improving data accuracy, or speeding up a process.

B. Select Appropriate Triggers and Actions

- Select a trigger that initiates the flow based on an event (e.g., receiving an email, creating a new item in SharePoint, modifying a row in Dataverse, etc.).

- Use Copilots to identify and add the necessary actions that the flow should perform (e.g., sending notifications, updating records, initiating an approval, etc.).

C. Incorporate Conditions and Loops

- Use conditional logic to specify different actions based on certain criteria (e.g., if-else statements). Copilots can suggest appropriate conditions based on the workflow context. If using formulas to define the condition checks, Copilots can process natural language and provide an expression that can be used for the condition mapping.

- Add loops to iterate over a collection of items. Copilots can help determine when to use loops and how to structure them for optimal performance.

D. Integrate with Other Services

- Leverage Power Automate's extensive library of connectors to integrate with various services and applications. Copilots can recommend connectors that fit the flow's requirements.

- Design workflows that span multiple platforms and applications, ensuring seamless data transfer and process automation.

E. Optimize and Validate the Flow

- Use Copilots to identify bottlenecks and suggest optimizations, such as parallel processing or efficient data handling techniques.

- Implement error handling mechanisms to manage exceptions gracefully. Copilots can suggest error handling strategies and actions to take when errors occur.

Example: Automating Employee Onboarding

A. Flow Objective

- Automate the employee onboarding process, including sending welcome emails, creating user accounts, and assigning training tasks.

B. Select Appropriate Triggers and Actions

- Trigger
    - When a new employee is added to the HR system (trigger from a database like SharePoint or Dataverse or HR application like Power Apps).

- Actions
    - Send a welcome email to the new employee using Outlook.
    - Create user accounts in Active Directory and other necessary systems using Azure AD (Entra ID) connectors and connectors corresponding to the services to be used.
    - Assign initial training tasks in the company's task tracking systems like Planner, Azure DevOps, Jira, etc.

C. Incorporate Conditions and Loops

- Condition
    - Check the employee's role to customize the onboarding process.
    - If the role is "Manager," assign additional training modules and tasks.

- Loop
    - Iterate over a list of training modules or tasks and assign each one to the new employee.

D. Integrate with Other Services

- Connectors
  - Use connectors for email, Active Directory (Entra ID), Planner, Azure DevOps, SharePoint, MS Forms, etc.
- Cross-Platform Automation
  - Ensure that data flows seamlessly between the HR system, Active Directory, SQL Server, Excel etc., based on the application dependencies.

E. Optimize and Validate the Flow

- Optimization
  - Use Copilots to identify any redundant steps and streamline the flow.
- Error Handling
  - Implement error handling to manage issues like failed account creation or email delivery. For multiple actions related to each other, containerize them into a scope control and implement error handling as required.

Best Practices for Flow Design Using Copilots

A. Modular Design

- Divide complex workflows into smaller, manageable subflows. Copilots can help identify logical breakpoints and modularize the workflow.

- Create reusable components that can be used across multiple flows to maintain consistency and reduce duplication.

B. Error Handling

- Configure flows to send notifications when errors occur, providing detailed information for troubleshooting. You can also add the link to the flow run history in the notification for easy access to the failed runs.

- Implement retry mechanisms to handle transient errors, ensuring the flow can recover from temporary issues. It is recommended to carefully configure retry logic as it may cause issues on the service like throttling, too many failures, etc., resulting in the API not functioning as expected.

C. Performance Optimization

- Use parallel branches to perform independent tasks simultaneously, reducing the overall execution time. Ensure that the variables and any dependent actions are correctly configured to avoid improper data references.

- Optimize data handling by minimizing data transfers and using efficient data structures. Copilots can suggest best practices for data management.

D. Security and Compliance

- Ensure that only authorized users have access to sensitive data and flow configurations. You can validate these settings while sharing the flows with other users.

- Implement data encryption to protect sensitive information during transit and at rest. You can configure the visibility of input and output of an action for the run-only users of the flow in order to maintain data security.

- Regularly review and update flows to ensure compliance with organizational policies and regulatory requirements.

In summary, the integration of Copilots in Microsoft Power Automate significantly enhances the flow design process by providing intelligent guidance and real-time assistance. By leveraging Copilots, users can create advanced, efficient, and robust workflows that automate complex business processes.

From selecting appropriate triggers and actions to optimizing performance and ensuring security, Copilots enable users to harness the full potential of Power Automate. As organizations continue to adopt automation, Copilots will play a crucial role in simplifying the design of sophisticated flows, driving innovation, and improving operational efficiency.

CHAPTER 8 WORKFLOW AUTOMATION USING POWER AUTOMATE

Integration with Power Apps

Microsoft Power Platform is a suite of applications that enables organizations to automate business processes, develop custom applications, and analyze data. Two key components of this suite are Power Automate and Power Apps.

Power Automate is a service for automating workflows between various applications and services, while Power Apps is a low-code platform for building custom business applications. Integrating Power Automate with Power Apps allows users to enhance their applications with automated workflows, making them more dynamic, responsive, and capable of handling complex business logic.

Benefits of Integrating Power Automate with Power Apps

Developers can leverage Power Automate to automate business processes in parallel or in sequence based on the actions performed by a user on the app. Here are some advantages of integrating Power Automate with Power Apps:

A. Enhanced Automation

- Automate complex business processes directly within your apps. Developers can configure functionality to call flows when users
  - Click a button
  - Click an icon or an image
  - Change the values of a drop-down, combo-box, or date controls
  - When the app is launched or when there is screen transition, etc.

B. Improved Efficiency

- Reduce manual tasks and streamline workflows, improving operational efficiency.

- Cloud flows can be set up to list records from different sources and return the data to canvas apps. This improves the efficiency by reducing the overall load time of the app.

- Bulk actions for creating or updating records can also be done through Power Automate. Developers can set up flows integrated with apps to perform bulk actions in the background, thereby allowing users to interact with other functionalities on the app.

C. Real-Time Updates

- Integrating Power Automate flows with Power Apps and Dataverse helps ensure that apps are always up-to-date with real-time data synchronization.

D. Simplified Development

- Developers can leverage low-code tools to build powerful, automated solutions without extensive coding.

- Power Automate can use multiple connectors and supports parallel processing of actions that can be leveraged to easily automate processes that can be complex to build directly in the apps.

Integration Scenarios

There are various scenarios where integrating Power Automate with Power Apps can reduce the overall work load and optimize the overall business process. Here are some common integration scenarios for Power Apps and Power Automate:

A. Form Submission and Approval Workflows

- Automate the approval process for submitted forms.
- Send notifications and updates to stakeholders.

B. Data Synchronization

- Sync data between Power Apps and other data sources, ensuring consistency.
- Utilize data manipulation techniques in Power Automate to merge complex data and return that to the app.

C. Task Automation

- Automate repetitive tasks such as data entry, report generation, and more.

D. Notifications and Alerts

- Trigger notifications based on specific events or changes in data.
- Notifications can be delivered through emails, Teams messages, notifications on mobile phones, etc., based on the requirements.

E. Advanced Business Logic

- Implement complex business rules and logic using automated workflows.

- Developers can leverage Power Automate cloud flows for automating dependent processes, data validation, filtering, etc. for enhancing the user experience on apps.

Steps to Integrate Power Automate with Power Apps

A. Create a Flow in Power Automate

- Navigate to make.powerautomate.com (Power Automate maker portal) to login and start creating a flow.

- It is mandatory to have a work or a school Microsoft account to create Power Automate flows.

- Ensure that you are in the right environment while creating the flow.

- Click Create in the left-hand navigation pane to start creating a new cloud flow. You will see options for the type of flow you want to create.

- Select Instant Cloud Flow to create a flow that can be triggered from Power Apps.

- Select PowerApps as the trigger. This allows the flow to be initiated from a Power App.

- Configure the trigger to request inputs as required from the app. These inputs will be required while configuring the flow in the app.
- Add the necessary actions to the flow. These could include data operations, sending notifications, calling APIs, etc.
- Provide a meaningful name to the flow and click Save.

B. Connect the Flow to Canvas Power Apps

- Navigate to make.powerapps.com (Power Apps maker portal) to login and start creating a new app or edit an already existing one.
- Ensure that you are in the right environment while creating or editing the app. It is mandatory to have the flow to be integrated with the app in the same environment.
- Add a button or other control (icon, image, checkbox, etc.) to the app that will trigger the flow.
- Select the control and open the OnSelect property. OnSelect property may not be available on all controls. For button and icon controls, OnSelect property can be configured to call a flow.
- Use the Flow function to connect the flow to the control. For example
- SendEmailNotification.Run(To,Subject,Body) (To, Subject, and Body are the input parameters of the flow and can be configured to map details from the existing controls on the app)

- Once the flow is added, click Save to save the app and then Publish so that the app can be run in play mode with the latest updates.

C. Test the Integration

- Run the Power Apps and interact with the control to trigger the flow.
- Check Power Automate to ensure the flow executed correctly and performed the desired actions.
- Debug any issues and refine the flow or app as needed to ensure smooth operation.
- In the connection settings of the flow, you can define whose connections will be used on the actions in the flow.

Best Practices for Integrating Power Automate with Power Apps

A. Design Considerations

- It is a recommended best practice to ensure that the integration enhances the user experience by making interactions smoother and more intuitive.
- Developers must focus on optimizing the flow and app for performance, especially when dealing with large datasets or complex workflows.
- As a best practice, developers must implement robust error handling in both the flow and the app to manage and recover from failures gracefully.

B. Security and Compliance

- Data protection is a critical aspect, and as a best practice, developers must ensure that data is securely transmitted and stored, adhering to organizational and regulatory requirements.

- It is recommended to implement proper access controls to restrict who can trigger flows and access data.

- It is important to ensure that the end users of the application who will trigger flows based on actions in the app have required security roles and access to the services used in the flow. If they do not have access, the flows will fail.

- Developers can also set up auditing and monitoring to track flow executions and troubleshoot issues. This enables to identify which user triggered the flow and track down issues on actions by going through the failed actions in the run history of the failed flow run.

- To restrict app users from viewing data in the flow run history, developers can leverage the Secure Input and Secure Output features on individual actions that might have sensitive data.

C. Maintenance and Updates

- As a general best practice, it is advised that the developers regularly review and update flows and apps to ensure they remain aligned with business requirements and leverage the latest features.

- It is important to maintain thorough documentation for both the flow and the app to facilitate maintenance and updates.

- Before rolling out the application to end users, it is recommended to provide training for users and ensure that they understand how to use the integrated solution effectively.

- Power Automate flows are automatically turned off if they are not triggered for a given amount of time or if there are continuous failures. As a best practice, developers must ensure that the flows are turned on so that it does not affect the intended usage of the application.

D. Package the Solution

- There might be multiple apps and flows in an environment for various use cases. As a recommended best practice, developers should leverage solutions as much as possible to package the app and the flow in the same solution to easily identify the dependencies.

- This also enables developers to easily export and import solution packages from one environment to another and also during cross-tenant deployments.

In summary, integrating Power Automate with Power Apps unlocks powerful capabilities for automating and enhancing business processes. By combining the flexibility of Power Apps with the automation prowess of Power Automate, organizations can create sophisticated solutions that streamline operations, improve efficiency, and provide a seamless user experience.

CHAPTER 8   WORKFLOW AUTOMATION USING POWER AUTOMATE

From simple notifications to complex approval workflows, the integration of these two platforms enables businesses to achieve more with less effort, paving the way for digital transformation and innovation.

Data Connectivity and Transformations

Microsoft Power Automate is a versatile platform designed to automate a wide range of business processes. A crucial aspect of creating effective workflows in Power Automate is the ability to connect to various data sources, transform data to fit the needs of the workflow, and manipulate this data to achieve desired outcomes. This process enables businesses to optimize their operations, ensure data consistency, and enhance decision-making.

Data Connectivity in Power Automate

Data connectivity refers to the capability of Power Automate to connect with various data sources, such as databases, cloud services, APIs, and on-premises systems. Power Automate provides a rich set of connectors to facilitate this integration.

Connectors in Power Automate

Power Automate offers over 1000 connectors, which can be categorized into the following types:

- A. Microsoft Connectors
    - These are Microsoft-provided connectors that enable developers to connect with Microsoft services.
    - For example, SharePoint, OneDrive, Outlook, Dynamics 365, Azure SQL Database, Azure Entra ID, Dataverse, Azure Blob, Planner, and more.

B. Third-Party Connectors

- These are third-party services that have APIs for their services and have corresponding connectors that users can use in Power Platform.

- For example, Salesforce, Google Drive, Dropbox, Twitter, DocuSign, Trello, Asana, Encodian, PlumSail, Adobe, and others.

C. Custom Connectors

- For products and services that have APIs for their services but do not have connectors in Power Platform, developers can leverage custom connectors to integrate with these APIs and set up triggers and actions as required.

- For example, if an organization has an internal service that has an API, developers can use the applicable authentication mechanism and create a custom connector with actions and triggers to consume the service.

Setting up Connections in Power Automate

To set up a connector for use in a Power Automate flow, developers need to follow the steps as mentioned below:

A. Authentication

- Depending on the connector, connections can be created by authenticating the connector using credentials, OAuth tokens, API keys, etc.

CHAPTER 8 WORKFLOW AUTOMATION USING POWER AUTOMATE

B. Permissions

- Users creating the connections must have required security roles and access to the service that they are trying to utilize.

C. Configuration

- Developers can configure the connector settings, such as specifying endpoints, parameters, filters, and other relevant options.

Example

To connect to a Dataverse table, follow the steps below:

- In Power Automate, create a new flow and choose the appropriate trigger (e.g., "When a row is added, modified, or deleted").
- Authenticate using the credentials (either service principal or user credentials) to create a connection to Dataverse.
- Once authenticated, you can select the table and the action on which the flow needs to trigger.
- You can add actions like Update a row, Add a new row, etc., from Dataverse connector to the flow and notice that the actions are authenticated. To use a different connection, select the ellipses on the action, and you can then select from the available connections or add a new one.

Data Transformation in Power Automate

Data transformation involves converting data from one format or structure to another to meet the requirements of the workflow or the target system. This can include filtering, aggregating, reshaping, or enriching data.

Developers can leverage the below tools and techniques to transform data.

Built-In Actions

Power Automate provides a variety of built-in actions for data transformation. Some of the most commonly used actions are

  A. Compose

  - Compose behaves like a temporary variable. Create and manipulate data structures of all data types including string, integer, object, array, etc.

  B. Filter Array

  - This action can be used to filter elements in an array output based on conditions. Users can leverage advanced conditions in filter array actions to combine multiple filter conditions.

  C. Select

  - The Select action helps in selecting specific properties as defined by the user from an array of objects.

  D. Join

  - The Join function can be used to concatenate array elements into a single string with the specified delimiter.

CHAPTER 8　WORKFLOW AUTOMATION USING POWER AUTOMATE

E. Parse JSON

- This is one of the most used actions when dealing with objects or array of objects. Developers can leverage the Parse JSON action to convert JSON strings into structured data.

- It employs a no-code method for users where the users can provide a sample of the JSON structure and the input data, and the action returns structured JSON based on the inputs.

Expressions

Developers can leverage expressions to perform calculations, manipulate strings, or work with dates and times. Power Automate expressions are based on Azure Logic Apps workflow definition language. Some commonly used expressions for data transformation are

A. String

- The string function can be used to convert a data type to string data type. For example, if the requirement is convert "1121" to string, the expression string("1121") can be used, and it returns the value as "1121".

B. Int

- Similar to the string function, the int function can be used to convert a valid data type to int. For example, to convert a string "1121" to int, the expression int("1121") can be used, and it returns the value as "1121".

C. Split

- The split function can be used to split data based on a delimiter. For example, if there is a string "ABC-DEF-GHI" and the requirement is to split the string and return a single string with all the alphabets, the expression join(split('ABC-DEF-GHI','-'),'') can be used, and the output returned is "ABCDEFGHI".

D. FormatDateTime

- The formatDateTime function can be used to format an ISO8061-formatted date time string to a format of choice. For example, if the date time value 1990-01-01T12:00:00 needs to be converted, the expression formatDateTime('1990-01-01T12:00:00', 'MM/dd/yyyy HH:mm') returns the output as '01/01/1990 12:00'.

AI Builder

- Power Automate flows have capabilities to integrate with AI Builder models. Developers can leverage these models to transform unstructured data into structured data.

- For example, developers can process an image file through an AI model to extract all the text required from the image. Similarly, models can be trained to extract text in the form of key value pairs or tables from PDFs, images, etc. by training the model as required.

Example

- To transform data from a Dataverse table and send a summary email, follow the steps below:
- Create a flow that uses a manual button trigger.
- Add an action to list rows from a Dataverse table. Use appropriate filtering to get a filtered list of data. For example, to get all active items, you can use the filter query as statecode eq 0.
- Use the Select action to reshape the data, picking only the relevant fields (e.g., Name, Created on Date, Description, etc.).
- Use the create HTML table action and pass the outputs of the select action to create an HTML table with the selected data.
- Use the send email using outlook action and configure the action based on the outputs of the previous action from the dynamic selector to send the summary email.

Data Manipulation in Power Automate

Data manipulation involves performing operations on data to modify, update, or enhance it as part of the workflow. This can include updating records, creating new entries, deleting data, and more.

Developers can leverage the below tools and techniques to manipulate data:

- Power Automate supports CRUD (Create, Read, Update, Delete) operations on connected data sources based on the connector actions.

- For example, if the requirement is to create an item in SharePoint, update an item in Dataverse, list rows from a table in Dataverse, or delete a file in SharePoint, developers can leverage the actions provided by these connectors, respectively, with appropriate data mapping.

- Power Automate supports variables with all data types including Boolean, string, int, object, array, etc. that can be used to store and manipulate data within the flow.

- Further, based on the retrieved data from data sources or additional conditions, developers can implement control actions like conditionals (if-else), loops (apply to each), and switches to manipulate data.

Workflow Example

Let's take an example of a company that wants to automate the process of approving expense reports. Employees submit expense reports via a Power Apps form, which are then reviewed and approved or rejected through an automated workflow.

Here are the steps that you can follow to create a workflow for automating the process:

A. Submission

- Employee submits an expense report via a Power Apps form.

B. Trigger

- A flow is triggered when a new item is created in the SharePoint list where expense reports are stored.

C. Data Retrieval

- Retrieve the new expense report details from the SharePoint list.

D. Data Transformation

- Use the Parse JSON action to parse the expense report details.
- Use the Select action to extract relevant fields (e.g., Employee Name, Amount, and Date).

E. Approval Process

- Send an approval request to the manager using the Approvals connector.
- Wait for the manager's response.

F. Conditional Logic

- If the manager approves the expense report, update the status in the SharePoint list and send a notification to the employee.
- If the manager rejects the expense report, update the status in the SharePoint list and send a notification to the employee with the reason for rejection.

G. Data Manipulation

- If approved, create a record in the financial system using a SQL connector or another relevant data source.

H. Error Handling

- Implement error handling to manage any issues that arise during the workflow, such as connectivity problems or invalid data.

Best Practices for Data Connectivity, Transformation, and Manipulation in Power Automate

A. Data Connectivity

- It is critical to ensure that all connections are secure, using encryption and secure authentication methods.

- As a recommended best practice, developers should focus on retrieving only the necessary data to minimize load times and improve performance.

- To drive user adoption and ensure that the flows are working as expected, it is advised to regularly monitor the status of connections and manage connection settings.

B. Data Transformation

- As a standard best practice, developers must ensure to optimize data transformations and reduce processing time to improve flow efficiency.

- It is recommended to ensure that data is validated and sanitized during transformation to prevent errors and ensure data integrity.

- To enhance data transformation processes, it is recommended to utilize AI Builder and other AI capabilities.

C. Data Manipulation

- Developers must ensure that all data manipulation actions have proper error handling to manage exceptions and retries.
- As a standard best practice, it is recommended to ensure that data is consistently updated across all connected systems to avoid discrepancies.
- Developers can leverage auditing and logging to track data manipulation actions and monitor workflow performance.

In summary, integrating data connectivity, transformation, and manipulation within Power Automate enables organizations to build comprehensive workflows that automate complex business processes efficiently. By leveraging the extensive connectors, powerful transformation tools, and robust data manipulation capabilities of Power Automate, businesses can optimize operations, ensure data consistency, and improve overall productivity.

Adopting best practices for each aspect of workflow creation further enhances the reliability and performance of automated processes, driving better business outcomes, and fostering a more agile and responsive organization.

Error Handling and Troubleshooting in Power Automate

Power Automate is a powerful tool for automating workflows and integrating various services and applications. However, like any automated system, errors and issues can arise. Effective error handling and troubleshooting are essential to ensure that workflows run smoothly and to quickly resolve any issues that occur.

Error handling in Power Automate involves anticipating possible points of failure and implementing strategies to manage errors gracefully. This includes setting up actions to handle errors, notifying stakeholders, and ensuring that workflows can continue or fail gracefully without causing major disruptions.

In this section, we will cover error handling techniques, common issues and their troubleshooting steps, and best practices to maintain reliable and efficient workflows.

Here are some techniques and actions that developers can leverage for better error handling in Power Automate flows:

A. Configure Run After

- The Configure run after option allows developers to specify actions to be taken after a previous action has failed, is skipped, has timed out, or has been successful. Using this, developers can set up alternative flows or actions to handle errors. To set up the configure run after sequence
    - Click the three dots (ellipsis) on an action.
    - Select "Configure run after."
    - Choose the conditions (e.g., "has failed").
    - Add subsequent actions based on these conditions.

- For example, if a step to update a row in a Dataverse table fails, you can configure a "Send Email" action to notify an administrator or the flow owner.

B. Scope Action

- The Scope action groups multiple actions together. Developers can leverage scope actions to apply error handling on the entire group, making it easier to manage complex workflows. To set up the scope action
    ○ Add a Scope action to your flow.
    ○ Place multiple actions inside the Scope. You can either add new actions or simply drag and drop the existing ones.
    ○ Use "Configure run after" on the Scope to handle errors for all included actions.
- For example, group all actions that update various systems within a single Scope (create a row in a Dataverse table, add a new SharePoint file to a document library, and send an email). If any action fails, you can handle the error at the Scope level.

C. Terminate Action

- The Terminate action allows developers to stop the flow and set a status (Succeeded, Failed, and Canceled) when an error occurs. This can be useful for explicitly defining the flow's end state. To set up the terminate action
    ○ Add a Terminate action where you want to end the flow.

CHAPTER 8 WORKFLOW AUTOMATION USING POWER AUTOMATE

- Set the status and provide a custom error message if needed.
- For example, if a required API call fails, you can add a Terminate action after the API call action and use configure run after to set the status to "Failed" with a detailed error message.

D. Parallel Branching

- Developers can leverage parallel branching to run multiple actions concurrently. If one branch fails, you can handle errors in the other branches without stopping the entire flow. To add parallel branching in a flow
    - Add a parallel branch to your flow below the action where the output can define which way the flow should proceed.
    - Configure actions in each branch.
    - Use error handling actions within each branch as needed.
- For example, send notifications and update databases in parallel branches. If the database update fails, the notification branch can still proceed.

CHAPTER 8   WORKFLOW AUTOMATION USING POWER AUTOMATE

Examples of Error Handling

A. API Call Failure Handling

- Scenario
  - An API call to an external service fails.
- Solution
  - Use "Configure run after" to detect failure.
  - Add a "Retry" mechanism or an alternative action (e.g., log the error and notify an admin).

B. Data Validation

- Scenario
  - User submits invalid data in a form.
- Solution
  - Validate data at the beginning of the flow.
  - If validation fails, use the Terminate action to stop the flow and notify the user.

Troubleshooting in Power Automate

A. Authentication and Permissions

- Issue
  - Authentication failures, insufficient permissions, empty response.
- Solution

CHAPTER 8   WORKFLOW AUTOMATION USING POWER AUTOMATE

- º Ensure correct authentication details are used (e.g., API keys, OAuth tokens).
- º Verify permissions for accessing the data sources and actions used in the flow.
- º Re-authenticate or update permissions as needed.

B. Connector Issues

- Issue
  - º Connectors not working or returning errors (internal server errors, continuous retry mode, and unexpected errors)
- Solution
  - º Check the connector status on the Power Automate status page.
  - º Verify the configuration of the connector.
  - º Ensure that the connected service is operational.

C. Timeouts and Delays

- Issue
  - º Actions timing out or experiencing significant delays (throttling issues)
- Solution
  - º Increase the timeout setting for actions if applicable.
  - º Optimize the flow to reduce processing time.
  - º Use parallel branching to distribute workload.

CHAPTER 8   WORKFLOW AUTOMATION USING POWER AUTOMATE

- ○ Check for any throttling issues on the connector or service.

D. Incorrect Data Handling

- Issue
  - ○ Data is not being processed or transformed correctly.
- Solution
  - ○ Verify the data schema and ensure that the correct fields are being used.
  - ○ Use the "Compose" action to debug data at various stages.
  - ○ Implement data validation checks.

E. Flow Not Triggering

- Issue
  - ○ Flow is not being triggered as expected.
- Solution
  - ○ Check the trigger configuration and ensure conditions are met.
  - ○ Verify that the trigger service is operational.
  - ○ Review the flow's run history to identify any issues with trigger conditions.
  - ○ In worse case scenarios, you may have to delete the trigger and add it again to the flow.

Debugging Tools and Techniques

A. Run History

- View the run history of a flow to see detailed information about each run, including inputs, outputs, and errors. To review the flow run history
    - Go to the flow in Power Automate.
    - Click "Run History."
    - Select a specific run to view detailed information.

B. Action Outputs

- Inspect the outputs of each action to verify that data is being processed correctly. To debug flow issues with action outputs
    - Click on an action in the run history.
    - Review the inputs and outputs sections for the action.

C. Logging and Notifications

- Implement logging and notifications to track the flow's progress and identify where issues occur. To leverage logging and notifications
    - Use the "Compose" action to log important data points.
    - You can also use variables to test.
    - Send notifications at critical stages to alert stakeholders of the flow's status.

CHAPTER 8   WORKFLOW AUTOMATION USING POWER AUTOMATE

- D. Testing with Sample Data
  - Test the flow with sample data to ensure it behaves as expected before deploying it to production. To test out flows with sample data
    - Use the "Test" feature in Power Automate to run the flow with sample data.
    - Analyze the results and make necessary adjustments.

Best Practices for Troubleshooting and Error Handling in Power Automate

- A. Proactive Error Handling
  - As a standard best practice, it is recommended to implement error handling at every critical step of the flow.
  - Developers can leverage "Configure run after," Scope, and Terminate actions to manage errors.
  - As discussed in the previous section, developers can also leverage parallel branching in Power Automate to create separate branches and handle the errors in the subsequent actions.
- B. Detailed Logging
  - It is recommended to log important data points and error messages to facilitate troubleshooting.
  - As a work around to review the data pointers, developers can use the "Compose" action to capture and log data at various stages.

C. Notifications

- It is generally recommended to set up notifications to alert stakeholders of errors and flow statuses.

- Developers can leverage email, Teams notifications, or other communication channels to timely notify the key stakeholders about errors and issues.

D. Regular Monitoring

- As a best practice, it is advised that developers regularly monitor the flow's run history and performance.

- Developers should focus on setting up alerts for any unusual activity or failures of the flow during the design phase itself.

- Microsoft generally sends out a consolidated email with failed runs to flow owners for all the flows owned by them.

E. Documentation

- It is recommended to document the flow design, including error handling strategies and known issues. This will help the teams that triage the flow run issues to accurately identify critical issues.

- As a standard best practice, teams should maintain a knowledge base of common issues and their solutions.

- Centralized documentation of all artifacts can also help teams to quickly triage the errors or issues on flows.

- Teams can also refer to the Microsoft Community Forums to compare similar issues and explore solutions to quickly fix issues.

F. Testing and Validation

- Before rolling out the flow on production data, it is advised to thoroughly test the flows with different data sets and scenarios.
- As a best practice, developers must validate data at multiple stages to ensure consistency and correctness.

In summary, error handling and troubleshooting are critical aspects of building robust and reliable workflows in Power Automate. By implementing proactive error handling techniques, using detailed logging and notifications, and following best practices, you can ensure that your workflows run smoothly and efficiently.

Regular monitoring and thorough testing further enhance the reliability of your automated processes, enabling you to quickly identify and resolve issues, minimize disruptions, and optimize business operations.

Power Automate Best Practices

Creating efficient and reliable flows in Power Automate requires adherence to best practices that ensure performance, maintainability, and scalability.

In this section, we will delve into various best practices for designing, developing, and managing flows, covering aspects such as planning, design, implementation, testing, and maintenance.

CHAPTER 8 WORKFLOW AUTOMATION USING POWER AUTOMATE

A. Define Objectives

- Power Automate enables developers to automate multiple services and build comprehensive processes for business solutions. However, to manage timelines for projects, it is recommended to clearly define the outcome to be achieved with the flow.

- It is important to have a clear understanding of the business problem or process that needs to be automated.

B. Map the Workflow

- To better understand the overall process flow of a business process, before creating the flow, it is recommended to create a flowchart or diagram of the process to visualize the steps and decision points.

- Developers can leverage tools like Microsoft Visio to create a process flow and define the data inputs, outputs, any intermediate storage, connection to services, logical implementations, etc.

- It is recommended to thoroughly study the process and then choose the right trigger and actions in Power Automate. Developers should avoid using unnecessary actions that can slow down the flow.

C. Modularize Flows

- Flows can have certain repetitive sections that can be used across at different stages. As a general best practice, it is recommended to break down complex flows into smaller, manageable scopes or child flows. This improves the readability and maintainability of the entire setup.

- Developers must focus on creating reusable components or templates for common tasks wherever applicable.

D. Error Handling

- Another critical aspect of building flows is error handling. As covered in the previous sections, developers must ensure to implement effective error handling by leveraging Configure Run After Settings, Scope actions, and error logging wherever applicable.

E. Optimize Performance

- As a standard best practice, it is recommended to minimize the number of data operations, such as querying databases or calling APIs.

- Developers can leverage parallel branching to run independent actions in parallel and reduce the overall execution time.

- It is advised to use event-driven triggers instead of polling triggers to reduce unnecessary checks and delaying of flow triggers.

F. Validate Data

- Developers must ensure that they validate inputs in order to meet the expected format and constraints before processing.

- It is advised to remove or escape any potentially harmful data to prevent security issues.
- In order to maintain data integrity, it is recommended to ensure that operations are atomic, meaning they are completed fully or not at all.
- Developers can also leverage concurrency settings in loops and triggers to handle concurrent data modifications.

G. Secure Connections

- It is recommended to utilize OAuth, API keys, or other secure authentication methods. Try to avoid unsecure APIs in order to maintain data security and process integrity.
- Developers must ensure that data is encrypted both in transit and at rest to avoid any unnecessary issues.

H. Manage Permissions

- Power Automate allows team members to share flows and run them. As a recommended best practice, developers must ensure that they grant only the necessary permissions to users and services.
- It is recommended to regularly review and update permissions to ensure they are still appropriate.

CHAPTER 8 WORKFLOW AUTOMATION USING POWER AUTOMATE

I. Audit and Compliance

- It is a standard best practice to enable auditing to track changes and access to critical data. This enables organizations to easily monitor and track changes to data and identify any issues through the process.

- Developers must ensure that the flows they create follow and comply with relevant regulations and standards (e.g., GDPR and HIPAA).

J. Testing

- Before rolling out the flows on production data or for production use, it is recommended to thoroughly test all the components of the flow.

- As a recommended best practice, developers and testing teams must test the individual components or actions of the flow in isolation and also test the entire flow end-to-end with realistic data.

- Developers can set up separate environments for development, testing, and production and deploy changes to production after thorough testing.

- Developers must ensure that they regularly check the run history and analytics to monitor flow performance and identify issues.

- It is recommended to use logging actions to capture detailed information about the flow's execution.

CHAPTER 8   WORKFLOW AUTOMATION USING POWER AUTOMATE

K. Documentation

- One of the most critical aspects of application development, solution design, or automation is clear and concise documentation of individual features and processes.

- Power Automate provides with the capability to add comments and notes on individual actions. It is a recommended best practice that developers leverage these features to explain complex logic and decisions.

- For end users, developers should keep in mind to educate on and maintain external documentation that provides an overview, usage instructions, and troubleshooting tips.

- It is a recommended best practice to keep track of different versions of your flows. Use meaningful version numbers and descriptions for other users to better understand the setup.

- Developers should also focus on periodically reviewing and optimizing flows based on performance data and user feedback.

In summary, adhering to best practices for creating flows in Power Automate ensures that your workflows are efficient, reliable, and maintainable. By planning meticulously, implementing robust error handling, optimizing data management, securing connections, and regularly testing and documenting your flows, you can create powerful automated processes that drive business efficiency and productivity.

CHAPTER 8   WORKFLOW AUTOMATION USING POWER AUTOMATE

Continuous monitoring and improvement further enhance the effectiveness of your workflows, allowing you to adapt to changing requirements and leverage new features in Power Automate.

Summary

Workflow automation using Power Automate has revolutionized how businesses manage and streamline their processes. Throughout this chapter, we have explored the essential aspects of designing, implementing, and optimizing workflows with Power Automate, focusing on its capacity to integrate various services, automate repetitive tasks, and enhance productivity.

Power Automate supports a wide range of connectors, allowing seamless integration with popular applications like SharePoint, Dynamics 365, Office 365, and various third-party services. This versatility enables businesses to create workflows that cater to diverse operational needs.

The intuitive, no-code/low-code interface of Power Automate empowers users with varying technical expertise to design and deploy workflows. This democratization of automation helps organizations to involve a broader range of employees in process optimization efforts.

Robust error handling and troubleshooting mechanisms are crucial for maintaining reliable workflows. Power Automate provides tools like "Configure run after," logging, and detailed run histories, which aid in diagnosing issues and ensuring smooth operations.

Adhering to best practices is essential for creating efficient and maintainable flows. This includes planning and designing workflows with clear objectives, modularizing complex flows, optimizing data management, ensuring security, and implementing thorough testing and validation.

The implementation of Power Automate has profound implications for businesses. By automating repetitive and time-consuming tasks, organizations can significantly reduce operational costs and free up human resources for more strategic activities. Automation also enhances process consistency and accuracy, leading to improved service delivery and customer satisfaction.

Furthermore, the ability to quickly adapt and modify workflows in response to changing business requirements provides a competitive edge. Businesses can remain agile and responsive in a dynamic market environment, continually refining their operations for better efficiency and effectiveness.

As Power Automate continues to evolve, we can anticipate even more powerful features and integrations. The future of workflow automation will likely see greater incorporation of AI and machine learning, enabling predictive and prescriptive automation. Businesses that invest in mastering Power Automate today will be well-positioned to leverage these advancements and maintain their competitive advantage.

In conclusion, workflow automation with Power Automate is not just a technical endeavor but a strategic initiative that transforms how businesses operate. By embracing this technology, organizations can achieve unprecedented levels of efficiency, accuracy, and agility. The journey of mastering Power Automate is ongoing, with continuous learning and adaptation being key to unlocking its full potential. As we move forward, the principles and practices discussed in this chapter will serve as a foundation for building robust, scalable, and impactful automated workflows.

CHAPTER 9

Integrating AI with Power Platform: AI Builder

The objective of this chapter is to equip readers with a comprehensive understanding of how AI Builder can be utilized to enhance business applications, streamline workflows, and drive operational efficiency. This chapter will provide practical insights into leveraging AI Builder's prebuilt and custom models within Power Platform tools such as Power Automate and Power Apps, demonstrating how AI capabilities can be seamlessly integrated to solve real-world business problems.

Key Learning Outcomes

1. **Understanding AI Builder**: Gain a foundational knowledge of AI Builder, its features, and its integration within the Power Platform.

2. **Exploring Pre-Built AI Models**: Learn about the various prebuilt AI models available in AI Builder and their applications in business scenarios.

3. **Creating Custom AI Models**: Discover how to build and train custom AI models using proprietary data to address specific business needs.

4. **Using Prompts Effectively**: Understand the concept of prompts, how to create them using the prompt builder, and their role in automating tasks.

5. **Using AI Models in Power Automate**: Learn how to integrate AI models into Power Automate workflows and Power Apps to enhance automation and decision-making.

6. **Using AI Models in Power Apps**: Explore how to embed AI models into Power Apps to create intelligent applications that leverage AI for enhanced functionality and user experience.

7. **Using AI Models in Copilot Studio**: Understand how to utilize AI capabilities in Copilot Studio to improve interaction and productivity within the development environment.

8. **Case Studies and Examples**: Review real-world case studies and examples that illustrate the successful implementation of AI Builder in various business contexts.

9. **Best Practices**: Identify best practices for deploying AI solutions using AI Builder, including data preparation, model training, and performance monitoring.

10. **Future Trends**: Explore the future trends in AI and how AI Builder is evolving to meet the growing demands of businesses.

By the end of this chapter, readers will be equipped with the knowledge and skills to effectively harness the power of AI Builder to transform their business applications, driving greater efficiency, accuracy, and innovation.

Introduction to AI Builder

The Power of AI in Business

Artificial Intelligence (AI) has rapidly transformed various industries, enabling businesses to automate processes, gain insights from data, and enhance customer experience.

AI Builder, a Microsoft Power Platform tool, democratizes AI, making it accessible to organizations of all sizes without requiring extensive programming skills or data science expertise. This chapter explores the foundational aspects of AI Builder and its significant impact on business operations.

The History of AI

Artificial Intelligence (AI) has a rich and fascinating history, tracing its origins back to ancient times when humans first dreamed of creating intelligent machines. Here's a detailed look at the history of AI.

Ancient Times to Early Modern Period

- **Mythology and Fiction**: Concepts of artificial beings and mechanical men appeared in ancient Greek myths, such as the story of Pygmalion and Galatea, and in early science fiction works like Mary Shelley's "Frankenstein."

Twentieth-Century Beginnings

- **1920s:** The term "robot" was introduced by Czech writer Karel Čapek in his play "R.U.R." (Rossum's Universal Robots), envisioning mechanical beings with human-like intelligence.

- **1940s and 1950s:**

    - **Turing Test:** In 1950, British mathematician and logician Alan Turing proposed the Turing Test to determine if a machine could exhibit intelligent behavior indistinguishable from that of a human.

    - **Foundational Work:** Warren McCulloch and Walter Pitts created the first conceptual model of artificial neurons in 1943, laying the groundwork for neural networks.

The Birth of AI as a Field

- **1956: Dartmouth Conference:** The term "artificial intelligence" was coined during the Dartmouth Conference, organized by John McCarthy, Marvin Minsky, Nathaniel Rochester, and Claude Shannon. This event is considered the birth of AI as an academic discipline.

- **Early AI Programs**

    - **Logic Theorist (1956):** Created by Allen Newell and Herbert A. Simon, this program proved mathematical theorems.

- **General Problem Solver (1957)**: Another program by Newell and Simon aimed to mimic human problem-solving.

The Rise and Fall of AI (1950s–1970s)

- **Optimism and Early Successes**: Initial successes in AI led to high optimism, with researchers believing that human-level intelligence was just around the corner.
- **Challenges and AI Winters**: By the late 1960s and 1970s, AI research faced significant challenges due to limitations in computing power and overly ambitious goals. This led to periods of reduced funding and interest, known as "AI winters."

Revival and Modern AI (1980s–Present)

- **Expert Systems (1980s)**: AI saw a resurgence with the development of expert systems, which used rule-based systems to mimic human expertise in specific domains.
- **Machine Learning (1990s–2000s)**
  - **Data and Algorithms**: The availability of large datasets and advances in algorithms, such as decision trees, support vector machines, and early neural networks, revitalized AI research.
  - **IBM's Deep Blue**: In 1997, IBM's Deep Blue defeated world chess champion Garry Kasparov, showcasing the potential of AI in complex problem-solving.

- **Deep Learning and AI Boom (2010s–Present)**

    ◦ **Deep Learning**: Advances in deep learning, a subset of machine learning, have driven the current AI boom. Techniques like convolutional neural networks (CNNs) and recurrent neural networks (RNNs) have achieved significant breakthroughs in image and speech recognition.

- **Notable Achievements**

    ◦ **AlphaGo**: In 2016, DeepMind's AlphaGo defeated Go champion Lee Sedol, demonstrating AI's capabilities in mastering complex games.

    ◦ **GPT-3**: OpenAI's GPT-3, released in 2020, showcased the power of large-scale language models in generating human-like text.

Current and Future Trends

- **AI Integration**: AI is now integrated into various industries, including healthcare, finance, retail, and autonomous vehicles.

- **Ethics and Regulation**: As AI becomes more prevalent, ethical considerations and regulations around AI's use, bias, and impact on employment are gaining importance.

- **General AI**: The quest for artificial general intelligence (AGI), where machines possess human-like cognitive abilities, remains a long-term goal for researchers.

Key Milestones in AI History

- **1950**: Alan Turing proposes the Turing Test.
- **1956**: Dartmouth Conference establishes AI as a field.
- **1966**: ELIZA, an early natural language-processing program, is developed.
- **1970s**: The first AI winter due to unmet expectations and funding cuts.
- **1980s**: Rise of expert systems and the second AI winter.
- **1997**: IBM's Deep Blue defeats Garry Kasparov.
- **2011**: IBM Watson wins "Jeopardy!" against human champions.
- **2016**: DeepMind's AlphaGo defeats Go champion Lee Sedol.
- **2023 +** : Generative AI and Copilots.

Understanding AI Builder

AI Builder is a powerful tool within the Microsoft Power Platform suite that allows users to add AI capabilities to their apps and workflows without writing code. It leverages prebuilt and customizable AI models to solve common business problems such as object detection, form processing, text recognition, and prediction.

Figure 9-1 demonstrates the AI Builder home page.

CHAPTER 9   INTEGRATING AI WITH POWER PLATFORM: AI BUILDER

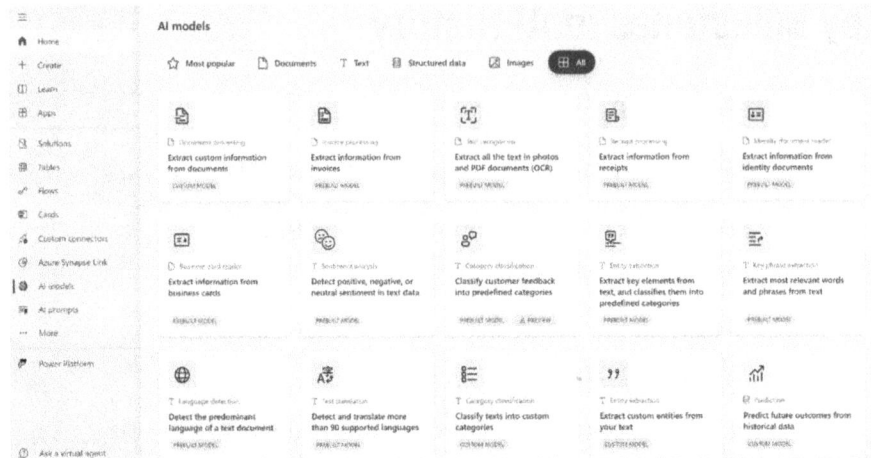

Figure 9-1. AI Builder home page screenshot

Transformative Impact on Business Processes

Automation of Routine Tasks: AI Builder automates repetitive and mundane tasks, freeing employees to focus on more strategic activities. For example, it can automate data entry by extracting information from documents and forms.

>**Improved Decision-Making**: By providing predictive analytics and insights, AI Builder helps businesses make informed decisions. For instance, it can analyze historical sales data to forecast future trends.
>
>**Enhanced Customer Experience**: AI Builder enables personalized customer interactions through features like sentiment analysis and language detection, allowing businesses to tailor their services to individual needs.

Increased Efficiency: AI Builder's capabilities streamline processes, reduce errors, and improve overall efficiency. For example, its object detection feature can be used in quality control processes to identify defects in products.

Examples of Few Real-World Applications

Finance: Automating invoice processing and extracting key data points for faster approvals.

Retail: Enhancing inventory management through object detection and predictive modeling.

Healthcare: Streamlining patient data entry and processing medical forms.

Customer Service: Analyzing customer feedback and sentiment to improve service quality.

Role of AI in the Power Platform

The Microsoft Power Platform is a suite of tools that empower organizations to build custom apps, automate workflows, and analyze data. AI Builder enhances the capabilities of the Power Platform by adding AI-driven insights and automation. This chapter delves into how AI Builder integrates with the Power Platform to provide comprehensive business solutions.

AI Builder Key Features

Custom AI Models: Users can create custom AI models tailored to their specific business needs using AI Builder's guided interface.

Prebuilt AI Models: AI Builder offers prebuilt models for common scenarios such as text classification, object detection, and form processing, which can be easily integrated into the Power Platform.

Model Training and Deployment: AI Builder simplifies the process of training, testing, and deploying AI models, ensuring they are accurate and reliable.

Use Cases

1. **Automated Document Processing**: Using AI Builder with Power Automate to extract data from invoices and update records in a Power Apps database.

2. **Predictive Maintenance**: Integrating AI Builder with Power Apps to predict equipment failures based on sensor data and schedule maintenance activities.

3. **Customer Feedback Analysis**: Combining AI Builder with Power BI to analyze customer reviews and sentiment, providing actionable insights for improving products and services.

4. **Unified Platform**: AI Builder's seamless integration with the Power Platform provides a unified environment for building, deploying, and managing AI solutions.

5. **Enhanced Capabilities**: By leveraging AI Builder, businesses can enhance their existing Power Platform solutions with advanced AI features, driving greater value and efficiency.

6. **Scalability and Flexibility**: AI Builder's models are scalable and can be customized to fit various business scenarios, making it a flexible tool for different industries.

AI Builder vs. Azure AI Studio: Key Differences

Both AI Builder and Azure AI Studio are powerful AI tools offered by Microsoft, each tailored to different user needs and functionalities. Here's a detailed comparison to understand their distinct features.

Target Audience and Usability

AI Builder

AI Builder is designed for business users, citizen developers, and makers who may not possess deep technical expertise. It offers a user-friendly, low-code/no-code interface integrated with the Power Platform. This integration makes it accessible for nontechnical users to easily create and deploy AI models, facilitating rapid implementation and iteration.

Azure AI Studio

Azure AI Studio which is not part of Power Platform but available as Azure services caters to data scientists, developers, and AI professionals with a technical background. It provides a more complex and customizable environment for building, training, and deploying sophisticated AI models. Azure AI Studio offers advanced tools and services that require a higher level of technical knowledge, allowing for greater flexibility and control over AI development processes.

Functionality and Features

AI Builder

AI Builder focuses on simplicity and ease of use, offering prebuilt AI models for common business scenarios such as text recognition, sentiment analysis, and document processing. Users can also create custom AI models using a guided no-code/low-code wizard. Its integration with Power Apps, Power Automate, and Copilot Studio enhances automation and decision-making in business processes.

Azure AI Studio

Azure AI Studio provides a comprehensive suite of tools for end-to-end AI development. It supports advanced functionalities such as custom model creation, model training, and deployment using machine learning frameworks like TensorFlow and PyTorch. Azure AI Studio also offers robust capabilities for data preprocessing, feature engineering, and model evaluation, making it ideal for complex AI projects.

Integration and Ecosystem

AI Builder

AI Builder seamlessly integrates with the Microsoft Power Platform, enabling users to incorporate AI capabilities into Power Apps, Power Automate, and other Microsoft services. This integration streamlines the development of intelligent applications and workflows without requiring extensive coding knowledge.

Azure AI Studio

Azure AI Studio integrates deeply with the Azure ecosystem, providing access to a wide range of Azure services, including Azure Machine Learning, Azure Databricks, and Azure Synapse Analytics. This integration allows for scalable and secure AI model deployment, leveraging Azure's cloud infrastructure and services for comprehensive data management and analytics.

Customization and Control

AI Builder

AI Builder offers a straightforward approach to AI, focusing on prebuilt models and easy customization through a guided interface. While it provides sufficient flexibility for many business applications, it may not offer the same level of granular control and customization as Azure AI Studio.

Azure AI Studio:

Azure AI Studio excels in offering extensive customization and control over the AI development process. Users can fine-tune models, implement custom algorithms, and manage the entire machine learning lifecycle. This level of control is ideal for advanced users looking to develop highly specialized and optimized AI solutions.

AI Builder and Azure AI Studio serve different purposes within the Microsoft AI ecosystem. AI Builder is perfect for business users and citizen developers seeking to integrate AI into their applications with minimal coding effort, while Azure AI Studio is tailored for technical professionals who require a sophisticated and customizable environment for advanced AI development. Together, they provide a comprehensive suite of AI tools that cater to a wide range of user needs and expertise levels.

Introduction to Prompt Engineering

Prompt engineering is the process of crafting inputs, or "prompts," to interact effectively with AI models like GPT-4 Turbo. The goal is to get the desired output by providing clear and structured prompts. Prompt engineering is essential for leveraging AI capabilities in various applications, from natural language processing to creative tasks.

Key Elements of a Prompt

1. **Instruction**: Clearly state what you want the model to do. It can be a question, a command, or a request.

2. **Context**: Provide any necessary background information to help the model understand the task. This can include examples, definitions, or specific details relevant to the prompt.

3. **Input Data**: Include any data or text that the model needs to process. This could be a list, a paragraph, or structured data like JSON.

4. **Output Format**: Specify the desired format of the output. This could be a bullet-point list, a paragraph, code, or a specific structure like a table.

5. **Constraints or Rules**: Set any limitations or rules the model should follow. This could be word limits, style guidelines, or content restrictions.

Types of Prompts

Prompt Engineering Method	Description	Example
Zero-Shot Learning	Involves giving the AI a task without any prior examples. You describe what you want in detail, assuming the AI has no prior knowledge of the task.	**Prompt:** "What are the environmental impacts of deforestation?"
One-Shot Learning	You provide one example along with your prompt. This helps the AI understand the context or format you're expecting.	**Prompt:** "A solar eclipse occurs when the moon passes between the Earth and the sun, casting a shadow on Earth. Explain how a lunar eclipse occurs."
Few-Shot Learning	Involves providing a few examples (usually 2–5) to help the AI understand the pattern or style of the response you're looking for.	**Prompt:** "Newton's laws of motion describe the relationship between a body and the forces acting upon it. How do Einstein's theories of relativity build on or differ from Newton's work?"
Chain-of-Thought Prompting	Here, you ask the AI to detail its thought process step-by-step. This is particularly useful for complex reasoning tasks.	**Prompt:** "Describe the steps involved in the scientific method, from forming a hypothesis to drawing a conclusion."

Best Practices of Prompt Engineering

Prompt engineering involves crafting effective prompts to guide AI models in generating the desired responses. Here are some best practices for good prompt engineering:

1. Clarity and Specificity

   Be Clear and Specific: Clearly define the task or question in the prompt. Avoid ambiguity to ensure the model understands exactly what is expected.

   Use Explicit Instructions: Provide explicit instructions or constraints to guide the model's response. For example, specify the format or length of the response if needed.

2. Context Provision

   Provide Relevant Context: Include necessary context or background information in the prompt to help the model generate accurate and relevant responses.

   Use Data Augmentation: Leverage external data or context through Data Retrieval Augmented Generation (RAG) to enhance the model's knowledge and response accuracy.

3. Iteration and Refinement

   Iterate and Refine Prompts: Continuously test and refine prompts based on the responses generated. Make adjustments to improve clarity, specificity, and relevance.

Experiment with Variations: Try different phrasings and structures to see what works best for the given task.

4. Balance and Neutrality

    Maintain Balance: Avoid overly complex or overly simplistic prompts. Strive for a balance that provides enough guidance without being restrictive.

    Ensure Neutrality: Craft prompts that are neutral and unbiased to avoid influencing the model's response in unintended ways.

5. Incorporate Examples

    Provide Examples: Include examples in the prompt to illustrate the desired type of response. Examples help the model understand the expected output.

    Use Few-Shot Learning: Provide a few examples (few-shot learning) to guide the model in generating responses that align with your requirements.

6. Consistency

    Maintain Consistency: Ensure consistency in the wording and structure of prompts, especially when used in a series of related tasks or questions.

    Standardize Prompts: Develop standardized prompts for common tasks to ensure uniformity and reliability in responses.

7. Feedback and Adaptation

    Gather Feedback: Collect feedback on the generated responses to understand how well the prompt is working and identify areas for improvement.

    Adapt to Changes: Be flexible and adapt prompts as the task or context evolves. Regular updates can help maintain prompt effectiveness.

8. Testing and Validation

    Thorough Testing: Rigorously test prompts across different scenarios to ensure they work well under various conditions.

    Validate Responses: Validate the responses generated by the model to ensure they meet the expected standards and requirements.

By following these best practices, you can craft effective prompts that guide AI models to generate accurate, relevant, and high-quality responses tailored to your specific needs.

AI Builder Prompts

AI Builder is a feature within Microsoft's Power Platform that allows users to easily add AI capabilities to their apps and workflows. Prompts play a crucial role in AI Builder by guiding the AI models to perform specific tasks effectively. Here's how prompts are useful in AI Builder:

1. **Guiding AI Models:** Prompts help define what you want the AI to do, whether it's processing text, recognizing images, predicting outcomes, or automating workflows.

2. **Customizing Outputs**: By crafting specific prompts, users can tailor the AI's output to meet their unique requirements, making the solutions more relevant and useful.

3. **Simplifying Complex Tasks**: Prompts can break down complex AI tasks into simpler instructions, making it easier for users to implement AI without deep technical knowledge.

4. **Enhancing Accuracy**: Clear and detailed prompts help improve the accuracy of AI models by reducing ambiguity and providing context.

5. **Improving Efficiency**: Well-crafted prompts can save time by reducing the need for multiple iterations and refinements, leading to quicker and more effective solutions.

Using Prompts for Automation

Prompts can be integrated into flows to build intelligent hands-off automation. Makers can also build advanced generative AI capabilities for their applications by describing them as natural language prompts. These prompts can also be used to extend Copilot action and topics, thereby streamlining your daily business operations and boosting efficiency.

Prerequisites

To use AI builder prompts in Power Platform, ensure you have the following:

- An environment in a region where prompts are available https://learn.microsoft.com/en-us/ai-builder/availability-region.

- You have a Power Apps or Power Automate license.

- A Dataverse database installed on the environment.

- An AI Builder add-on.

Prebuilt AI Prompts

The Power Platform empowers makers with prebuilt prompts for common business scenarios such as summarizing, classifying, extracting entities, translating, assessing sentiment, or drafting replies. These prebuilt prompts allow you to generate AI-driven responses without the need to manually create a prompt. Instead of specifying both the prompt and the text to process, you can simply provide the text you want to analyze, and the AI generates the desired output.

Available Prebuilt Prompts

- **AISummarize**: Generates concise summaries from larger texts.

- **AISentiment**: Analyzes and determines the sentiment of a given text.

- **AIReply**: Drafts automated replies based on the context of the input text.

CHAPTER 9   INTEGRATING AI WITH POWER PLATFORM: AI BUILDER

- **AITranslate**: Translates text from one language to another.

- **AIClassify**: Categorizes text into predefined categories.

- **AIExtract**: Extracts specific entities or data points from text.

Figure 9-2 shows prebuilt prompts available in AI Builder.

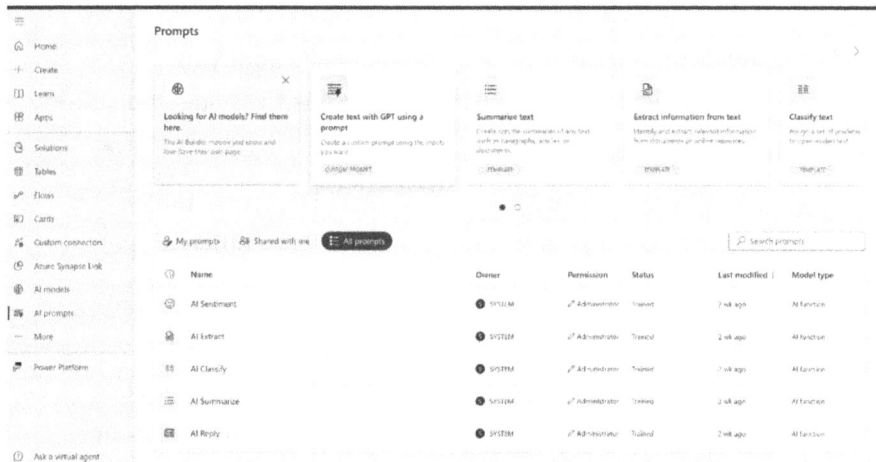

Figure 9-2. *AI Builder prompts*

By leveraging these prebuilt prompts, makers can streamline their workflows and enhance their business applications with powerful AI capabilities.

Custom Prompts

The Prompt Builder in AI Builder used to create custom prompts, allowing makers to instruct the GPT model to behave in a certain way or perform a specific task. By carefully crafting prompts, you can generate responses tailored to your specific business needs. This transforms the GPT model into a versatile tool capable of accomplishing various tasks.

Key Features

- **Generative AI Customization**: Custom prompts enable the creation of specific instructions for AI models, allowing them to perform tasks or generate responses suited to unique business requirements.

- **Data Retrieval Augmented Generation (RAG)**: This feature allows the integration of external data into the AI model's responses, enhancing its ability to provide accurate answers based on business-specific information.

- **Data Integration**: Makers can select Dataverse tables to provide contextual data, which the generative model uses to improve its responses.

- **Data Filtering**: Users can filter data from selected tables, refining the information used by the AI model. Filters can be set using free-form text, prompt inputs, or predefined choices and option sets.

- **Data References**: Multiple data and related table references can be inserted into prompts, enabling the AI to use comprehensive and relevant information from various sources.

How to Use Prompt Builder

Think of a prompt as a task or a goal you give to the large language model (LLM). With the prompt builder, you can build, test, and save your custom prompts. You can also use input variables and Dataverse data to provide dynamic context data at runtime. You can share these prompts with others and use them in Power Automate, Power Apps, or Copilot Studio.

For instance, you could make a prompt to pick out action items from your company emails and use it in a Power Automate flow to build an email-processing automation.

Features of Prompt Builder

1. **Custom Prompt Creation**: Enables makers to devise custom prompts that cater to their specific business needs using natural language.

2. **Dynamic Context**: Use input variables and Dataverse data to provide dynamic context data at runtime.

3. **Integration**: Prompts can be shared and used in Power Automate, Power Apps, or Copilot Studio.

4. **Task Variety**: Prompts can be employed for many tasks or business scenarios, such as

   - Summarizing content
   - Categorizing data
   - Extracting entities
   - Translating languages
   - Assessing sentiment
   - Formulating responses to complaints

Create a GPT Prompt

Prompt builder provides the flexibility to create your own custom prompt by defining input variables that enable incorporating dynamic runtime content within a prompt. It gives you the ability to validate the prompt with **Test your prompt**, ensuring optimal prompt performance and correctness of the response before integration into your business solutions.

CHAPTER 9 INTEGRATING AI WITH POWER PLATFORM: AI BUILDER

1. Sign in to Power Apps, Power Automate, or Copilot Studio.

2. On the left pane, select **AI prompts** or **Prompts ➤ Create text with GPT using a prompt**.

    a. For Power Apps and Power Automate, first select **AI hub** on the left pane.

3. On the lower-right corner, select **Create custom prompt**.

Figure 9-3 demonstrates how to create a custom prompt in AI Builder.

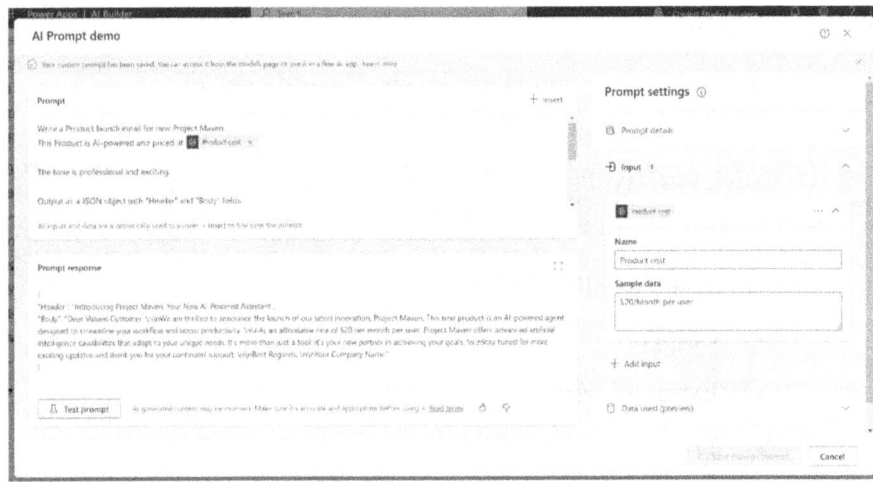

Figure 9-3. Demo of a custom prompt

Use Your Own Data in a Prompt

Custom prompts enable makers to utilize generative AI models for various content generation scenarios. These models leverage their built-in knowledge from training data to provide answers. However, this built-in knowledge may not be sufficient for use cases that require specific business data context.

CHAPTER 9   INTEGRATING AI WITH POWER PLATFORM: AI BUILDER

This is where Data Retrieval Augmented Generation (RAG) comes in, allowing you to augment the model's knowledge with external information to get the precise answers you need.

Add Data and Filter

Makers can use the "Data used" option to select a Dataverse table. The fields from the active view of this table are utilized by the generative model to enhance its knowledge when responding based on the custom prompt defined and inputs provided.

Figure 9-4 shows the screenshot of how to select a Dataverse table as data to be used in the prompt builder.

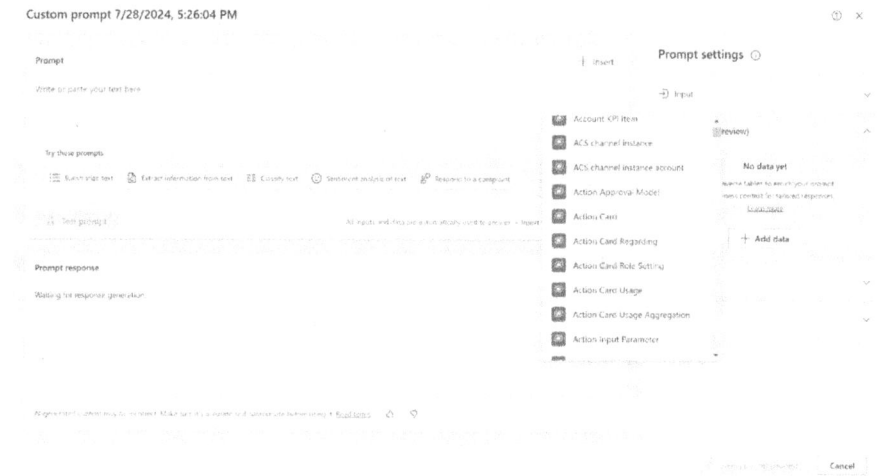

Figure 9-4. *Add Dataverse tables for data grounding*

You can filter the retrieved data by expanding the table and selecting the desired field and filter value. The filter value can be free-form text, an input for the prompt, or a named value when filtering on a choice or option set.

CHAPTER 9 INTEGRATING AI WITH POWER PLATFORM: AI BUILDER

Summary

Custom prompts in AI Builder empower makers to leverage generative AI models for tailored content generation scenarios. These models use their built-in training data to generate responses, but for specific business needs, additional context is often required.

AI Builder Models

AI Builder is a powerful feature within the Microsoft Power Platform that enables businesses to harness the capabilities of artificial intelligence without requiring deep technical expertise. It offers a variety of prebuilt and custom AI models that can be integrated into workflows and applications, enhancing automation and decision-making processes.

In AI Builder, prebuilt AI models are ready-to-use solutions designed for common business scenarios. They do not require any training or configuration, allowing users to quickly deploy AI capabilities such as text recognition, sentiment analysis, and invoice processing. These models are ideal for users looking for immediate and straightforward AI integration without the need for customization.

On the other hand, custom AI models in AI Builder are tailored solutions that require training with your proprietary data. These models are designed to meet specific business needs and can be customized for unique tasks like custom document processing, entity extraction, or object detection. While they require more effort to set up and train, custom models offer greater flexibility and precision by leveraging data that is specific to your organization's context and requirements.

Below is a table that categorizes the available AI models by data type, along with their descriptions and AI template mappings.

Data Type	Model Type	AI Template	Build Type	Description
Documents	Business Card Reader	BusinessCard	Prebuilt	Extracts contact information from business cards for automating contact lists.
	Document Processing	DocumentScanning, Document LayoutAnalysis	Custom	Extracts custom information from documents tailored to specific business needs.
	Text Recognition	TextRecognition	Prebuilt	Recognizes and extracts text from images like printed documents or notes.
	Receipt Processing	ReceiptScanning	Prebuilt	Extracts data from receipts to simplify expense report automation.
	Invoice Processing	InvoiceProcessing	Prebuilt	Extracts information from invoices to automate accounts payable processes.

(*continued*)

Data Type	Model Type	AI Template	Build Type	Description
	ID Reader	IdentityDocument	Prebuilt	Extracts information from identity documents such as passports and licenses.
Text	Text Generation (Preview)	GptPowerPrompt, GptPrompt Engineering (Preview)	Prebuilt	Generates text based on input prompts for content creation and other tasks.
	Category Classification	TextClassificationV2	Prebuilt (Preview) and Custom	Classifies text into predefined or custom categories.
	Entity Extraction	EntityExtraction	Prebuilt and Custom	Identifies and extracts specific data points or entities from text.
	Key Phrase Extraction	KeyPhrase Extraction	Prebuilt	Identifies and extracts significant phrases from text.
	Language Detection	LanguageDetection	Prebuilt	Detects the language of a given text to route it appropriately.
	Sentiment Analysis	SentimentAnalysis	Prebuilt	Analyzes text to determine sentiment (positive, negative, and neutral).

(continued)

CHAPTER 9 INTEGRATING AI WITH POWER PLATFORM: AI BUILDER

Data Type	Model Type	AI Template	Build Type	Description
	Text Translation	TextTranslation	Prebuilt	Translates text from one language to another for better communication.
Structured Data	Prediction	BinaryPrediction, GenericPrediction	Custom	Uses historical data to predict future outcomes or trends.
Images	Object Detection	ObjectDetection, ObjectDetection Proposal	Custom	Identifies and locates specific objects within images for inventory management.
	Image Description	ImageDescription	Prebuilt (Preview)	Generates descriptions for images to aid in content management and accessibility.
	Text Recognition	TextRecognition	Prebuilt	Recognizes and extracts text from images for digitizing physical documents.
Preview Versions	Copilot (Preview)	CopilotSidePane Predict	Prebuilt (Preview)	Provides AI assistance in applications using Copilot side pane predictions.

This table summarizes various AI models available in AI Builder, including their types, templates, and descriptions, highlighting their applications in business processes.

CHAPTER 9 INTEGRATING AI WITH POWER PLATFORM: AI BUILDER

Prebuilt AI Models

These models are ready-to-use and designed to handle common business tasks, making it easy to incorporate AI into your processes.

Prebuilt AI models are ready to use out of the box and don't require any training.

You can invoke them directly from Power Automate or Power Apps to build intelligent apps and workflows.

For example: Sentiment analysis

Figure 9-5 shows the sentiment analysis prebuilt model.

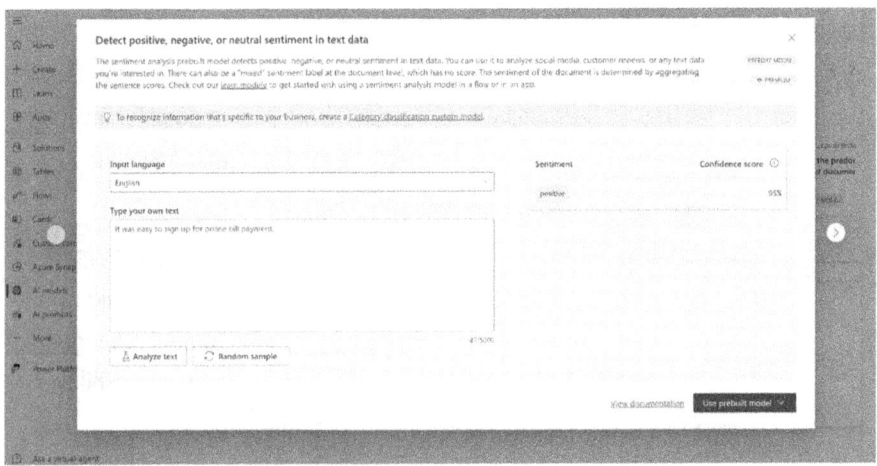

Figure 9-5. *Demonstration of the prebuilt AI model*

Below are the list of prebuilt models available in AI Builder.

> **Business Card Reader**: Pull contact information from business cards and import it into your CRM system.
>
> **Sentiment Analysis**: Detect positive, negative, neutral, and mixed sentiments in social media, customer reviews, or any text data.

Key Phrase Extraction: Extract the main points and key phrases in text documents.

Language Detection: Use this model to identify the predominant language of a text document.

Text Recognition: Extract printed and handwritten text from documents and images into machine-readable character streams.

Entity Extraction: Extract entities and their types from text.

Category Classification: Categorize customer feedback text by its meaning.

Invoice Processing: Save time on your expenses. Use AI to extract and save receipt data automatically.

Translation: Translate your text data across more than 60 languages.

Identity Document Reader: Extract information from passports and US driver licenses.

Custom AI Models

Custom AI models allow businesses to train AI models using their proprietary data to address unique business needs. These models provide flexibility and specificity, ensuring that AI capabilities align closely with organizational requirements.

Custom AI models in AI Builder are tailored solutions designed to meet unique business needs by leveraging the organization's proprietary data. The process of creating these models involves training them with historical data specific to the task at hand. This enables the model to learn and understand the nuances of the data it will be working with, making it highly effective for specialized tasks.

The training process is facilitated by a no-code wizard, which guides users step-by-step through the setup, ensuring that even those without extensive technical expertise can build and deploy custom AI models. This user-friendly approach democratizes AI, allowing businesses to harness advanced machine learning capabilities without the need for in-depth coding knowledge.

For instance, a company can train a custom AI model to understand and process purchase orders based on a specific company template. This involves feeding the model historical purchase order data, teaching it to recognize relevant fields, and defining the logic for extracting and interpreting the information. Once trained, the model can accurately process new purchase orders, extracting the necessary data and streamlining the workflow.

The screenshot in Figure 9-6 shows how to create a custom model. Go to AI builder ➤ Models ➤ click "models supports custom model" (in this screen, it's Extract custom information from documents) ➤ click "Create Custom Model."

CHAPTER 9   INTEGRATING AI WITH POWER PLATFORM: AI BUILDER

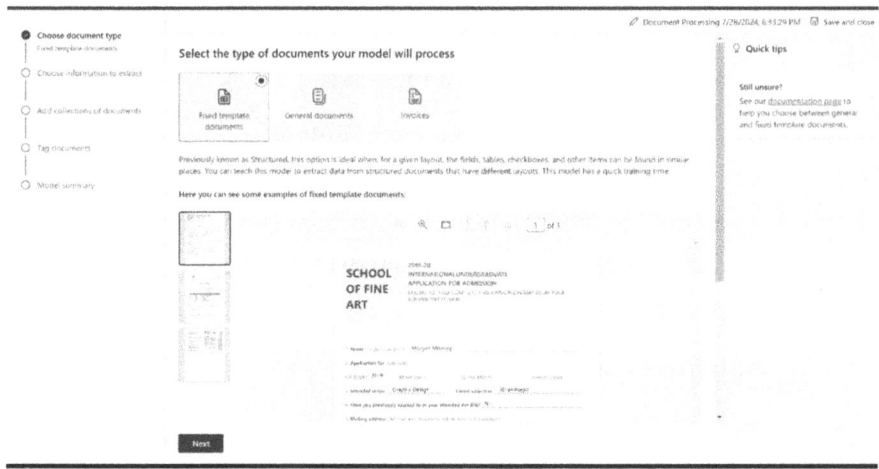

Figure 9-6. *Custom AI model*

The benefits of using custom AI models in AI Builder include improved accuracy and relevance of AI-driven tasks, as the models are fine-tuned to the specific context and requirements of the business. This leads to enhanced efficiency, reduced manual effort, and the ability to tackle complex scenarios that generic, prebuilt models might not handle as effectively.

Common Business Scenarios with AI Builder Models

AI Builder offers a range of AI models that enhance business processes without requiring extensive coding or data expertise. Here are some common business scenarios along with brief descriptions and the preferred AI model types for addressing them:

1. **Automate Customer Application Processing**

   a. **Model Type:** Document Processing

   b. **Description:** Streamline the handling of customer applications by automatically extracting relevant information from submitted documents, reducing manual data entry and processing time.

2. **Automate Expense Reports**

   a. **Model Type:** Receipt Processing

   b. **Description:** Simplify the management of expense reports by automatically extracting details from receipts, such as date, amount, and merchant name, and populating expense forms.

3. **Categorize User Feedback Based on Their Focus**

   a. **Model Type:** Category Classification

   b. **Description:** Analyze and categorize user feedback into predefined categories, enabling better understanding of customer concerns and priorities.

4. **Extract Insights from Product Reviews**

   a. **Model Type:** Entity Extraction

   b. **Description:** Identify and extract key insights and entities (e.g., product features and sentiments) from product reviews to gain a deeper understanding of customer opinions.

5. **Identify Language of Text**

    a. **Model Type:** Language Detection

    b. **Description:** Automatically detect the language of incoming text, such as emails or support tickets, to route them to the appropriate language-specific team or tool.

6. **Identify and Classify Customer Feedback**

    a. **Model Type:** Sentiment Analysis

    b. **Description:** Determine the sentiment of customer feedback (positive, negative, and neutral) to quickly gauge customer satisfaction and identify areas for improvement.

7. **Translate Support Requests into Your Language**

    a. **Model Type:** Text Translation

    b. **Description:** Translate support requests or other text-based communications into your preferred language, facilitating better communication with customers from different linguistic backgrounds.

8. **Identify Fraudulent Transactions**

    a. **Model Type:** Prediction

    b. **Description:** Use historical data to predict and identify potentially fraudulent transactions, enhancing security and reducing financial risks.

9. **Get Alerted to Social Media Posts Referencing Your Brand**

   a. **Model Type:** Key Phrase Extraction

   b. **Description:** Monitor social media for posts mentioning your brand by extracting key phrases, allowing you to respond promptly to customer comments or concerns.

10. **Automate Contact List Management**

    a. **Model Type:** Business Card Reader

    b. **Description:** Automate the creation and updating of contact lists by extracting contact information from business cards, improving accuracy and efficiency.

11. **Automate Inventory Taking**

    a. **Model Type:** Object Detection

    b. **Description:** Use object detection to automate inventory management by identifying and counting items in stock, reducing manual inventory checks.

12. **Take a Photo of Text and Save It to a Database**

    a. **Model Type:** Text Recognition

    b. **Description:** Capture text from images (e.g., handwritten notes and printed documents) and save the recognized text to a database, facilitating digital record-keeping.

By leveraging these AI models, businesses can enhance efficiency, improve decision-making, and provide better customer experiences across various scenarios.

Summary

Custom AI models in AI Builder allow enterprises to leverage their proprietary data to create tailored AI solutions for document processing, text classification, entity extraction, prediction, object detection, and more. The prompt builder feature empowers users to create, test, and deploy custom prompts, integrating them seamlessly into Power Automate, Power Apps, and Copilot Studio to enhance automation and operational efficiency. By leveraging these capabilities, businesses can streamline processes, improve accuracy, and make data-driven decisions more effectively.

AI Builder Architecture and Integration
Overview of AI Builder Architecture

AI Builder is a comprehensive AI solution within Microsoft Power Platform that allows users to create, train, and deploy machine learning models. It leverages Microsoft's Azure AI capabilities to provide a user-friendly, no-code/low-code environment for building and integrating AI models. The architecture of AI Builder can be broadly understood in terms of its core components and how it integrates with other Power Platform services.

Core Components of AI Builder

1. **Model Training and Deployment**

    - **Prebuilt Models**: These are ready-to-use AI models for common scenarios such as text recognition, sentiment analysis, and invoice processing.

    - **Custom Models**: Users can create custom AI models tailored to their specific business needs by training them with their proprietary data.

2. **Data Sources**

   - **Dataverse**: AI Builder utilizes Dataverse as the primary data storage and management solution, allowing seamless access to data across different Power Platform services.

3. **No-Code/Low-Code Environment**

   - **Model Builder Interface**: A user-friendly interface that guides users through the process of creating and training AI models without requiring coding expertise.

Figure 9-7 shows the architecture and integration of AI Builder in Power Platform ecosystem.

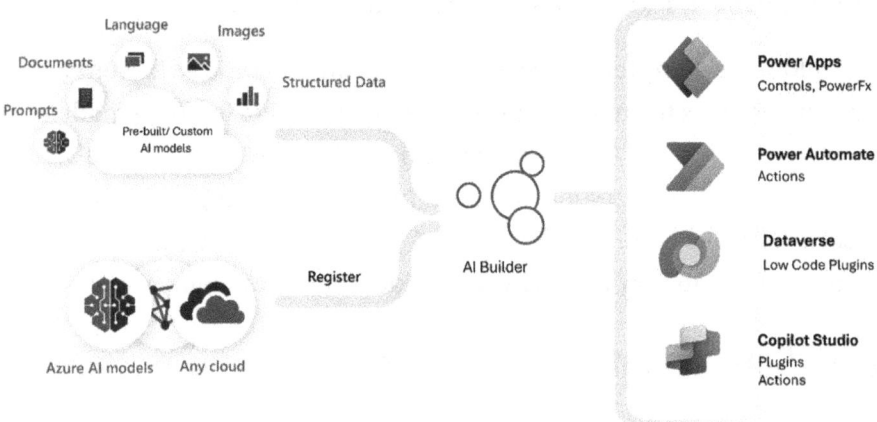

Figure 9-7. AI Builder integration architecture

Integration with Power Platform Services

AI Builder is tightly integrated with other Power Platform services, enhancing the overall capabilities of the platform and providing a unified environment for building intelligent applications and workflows.

AI Builder Integration in Power Automate

AI Builder models can be used in automated workflows. For example, a workflow can automatically process and categorize emails based on their content. Power Automate prompts in Power Automate are available as AI Builder actions, enabling you to automate complex workflows with ease.

> **AI Model Integration**: AI Builder models can be easily integrated into Power Automate workflows. For example, a sentiment analysis model can be used to automatically analyze customer feedback and trigger specific actions based on the results.
>
> **Automation**: Users can create automated workflows that leverage AI to perform tasks such as data extraction, categorization, and translation, thereby enhancing efficiency and reducing manual effort.

Add an AI Model As Action

1. Sign in to Power Automate (`https://flow.microsoft.com/`).

2. Select **My flows** in the left pane and then select **New flow ➤ Instant cloud flow**.

3. Name your flow, select **Manually trigger a flow** under **Choose how to trigger this flow**, and then select **Create**.

4. Expand **Manually trigger a flow**, and then select **+Add an input ➤ Text** as the input type.

CHAPTER 9 INTEGRATING AI WITH POWER PLATFORM: AI BUILDER

5. Replace the word **Input** with **My Text** (also known as the title).

6. Select **+ New step ➤ AI Builder**, and then select **one of your custom models** in the list of actions.

The screen in Figure 9-8 shows "**categorize text**" AI model to analyze incoming emails and route them accordingly.

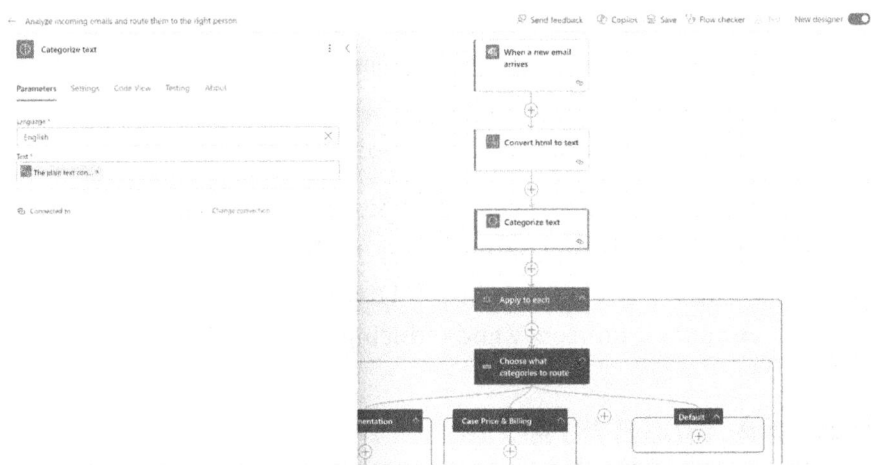

Figure 9-8. Integrating AI models in Power Automate

AI Builder Integration in Power App

AI Builder allows users to embed AI models directly into their apps. For instance, a field service app can use object detection to identify equipment issues on-site. In Power Apps, you can easily add prompts as AI models, similar to other AI models. By using Power Fx, you can invoke these custom prompts, bringing smart features into your business applications.

CHAPTER 9 INTEGRATING AI WITH POWER PLATFORM: AI BUILDER

Add an AI Model as a Data Source

The following example creates a simple app that answers a question entered in a text box:

1. Sign in to Power Apps (https://make.powerapps.com/).

2. On the left navigation pane, select **Apps**.

3. On the menu at the top, select **+ New app ➤ Canvas**.

4. Enter a name for the app and choose between **Tablet** and **Phone** for the format of the app.

5. Select **Create**.

6. On the list of icons to the left of the **Tree view**, select **Data ➤ Add data ➤ AI models**.

The screenshot in Figure 9-9 shows how to add AI model as a data source.

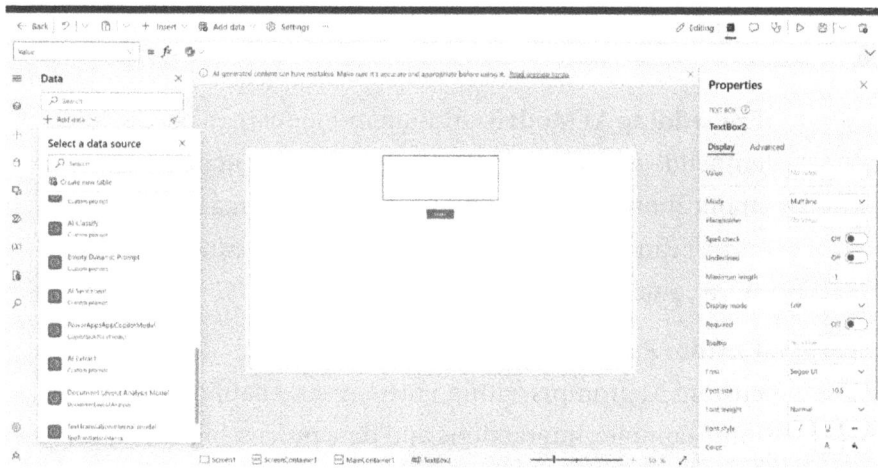

Figure 9-9. *Integrating AI models in Power Apps*

CHAPTER 9　INTEGRATING AI WITH POWER PLATFORM: AI BUILDER

For instance, below example code invoked on button click to summarize input given in the textbox.

Button ➤ OnSelect event

```
Set(TextCompletionResult, 'AI Summarize'.Predict(TextBox2.
Value));
```

Binding the result to a label is shown in the screenshot in Figure 9-10.

Figure 9-10. *Demo of AI models in Power Apps*

>**Embedding AI Models**: AI Builder models can be embedded into Power Apps to add intelligence to applications. For instance, a business card reader model can be incorporated into an app to scan and store contact information directly.
>
>**Custom Prompts**: Users can define and use custom AI prompts within Power Apps, enabling more complex interactions and data processing capabilities.

AI Builder Integration in Copilot Studio

AI Builder enhances chatbots by adding natural language processing capabilities, enabling more intelligent and context-aware conversations. Copilot Studio prompts can be saved as plugins to enhance your Copilot, much like adding new skills to a toolbox. These plugins, built with prompts, help extend your Copilot with additional functions and expertise.

> **Power Automate Action**: Custom AI prompts in Copilot Studio enable users to leverage generative AI models for various content generation tasks, enhancing the functionality of applications built within the platform.
>
> **Plugins Action**: Integration with Dataverse allows Copilot Studio to dynamically use data to provide contextually accurate responses, making interactions more relevant and personalized.

Steps to Create Power Automate Actions in Copilot Studio

Sign in to Copilot Studio (`https://copilotstudio.microsoft.com/`), select "Create" from the side navigation pane. Choose "New Copilot" and then Choose "Actions" ➤ Flows, as shown in Figure 9-11.

CHAPTER 9　INTEGRATING AI WITH POWER PLATFORM: AI BUILDER

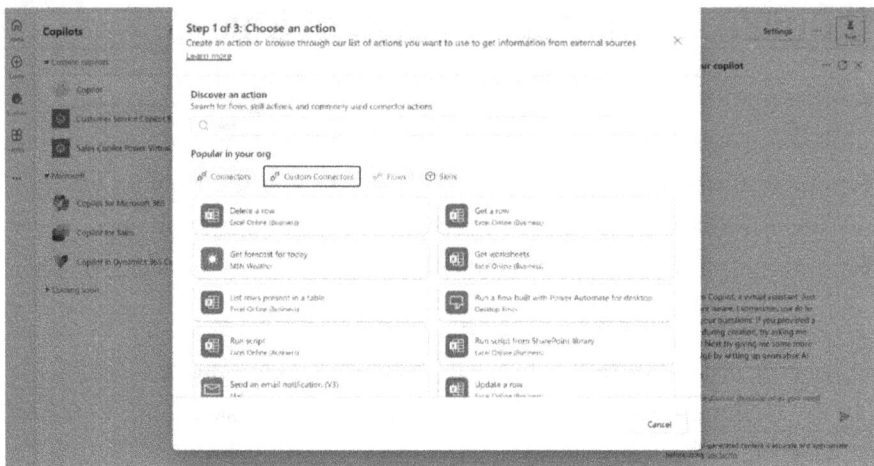

Figure 9-11. *Integrating AI models in Copilot Studio*

Steps to Create Prompt Actions in Copilot Studio

- Sign in to Copilot Studio (https://copilotstudio.microsoft.com/), select "Library" from the side navigation pane.

- Click "+ Add an item," choose a Microsoft Copilot to extend.

- Select "New action" for Copilot for Microsoft 365, choose "Prompt" from the "New action" menu, enter a name and description for your prompt, add input variables and sample data, define context data by adding input variables under "Prompt."

- Optionally add Dataverse tables as grounding data, test the prompt, review details by selecting "Finalize prompt," and save your prompt action by clicking "Create prompt action." as shown in Figure 9-12.

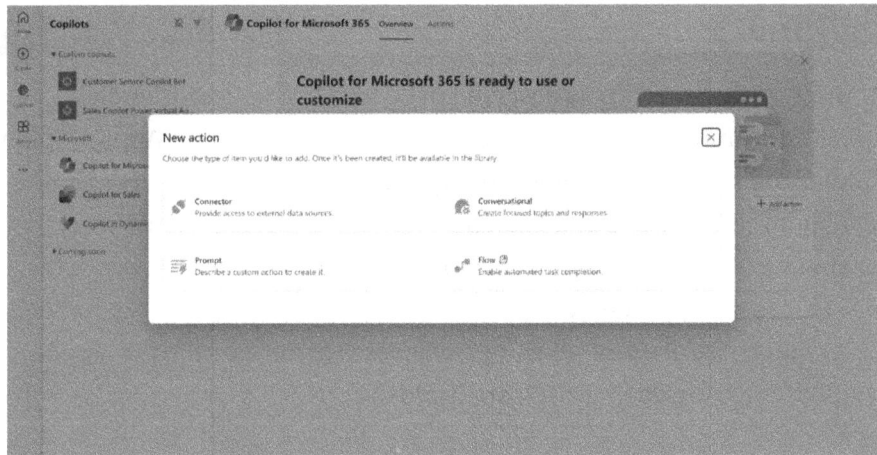

Figure 9-12. Integrating prompts as actions in Copilot Studio

AI Builder Integration in Dataverse Plugins

Low-code plugins in Dataverse allow makers and developers to extend the functionality of their applications without extensive coding. These plugins enable the integration of custom logic, automation, and complex workflows directly into Dataverse, leveraging its robust data management and storage capabilities.

> **Low-Code Plugins**: AI Builder supports the integration of prebuilt AI models into Dataverse low-code plugins, allowing users to enhance their data-driven applications with AI capabilities.
>
> **Data-Driven Insights**: By utilizing AI models within Dataverse plugins, users can extract insights and perform actions based on real-time data analysis, improving decision-making processes.

Summary

AI Builder's architecture is designed to be robust and user-friendly, enabling seamless integration with Power Automate, Power Apps, Copilot Studio, and Dataverse plugins. This integration empowers users to build intelligent applications and automate workflows with AI capabilities, leveraging the extensive data management and processing power of the Power Platform. The no-code/low-code approach ensures accessibility for a wide range of users, allowing businesses to harness the power of AI without requiring deep technical expertise.

Security and Governance

AI Builder, integrated within the Microsoft Power Platform, provides a comprehensive framework for security and governance. This includes leveraging Microsoft Dataverse for application lifecycle, storage, and security capabilities.

Overview

AI Builder relies on Dataverse to handle security, data storage, and application lifecycle management. When AI models are created, they utilize Azure infrastructure, but the data required for training the models stays within the environment's geography and is deleted after the model is created, ensuring data privacy and security.

Personas and Roles

There are distinct personas and roles in AI Builder, each with specific permissions and capabilities:

1. **Maker**: Involved in building and deploying models and applications.

2. **Model Owner**: Builds and owns the AI models.

3. **App/Flow Builder**: Uses models to build Power Apps or Power Automate flows.

4. **Business User**: Uses the applications or flows that include AI models and consumes the predictions generated by these models.

Data Security and Privacy

AI Builder supports real-time and batch predictions. In real-time prediction scenarios, the input and output data are not persisted in Dataverse, enhancing data privacy. Batch predictions, which process rows of data tables, only require access to view the predicted data without needing model access.

Model Accessibility and Permissions

By default, AI models are only accessible to their creators. To share models with other users, explicit sharing actions must be taken. AI Builder uses several Dataverse tables to store model configurations and training data, with specific permissions set for each table to control access. For instance:

1. **AI Builder Dataset**: Stores model training configurations.

2. **AI Builder Dataset File**: Contains training files.

3. **AI Configuration**: Holds model versions.

These tables ensure that only authorized users have access to specific data, maintaining data security and integrity.

Roles and Permissions Mapping

AI Builder permissions are mapped to standard Dataverse roles:

1. **System Administrator**: Full access to all AI Builder features.

2. **System Customizer**: Can create and modify models but may have limited access to some features.

3. **Environment Maker**: Limited to creating and using models within their own environment.

4. **Dataverse User**: Basic access to use shared models.

These roles ensure that users have the appropriate level of access based on their responsibilities.

Data Loss Prevention (DLP)

DLP policies in the Power Platform admin center allow administrators to categorize connectors into Business, Non-Business, and Blocked categories. This prevents data from being shared between Business and Non-Business connectors, enhancing data security. For example, if Dataverse is categorized as Business and Outlook as Non-Business, data from AI Builder cannot be sent to Outlook.

Model Lifecycle Management

AI models go through various states, from draft to published. This lifecycle is managed within the Dataverse environment, ensuring that models are only deployed once they meet the necessary criteria for production use. Key states include:

Draft: Initial state when a model is created.

Training: Transient state during model training.

Trained: Model is trained but not yet deployed.

Published: Model is live and can be used in applications.

Models are managed through solutions in Power Platform, allowing for controlled deployment across different environments, such as Development, Testing, and Production.

Capacity Management

AI Builder uses a subscription model for capacity management, where credits are allocated to environments. Administrators can allocate these credits based on the expected usage, ensuring efficient resource management. Consumption reports help administrators monitor and adjust credit allocation as needed.

Monitoring and Compliance

Administrators can monitor AI Builder usage and manage licensing through the Power Platform admin center. This includes tracking credit consumption and ensuring compliance with organizational policies.

By implementing these security and governance practices, AI Builder ensures that AI models are managed securely, data privacy is maintained, and organizational compliance requirements are met.

CHAPTER 9 INTEGRATING AI WITH POWER PLATFORM: AI BUILDER

Responsible AI

Responsible AI refers to the practice of developing and deploying artificial intelligence systems in a manner that is ethical, fair, and transparent. This approach ensures that AI technologies respect human rights, avoid bias, and contribute positively to society. Central to responsible AI is the commitment to transparency, where the functioning of AI systems is made clear to users and stakeholders, enabling them to understand how decisions are made.

Fairness is another critical aspect, as it involves ensuring that AI systems do not perpetuate or amplify existing biases or inequalities. This requires rigorous testing and validation to identify and mitigate potential biases in data and algorithms. Privacy and security are also paramount in responsible AI, demanding robust measures to protect sensitive information and prevent unauthorized access.

Accountability is essential, meaning that developers, organizations, and stakeholders are held responsible for the outcomes of AI systems. This involves setting up mechanisms for oversight and establishing clear guidelines and standards for AI development and deployment. Inclusivity is a core principle, ensuring that AI technologies are accessible and beneficial to all segments of society, including marginalized and underrepresented groups.

In a nutshell, responsible AI emphasizes the importance of continual monitoring and evaluation to adapt to new challenges and ensure that AI systems remain aligned with ethical standards and societal values. By adhering to these principles, responsible AI seeks to build trust and promote the positive impact of artificial intelligence on society.

Summary

This chapter explores AI Builder within the Microsoft Power Platform, highlighting its architecture, capabilities, and integrations. AI Builder enables users to create, train, and deploy AI models using a no-code/low-code environment, making advanced AI accessible to a broad range of users. It offers both prebuilt and custom AI models that can be used for various tasks such as text recognition, sentiment analysis, document processing, and more.

The integration of AI Builder with Power Automate, Power Apps, and Copilot Studio enhances automation and decision-making processes. In Power Automate, AI models can be embedded in workflows to perform tasks like data extraction and translation. Power Apps allows for the incorporation of AI-driven functionalities, such as scanning business cards or analyzing feedback. Copilot Studio leverages custom prompts for generative AI, enabling dynamic and contextually accurate responses in applications.

The chapter delves into the architectural components of AI Builder, including its use of Dataverse for data management and storage. It explains how users can train custom models using their proprietary data and the role of the no-code wizard in simplifying this process. The chapter also touches on the ethical considerations and best practices of using AI responsibly, ensuring fairness, transparency, and accountability.

In summary, AI Builder in Power Platform empowers users to harness the power of AI without requiring deep technical expertise, enabling the creation of intelligent applications and automated workflows that drive efficiency and innovation.

CHAPTER 10

Solutions Overview and ALM Strategy

The goal of this chapter is to provide readers with a comprehensive understanding of solution architecture and Application Lifecycle Management (ALM) within the Power Platform. By the end of this chapter, readers should have a comprehensive understanding of ALM best practices, strategies, and a clear vision for implementing robust ALM processes in Power Platform projects.

Introduction to Application Lifecycle Management (ALM)

Application Lifecycle Management (ALM) is a structured approach to managing the entire lifespan of an application, from its initial conception through to its eventual retirement. It encompasses various disciplines and processes, aiming to enhance collaboration, improve efficiency, and ensure high-quality software delivery. ALM integrates governance, development, and maintenance activities to streamline software production and operations.

CHAPTER 10   SOLUTIONS OVERVIEW AND ALM STRATEGY

Key Areas of ALM

Governance

Requirement Management: Documenting, analyzing, and managing the needs and requirements of stakeholders

Resource Management: Efficient allocation and management of resources such as personnel, tools, and infrastructure

System Administration: Managing data security, user access, change tracking, review, audit, deployment control, and rollback mechanisms

Application Development

Problem Identification: Recognizing and documenting current issues or opportunities for improvement

Planning and Design: Outlining the project scope, creating detailed designs, and preparing for development

Building: Actual development of the application, involving coding and integration of components

Testing: Ensuring the application meets all requirements and is free of defects through various testing methodologies

Continuous Improvement: Ongoing updates and enhancements based on feedback and performance metrics

CHAPTER 10 SOLUTIONS OVERVIEW AND ALM STRATEGY

Maintenance

Deployment: Releasing the application into the live environment and ensuring it runs smoothly

Maintenance of Technologies: Keeping optional and dependent technologies up to date and functional

Support: Providing user support and managing any issues or bugs that arise post-deployment

Application Lifecycle

The application lifecycle is a cyclic process that includes the following stages as shown in Figure 10-1:

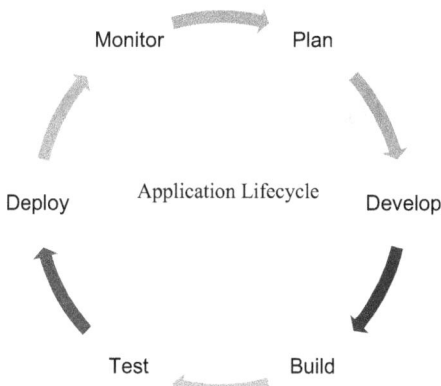

Figure 10-1. *Application Lifecycle*

- **Plan and Track**: Defining project objectives, scope, and timelines, and tracking progress

- **Develop**: Writing code, integrating components, and creating the application

- **Build and Test**: Compiling the application and conducting various tests to ensure quality

- **Deploy**: Releasing the application to the production environment

- **Operate**: Managing day-to-day operations of the application in the live environment

- **Monitor**: Continuously observing the application's performance and user feedback

- **Learn from Discovery**: Analyzing the collected data to make informed decisions for future improvements

ALM for Power Apps, Power Automate, Microsoft Copilot Studio, and Dataverse

The Microsoft Power Platform, including Power Apps, Power Automate, Microsoft Copilot Studio, and Dataverse, provides a robust environment for ALM. Dataverse plays a central role by securely storing and managing data and processes used by business applications. Here's how ALM is implemented using these tools.

CHAPTER 10   SOLUTIONS OVERVIEW AND ALM STRATEGY

Solutions

Mechanism for ALM: Solutions are packages that contain all the components of your application. They enable the distribution of these components across different environments through export and import.

Components: Anything that can be included in a solution is considered a component, such as tables, columns, canvas and model-driven apps, Power Automate flows, chatbots, charts, and plugins.

Dataverse

Central Repository: Dataverse acts as the central storage for all artifacts, including solutions and deployment pipelines, ensuring secure and organized data management.

Source Control

Collaboration and Versioning: Source control systems like Git provide a collaborative platform for developers, enabling version control, branching, and merging of components. This ensures that the source code remains the single source of truth.

CHAPTER 10   SOLUTIONS OVERVIEW AND ALM STRATEGY

Continuous Integration and Continuous Delivery (CI/CD)

Automation: CI/CD platforms, such as Azure DevOps, automate the build, test, and deployment processes. This automation reduces manual errors, increases deployment speed, and ensures consistent quality.

In-Product Pipelines: These can be integrated with CI/CD tools to further streamline the deployment process, allowing for seamless transitions from development to production environments.

Benefits of ALM

Application Lifecycle Management (ALM) significantly improves various aspects of software development and operations. ALM tools enhance collaboration by fostering better communication among development teams and other departments such as testing and operations. This collaborative environment ensures that all parties are aligned and working toward common goals, reducing misunderstandings and streamlining workflows.

Moreover, ALM boosts efficiency by standardizing processes and automating repetitive tasks. This automation not only speeds up the development process but also minimizes human errors, leading to increased productivity. Continuous testing and integration, integral components of ALM, guarantee that the final product adheres to high standards of quality and reliability, ensuring that any issues are promptly identified and resolved.

The structured approach of ALM leads to predictable and repeatable software delivery, reducing surprises and last-minute issues. This predictability helps in better planning and resource allocation, ultimately resulting in smoother project execution. Furthermore, robust governance practices within ALM ensure comprehensive monitoring, control, and documentation of all aspects of the software lifecycle. This thorough oversight enhances compliance and security, providing a more secure and well-regulated development environment.

In summary, ALM is a holistic approach that integrates multiple disciplines and tools to manage the entire lifecycle of an application, from inception to retirement, with a focus on improving efficiency, collaboration, and quality in software development and operations.

ALM Basics with Microsoft Power Platform

Environments in Microsoft Power Platform are essential for storing, managing, and sharing your organization's business data, applications, and processes. They act as containers that help segregate apps based on different roles, security requirements, or target audiences. Each environment can contain only one Microsoft Dataverse database, ensuring data is managed within a specific context.

Environments

Types of Environments Used in ALM

Using the Power Platform admin center, you can create the following types of environments:

> **Sandbox**: This nonproduction environment is isolated from the production environment, providing a safe space to develop and test

application changes without risking production data. Sandbox environments support operations like reset, delete, and copy, which would be unsafe in a production environment.

Production: This environment is where applications and other software are deployed for their intended operational use.

Developer: The Power Apps Developer Plan grants access to Power Apps premium functionality, Dataverse, and Power Automate for individual use. This plan is primarily for building and testing applications, as well as for learning purposes. A developer environment is meant for a single user and cannot run or share production apps.

Default: Automatically created for each tenant, this environment is shared by all users within the tenant. The default environment is named "{Microsoft Entra tenant name} (default)" and is located in the closest region to the default region of the Microsoft Entra tenant. New Power Apps users are automatically added to the Maker role of this environment.

Purpose and Usage of Environments

Environments should be created and used based on specific purposes, such as development, testing, or production. A Power Platform environment serves as a space to store, manage, and share business data, apps, chatbots, and flows, while also separating applications based on their roles, security requirements, or target audiences:

CHAPTER 10 SOLUTIONS OVERVIEW AND ALM STRATEGY

Single Environment Use: Some organizations may choose to build all their apps or chatbots within a single environment.

Separate Environments for Testing and Production: Others may create distinct environments to segregate the test and production versions of their apps or chatbots.

Department-Specific Environments: Companies might create environments for specific teams or departments, each containing relevant data and apps for the intended audience.

Global Branch Environments: Organizations with multiple global branches may set up separate environments for each branch.

Figure 10-2 depicts the high-level environment strategy.

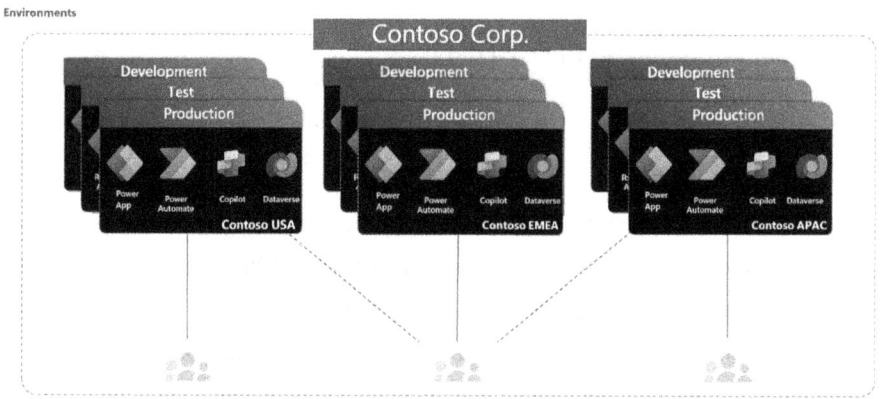

Figure 10-2. Environment strategy

Scope of Power Platform Environments

Each environment is created under a Microsoft Entra tenant, and only users within that tenant can access its resources. An environment is also tied to a geographic location, such as the United States. When an app is created in an environment, it is routed to datacenters in that specific geographic location. All items created within an environment, including chatbots, connections, gateways, and Power Automate flows, are bound to the environment's location.

Each environment can have zero or one Microsoft Dataverse database, which provides storage for apps and chatbots. Whether you can create a database in an environment depends on your Power Apps license and your permissions within that environment.

When an app is created in an environment, it can only connect to data sources deployed within that same environment, including connections, gateways, flows, and Dataverse databases. For instance, if you have two environments named Test and Dev, each with its own Dataverse database, an app created in the Test environment will only be able to connect to the Test database and not to the Dev database.

Solutions

Solutions serve as the primary mechanism for implementing Application Lifecycle Management (ALM) in Microsoft Power Platform. Understanding key solution concepts is essential for managing the lifecycle of applications effectively. Solutions are used to package and maintain components that make up one or more PowerApps, Power Automate, Copilots, or Power Pages.

This section discusses several critical aspects of solutions, including the types of solutions, solution components, the lifecycle of a solution, solution publishers, dependencies, and the distinction between managed and unmanaged solutions.

CHAPTER 10 SOLUTIONS OVERVIEW AND ALM STRATEGY

Solution Components

Solutions comprise various components, including tables, columns, forms, views, and business rules. Understanding how these components interact and function within a solution is vital for effective management and development.

Lifecycle of a Solution

The lifecycle of a solution involves multiple stages, including development, testing, deployment, and maintenance. Each stage requires careful planning and execution to ensure a successful application lifecycle.

Solution Publisher

A solution publisher is the entity responsible for creating and managing the solution. This includes defining the solution's identity and versioning, which helps in tracking changes and updates over time.

Solution and Solution Component Dependencies

Solutions can have dependencies on other solutions or components. When a dependency exists, certain constraints are placed on the uninstallation or modification of solutions. For example, managed solutions cannot be uninstalled if there are dependencies linked to unmanaged customizations.

CHAPTER 10   SOLUTIONS OVERVIEW AND ALM STRATEGY

Key Solution Concepts

Unmanaged Solutions

Unmanaged solutions are actively developed and are utilized in development environments. They allow for modifications and serve as the primary source of Microsoft Power Platform assets. Exported unmanaged solutions should be tracked in a source control system. These are typically used during the development phase. They allow for modifications and changes to be made easily as developers work on the application. Unmanaged solutions can be exported either as unmanaged or managed. It is essential to check exported unmanaged versions into a source control system, as they represent the source for Microsoft Power Platform assets. If an unmanaged solution is deleted, only the solution container for any customizations is removed, while all unmanaged customizations remain effective and belong to the default solution.

Managed Solutions

Managed solutions are intended for deployment in production and other nondevelopment environments. They cannot be edited directly. If changes are needed, components must first be added to an unmanaged solution. This process creates a dependency that prevents uninstallation of the managed solution until the dependency is removed. These are deployed in environments other than development, such as testing, User Acceptance Testing (UAT), System Integration Testing (SIT), and production environments. Managed solutions can be serviced independently from other managed solutions within the same environment. As a best practice for ALM, managed solutions should be generated by exporting an unmanaged solution as managed, effectively serving as a build artifact.

All the components go into solution based on the app design outlined in Figure 10-3.

CHAPTER 10 SOLUTIONS OVERVIEW AND ALM STRATEGY

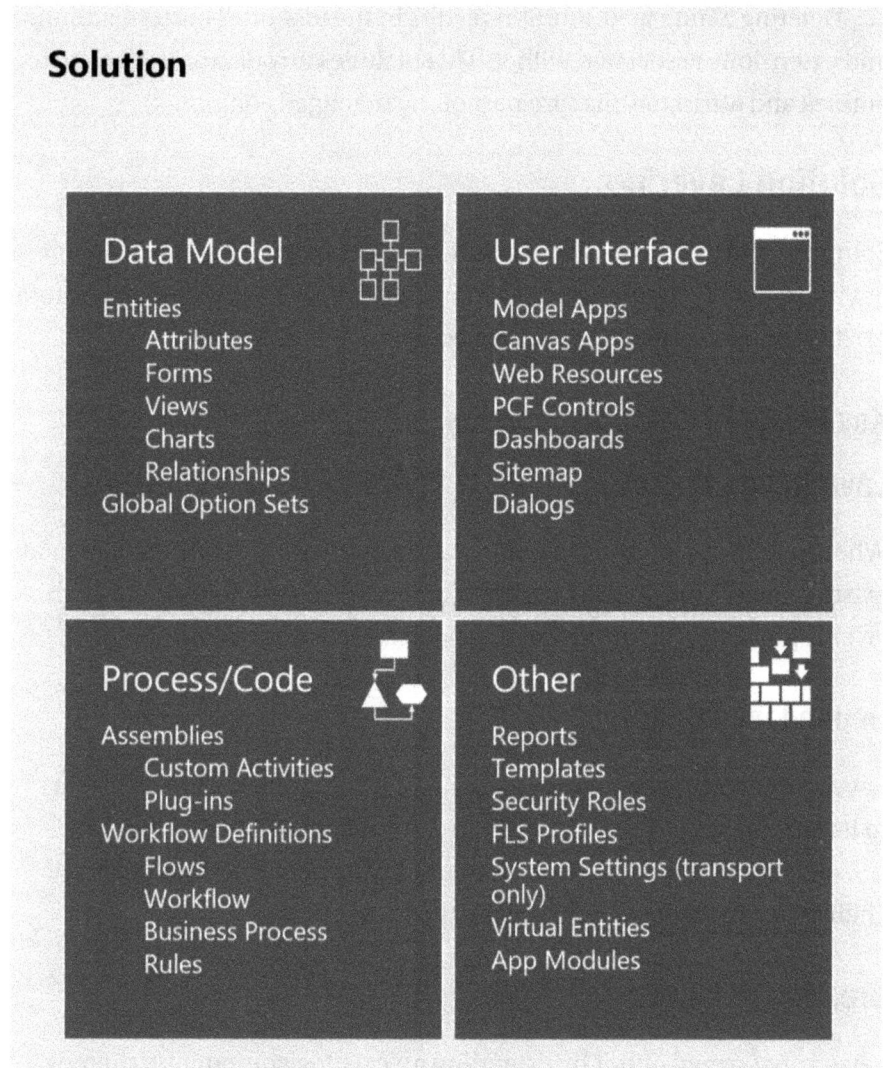

Figure 10-3. Solution components

It is crucial to note that you cannot export a managed solution once it has been created, nor can you import a managed solution into the same environment that houses the original unmanaged solution. Instead, a separate environment is required for testing a managed solution.

CHAPTER 10   SOLUTIONS OVERVIEW AND ALM STRATEGY

Deleting a managed solution results in the loss of all customizations and extensions associated with it. This includes any data stored in custom entities and attributes that are part of the managed solution.

Solution Layering

Solution layering occurs when solutions are imported into an environment. Each imported solution can add new components or modify existing ones, creating a layered structure of dependencies.

Key Points of Solution Layering

Layering on Import

When solutions are imported, they can introduce new components or alter existing ones. This process creates a hierarchical structure where each layer represents a solution that has been added or modified.

Dependency Chain

Layers describe the dependency chain of a component from its origin to its current state. The root solution introduces the component, and subsequent solutions can extend or modify its behavior. This creates a chain where each layer depends on the previous one.

Creation of Layers

Layers are formed either by extending an existing component, thereby taking a dependency on it, or by creating new components or versions of a solution. This means any change or addition to a component in a new solution will form a new layer on top of the existing ones.

How Layers Work?

Root Solution: This is the original solution that introduces a component. It represents the base layer.

Extensions and Changes: Subsequent solutions can extend or modify the component introduced by the root solution. Each change or extension creates a new layer, building on the previous ones.

Dependencies: Each layer is dependent on the layers beneath it. If a solution at a higher layer (more recent) relies on a component from a lower layer (earlier solution), it creates a dependency chain.

Example Scenario

Initial Import: Solution A is imported, introducing Component X. This is the root layer.

Modification: Solution B is then imported, which modifies Component X. This creates a new layer on top of the root layer.

Further Extension: Solution C is imported, extending Component X further. This adds another layer on top of the previous two.

If Solution C depends on the changes made in Solution B, and Solution B depends on the original Component X from Solution A, this forms a dependency chain. Each layer must be intact for the component to function correctly.

Importance of Understanding Layers

Impact on Uninstallation: If there are dependencies between layers, uninstalling a lower-layer solution (e.g., Solution A) can affect all higher-layer solutions (e.g., Solutions B and C) that depend on it.

Managing Changes: Understanding layering helps manage changes more effectively. It ensures that modifications and extensions are made with the awareness of existing dependencies, preventing unintended disruptions.

By comprehensively understanding solution layering, you can better manage Application Lifecycle Management (ALM) in Power Platform, ensuring smooth and effective deployment, modification, and maintenance of solutions.

Solution Segmentation and Upgrades

With segmentation, you can export solutions with selected table assets such as columns, forms, and views. This capability allows for a more granular approach to solution management, where you can focus on specific components of a table without having to include the entire table. This is useful for managing dependencies and maintaining a streamlined solution structure.

When it comes to solution upgrades, the default option upgrades your solution to the latest version and rolls up all previous patches in one step. This process ensures that your solution is always up-to-date, integrating all previous patches and enhancements into a single, cohesive version. This simplifies maintenance and ensures consistency across environments, reducing the risk of conflicts and errors that might arise from fragmented updates.

ALM Strategy in Power Platform

The Application Lifecycle Management (ALM) strategy in Power Platform is a comprehensive approach designed to streamline the development, deployment, and management of applications. This strategy involves several key stages, each with specific roles and actions to ensure a smooth and efficient process from planning to release.

There are quite a few challenges listed below in the implementation of ALM in Power Platform.

Challenges in the Implementation of ALM in Power Platform

Complexity in Managing Multiple Environments

- Difficulty in maintaining consistency across development, testing, and production environments
- Ensuring environment configurations are synchronized and up-to-date can be challenging
- Management of solution layers and dependencies becomes complex with multiple environments

Customization and Configuration Management

- Handling customizations and configurations effectively to prevent conflicts during deployments
- Keeping track of changes and ensuring they are appropriately documented and tested

CHAPTER 10 SOLUTIONS OVERVIEW AND ALM STRATEGY

Security and Compliance

- Ensuring that all components meet security and compliance standards across different environments
- Managing security roles and permissions to avoid unauthorized access or data breaches

Integration with Other Systems

- Integrating Power Platform solutions with other enterprise systems can be complex and prone to errors.
- Ensuring seamless data flow and compatibility between different systems and platforms.

Data Management

- Managing data consistency and integrity during the migration and deployment processes
- Handling large volumes of data efficiently without impacting performance

Tooling and Automation

- Limited or complex automation capabilities for deployment and testing.
- Integration of ALM tools and automation scripts to streamline the development and deployment processes can be challenging.

CHAPTER 10   SOLUTIONS OVERVIEW AND ALM STRATEGY

Version Control and Source Code Management

- Managing version control effectively, especially with multiple developers working on the same solution
- Ensuring that all changes are tracked and can be rolled back if necessary

The ALM process begins with the planning phase, where best practices are established, and a solid plan is developed. This phase is crucial as it sets the foundation for the entire lifecycle. It involves defining policies, default settings, and ensuring a healthy environment for app development. The planning phase also includes creating necessary configurations and setting up the ALM infrastructure, such as source code repositories and environments.

Once the planning is complete, the build phase begins. This phase focuses on the actual development of the application. Makers, who are primarily responsible for creating new apps, start building the application using core solutions and source code control. This phase emphasizes the importance of having ALM active behind the scenes from the beginning, ensuring that all changes are tracked and managed effectively. The build phase also involves synchronizing maker changes with the source code repository, creating managed solutions, and validating the solution through automated tests.

After the build phase, the application moves to the test phase. This phase involves deploying the application to test environments for necessary review and validation. Automated testing tools, such as Solution Checker, are used to ensure the application meets quality standards. Manual testing is also conducted to validate the application's functionality and performance. The test phase is critical for identifying and resolving any issues before the application is deployed to production environments.

The release phase follows the test phase, where the application is deployed to different environments, such as test and production,

CHAPTER 10 SOLUTIONS OVERVIEW AND ALM STRATEGY

in a controlled manner. This phase involves importing the tested solution to the production environment and ensuring that all necessary configurations are in place. Stakeholders are involved in this phase to provide feedback and ensure that the application meets their requirements. The release phase also includes monitoring the deployment process to ensure a smooth transition to the production environment.

Throughout the ALM process, different actors play specific roles. Makers focus on creating new apps and ensuring they adhere to the defined policies and standards. Power Platform administrators and IT professionals manage the ALM infrastructure, including source code repositories and environments. Admins, business managers, and multidiscipline subject matter experts create policies and guardrails for makers, ensuring that all projects adhere to the same standards and best practices.

The ALM strategy in Power Platform emphasizes the importance of having a structured and well-defined process for managing app development. By following a systematic approach, organizations can ensure that their applications are developed, tested, and deployed efficiently and effectively. This strategy also highlights the importance of collaboration between different roles, ensuring that all stakeholders are involved in the process and that their feedback is incorporated into the final product.

The ALM strategy for the Power Platform is outlined in Figure 10-4.

CHAPTER 10 SOLUTIONS OVERVIEW AND ALM STRATEGY

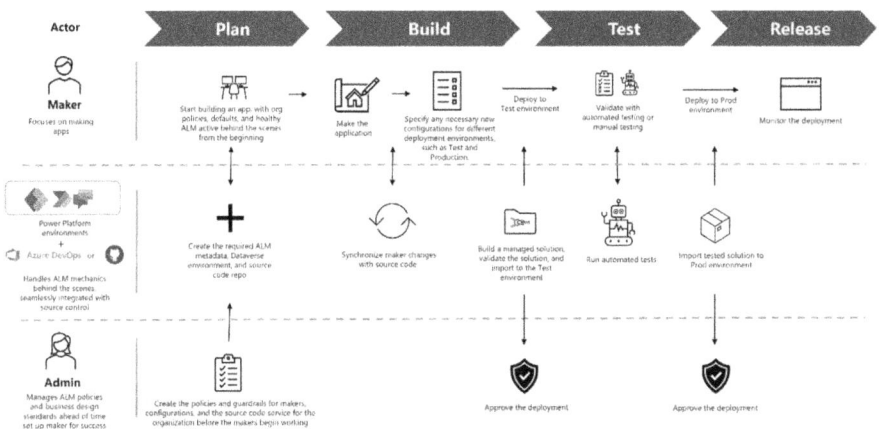

Figure 10-4. ALM strategy for Power Platform

In conclusion, the ALM strategy in Power Platform is a comprehensive approach that covers all stages of the application lifecycle, from planning to release. It involves defining best practices, creating necessary configurations, developing the application, testing it thoroughly, and deploying it to production environments. By following this strategy, organizations can ensure that their applications are developed efficiently, meet quality standards, and are deployed smoothly to production environments.

Automate Deployments with Pipelines for Power Platform

Pipelines for Power Platform are a powerful feature designed to streamline and automate the Application Lifecycle Management (ALM) process. They bring continuous integration and continuous delivery (CI/CD) capabilities to Power Platform and Dynamics 365, making it easier for makers, admins, and developers to manage and deploy solutions.

Here's an in-depth look at how pipelines work and their benefits.

Overview of Pipelines

Pipelines in Power Platform aim to democratize ALM by providing a more approachable way to implement automation and CI/CD. This is particularly beneficial for organizations looking to improve their development processes without requiring extensive domain knowledge.

Key Components

Admins Centrally Manage and Govern Pipelines

Centralized Governance: Admins can set up safeguards to govern solution development, testing, and delivery across the organization. This ensures that all projects, whether led by citizen developers or professional developers, adhere to the same standards.

Lower Total Cost of Ownership: By improving productivity and reducing the effort required to manage ALM processes, pipelines help lower the overall cost of ownership.

Scalability: Pipelines can be extended to accommodate evolving business needs, making it easier to scale ALM processes as the organization grows.

Makers Run Preconfigured Pipelines

Ease of Use: Makers can initiate deployments directly from their development environments with just a few clicks. This intuitive user experience eliminates the need for deep knowledge of ALM processes.

Preconfigured Pipelines: Once pipelines are set up, makers can use them to deploy solutions without needing to configure them each time.

Developers Can Use and Extend Pipelines

Extensibility: Professional developers can extend pipelines using the Power Platform command line interface (CLI) to meet specific requirements.

Integration with DevOps: Pipelines can be integrated with Azure DevOps, allowing teams to use Power Platform Build Tools tasks alongside other Azure DevOps tasks to create comprehensive build and release pipelines.

Setting Up Pipelines

There are two main ways to set up pipelines in Power Platform.

Platform Host

Default Tenant-Wide Host: This is the default method where the platform host is provisioned for everyone in the tenant to use. It can be configured by makers from their development environments.

Personal Pipelines: Makers can create personal pipelines from their development environments to target environments they have access to. This setup includes benefits like deployment scheduling, inline validation, and Copilot-generated deployment notes.

Custom Host

Admin Configuration: Admins can configure a custom host to centrally govern projects. This method provides more control and customization options for managing pipelines.

Benefits of Pipelines

1. Improved Productivity

   a. **Automation**: Pipelines automate many of the repetitive tasks involved in ALM, freeing up time for makers and developers to focus on more strategic work.

   b. **Faster Time to Market**: By streamlining the deployment process, pipelines help bring business solutions to market faster.

2. Enhanced Quality and Compliance

   a. **Built-in Safeguards**: Pipelines include safeguards to ensure that deployments meet quality and compliance standards. This includes secure production environments, approval-based delegated deployments, and automatic audit logs.

b. Visibility and Monitoring: Out-of-the-box analytics and Power BI reports provide better visibility into the deployment process, helping teams monitor and manage their pipelines more effectively.

3. Cost Savings

   a. **Reduced Maintenance Effort**: The system handles much of the heavy lifting and ongoing maintenance, reducing the effort required to manage ALM processes.

   b. **Lower Total Cost of Ownership**: By improving productivity and reducing the effort required to manage ALM processes, pipelines help lower the overall cost of ownership.

Practical Use Cases Based on Persona Makers

Simplified Deployment: Makers can use preconfigured pipelines to deploy their solutions without needing to understand the complexities of ALM.

Focus on Innovation: By automating the deployment process, pipelines allow citizen developers to focus on creating innovative solutions rather than managing deployments.

Professional Developers

Customizable Pipelines: Professional developers can extend and customize pipelines to meet specific project requirements, integrating them with existing DevOps processes.

Enhanced Collaboration: Pipelines facilitate better collaboration between different teams by providing a standardized deployment process.

Admins

Centralized Management: Admins can centrally manage and govern all pipelines, ensuring that all projects adhere to the same standards and best practices.

Scalability: Pipelines can be scaled to accommodate the growing needs of the organization, making it easier to manage ALM processes as the organization evolves.

Summary

Pipelines for Power Platform are a game-changer for organizations looking to improve their ALM processes. By providing a more approachable way to implement automation and CI/CD, pipelines help democratize ALM, making it accessible to all makers, admins, and developers. With benefits like improved productivity, enhanced quality and compliance, and cost savings, pipelines are an essential tool for any organization using Power Platform and Dynamics 365.

Best Practices for ALM with Solutions

Develop and Test in Unmanaged Solutions: Makers and developers should work in development environments using unmanaged solutions. Once the application has been refined and tested, it can be imported into downstream environments (e.g., testing or production) as a managed solution.

Manage Dependencies Carefully: Keep track of dependencies between managed and unmanaged solutions to avoid complications during updates or uninstallation.

Use Separate Environments for Testing: Always use a separate environment to test managed solutions to prevent conflicts with unmanaged solutions. Never lose your source or solution files. This practice helps maintain version history and facilitates collaboration among team members.

Plan Your Publishers: Use the same publisher when organizing solutions. Reorganizing solutions across different publishers can be problematic and lead to dependency issues.

Environment Planning: Plan your environments carefully, as cross-solution dependencies can be challenging to manage. Ensure each environment serves a specific purpose (development, test, and production) to maintain clarity and control.

Avoid Unmanaged Changes Upstream: Do not make unmanaged changes in upstream environments (such as test or production). Always make changes in the development environment and promote them through managed solutions.

Know Your Dependencies: Keep your development environments clean and free of unnecessary dependencies. Understanding and managing dependencies is crucial for maintaining a stable and reliable solution.

Use Connection References and Environment Variables Strategically: Leverage connection references and environment variables to manage configurations across different environments. This practice ensures that your solutions are adaptable and easier to maintain.

Solution Updates and Upgrades: Use solution updates for incremental changes and solution upgrades when you need to delete or significantly modify components. Upgrades integrate all previous patches and enhancements into a single version, ensuring consistency and reducing errors.

Manage Layers: Avoid using too many layers, as they add complexity. However, some layers can be very useful for managing dependencies and organizing your solution components effectively.

By understanding these key concepts and adhering to best practices, organizations can effectively implement ALM in the Power Platform, ensuring a smooth application lifecycle from development through to deployment and maintenance.

Tools

The ALM Accelerator for Power Platform is a comprehensive tool designed to streamline the Application Lifecycle Management (ALM) process for Power Platform solutions. It provides a simplified interface to Azure Pipelines and Git source control, making it easier for makers and developers to manage their solutions from creation to deployment. This accelerator is a reference implementation of ALM patterns and practices, leveraging built-in platform capabilities to help users get started with ALM in Power Platform.

The ALM Accelerator is particularly beneficial for organizations looking to implement ALM without requiring extensive domain knowledge. It is built using a combination of low-code maker- and administrator-focused canvas apps, along with Azure Pipelines YAML and PowerShell templates. This combination allows makers to perform source control, enable version history, and deploy their solutions within Power Platform. To use the ALM Accelerator, all Power Platform components, including apps, flows, and customizations, must be contained in a solution. This requirement ensures that all changes are tracked and managed effectively.

One of the key features of the ALM Accelerator is its ability to provide a simplified interface for makers to regularly export components in their Power Platform solutions to source control. This feature is particularly useful for makers who are unfamiliar with ALM concepts but want to save their work, along with a history of changes, and share those changes with other users. The accelerator also supports advanced makers who are comfortable with using Git and want to work in a familiar way with source control and deployment automation. These advanced makers can use the accelerator to create pull requests, branch, merge, and perform other Git-related tasks.

CHAPTER 10   SOLUTIONS OVERVIEW AND ALM STRATEGY

The ALM Accelerator also includes customizable templates for Azure Pipelines, which automate ALM tasks and support a staged deployment from development to production. This automation helps streamline the deployment process, reducing the time and effort required to move solutions from development to production environments. The accelerator also provides a canvas app that sits on top of Azure DevOps Pipelines and Git source control, offering a simplified interface for makers to create deployment requests and have their work reviewed before deploying to target environments.

To set up and configure the ALM Accelerator, users should have a basic understanding of Power Platform environments, solutions, and Azure Pipelines. They should also be familiar with Microsoft Entra and Dataverse administration. The setup process involves creating the required ALM metadata in Dataverse, synchronizing maker changes with source control, and building managed solutions. Once the setup is complete, makers can use the accelerator to import solutions from source control, export changes to source control, and create pull requests to merge changes.

The ALM Accelerator is designed to be used by Power Platform makers and maker teams. It provides a solution for setting up an enhanced ALM experience for both code-first and low-code developers. Within this single accelerator, there are capabilities for both simplified and advanced experiences. For those who want to get started with ALM, the accelerator offers a simplified experience that does not require advanced knowledge of ALM concepts. For advanced makers, the accelerator provides capabilities to work the way they want, using Git, Azure DevOps, and basic ALM concepts such as source control, pushes, pull requests, branching, merging, and continuous integration/continuous deployment (CI/CD).

The ALM Accelerator is part of the Center of Excellence (CoE) Starter Kit, download the Center of Excellence (CoE) Starter Kit from the following link: `https://aka.ms/CoEStarterKitDownload`, which provides a set of tools and best practices for managing Power Platform environments. The accelerator was originally developed to facilitate ALM

CHAPTER 10 SOLUTIONS OVERVIEW AND ALM STRATEGY

for the CoE Starter Kit team and has since been open-sourced to help other organizations understand how to apply ALM patterns and practices with the Power Platform. Organizations can use the ALM Accelerator as is, customize it to meet their requirements, or use it as a reference implementation to see how ALM scenarios can be addressed.

One of the main benefits of the ALM Accelerator is that it helps organizations streamline their ALM processes, improve efficiency, and ensure the quality of their Power Platform solutions. By providing a simplified interface to Azure Pipelines and Git source control, the accelerator makes it easier for makers and developers to manage their solutions from creation to deployment. This streamlined process helps reduce the time and effort required to move solutions from development to production environments, allowing organizations to bring their solutions to market faster.

The ALM Accelerator also helps improve collaboration between different teams by providing a standardized deployment process. This standardization ensures that all projects adhere to the same best practices and quality standards, reducing the risk of errors and inconsistencies. The accelerator also provides better visibility into the deployment process, allowing teams to monitor and manage their pipelines more effectively.

The ALM Accelerator is also designed to be scalable, making it easier for organizations to manage their ALM processes as they grow. The accelerator can be extended to accommodate evolving business needs, allowing organizations to scale their ALM processes as their requirements change. This scalability ensures that organizations can continue to manage their Power Platform solutions effectively, even as their needs evolve.

In conclusion, the ALM Accelerator for Power Platform is a comprehensive tool that helps organizations streamline their ALM processes, improve efficiency, and ensure the quality of their Power Platform solutions. By providing a simplified interface to Azure Pipelines and Git source control, the accelerator makes it easier for makers and developers to manage their solutions from creation to deployment.

CHAPTER 10   SOLUTIONS OVERVIEW AND ALM STRATEGY

With benefits like improved productivity, enhanced collaboration, and better quality assurance, the ALM Accelerator is an essential tool for any organization using Power Platform. Whether used as is, customized to meet specific requirements, or used as a reference implementation, the ALM Accelerator provides a valuable solution for managing the lifecycle of Power Platform solutions.

Summary

Application Lifecycle Management (ALM) in Power Platform is a structured approach to managing the development, deployment, and maintenance of applications. It encompasses a series of processes and tools designed to ensure that applications are developed efficiently, tested thoroughly, and deployed smoothly.

The ALM process in Power Platform begins with the planning phase, where best practices and policies are established. This phase sets the foundation for the entire lifecycle by defining the necessary configurations and setting up the ALM infrastructure, such as source code repositories and environments.

Next is the build phase, where makers and developers create the application using core solutions and source code control. This phase emphasizes the importance of having ALM active from the beginning to ensure all changes are tracked and managed effectively. Synchronizing maker changes with the source code repository and validating the solution through automated tests are key activities in this phase.

The test phase follows, involving the deployment of the application to test environments for review and validation. Automated testing tools, such as Solution Checker, and manual testing are used to ensure the application meets quality standards. This phase is crucial for identifying and resolving any issues before the application is deployed to production environments.

In the release phase, the application is deployed to different environments, such as test and production, in a controlled manner. This phase includes importing the tested solution to the production environment, involving stakeholders for feedback, and monitoring the deployment process to ensure a smooth transition.

Throughout the ALM process, different roles play specific parts. Makers focus on creating new apps, Power Platform administrators manage the ALM infrastructure, and admins and business managers create policies and guardrails to ensure all projects adhere to the same standards.

The ALM Accelerator for Power Platform is a tool that simplifies this process by providing a user-friendly interface to Azure Pipelines and Git source control. It helps streamline the ALM process, improve efficiency, and ensure the quality of Power Platform solutions. By automating many repetitive tasks, the ALM Accelerator allows makers and developers to focus on more strategic work, improving productivity and collaboration.

In summary, ALM in Power Platform is a comprehensive approach that covers all stages of the application lifecycle, from planning to release. It ensures that applications are developed efficiently, meet quality standards, and are deployed smoothly to production environments, ultimately helping organizations manage their Power Platform solutions effectively.

CHAPTER 11

Power Pages for External Websites

This chapter is dedicated to empowering users—both low-code makers and professional developers—in harnessing the capabilities of Microsoft Power Pages for creating, hosting, and administering secure and modern external-facing business websites. In this chapter, we will understand Microsoft Power Pages, high-level architectural overview, why one should use Power Pages, security governance, low-code design principles, integration with external websites, and configuring for cross-browser capability.

Power Pages for External Websites

Microsoft Power Pages, a key component of the Microsoft Power Platform, is a unique tool that empowers both low-code creators and professional developers. It enables the development, hosting, and management of secure, modern, and user-friendly external-facing business websites.

This chapter provides a comprehensive understanding of Power Pages, delving into its unique architecture, advantages, security features, design principles, integration capabilities, and cross-browser compatibility.

CHAPTER 11   POWER PAGES FOR EXTERNAL WEBSITES

At its core, Microsoft Power Pages is designed with a robust framework that emphasizes a low-code approach, making it accessible for users with varying levels of technical expertise. The platform's intuitive interface and drag-and-drop functionalities empower low-code makers to construct websites without the need for deep coding knowledge. Simultaneously, it provides the flexibility for professional developers to leverage their coding skills to create more complex and customized web solutions.

The architecture of Power Pages is built to support scalability, security, and seamless integration with other Microsoft Power Platform components such as Power Automate, Power Apps, and Power BI. This integration facilitates the creation of comprehensive business solutions that can effectively collect, analyze, and visualize data. Additionally, Power Pages supports connectors to various external data sources, enhancing its versatility in handling diverse business needs.

One of the primary benefits of using Microsoft Power Pages is its efficiency in streamlining the development process, significantly reducing the time and effort required to create functional and attractive business websites. The platform's low-code environment accelerates development cycles, enabling rapid prototyping and deployment. This efficiency is particularly advantageous for businesses looking to quickly adapt to changing market conditions or customer demands.

Security is a paramount consideration in developing and managing external-facing business websites. Microsoft Power Pages incorporates robust security features to protect websites against potential threats. The platform includes built-in security measures such as authentication and authorization protocols, data encryption, and industry standards and regulations compliance. Additionally, Power Pages supports role-based access control, allowing administrators to define user permissions and ensure that sensitive information is accessible only to authorized personnel.

CHAPTER 11   POWER PAGES FOR EXTERNAL WEBSITES

Adhering to low-code design principles, Power Pages promotes ease of use and accessibility. The platform offers predesigned templates and components that are easily customized to fit specific business requirements. This approach simplifies the design process and ensures that websites are consistent and visually appealing. Moreover, Power Pages' responsive design capabilities guarantee that websites are accessible and functional across different devices and screen sizes.

Microsoft Power Pages's crucial strength is its integration capabilities. The platform seamlessly connects with various external systems and applications, enabling businesses to create integrated solutions that enhance operational efficiency and customer experience. Whether integrating with CRM systems, ERP platforms, or third-party services, Power Pages facilitates smooth data flow and interoperability.

Cross-browser compatibility is another critical feature of Microsoft Power Pages. Ensuring that websites perform consistently across different web browsers is essential for providing a positive user experience. Power Pages is designed to support all major web browsers, ensuring that users can access and interact with websites without compatibility issues.

Microsoft Power Pages is a powerful tool that empowers users to create secure, modern, and user-friendly business websites. Its comprehensive architecture, robust security features, low-code design principles, and seamless integration capabilities make it an ideal choice for businesses developing and managing external-facing websites efficiently. By leveraging Microsoft Power Pages' strengths, businesses can enhance their online presence, improve customer engagement, and achieve their digital transformation goals.

In this chapter, we will cover

- Understanding Microsoft Power Pages
  - Overview
  - Key Features

CHAPTER 11 POWER PAGES FOR EXTERNAL WEBSITES

- High-Level Architectural Overview
  - Key Components
  - Data Flow
- Why Use Power Pages?
  - Business Benefits
  - User Experience
- Security Governance
  - Built-In Security Features
  - Compliance and Standards
- Low-Code Design Principles
  - Simplifying Development
  - Enhancing Collaboration
- Integration with External Websites
  - Connecting to Third-Party Services
  - Embedding External Content
- Configuring for Cross-Browser Capability
  - Ensuring Compatibility
  - Performance Optimization
- Conclusion
- Key Takeaways

CHAPTER 11 POWER PAGES FOR EXTERNAL WEBSITES

Understanding Power Pages—An Overview

Microsoft Power Pages (refer to product page: https://www.microsoft.com/en-us/power-platform/products/power-pages) is a sophisticated, enterprise-grade, low-code platform for creating, hosting, and managing external business websites. It is a pivotal tool for novice and experienced developers in organizations and government entities, offering a versatile environment to build and deploy custom web applications swiftly and securely.

Power Pages addresses many users, including external customers, partners, community members, and internal personnel. The platform's key strength lies in its user-centric design, simplifying web development. It allows individuals with varying degrees of technical expertise to contribute to creating functional and aesthetically pleasing websites. For those with limited coding skills, the platform provides an intuitive drag-and-drop interface and a variety of prebuilt templates, facilitating the construction of web pages with minimal effort. This aspect of Power Pages democratizes web development, enabling individuals who may not have a traditional technical background to produce high-quality websites.

On the other hand, professional developers can leverage Power Pages' advanced features to address more complex requirements. The platform supports sophisticated integrations with diverse data sources and implements custom code, catering to more nuanced needs. Additionally, it includes robust security measures that ensure the safety and integrity of web applications. By supporting these dual capabilities—one for less technical users and one for seasoned developers—Power Pages bridges the gap between different levels of expertise within an organization.

A significant advantage of Power Pages is its rapid deployment capability. This feature is crucial for organizations that need to quickly launch new web applications to meet business demands or respond to market changes. The platform's design facilitates the swift rollout of new initiatives, reducing the market time. This agility is particularly

CHAPTER 11 POWER PAGES FOR EXTERNAL WEBSITES

advantageous in industries where the ability to make timely updates or introduce new features can offer a competitive edge. The ability to rapidly deploy new solutions accelerates project timelines and enhances an organization's capacity to adapt to evolving circumstances and seize new opportunities.

Security is a core component of Power Pages, reflecting its importance in safeguarding data and ensuring compliance with regulatory standards. The platform incorporates a suite of security features designed to protect sensitive information and maintain a secure environment for users and administrators. Secure user authentication mechanisms and role-based access control are built into the platform, allowing organizations to manage permissions effectively. Data encryption is also fundamental, ensuring that information remains protected in transit and at rest. These security measures are integral to maintaining the integrity and confidentiality of web applications and reassuring users about the safety of their data.

Power Pages seamlessly integrates with other Microsoft Power Platform ecosystem tools, such as Power Apps, Power Automate, and Power BI. This integration enhances the platform's utility, allowing organizations to develop comprehensive digital solutions that extend beyond web development. For instance, integration with Power Apps enables the incorporation of custom applications into websites, while Power Automate facilitates the automation of workflows and business processes. Power BI integration provides advanced data analytics and reporting capabilities, offering valuable insights that can drive informed decision-making. This interconnectedness between Power Pages and other Microsoft tools fosters a cohesive digital environment, enhancing operational efficiency and creating opportunities for more streamlined business processes.

The versatility of Power Pages is evident in its ability to cater to a wide range of needs and use cases. Whether it is developing a customer-facing portal, a partner collaboration site, a community engagement platform, or an internal resource hub, the platform's features and capabilities can be tailored to meet specific requirements. This adaptability makes Power Pages a valuable asset for modern businesses and governmental entities seeking to enhance their online presence and digital interactions.

Microsoft Power Pages is a powerful and flexible tool for creating and managing external business websites. Its low-code accessibility enables users with varying levels of technical expertise to participate in web development, while its rapid deployment capabilities allow organizations to launch new initiatives swiftly. The platform's robust security features ensure that data is protected and compliant with regulatory standards. At the same time, its integration with other Microsoft Power Platform tools extends its functionality and enhances overall operational efficiency. With these attributes, Power Pages is an invaluable resource for organizations developing sophisticated, secure, and practical web applications.

Key Features of Microsoft Power Pages

Before diving into the architectural components and core elements of Power Pages, let us examine its key features (Figure 11-1) with a real-world example to illustrate their practical application:

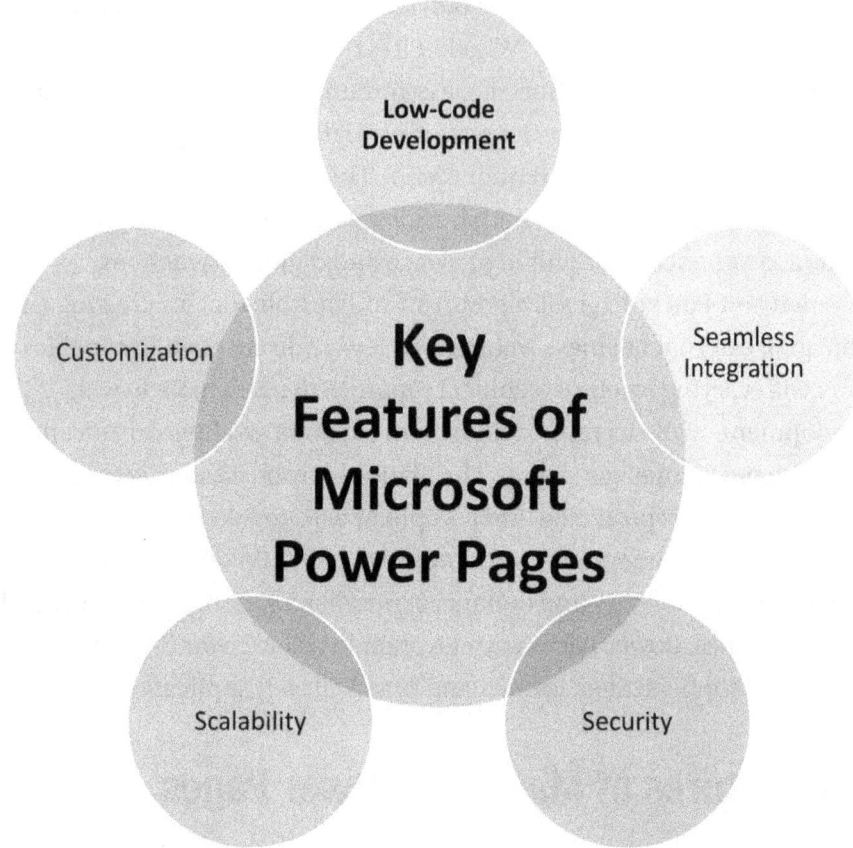

Figure 11-1. Key features of Power Pages

Low-Code Development

Microsoft Power Pages revolutionzses website creation by providing a user-friendly interface that leverages drag-and-drop functionality and prebuilt templates. This streamlined approach not only allows individuals with minimal or no coding expertise to craft sophisticated and professional websites efficiently but also empowers them with a sense of capability and

CHAPTER 11 POWER PAGES FOR EXTERNAL WEBSITES

confidence. For example, consider a local government agency tasked with developing a public service portal. Traditionally, creating such a portal would involve significant time and financial resources, often necessitating the involvement of skilled web developers. However, with Power Pages, the agency's nontechnical staff could manage the entire process, gaining a new level of confidence and control over their online presence.

The platform's drag-and-drop functionality enables users to select and position various elements—such as text blocks, images, and forms—without writing code. Users drag components from a palette onto the website canvas and arrange them according to their preferences. This intuitive method eliminates the complexity usually associated with web design, allowing individuals unfamiliar with coding to achieve a polished and functional result.

Additionally, Power Pages offers a range of prebuilt templates tailored for various purposes, including public service portals, e-commerce sites, and informational blogs. These templates provide a solid foundation, ensuring that even users with no prior experience can produce a website that adheres to best practices and professional standards. Users can customize their sites using these templates to reflect their unique needs while avoiding the pitfalls of starting from scratch.

For instance, the local government agency used Power Pages to develop a portal facilitating public access to various services. The platform's ease of use allowed staff members to create and publish pages for permit applications, community event registrations, and other essential functions without requiring technical assistance. The ability to build and modify these pages quickly and efficiently not only reduced the time and expense typically associated with website development but also brought a sense of relief and reassurance. The agency could now focus more on delivering value to the public rather than managing technical challenges.

The efficiency gained from using Power Pages translates into a more agile response to evolving needs and opportunities. For the government agency, this meant that updates and additions to the portal could be made swiftly, reflecting changes in services or community requirements without the delays inherent in traditional development processes. By empowering nontechnical staff to handle these updates, the agency could allocate its resources more effectively and focus on delivering value to the public rather than managing technical challenges. This adaptability of Power Pages invokes a sense of readiness and preparedness in the audience.

Employing Power Pages in this scenario resulted in a well-functioning public service portal that met the agency's needs without overextending its budget or relying heavily on external developers. The platform's design principles facilitated a straightforward and efficient development process, demonstrating how accessible and impactful Power Pages can be for organizations aiming to enhance their online presence while maintaining control over the content and functionality of their websites.

Seamless Integration

The platform seamlessly integrates with Microsoft Dynamics 365, Power BI, Power Apps, and other services, allowing users to harness existing data and functionalities within their Microsoft ecosystem. This integration capability empowers businesses to create interconnected solutions that drive efficiency and innovation.

For example, a manufacturing company implemented Power Pages to develop a sophisticated supplier portal. This portal was designed to integrate directly with Dynamics 365, facilitating real-time inventory tracking and streamlined order management. By leveraging Dynamics 365, the portal provided suppliers with immediate access to critical information such as current inventory levels, pending orders, and delivery schedules.

This real-time data access transformed the company's supply chain operations. Suppliers no longer had to rely on periodic updates or manual communication to stay informed about inventory needs and order statuses. Instead, they could log into the portal anytime to view accurate, up-to-date information. This transparency significantly improved the efficiency of the supply chain process, reducing delays and errors associated with outdated information.

The integration also enabled automated order management processes. When inventory levels reached a certain threshold, the system could automatically generate purchase orders and notify suppliers through the portal. This automation reduced the administrative burden on the company's procurement team, allowing them to focus on strategic tasks rather than routine order processing. Additionally, it ensured that inventory levels remained optimal, preventing stockouts and overstock situations that could disrupt production schedules.

Furthermore, the supplier portal offered a centralized platform for communication and collaboration. Suppliers could use the portal to submit invoices, track payments, and resolve real-time discrepancies. This direct communication channel minimized the back-and-forth emails and phone calls that often characterize supplier interactions, leading to faster issue resolution and improved supplier relationships.

The company also benefited from enhanced data analytics capabilities through Power BI integration. By analyzing the data collected from the supplier portal, the company could identify trends, monitor supplier performance, and make data-driven decisions to optimize its supply chain. For instance, they could pinpoint suppliers consistently meeting delivery deadlines and those frequently causing delays, allowing them to take corrective actions or renegotiate terms.

Security

Security is paramount in today's digital landscape, and Microsoft Power Pages addresses this concern comprehensively with its built-in security features. These features ensure that websites created with Power Pages are functional but also secure and compliant with industry standards.

CHAPTER 11 POWER PAGES FOR EXTERNAL WEBSITES

One of Power Page's critical security features is its support for multiple authentication methods. These include Azure Active Directory (AD), OAuth, and social logins. Azure AD provides a robust and scalable identity management solution, ensuring only authorized users can access the website. OAuth, an open-standard authorization protocol, allows users to securely authenticate with external systems without exposing their credentials. Social logins enable users to authenticate using their existing social media accounts, simplifying the login process while maintaining security.

In addition to authentication, Power Pages implements role-based access control (RBAC). RBAC allows administrators to define roles with specific permissions, ensuring that users have access only to the resources they need. This minimizes the risk of unauthorized access and helps maintain the principle of least privilege, essential for reducing potential security breaches. Organizations can enforce security policies that align with their operational requirements and compliance obligations by carefully assigning roles and permissions.

Data encryption is another critical security feature in Power Pages. Data is encrypted both in transit and at rest, protecting sensitive information from unauthorized access and potential breaches. In-transit encryption ensures that data is securely transmitted between the client and server, preventing interception by malicious actors. At-rest encryption safeguards data stored on servers, ensuring that the data remains protected even if the physical storage is compromised. This dual approach to encryption ensures comprehensive data security, addressing network-based and physical threats.

A practical example of the effectiveness of these security features can be seen in the case of a financial services firm that adopted Power Pages to launch a customer portal. This portal allowed clients to view account information and perform transactions online. Given the sensitive nature of financial data, security was a top priority. The firm's IT department leveraged Power Pages' robust authentication methods to ensure only

CHAPTER 11 POWER PAGES FOR EXTERNAL WEBSITES

verified users could access the portal. RBAC restricted access based on user roles, ensuring clients could only view and manage their accounts. Data encryption provided an additional layer of security, protecting financial information during transmission and stored on servers.

These security measures ensured that the firm's customer portal complied with industry regulations, such as the Payment Card Industry Data Security Standard (PCI DSS), and the General Data Protection Regulation (GDPR). Compliance with these regulations safeguarded customer data and helped the firm avoid potential legal penalties and build trust with its clients.

Scalability

Microsoft Power Pages is built to manage high traffic and extensive data handling, making it particularly well-suited for large enterprises. As a business grows, its digital infrastructure needs to scale accordingly, ensuring its online presence remains performant and reliable. Power Pages is designed with scalability at its core, allowing businesses to expand their web capabilities seamlessly in response to increasing user demand.

A practical example of this can be seen in the experience of a large e-commerce retailer. This retailer faced the challenge of managing significant traffic surges during seasonal sales. Typically, these spikes in activity could overwhelm less robust systems, leading to slow load times, crashes, and, ultimately, lost sales. However, utilizing Power Pages, the retailer could ensure their website remained fully operational, even under the heaviest loads.

The scalable architecture of Power Pages allowed the retailer to adjust resources dynamically in response to real-time demand. During peak shopping times, such as Black Friday or holiday sales, the platform could handle increased traffic volumes without compromising performance. This capability was crucial in maintaining a smooth and responsive user experience, retaining customer satisfaction, and driving sales.

Moreover, the retailer could integrate its website with other critical systems, such as inventory management and payment processing, without worrying about performance bottlenecks. Power Pages' integrated nature with the broader Microsoft ecosystem ensured that all parts of the retailer's operations were synchronized, providing a cohesive and efficient workflow.

The reliability of Power Pages significantly bolstered the retailer's confidence in managing peak periods—Pages' reliability. Instead of diverting resources to crisis management during busy times, the business could focus on strategic initiatives like marketing and customer engagement. This shift improved operational efficiency and allowed the retailer to maximize revenue opportunities during their busiest seasons.

Additionally, Power Pages provided robust analytics and monitoring tools, enabling the retailer to gain insights into traffic patterns and user behavior. These insights were instrumental in anticipating future demand and planning accordingly. By understanding how their website performed under various conditions, the retailer could make informed decisions about further scaling their infrastructure and optimizing their digital strategy.

Customization

Microsoft Power Pages is crafted to be intuitive for low-code users, yet it retains the flexibility necessary for professional developers to enhance its functionalities using custom code and APIs. This blend of accessibility and extensibility makes it possible to meet complex requirements without compromising simplicity.

For instance, a healthcare provider leveraged Power Pages to develop a comprehensive patient portal. They aimed to streamline the patient experience by integrating scheduling features and connecting with third-party health information systems—the basic framework created using the platform's low-code capabilities, allowing for quick development

CHAPTER 11 POWER PAGES FOR EXTERNAL WEBSITES

and deployment. However, the project required more sophisticated functionalities to meet specific needs and provide a superior user experience.

To achieve this, professional developers enhanced the portal. They integrated bespoke functionalities, such as advanced scheduling algorithms that accommodated various healthcare provider schedules and patient preferences. They also incorporated third-party health information systems, ensuring patients could access their medical records seamlessly. These enhancements transformed the portal into a personalized hub where patients could manage appointments, view test results, and communicate with their healthcare providers efficiently.

The result was a patient portal that was not only functional but also intuitive and user-friendly. Patients could easily navigate the portal to find the needed information, schedule appointments, and access their health data without technical difficulties. The integration with external systems ensured that the data was always up-to-date and accurate, fostering trust and reliability.

The healthcare provider created a solution that met their advanced requirements by leveraging the core features of Power Pages alongside custom development. This approach allowed them to deliver a robust and secure platform that scaled with their needs and integrated seamlessly with existing systems. The portal's development demonstrated how Power Pages could be used to build and manage external business websites that cater to complex needs while remaining accessible to users with varying levels of technical expertise.

Organizations benefit significantly from this dual approach. Low-code capabilities allow for rapid development and deployment, reducing the time and resources needed to launch a functional website. At the same time, the option to extend functionalities through custom code ensures that the platform can adapt to specific business needs and integrate smoothly with existing infrastructures. This adaptability makes Power

Pages an ideal solution for creating external-facing business websites that are secure, scalable, and tailored to meet diverse organizational goals.

How to start with Power Pages?

In case you don't have Power Pages access, no worries, you can start with Power Pages Trial account; follow these steps to start your 30 days' trial. Refer Microsoft Learning website: `https://learn.microsoft.com/en-us/power-pages/getting-started/trial-signup`

Low-Code Design Principles

Microsoft Power Pages offers a robust, low-code platform that empowers users to craft, construct, and oversee professional, secure, and scalable websites with minimal coding. Embracing low-code design principles with Power Pages not only streamlines the development process but also ensures that websites are not just functional but also user-friendly.

Below, we delve into key low-code design principles (Figure 11-2), complete with practical examples to illustrate their application.

CHAPTER 11 POWER PAGES FOR EXTERNAL WEBSITES

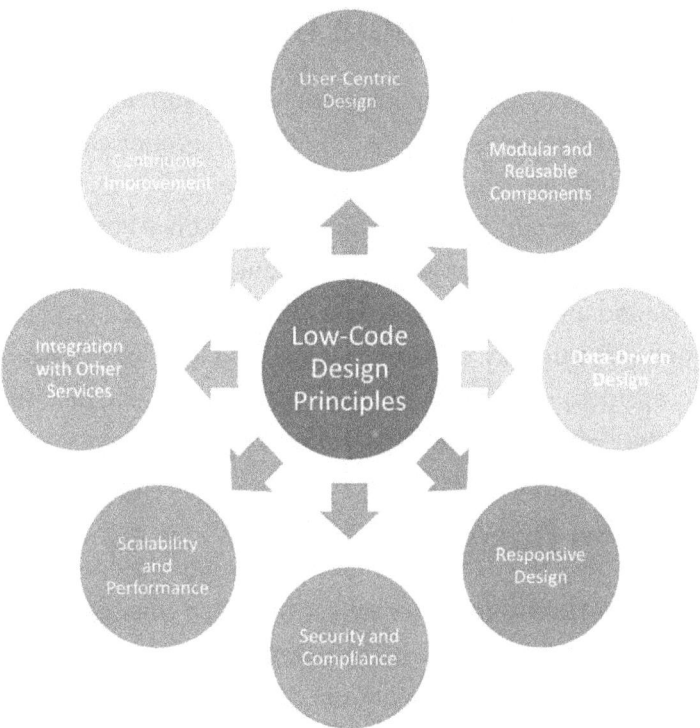

Figure 11-2. Low-code design principles

User-Centric Design

Adopt a user-centric design approach that focuses on the needs and experiences of end-users. By ensuring the website is intuitive, accessible, and provides a seamless user experience, you can create a positive impact and show empathy toward your users.

For instance, a healthcare provider can harness Power Pages to create a patient portal. This portal, designed with ease of navigation in mind, features user-friendly interfaces and accessible features for individuals with disabilities. This practical approach ensures that the portal is not just theoretical but practical for all users, thereby enhancing their overall experience.

Modular and Reusable Components

Design websites using modular components that can be reused across various pages and projects. This method promotes consistency, reduces development time, and simplifies maintenance.

For example, an educational institution might use Power Pages to build a course registration system with modular components like forms, lists, and calendars. These components can be replicated for different courses and departments, ensuring a consistent user experience and streamlining updates. By using reusable components, the institution saves time and effort while maintaining a uniform design.

Data-Driven Design

Integrating with Microsoft Dataverse allows you to leverage data to drive website design and functionality. This approach allows for secure and efficient interaction with organizational data.

For example, a retail company can create a customer loyalty portal with Power Pages that pulls data from Dataverse to offer personalized promotions, display purchase history, and track reward points. Using a data-driven approach, the portal delivers relevant and timely information to customers, enhancing engagement and satisfaction with the brand.

Responsive Design

Ensure the website is responsive and performs well on various devices, including desktops, tablets, and smartphones. Utilize Power Pages' responsive design framework to adapt the site layout to different screen sizes.

For example, an e-commerce website developed with Power Pages should automatically adjust its layout and features to provide an optimal shopping experience across devices. This includes resizing images, reconfiguring navigation menus, and ensuring that interactive elements are touch-friendly. A responsive design ensures a seamless shopping experience, regardless of the device used.

Security and Compliance

Incorporate robust security measures and ensure compliance with relevant regulations. Use Power Pages' built-in security features to protect user data and maintain trust.

For example, a financial services company can use Power Pages to build a secure client portal that is compliant with GDPR and ISO/IEC 27001 standards. The portal can include multifactor authentication, role-based access control, and data encryption to safeguard sensitive information. These security measures help maintain regulatory compliance and protect user data from unauthorized access.

Scalability and Performance

Design websites to scale effectively, accommodating growing user bases and increased traffic. Optimize performance to ensure fast load times and a smooth user experience.

For example, a government agency can create a public service portal with Power Pages that handles high traffic during peak periods, such as tax filing season. By optimizing the website's performance and scalability, the agency can provide reliable and efficient service to citizens, even under heavy demand.

Integration with Other Services

Integrate the website with Microsoft services and third-party applications to enhance functionality and streamline workflows. This integration can expand the website's capabilities and improve operational efficiency.

For example, a nonprofit organization can integrate its Power Pages website with Microsoft Teams and Power Automate to manage volunteer activities. Volunteers can sign up for events through the website, and the information can be automatically synchronized with Teams for effective coordination and communication. This integration simplifies management and enhances organizational efficiency.

Continuous Improvement

Regular updates and refinements based on user feedback and analytics are crucial for the success of any website. With Power Pages' analytics tools, you can monitor performance and identify areas for enhancement, ensuring that your website is always evolving to effectively meet user needs.

For example, an online learning platform using Power Pages can track student engagement and performance. By analyzing data on course popularity and areas where students face challenges, the platform can make informed improvements to enhance the learning experience. This continuous improvement approach ensures that the platform evolves to effectively meet user needs.

Adhering to these low-code design principles allows you to leverage Microsoft Power Pages to create effective, user-friendly, and secure websites that align with your organization's needs and goals. In coming sections, we will see how Power Pages adhere these low-code design principles to provide the easiest way to work.

High-Level Architectural Overview

Learning the architecture of Microsoft Power Pages is not just beneficial; it is also required to understand its core building blocks. It is the key to unlocking the platform's full potential in building robust, scalable, and secure websites. This section provides a comprehensive view of the core architectural components of Power Pages, offering a deep understanding of how the frontend, backend, and database collaborate to deliver a seamless user experience. By dissecting these elements, users can gain valuable insights into the data flow and processing mechanisms that drive the platform's functionality. Figure 11-3 visualizes a high-level architecture of Power Pages.

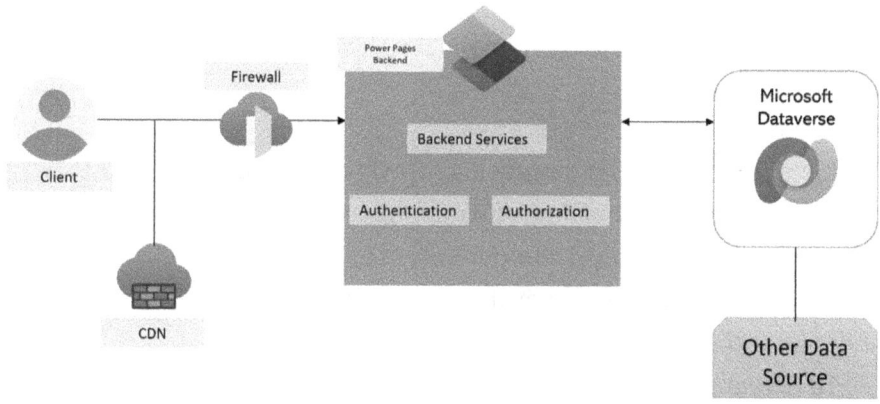

Figure 11-3. *Visualizing architecture of Power Pages*

Power Pages provides a secure, scalable, and highly available platform to build business-critical websites for various use cases. Power Pages' heart lies in a well-integrated structure combining user-friendly interfaces with robust backend services that you can trust. The frontend, built using standard web technologies such as HTML, CSS, and JavaScript, ensures an intuitive and responsive user experience. Meanwhile, the backend, powered by Azure services and Dynamics 365, handles complex business logic and data processing with unwavering efficiency. The database, managed through Microsoft Dataverse, ensures secure and consistent data storage and retrieval, seamlessly and reassuringly integrating with other components of the Power Platform.

Each production Power Pages website follows an architecture optimized for scalability and high availability. By understanding these architectural layers and their interactions, users—low-code makers or professional developers—can better design, develop, and optimize their websites. This knowledge enhances the creation process and ensures that the resultant websites are not just scalable but also secure and capable of meeting diverse business needs, giving you the confidence to tackle any project.

Key Components

Microsoft Power Pages is designed to provide a comprehensive platform for creating, hosting, and managing business-critical websites. Understanding the critical components of a Power Pages website helps leverage its capabilities effectively and ensure that each website is robust, scalable, and secure.

Here is an overview of the essential components.

Frontend

The frontend is the user-facing part of the website, responsible for delivering the visual and interactive elements that users interact with. Key aspects include

- **User Interface (UI)**: Built using HTML, CSS, and JavaScript, the UI provides a responsive and intuitive experience for users. It includes page layouts, navigation, forms, and interactive elements.

- **Responsive Design:** Ensures the website adapts to various screen sizes and devices, providing a consistent user experience across desktops, tablets, and smartphones.

- **Content Management**: Being a user-friendly system, it allows for easy content management and updating. Users can create, edit, and organize content without extensive technical knowledge, making the platform accessible and intuitive.

Backend

The backend handles the server-side logic, data processing, and integration with other systems. It includes

- **Business Logic**: Managed by Azure services and Dynamics 365, it is a robust layer that processes user requests, performs calculations, and executes workflows. It is responsible for managing data interactions and implementing core functionalities, ensuring the system's reliability.

- **Application Programming Interfaces (APIs)**: Facilitate communication between the frontend and backend and integration with external services and applications. RESTful APIs, a type of API that uses HTTP requests to GET, PUT, POST, and DELETE data, are commonly used to enable these interactions. They allow seamless data exchange and enable the frontend to access and manipulate data stored in the backend.

- **Custom Code**: Developers can extend functionalities through custom code, allowing for advanced features and integrations tailored to specific business needs

CHAPTER 11   POWER PAGES FOR EXTERNAL WEBSITES

Database

The database component is crucial for storing, managing, and retrieving data. Key aspects include the following:

- Microsoft Dataverse is the primary data storage solution used by Power Pages. It provides a secure and scalable environment for managing data and ensures seamless integration with other Power Platform components.

- Data Management, including schema definitions, data relationships, and data validation rules, is a comprehensive feature of Dataverse. It supports complex data models and relationships, enabling comprehensive data management and reporting, putting the audience in the driver's seat of their data.

Why Use Power Pages?

In a rapidly growing digital world, businesses are under constant pressure to deliver dynamic, engaging, and secure web experiences. Microsoft Power Pages, with its adaptability to a variety of business needs, emerges as a compelling solution for organizations looking to streamline their web development processes while maintaining high performance and security standards. The platform's ability to balance rapid development with robust functionality makes it an attractive choice for both low-code makers and professional developers, offering a flexible solution for all.

With Power Pages, businesses are empowered to swiftly create modern, responsive websites, all while keeping costs in check. This is made possible by a low-code approach that minimizes the need for extensive programming skills. The platform's seamless integration with other Microsoft services further enhances this sense of control, offering a cohesive and interconnected digital ecosystem. Crucially, Power Pages supports scalability, ensuring that businesses can expand their web presence without sacrificing performance or user experience in the long run.

This section will explore the compelling reasons to adopt Power Pages and highlight its key benefits, such as rapid development cycles, cost efficiency, and enhanced user experience. For instance, Power Pages can improve user experience by providing faster load times and smoother navigation. We will delve into how Power Pages addresses the demands of today's web environment and how it supports organizations in achieving their digital transformation goals.

Business Benefits

Microsoft Power Pages delivers substantial business advantages by streamlining the website development and reducing costs. This section explores how Power Pages accelerate time-to-market with low-code capabilities, enabling rapid deployment of functional and attractive websites. It also highlights the cost-effectiveness of the platform, which minimizes the need for extensive coding and specialized developer resources.

Furthermore, Power Pages' seamless integration with Microsoft services and scalability ensures that businesses can efficiently manage growing demands and leverage existing data. These benefits collectively enhance operational efficiency, drive innovation, and support strategic growth objectives.

Microsoft Power Pages offers several key benefits for businesses, making it a valuable tool for creating and managing external-facing websites. Here is an in-depth look at each benefit.

CHAPTER 11 POWER PAGES FOR EXTERNAL WEBSITES

Rapid Development

Power Pages significantly accelerates the website development process through its low-code environment. The platform allows users to quickly build and deploy websites without extensive coding by providing drag-and-drop interfaces, prebuilt templates, and customizable components. This rapid development capability is crucial in today's fast-paced digital landscape, where businesses must adapt quickly to market changes, customer needs, and emerging opportunities. With Power Pages, organizations can launch new sites or update existing ones more swiftly, reducing time-to-market and gaining a competitive edge.

For example, a retail company can use Power Pages to develop a new e-commerce site in weeks instead of months, enabling it to respond faster to seasonal trends and promotions.

Cost-Effective

The low-code nature of Power Pages reduces development costs by minimizing the need for extensive coding and highly specialized developers. Businesses can leverage prebuilt components and templates, lowering the barrier to entry and reducing the overall development cost. Additionally, the platform's integration with existing Microsoft services means companies can avoid the expenses of building custom integrations from scratch. This cost-effectiveness allows organizations to allocate resources more efficiently, focusing on innovation and other strategic initiatives rather than technical complexities.

For example, a small business can create a professional-looking website using Power Pages without hiring a full-time web developer, significantly reducing upfront development costs.

Seamless Integration

Power Pages integrates effortlessly with Microsoft services such as Dynamics 365, Power BI, and Power Apps. This seamless integration allows businesses to leverage existing data and functionalities across their Microsoft ecosystem, creating a unified experience. For example, integrating with Dynamics 365 enables real-time data updates and streamlined workflows, while Power BI integration provides powerful analytics and reporting capabilities. This interconnected approach enhances operational efficiency and ensures that the website can interact smoothly with other business systems.

For example, a company can integrate Power Pages with Dynamics 365 to automatically update customer information on the website, ensuring that users always see the most current data.

Scalability and Flexibility

Power Pages is designed to support both small- and large-scale websites, making it a scalable solution for businesses of all sizes. The platform can handle high traffic and extensive data management, allowing it to grow with the business's needs. This scalability ensures that as a company expands or its website traffic increases, Power Pages can accommodate these changes without compromising performance. Additionally, the platform's flexibility allows for customization and adaptation to meet evolving business requirements.

An enterprise can use Power Pages to manage a global website with multiple regional sections, handling high traffic volumes and complex data requirements without performance issues.

User Experience

Microsoft Power Pages stands out with its unique features that cater to both developers and nontechnical users, empowering them to create and maintain websites with confidence. The platform's intuitive interface, user-friendly design, and prebuilt templates simplify complex tasks and reduce the learning curve.

This inclusivity empowers a broader range of team members to participate in website development and maintenance, fostering greater collaboration and efficiency.

Intuitive Design

Power Pages offers a streamlined and intuitive user interface that significantly enhances the overall experience. Its robust drag-and-drop functionality and extensive library of prebuilt templates make website creation straightforward, even for those with minimal technical background.

Consider a small business owner with limited technical knowledge. With Power Pages, they can create a professional-looking website using predesigned templates. The platform's user-friendly approach, which allows easy addition and arrangement of content, images, and forms, significantly reduces the need for coding expertise. This enables business owners to concentrate on content and design, rather than the complexities of web development.

Imagine a marketing team within a large corporation. With Power Pages, they can quickly update website content and create landing pages for promotional campaigns, boosting their productivity. The platform's drag-and-drop editor allows efficient modification of page layouts, addition of banners, and insertion of call-to-action buttons, all without relying on IT support. This efficiency not only accelerates the development process but also enables marketing professionals to make timely updates that align with their campaign goals.

Responsive Layouts

Besides its user-friendly design, Power Pages ensures that websites are accessible and functional across various devices and screen sizes, providing a reliable user experience. The platform's responsive layouts automatically adjust to different resolutions, providing a seamless and consistent user experience whether accessed on a desktop, tablet, or smartphone.

For instance, a nonprofit organization using Power Pages to build its website will benefit from responsive design features. Visitors accessing the site from mobile devices will experience a fully optimized layout that adjusts images, text, and navigation menus to fit smaller screens. This responsiveness ensures users can easily navigate and interact with the site, leading to a more positive engagement experience.

Another example is an e-commerce company that uses Power Pages to manage its online store. As customers browse products on their smartphones or tablets, the responsive design ensures that product images, descriptions, and checkout processes are displayed correctly and efficiently. This adaptability improves the customer experience and helps reduce bounce rates and increase conversion rates by providing a smooth shopping experience across all devices.

Security Governance

Security governance is a comprehensive and robust cornerstone of Microsoft Power Pages. It ensures that websites and their data are safeguarded against threats and comply with relevant regulatory standards. The platform integrates a wide array of security features and practices to protect sensitive information and maintain user trust. This section explores the essential security elements of Power Pages, including authentication, authorization, data encryption, and adherence to industry compliance standards.

Power Pages is designed with a "Zero Trust" security approach, which assumes that every action on the platform, even by trusted users, might be a potential security breach. This mindset leads to the explicit verification of all activities and access attempts. The platform's security is further strengthened by a robust authorization model, ensuring that only authorized users can perform specific actions. This model verifies each access request, providing a layer of security that scrutinizes every interaction.

Power Pages adheres to the principle of Least Privilege Access, a key strategy in reducing the risk of unauthorized access. This principle ensures that users have only the minimum access levels necessary to perform their tasks. By limiting permissions, the platform reduces the risk of unauthorized access to sensitive website data and content. This approach enhances security and ensures that users interact with the platform in a controlled and safe manner, mitigating potential vulnerabilities.

Zero Trust Security

The Zero Trust security model is a strategic framework designed to protect organizational data and infrastructure by assuming threats can arise outside and within the network. Unlike traditional security models that trust users and devices within a defined perimeter, Zero Trust operates on "never trust, always verify." This means every access request, regardless of origin, is treated as potentially malicious. Figure 11-4 visualizes the principles of Zero Trust.

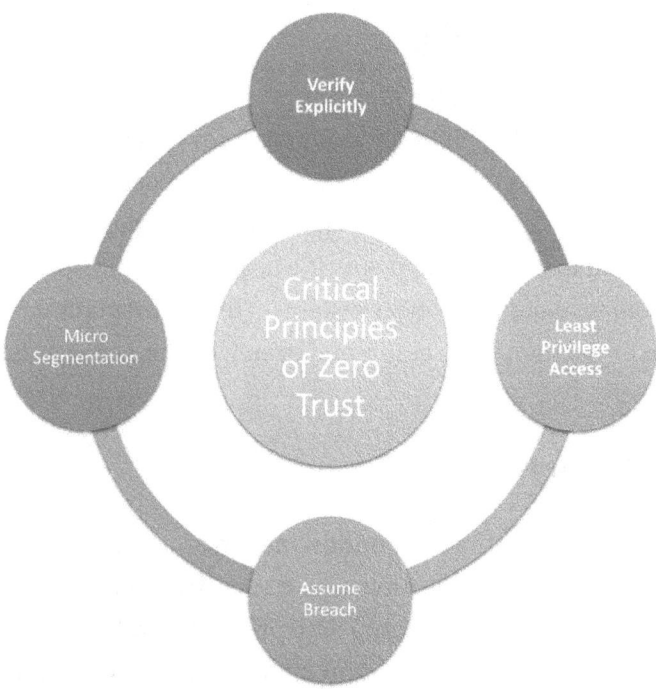

Figure 11-4. *Principles of Zero Trust*

Verify Explicitly

Zero Trust requires strict verification of every access attempt. This involves authenticating and authorizing every user and device before granting access to resources. Multifactor authentication (MFA), strong passwords, and other verification methods ensure that only legitimate users gain entry. Importantly, this continuous verification process, which also extends to monitoring user activity to detect and respond to unusual or unauthorized actions, underscores that security is always a top priority.

Least Privilege Access

The principle of least privilege limits users to the minimal level of access necessary for their role. This approach reassures organizations that they can minimize the potential impact of a security breach by reducing the number of permissions and access rights. Users are granted only the access required to perform their specific tasks, preventing unauthorized access to sensitive data or critical systems. This segmentation ensures that the potential damage is contained even if a user's credentials are compromised.

Assume Breach

Zero Trust operates on the assumption that an attack is always imminent or has already occurred. This proactive stance drives continuous monitoring, logging, and analyzing network traffic and user behavior. It's crucial for security teams to adopt an "assume breach" mentality, preparing them to quickly detect, isolate, and mitigate any threats that penetrate the network. This includes implementing robust incident response plans and regular vulnerability assessments to identify and address potential weaknesses.

Micro-segmentation

Zero Trust advocates for micro-segmentation, which involves dividing the network into smaller, isolated segments. This granular approach ensures that even if one segment is compromised, the threat cannot quickly move laterally across the network. Each segment requires separate authentication and authorization, limiting an attacker's potential reach.

CHAPTER 11　POWER PAGES FOR EXTERNAL WEBSITES

Built-In Security Features

Microsoft Power Pages is equipped with a comprehensive suite of built-in security features to ensure robust protection of sensitive data and secure user interactions. These features address various security concerns and provide a secure environment for managing and accessing website content.

Authentication

Power Pages provides multiple user-friendly authentication options to enhance security and user convenience. It supports Azure Active Directory (Azure AD) for enterprise-level authentication, OAuth for flexible third-party integration, and social logins like Google and Facebook for streamlined user access. For instance, an online retail site might allow customers to log in using their Google accounts. This method simplifies the login process and leverages Google's robust security features, offering users a seamless and secure experience.

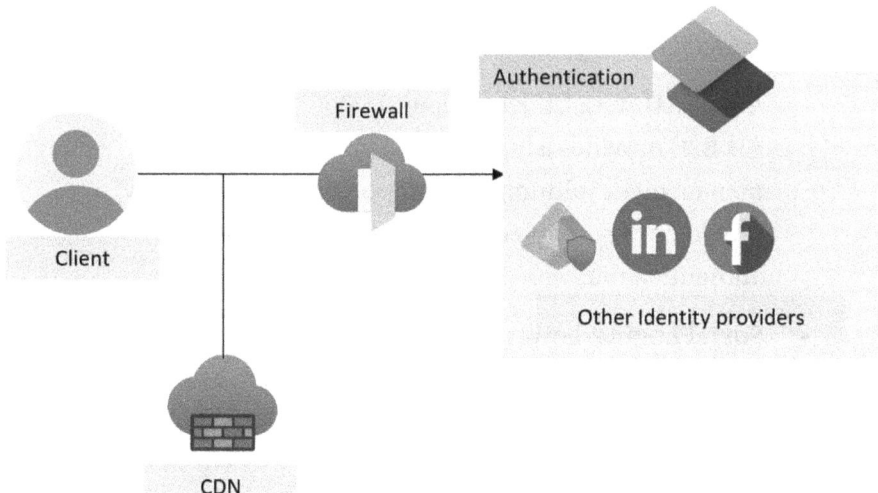

Figure 11-5. *Authentication in Microsoft Power Pages*

CHAPTER 11   POWER PAGES FOR EXTERNAL WEBSITES

Figure 11-5 refers to the overview of authentication in Power Pages; referring to this, we can say, Authentication in Microsoft Power Pages is fundamental to securing your site and managing user access effectively. Power Pages leverages Microsoft Dataverse contact records to link authenticated users with the website, ensuring a secure and personalized experience. Users must be assigned to specific web roles to obtain permissions beyond those available to unauthenticated users. This robust role-based access control system plays a key role in defining what users can see and do on the website, thereby maintaining a secure and organized structure.

Power Pages supports a variety of identity providers, enabling users to sign in using external accounts. This flexibility enhances user convenience and leverages existing security measures provided by these identity providers. Some of the shared identity providers supported by Power Pages include

- **Microsoft Entra ID**: This includes support for OpenID Connect, SAML 2.0, and WS-Federation protocols, allowing integration with Microsoft's robust identity management system.

- **Azure AD B2C**: Utilizing OpenID Connect, Azure AD B2C provides a highly customizable identity management solution that supports multiple identity providers and enables secure and scalable user authentication.

- **Social Logins**: Power Pages also supports authentication through social media platforms such as LinkedIn, Facebook, Google, and Twitter using the OAuth 2.0 protocol. This feature allows users to sign in with their existing social media accounts, simplifying the authentication process and enhancing user experience.

CHAPTER 11   POWER PAGES FOR EXTERNAL WEBSITES

Setting Up Authentication

Setting up authentication in Power Pages involves configuring several settings to align with the specific requirements of your site. For instance, if your site is a public blog, you might want to allow open registration. If it's an e-commerce site, you might want to enforce unique email requirements. Here are the steps to set up authentication:

- **Select General Authentication Settings**: This initial step involves configuring general authentication settings, such as turning external login options on or off, allowing open registration, and enforcing unique email requirements. These settings help define the site's overall authentication behavior and ensure it meets the desired security and user management standards.

- **Add Identity Providers**: After configuring the general settings, the next step is to choose and configure the specific identity providers used for authentication. This process involves setting up each provider according to their protocols and requirements. For instance, setting up Microsoft Entra ID or Azure AD B2C requires entering specific configuration details such as client IDs, secrets, and endpoint URLs. Similarly, setting up social logins with providers like LinkedIn, Facebook, Google, or Twitter involves configuring OAuth 2.0 settings and obtaining credentials from the respective platforms.

Each identity provider configuration must be meticulously entered to ensure seamless integration and secure user authentication. The setup process, which includes configuring scopes and claims, is a crucial step that defines the permissions and information the application will request from the identity provider during the authentication process. This attention to detail is essential for a robust authentication setup.

Importance of Authentication in Power Pages

Authentication is crucial for several reasons:

- **Security**: Proper authentication mechanisms ensure that only authorized users can access certain parts of the website, protecting sensitive information and preventing unauthorized access.

- **User Management**: Administrators can efficiently manage user permissions and access levels by associating authenticated users with Dataverse contact records and assigning them to web roles. This role-based access control helps maintain an organized and secure environment.

- **User Experience**: Supporting multiple identity providers and social logins enhances the user experience by offering flexible and convenient authentication options. Users can sign in with accounts they already use, reducing the friction often associated with creating new accounts and remembering additional credentials.

- **Compliance**: Implementing robust authentication practices helps ensure compliance with various data protection regulations and standards, which often require secure user authentication and access control measures

Authorization

Role-based access control (RBAC) is a fundamental security feature in Power Pages that empowers administrators to manage granular user permissions. With RBAC, administrators can assign specific roles to users, controlling their access to various sections and functionalities of the website. For example, in an internal company portal, access to sensitive financial reports can only be restricted to authorized finance team members. This ensures that critical information remains confidential and is only accessible to those with the appropriate permissions.

Authorization in Microsoft Power Pages is critical to its security architecture, ensuring that only authorized users can access specific pages, data, or functionalities. By assigning permissions based on user roles, Power Pages provides a structured and secure way to manage who can see and do what on a website. Figure 11-6 depicts authorization by assigning permissions.

Figure 11-6. *Authorization by assigning permissions*

This method protects sensitive information and enhances user experience by tailoring access according to user needs and responsibilities.

Web Roles

Web roles play a pivotal role in managing permissions for authenticated users in Power Pages. Each web role represents a set of permissions that dictate what users assigned to that role can access and perform on the website. For instance, a "Manager" role might have permission to access administrative pages and perform data entry tasks. In contrast, a "Customer" role may only have access to view product information and submit service requests.

Creating web roles is an empowering process that involves defining these roles based on the specific needs of your site. Once roles are defined, permissions are assigned to them, granting or restricting access to various pages and functionalities. This system allows for a granular level of control, ensuring that each user interacts with the site in a way that is consistent with their role and responsibilities.

Page Permissions

Page permissions in Power Pages control access to individual pages on your site. This means you can specify which users or groups of users (through their assigned web roles) can view or interact with specific pages. For example, you might have a page containing sensitive financial information that should only be accessible to users with a "Finance" web role.

Setting page permissions involves configuring the access levels for each page. You can grant access to specific web roles, ensuring only users with the appropriate role can see or interact with the page. Conversely, you can restrict access to certain users or groups, preventing them from accessing pages that are irrelevant to their role or contain sensitive information.

This level of control is beneficial in environments where information needs to be compartmentalized based on user roles. It ensures that users only have access to the information and functionalities they need, reducing the risk of unauthorized access and potential data breaches.

Entity Permissions

Entity permissions govern access to the data stored in Microsoft Dataverse, the underlying data platform used by Power Pages. These permissions are defined at the entity level, allowing for precise and meticulous control over who can read, create, update, or delete data within each entity.

- **Read**: This permission allows a user to view data within an entity. For example, users with read permissions on a customer entity can view customer details but not modify them.

- **Create**: Allows users to add new data to an entity. This is essential for roles that input new records, such as sales representatives entering new leads.

- **Update**: Permits modification of existing data. Users with this permission can edit records, making it suitable for roles like customer service representatives who need to update case details.

- **Delete**: This permission enables users to remove data from an entity. It should be granted sparingly to prevent the accidental or malicious deletion of essential records.

By defining entity permissions, you can ensure that users have the appropriate level of access to the data they need to perform their tasks while protecting the integrity and confidentiality of your data.

Setting Up Authorization

Setting up authorization in Power Pages involves several steps to ensure that users have the correct permissions based on their roles. This process includes creating web roles, assigning permissions, and linking users to the appropriate roles.

Create Web Roles

The first step in setting up authorization is to define web roles based on your site's needs. These roles should reflect the different types of users who will interact with your website and the specific permissions each type of user requires. For example, you might create roles such as "Administrator", "Editor," "'Viewer," and "Customer."

Each role should be carefully defined to accurately represent the access and actions that users in that role need to perform. This step is crucial for creating a secure, organized structure for permissions management.

Assign Permissions

Once web roles are defined, the next step is to assign permissions to each role. This involves configuring page and entity permissions for each role, specifying what users in that role can access and do on the site.

You will need to determine which pages each role should have access to for page permissions and set the appropriate permissions for those pages. For entity permissions, you will need to define the access levels for each entity, specifying whether users in each role can read, create, update, or delete data.

This step ensures that each role has the correct permissions, aligning with its users' tasks and responsibilities.

Assign Users to Roles

The final and crucial step in setting up authorization is assigning users to the appropriate web roles. This involves linking individual users to roles that match their responsibilities and access needs, underscoring the significance of each user's role in the process.

Assigning users to roles can be done through the Power Pages administration interface, where you can select and assign users to one or more roles. Reviewing and updating these assignments regularly is essential to ensure that users have the correct permissions based on changes in their roles or responsibilities.

Example to Implement Authentication

To illustrate how authorization in Power Pages works, let us consider a company implementing a Power Pages website to manage customer service interactions.

The company has defined several web roles: "Customer," "Customer Service Representative," and "Manager."

- **Customer**: This role is assigned to end-users who interact with the site to submit service requests and view their request status. Customers have read permissions for their data and created permissions to submit new requests.

- **Customer Service Representative**: This role is for employees who handle customer service requests. They have read and updated permissions to view and modify request details and create permissions to add notes or follow-up actions.

- **Manager**: This role is for supervisors who oversee the customer service team. Managers have full permissions, including read, create, update, and delete, to manage all aspects of customer service requests and data.

By assigning these roles and configuring the appropriate permissions, the company ensures that each user can perform their tasks effectively while maintaining the security and integrity of their data. Customers can only see and interact with their data, service representatives can manage service requests, and managers oversee the entire process.

Data Encryption

Microsoft Power Pages uses robust encryption protocols to protect data in transit and at rest. Figure 11-7 visualizes data encryption in Microsoft pages.

For example, a healthcare website using Power Pages can encrypt patient data to comply with Health Insurance Portability and Accountability Act (HIPAA)regulations. This encryption safeguards sensitive health information from unauthorized access and breaches, ensuring patient privacy.

Info *The Health Insurance Portability and Accountability Act (HIPAA), enacted in 1996, is a critical piece of legislation in the United States. It aims to safeguard sensitive patient information and ensure the privacy and security of healthcare data. HIPAA's primary objectives include improving the efficiency of healthcare delivery, but more importantly, it is dedicated to protecting patient rights and preventing healthcare fraud and abuse.*

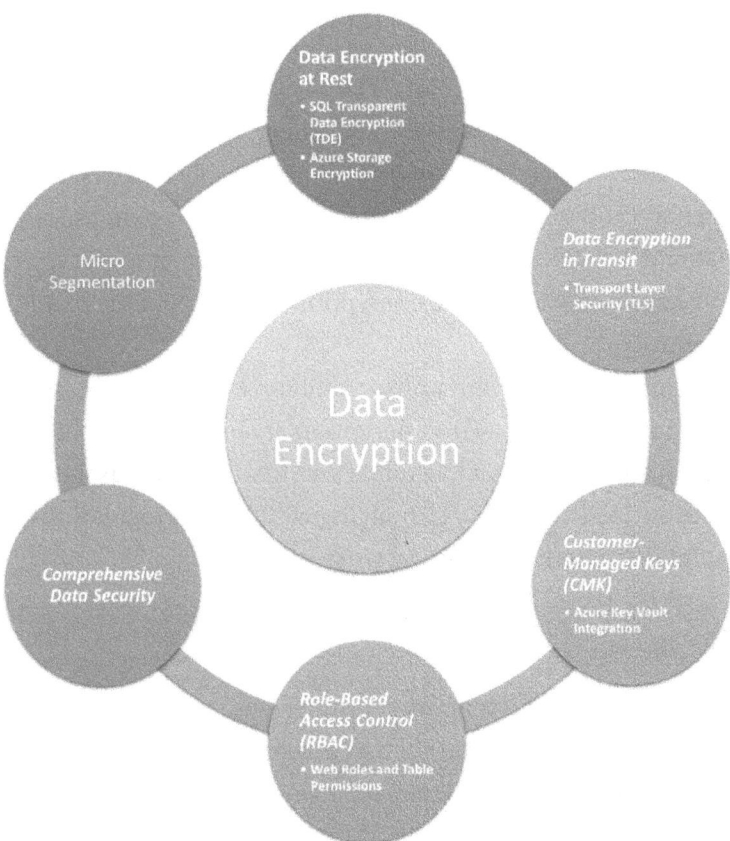

Figure 11-7. *Data encryption in Microsoft Power Pages*

By utilizing encryption methods like TLS (Transport et al.) for data in transit and AES (Advanced et al.) for data at rest, Power Pages ensures that data remains secure throughout its lifecycle.

Data Encryption at Rest

Data encryption at rest involves protecting data stored on a physical medium, ensuring that even if the storage is compromised, the data remains inaccessible without the proper decryption keys. Power Pages utilizes several sophisticated mechanisms to achieve this.

SQL Transparent Data Encryption (TDE)

SQL Transparent Data Encryption (TDE) is a security feature that encrypts relational data stored in databases. TDE encrypts the data as it is written to disk and decrypts it when read into memory. This ensures that the data remains encrypted while at rest on the storage medium. In the event of a physical breach, such as the theft of a storage device, the encrypted data cannot be accessed without the encryption keys, providing an additional layer of security.

For instance, a healthcare website built on Power Pages can use TDE to encrypt patient records. This encryption ensures that sensitive health information, such as medical histories and treatment plans, is protected from unauthorized access. By complying with HIPAA regulations, TDE helps maintain patient privacy and trust.

Azure Storage Encryption

Azure Storage encryption is another critical feature employed by Power Pages for securing binary data, such as images and documents. This encryption method ensures that all data stored in Azure Storage is encrypted using Microsoft-managed keys. The encryption is automatic and seamless, providing robust security without user intervention.

For example, a financial institution using Power Pages to store customer documents and transaction records can rely on Azure Storage encryption to protect this sensitive information. By encrypting data at rest, the institution ensures that even if the physical storage infrastructure is compromised, the data remains secure and unreadable without the proper decryption keys.

Data Encryption in Transit

Data encryption in transit is essential for protecting data as it moves between clients and servers, safeguarding it from interception and tampering during transmission. Power Pages employs Transport Layer Security (TLS) to achieve this.

Transport Layer Security (TLS)

TLS is a widely adopted encryption protocol for secure data transmission over the Internet. Power Pages uses TLS to encrypt data exchanged between clients and servers, ensuring that it remains confidential and protected from eavesdropping or tampering.

For example, when a user accesses a healthcare website built on Power Pages and submits sensitive information, such as personal details or medical data, TLS encrypts this information during transmission. This encryption ensures that malicious actors cannot intercept or alter the data, providing a secure communication channel between the user and the website.

Customer-Managed Keys (CMKs)

Power Pages offers additional security and control through the use of Customer-Managed Keys (CMKs), allowing organizations to manage their encryption keys.

Azure Key Vault Integration

Power Pages integrates with Azure Key Vault, enabling organizations to store and manage their encryption keys. This integration controls the keys to encrypt and decrypt data, including the ability to rotate or revoke keys as needed. By using CMKs, organizations can implement stringent security policies and maintain greater control over their data.

For instance, a legal firm using Power Pages to handle confidential client information can utilize Azure Key Vault to manage their encryption keys. This control ensures that the firm can enforce security policies, such as crucial rotation schedules, to enhance data protection and compliance with regulatory requirements.

Role-Based Access Control (RBAC)

Role-based access control (RBAC) is a security model that restricts access to data based on the roles of individual users within an organization. Power Pages employs RBAC to ensure that only authorized users can access sensitive information:

Web Roles and Table Permissions

Power Pages uses RBAC to define web roles and table permissions, controlling who can access or modify specific data. This approach ensures that users only have the necessary permissions to perform their tasks, minimizing the risk of unauthorized access.

For example, in an educational institution using Power Pages to manage student records, RBAC can be configured to ensure that only authorized staff members, such as administrators and faculty, can access sensitive data. Students and other users would have limited access based on their roles, protecting the confidentiality of personal information.

Comprehensive Data Security

Power Pages incorporates these robust encryption and security mechanisms to protect data. By encrypting data both at rest and in transit, utilizing Customer-Managed Keys, and implementing role-based access control, Power Pages ensures that data remains secure throughout its lifecycle.

These measures safeguard sensitive information from unauthorized access and breaches, ensuring compliance with industry standards and regulations. Whether a healthcare website protects patient data, a financial institution secures transaction records, or an educational platform safeguards student information, Power Pages provides the necessary tools and features to maintain data security and privacy.

Compliance and Standards

Ensuring compliance with regulatory standards is crucial to security governance, as it helps organizations adhere to legal requirements and industry best practices. Power Pages is designed to meet various compliance standards, providing a framework that supports data protection and regulatory adherence across different regions and sectors. This section examines how Power Pages aligns with critical regulatory requirements, including GDPR and ISO/IEC 27001, ensuring that your website meets the highest data security and privacy standards.

GDPR

Microsoft Power Pages adheres to the General Data Protection Regulation (GDPR), which governs the handling of personal data within the European Union. For instance, a European e-commerce site leveraging Power Pages can ensure customer data is processed in compliance with GDPR guidelines. This includes data access controls, the ability to delete or anonymize user data upon request, and transparent data processing practices to protect user privacy and meet legal obligations.

ISO/IEC 27001

Power Pages aligns with the ISO/IEC 27001 standard for information security management, which is recognized internationally for its rigorous security requirements. For example, a financial institution can utilize Power Pages to build a secure client portal, confident that the platform meets stringent security criteria. This certification ensures that Power Pages implements a robust information security management system (ISMS) that covers risk management, security controls, and continuous improvement practices.

User Education and Training

Effective security governance also involves educating users about best practices and potential security threats. Power Pages offers various resources and training materials to help users understand how to secure their websites and manage data responsibly. For instance, administrators and content creators can access guides on securing user accounts, managing permissions, and recognizing phishing attempts. By promoting awareness and best practices through these resources, organizations can mitigate the risk of human error, enhance overall security, and ensure that all team members contribute to maintaining a secure digital environment.

Microsoft Power Pages incorporate robust security features and adhere to international standards to protect data and ensure compliance. From multifaceted authentication options and role-based access control to comprehensive data encryption and adherence to GDPR and ISO/IEC 27001, Power Pages offers a secure and compliant platform for building and managing external-facing websites. The platform's commitment to continuous improvement in security practices ensures that it stays ahead of emerging threats. User education and training further bolster security by equipping individuals with the knowledge to safeguard their digital assets effectively.

Integration with External Websites

Microsoft Power Pages offers diverse methods for integrating with external websites and services, enhancing your site's functionality and interactivity. While these integration capabilities enable seamless data exchange, real-time updates, and improved user experiences, they also come with potential challenges such as API versioning, data security, and performance optimization.

Here is an in-depth look at how Power Pages facilitates integration with external content and services, along with strategies to overcome these challenges.

Connecting to Third-Party Services

Power Pages excels in this area, offering robust integration capabilities that allow users to extend the functionality of their websites by connecting with external applications and services. This section will explore how Power Pages facilitates these integrations through APIs and webhooks, enabling real-time data synchronization and enhanced interactivity. By leveraging these tools, businesses can enrich their websites with external data and services, driving greater efficiency and delivering a more comprehensive user experience.

APIs

Power Pages harnesses RESTful APIs to integrate with external applications and services, facilitating smooth data flow and dynamic content updates. For instance, a travel-booking website can integrate with an airline's API to retrieve real-time flight information. This integration lets users view up-to-date schedules, prices, and availability directly on the site, enhancing their booking experience with accurate and current data.

For example, imagine a travel website showing real-time flight data from multiple airlines. Using RESTful APIs, the site can automatically update flight schedules and ticket prices as they change, providing users with the latest information without needing to refresh or manually update the content. This real-time update feature ensures that users always have the most accurate and up-to-date information at their fingertips.

Webhooks

Power Pages utilizes webhooks for real-time data synchronization and event-driven communication. For example, an e-commerce site can use webhooks to update inventory levels automatically when a purchase is made. This ensures that stock information is accurate and current, reducing the risk of overselling products and improving customer satisfaction.

For example, a retail website integrated with a webhook system can instantly update its product inventory when items are sold. This proactive nature of webhooks ensures that the site's inventory is always up-to-date, and users can trust the availability of the products they see. Additionally, webhooks can be configured to trigger notifications or initiate workflows, such as sending a confirmation email or updating a CRM system with customer purchase details.

Embedding External Content

In today's interconnected digital landscape, seamlessly integrating and displaying external content within your website is crucial for delivering a cohesive user experience. Microsoft Power Pages facilitates this by offering robust options for embedding various external content types. Whether you need to incorporate data from third-party applications, display external web pages, or integrate interactive elements, Power Pages provides flexible tools and techniques to achieve these goals.

This section delves into the methods available for embedding external content, including iFrames, JavaScript integrations, and other approaches, enabling you to enrich your website's functionality and provide a more engaging user experience.

iFrames

Power Pages allows for embedding external web pages or applications using iFrames. This method enables you to integrate tools and services hosted elsewhere without redirecting users away from your site. For instance, a financial services website might embed a third-party mortgage calculator using an iFrame. This feature directly provides users with essential tools on the site, improving engagement and functionality.

For example, a real estate website can embed a property valuation tool through an iFrame, allowing users to estimate property values without leaving the site. This user-centric approach enhances the site's utility by incorporating valuable external resources, making the user experience more convenient and efficient.

JavaScript

Power Pages supports using custom JavaScript to interact with external systems and enhance site functionality. For instance, a customer support portal can integrate with a live chat service using JavaScript, offering real-time assistance to users. Additionally, JavaScript can fetch data from external APIs, validate user input, or create dynamic content based on user interactions. For example, JavaScript can be used to implement features like dynamic content updates, form validation, and interactive elements that improve the user experience.

For example, a website with a JavaScript integration for a live chat service can offer users instant support while they browse. JavaScript can also implement features like dynamic content updates, form validation, and interactive elements that improve the user experience.

CHAPTER 11 POWER PAGES FOR EXTERNAL WEBSITES

Configuring for Cross-Browser Capability

As technology evolves and new browser versions are released, the challenge of maintaining compatibility grows. Configuring for cross-browser capability is essential to address these challenges, ensuring that your Microsoft Power Pages website performs optimally regardless of the user's browser choice. This section delves into strategies and best practices for cross-browser compatibility, including responsive design principles, comprehensive testing methodologies, and performance optimization techniques. By implementing these approaches, you can guarantee a smooth and engaging experience for all users

Responsive Design

It employs responsive web design principles to ensure that your Power Pages site performs well across various devices and screen sizes. This approach ensures that the site adjusts its layout and functionality based on the device, whether a desktop, tablet, or smartphone.

For example, an e-commerce website built with Power Pages will display product images, navigation menus, and checkout forms in a way that is optimized for both desktop and mobile devices. This responsiveness ensures a consistent and user-friendly experience, regardless of the device used to access the site.

Cross-Browser Testing

Conducting thorough testing across different browsers is crucial for identifying and resolving compatibility issues. Tools such as BrowserStack or CrossBrowserTesting can test your Power Pages site on various browsers and operating systems, ensuring consistent user performance.

For example, using cross-browser testing tools, you can verify that your Power Pages site functions correctly on popular browsers like Chrome, Firefox, Safari, and Edge. This testing helps identify rendering issues or functionality problems that may arise due to differences in browser behaviors.

Performance Optimization

In today's fast-paced digital environment, website performance is crucial for delivering an exceptional user experience and maintaining engagement. Performance optimization involves various strategies and techniques to improve a website's speed, efficiency, and overall responsiveness. For Microsoft Power Pages users, ensuring their sites load quickly and function smoothly across all devices and browsers is essential. This section delves into the critical practices for optimizing performance within Power Pages, including caching mechanisms, minification of assets, and effective resource management. By focusing on these optimization strategies, businesses can enhance their website's performance, reduce load times, and provide a seamless experience for their users.

Caching

Implementing caching strategies enhances site performance and reduces load times by storing frequently accessed data. For instance, server-side caching can store static content or database query results, minimizing the need for repeated data retrieval and accelerating page load speeds.

For example, a news website using caching can quickly serve frequently viewed articles to returning visitors, reducing server load and improving the speed at which pages are displayed.

Minification

Reducing CSS, JavaScript, and HTML file sizes through minification helps improve loading speeds. This process involves removing unnecessary characters, such as whitespace and comments, from code files to make them more compact and faster to download.

For example, by minifying CSS and JavaScript files, a Power Pages site can decrease the amount of data that needs to be transferred to users' browsers, leading to quicker page load times and a smoother user experience.

By leveraging these integration methods, Power Pages enables the creation of feature-rich and interactive websites that perform well across different platforms and devices, ensuring a seamless and engaging user experience.

Challenges of Using Power Pages for External Websites

While Microsoft Power Pages offers numerous benefits for creating and managing external-facing business websites, users might encounter some challenges.

Understanding these challenges can help in planning and implementing solutions effectively.

Customization Limitations

Power Pages is designed to be accessible to low-code makers, prioritizing simplicity and ease of use. However, this can sometimes limit the level of customization that can be achieved compared to traditional web development. Users who require highly customized features or intricate designs may find the platform restrictive.

Learning Curve for Professional Developers

Professional developers accustomed to traditional coding and development environments might face a learning curve when transitioning to a low-code platform like Power Pages. While the platform simplifies many aspects of web development, it requires developers to adapt to a new set of tools and methodologies, which can initially slow down the development process.

Integration Complexities

Although Power Pages offers seamless integration with other Microsoft services and third-party applications, setting up these integrations can sometimes be complex. Ensuring that all systems communicate effectively and handle data correctly requires careful planning and technical expertise, particularly for complex or large-scale implementations.

Performance and Scalability Concerns

Performance and scalability can be concerns for websites with high traffic or extensive data-processing needs. While Power Pages is designed to handle significant workloads, optimizing the website to maintain performance under heavy load requires careful resource management and may necessitate additional infrastructure or configuration.

Security and Compliance Management

While Power Pages incorporates robust security features, managing security and compliance, especially in regulated industries like healthcare and finance, can be challenging. Ensuring the website meets all regulatory requirements, such as HIPAA for healthcare websites, requires continuous monitoring and updating security practices.

Cost Management

While Power Pages can be cost-effective by reducing the need for extensive coding, managing costs can still be challenging. Users must consider the costs of additional services, such as Azure storage and other Microsoft services, that integrate with Power Pages. Budgeting for these ongoing expenses is crucial to avoid unexpected costs.

Dependency on the Microsoft Ecosystem

Power Pages is deeply integrated with the Microsoft ecosystem, which can be a double-edged sword. While this integration offers many benefits, it also means that users are heavily dependent on Microsoft services. Any changes or disruptions within the Microsoft ecosystem can impact the functionality and performance of Power Pages websites.

Limited Offline Functionality

Power Pages is primarily designed for online use, and its functionality can be limited in offline scenarios. This can be a significant limitation for users who require extensive offline capabilities, necessitating additional development to implement offline features or fallback mechanisms.

Complexity in Role-Based Access Control (RBAC)

While RBAC provides robust security by limiting access based on user roles, setting up and managing these roles can be complex, especially in larger organizations with numerous users and varied access requirements. Ensuring that all permissions are correctly assigned and maintained requires ongoing administrative effort.

Support and Documentation

Although Microsoft provides extensive documentation and support for Power Pages, users may still encounter situations where finding specific information or resolving issues can be challenging. Access to timely and effective support is crucial, particularly during critical development phases or when addressing complex problems.

While Microsoft Power Pages is a powerful tool for creating and managing external websites, it is essential to know the potential challenges. By understanding and planning for these issues, users can better leverage the platform's capabilities while mitigating risks and ensuring successful website implementation.

Summary

This chapter explored Microsoft Power Pages as a dynamic and versatile tool for developing and managing external-facing business websites. Power Pages stands out for its ability to simplify the website creation process through its low-code environment, making it accessible to a broad range of users, from novices to seasoned developers. Its user-friendly interface and straightforward processes not only make it accessible but also reassure even those with limited technical expertise, instilling a sense of confidence in their ability to use the platform. This platform allows for rapidly constructing sophisticated, secure, and highly responsive websites without extensive coding. It effectively balances ease of use with powerful features, making it an attractive option for businesses seeking to enhance their online presence.

The chapter detailed the core architectural elements of Power Pages, shedding light on its structure and operational mechanisms. By understanding the interaction between the frontend, backend, and database, we gained insights into how Power Pages processes user

CHAPTER 11 POWER PAGES FOR EXTERNAL WEBSITES

requests and manages data flow. This architectural knowledge is crucial for effectively leveraging the platform, ensuring that websites not only meet aesthetic and functional requirements but also perform optimally.

Power Pages' integration with other Microsoft services was another focal point of the discussion. The platform's ability to seamlessly connect with tools such as Microsoft Dynamics 365, Power BI, and Power Apps illustrates its value in creating a cohesive digital ecosystem. This integration empowers users to harness existing data and functionalities, enhancing the capabilities of their websites and streamlining workflows. By drawing on these interconnected services, businesses can achieve higher efficiency and consistency across their digital operations, making them feel more empowered and efficient.

Security emerged as a critical strength of Power Pages. The platform offers robust security features designed to protect sensitive information and ensure compliance with industry standards. From authentication and authorization to data encryption, Power Pages provides a comprehensive security framework that addresses various aspects of data protection. These features are essential for safeguarding user data and maintaining trust, especially in an era where cybersecurity concerns are increasingly prominent. The robust security features of Power Pages instill a sense of security and trust in its users.

In addition to security, the chapter highlighted the importance of low-code design principles in Power Pages. The platform's drag-and-drop interfaces and prebuilt connectors simplify the development process, enabling users to build and customize websites without extensive technical expertise. This approach accelerates development and fosters collaboration among team members, making it easier to manage projects and iterate on designs. Including co-authoring and version control features further supports a collaborative development environment, ensuring that changes are tracked and managed effectively. This collaborative nature of Power Pages makes every team member feel included and part of the development process.

The chapter also covered Power Pages' capabilities for integrating with external systems and embedding external content. By utilizing APIs, webhooks, iFrames, and custom JavaScript, users can extend the functionality of their websites and incorporate data and services from other platforms. This flexibility is crucial for creating dynamic and interactive websites that meet specific business needs and adapt to evolving requirements. The platform's ability to adapt to changing needs and technologies instills confidence in its flexibility and future-proofing capabilities.

Ensuring cross-browser compatibility was another significant aspect discussed. Power Pages addresses this need through responsive design principles and rigorous cross-browser testing. By optimizing websites for various devices and browsers, the platform ensures a consistent user experience, regardless of the technology used to access the site. Performance optimization techniques, such as caching and minification, further enhance the efficiency and speed of the websites built with Power Pages.

As we conclude this chapter, we transition to the next topic, where we will delve into real-world industry use cases of Microsoft Power Pages. This forthcoming discussion will focus on various challenges faced by different sectors and how the Power Platform, with its modernization technology, has been leveraged to address these issues. Through these case studies, we will explore practical applications of Power Pages, offering insights into how businesses have successfully navigated their digital transformation journeys.

CHAPTER 11   POWER PAGES FOR EXTERNAL WEBSITES

Key Takeaways

- **Power Pages**: A low-code platform for creating and managing external-facing business websites.

- **Architectural Components**: Includes frontend, backend, and database, seamlessly integrated with Microsoft services.

- **Benefits**: Rapid development, cost-effectiveness, seamless integration, and intuitive design, all backed by the platform's scalability, ensuring your business's future-proofing.

- **Security**: Built-in features and compliance with international standards ensure data protection.

- **Low-Code Design**: With Power Pages, you can develop your business website with minimal coding. This not only speeds up the development process but also fosters collaboration among your team members, as it allows them to focus on the business logic and user experience rather than the technical details.

- **Integration**: Easily connects with third-party services and embeds external content.

- **Cross-Browser Compatibility**: Ensures websites are functional across various devices and browsers.

- **Real-World Applications**: Demonstrated through case studies, showcasing the practical benefits and lessons learned, inspiring you with the platform's potential.

References

- https://www.microsoft.com/en-us/power-platform/products/power-pages
- https://learn.microsoft.com/en-us/power-pages/security/table-permissions
- https://learn.microsoft.com/en-us/power-pages/security/table-permissions#additional-considerations
- OWASP Top Ten | OWASP Foundation
- Set column permissions | Microsoft Learn
- https://learn.microsoft.com/en-us/power-pages/security/create-web-roles
- https://learn.microsoft.com/en-us/entra/identity/conditional-access/overview
- https://learn.microsoft.com/en-us/power-pages/configure/configure-cdn
- https://learn.microsoft.com/en-us/power-apps/maker/data-platform/data-platform-intro
- https://learn.microsoft.com/en-us/power-automate/

CHAPTER 12

Real-World Use Cases and Success Stories

This chapter aims to illustrate the practical applications and benefits of Microsoft Power Platform through real-world use cases and success stories. By showcasing various industries and scenarios, readers will better understand how Power Platform can solve complex business problems, drive innovation, and enhance productivity.

Organizations are constantly in search of innovative solutions to stay competitive and drive growth in today's rapidly evolving business landscape. Microsoft Power Platform, a suite of tools that has proven its transformative potential, is here to empower businesses. It offers a unique adaptability that allows it to address the specific challenges of each business and capitalize on opportunities with unprecedented agility and efficiency. By integrating low-code development, automation, and advanced analytics, Power Platform enables users to build custom applications, automate workflows, and harness data insights without extensive coding expertise.

In this chapter, we will discuss real-world use cases to see the impact of Power Platform and illustrate its transformative potential through compelling success stories. We will discuss how the business, as per our use case for the manufacturing industry, has leveraged the Power Platform to solve complex problems, drive operational excellence, and enhance productivity.

CHAPTER 12   REAL-WORLD USE CASES AND SUCCESS STORIES

In this chapter, we understand how Power Platform revolutionizes business operations by providing low-code solutions that cater to the modern demands of agility and innovation.

Finally, we will discuss our use case from the manufacturing industry, showcasing how a firm overcame equipment performance and maintenance challenges through the strategic use of Power Platform tools.

In this chapter, we will cover

- Unveiling Power Platform Impact
    - Understanding the transformative impact of Power Platform in real-world business scenarios
    - Role of low code in modern business solutions
- Success Stories
    - Overview of success stories in various industries
- Use Case: Manufacturing Industry
    - **Problem Statement**: A manufacturing firm needed a solution to monitor equipment performance and predict maintenance needs to prevent downtime.
    - **Transformation Using Power Platform**: The firm deployed Power BI to analyze sensor data from equipment, Power Automate to trigger maintenance alerts, and Power Apps to log and track maintenance activities.
    - **Outcome and Benefits**: The predictive maintenance solution reduced unexpected equipment failures, improved operational efficiency, and decreased maintenance costs. The firm could maintain continuous production with minimal interruptions.

- Key Takeaways
- Conclusion

Unveiling Power Platform Impact

As businesses navigate an increasingly complex and dynamic environment, the need for agile and adaptable solutions has never been more critical. Microsoft Power Platform, standing at the forefront of this transformation, offers tools designed to empower organizations to overcome challenges and seize opportunities with unparalleled speed and efficiency. This section aims to unveil the profound impact of Power Platform on real-world business scenarios, highlighting its role in driving innovation, streamlining operations, and enhancing decision-making processes.

In the first part, we will explore how Power Platform's low-code approach has revolutionized modern business solutions. By enabling users to build custom applications, automate workflows, and analyze data without extensive coding knowledge, Power Platform has democratized technology and accelerated digital transformation. We will delve into the practical benefits of this approach, such as empowering organizations to create tailored solutions that address their unique needs, reduce development time, and minimize costs, thereby significantly impacting business operations.

Next, we will examine the transformative impact of Power Platform across various industries. From optimizing operations and improving customer experiences to ensuring regulatory compliance and driving data-driven decisions, Power Platform's capabilities extend far beyond traditional IT solutions. Through real-world examples and practical insights, we will demonstrate how businesses have leveraged Power

Platform to achieve significant improvements in efficiency, productivity, and overall performance and how it can do the same for your industry, making it a relevant and applicable solution for your business needs.

By understanding the transformative impact of Power Platform, readers will gain a clearer perspective on its potential to revolutionize business practices and drive meaningful change. This section sets the stage for a deeper exploration of success stories and use cases, illustrating how Power Platform can be a powerful enabler of innovation and operational excellence.

Role of Low Code in Modern Business Solutions

Low-code development has democratized application creation by enabling users with minimal coding experience to build sophisticated applications. Power Platform's low-code approach allows businesses to develop custom applications, automate workflows, and analyze data without extensive programming knowledge. This has accelerated digital transformation, reduced time-to-market for solutions, and lowered the development cost.

Low code is beneficial in various business solutions by having more competency as below.

Accelerated Development and Deployment

Low-code platforms enable users to design, build, and deploy applications quickly by providing prebuilt components, drag-and-drop interfaces, and visual development tools. This accelerated development process allows businesses to respond swiftly to new opportunities and challenges. Instead of waiting for months for a custom solution, organizations can develop and launch applications in weeks or even days, significantly reducing time-to-market.

Empowering Nontechnical Users

One of the most transformative aspects of low-code platforms is their ability to empower nontechnical users, such as business analysts and departmental managers, to create solutions without extensive coding knowledge. This democratization of technology recognizes the value of these employees, enabling them to design and implement solutions that address their specific needs. Low-code platforms foster greater collaboration and innovation by bridging the gap between IT and business users, highlighting the integral role of nontechnical users in problem-solving.

Cost Efficiency

Low-code development reduces the need for specialized coding skills and extensive IT resources, leading to cost savings in development and maintenance. With fewer resources for coding and debugging, businesses can allocate their budget more effectively and achieve a higher return on investment. Additionally, the ability to make rapid changes and updates to applications without significant rework further enhances cost efficiency.

Enhanced Flexibility and Customization

Low-code platforms offer a high degree of flexibility, allowing businesses to customize applications to meet their unique requirements. Users can easily modify workflows, integrate with existing systems, and add new features. This adaptability ensures that applications can evolve alongside changing business needs and technological advancements, providing a future-proof solution.

Automation

Automation is a vital benefit of low-code platforms. By automating repetitive tasks and processes, businesses can improve efficiency and reduce the risk of human error. For instance, Power Automate, part of the Microsoft Power Platform, enables users to create workflows that automate routine activities, such as data entry, notifications, and approvals. This not only saves time but also enhances productivity and consistency.

Collaboration and Innovation

Low-code platforms, with their intuitive, drag-and-drop interfaces, facilitate greater collaboration between IT and business teams. This allows business users to actively participate in application development, while IT ensures technical robustness. The result is faster and more effective solutions. Moreover, the shared development environment bridges communication gaps and aligns both teams toward common goals, encouraging a sense of unity and shared purpose. These tools enable stakeholders from different departments to collaborate more effectively by providing a common platform for developing and testing applications. This collaborative approach fosters innovation, as diverse perspectives contribute to creating more effective and comprehensive solutions.

Data-Driven Insights

Many low-code platforms integrate with advanced analytics and reporting tools, enabling businesses to leverage data for informed decision-making. For example, Power BI, another component of the Microsoft Power Platform, provides powerful data visualization and analysis capabilities. Businesses can make more informed decisions and drive better outcomes by embedding data insights directly into applications.

CHAPTER 12   REAL-WORLD USE CASES AND SUCCESS STORIES

Success Stories

In this section, we will explore real-world success stories of how various industries have harnessed the Power Platform to overcome challenges and achieve significant improvements. By examining detailed transformation journeys in healthcare, retail, and finance, we will illustrate the practical benefits and outcomes of implementing Power Platform solutions in diverse business contexts.

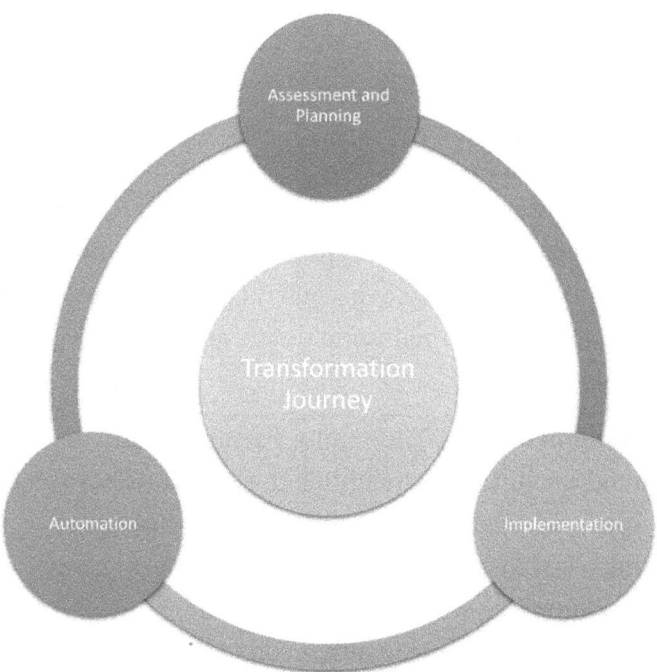

Figure 12-1. *Typical transformation journey of an industry*

Figure 12-1 visualizes a typical transformation journey of any industry. We will explore the industry success cases based on their journey.

CHAPTER 12 REAL-WORLD USE CASES AND SUCCESS STORIES

Healthcare Industry

A large healthcare provider managing multiple facilities and a high volume of patient interactions faced significant challenges with patient scheduling and medical record management. The reliance on manual scheduling led to frequent appointment conflicts, delays, and a higher rate of administrative errors. Managing medical records could have been more convenient and efficient, impacting operational efficiency and patient satisfaction.

Transformation Journey

- **Assessment and Planning**: The healthcare provider assesses pain points in the scheduling and records management processes. They engaged stakeholders, including administrative staff and healthcare providers, to gather requirements and define goals for the new system.

- **Implementation**: They chose Power Platform to build a solution to streamline these processes. Power Apps was used to create a custom scheduling app that allowed patients to book, reschedule, or cancel appointments easily. The app also integrates with the hospital's electronic health records (EHR) system to ensure up-to-date information.

- **Automation**: Power Automate was employed to automate routine tasks, such as sending appointment reminders, updating patient records, and managing administrative approvals. This automation helped reduce manual errors and ensured timely updates.

- **Integration**: The solution was integrated with the existing healthcare management systems, ensuring a seamless flow of information and reducing the need for duplicate data entry.

Outcome and Benefits

- **Efficiency**: The new system reduced administrative workload, allowing staff to focus on patient care. Scheduling conflicts decreased, and appointment management became more efficient.

- **Accuracy**: Automation minimized errors in patient records and scheduling, improving patient information accuracy.

- **Patient Satisfaction**: Patients experienced fewer appointment issues and received timely reminders, enhancing their overall satisfaction with the healthcare provider.

Retail Industry

A global retail chain with numerous outlets worldwide needed help managing sales data and understanding customer preferences. The existing approach to data analysis needed to be more cohesive, leading to delayed insights and suboptimal decision-making in inventory and marketing.

Transformation Journey

- **Assessment and Planning:** The retail chain needed a more integrated, real-time approach to analyzing sales and customer data. They set objectives to improve inventory management, enhance marketing strategies, and gain deeper insights into customer behavior.

- **Implementation:** The company implemented Power BI to aggregate and analyze sales data across all locations. Interactive dashboards were created to visualize trends, track performance metrics, and understand customer preferences.

- **Data Integration:** Power BI connects various data sources, including sales records, inventory systems, and customer feedback platforms. This integration provided a comprehensive view of operations and customer interactions.

- **Actionable Insights:** The insights derived from Power BI enabled the retail chain to optimize inventory levels, identify popular products, and tailor marketing campaigns based on customer preferences and buying patterns.

Outcome and Benefits

- **Sales Growth:** Improved inventory management and targeted marketing efforts increased sales and revenue.

- **Customer Loyalty:** Personalized marketing campaigns and better product availability enhanced customer satisfaction and loyalty.

- **Operational Efficiency**: Streamlined data analysis and decision-making processes improved operational efficiency and responsiveness to market trends.

Finance industry

A financial services firm faced challenges in managing compliance with regulatory requirements. Manual tracking and approval processes could have been faster and more error-prone, risking noncompliance and potential regulatory penalties.

Transformation Journey

- **Assessment and Planning**: The firm thoroughly reviewed its compliance processes and identified bottlenecks and areas prone to errors. They defined objectives to automate workflows, improve tracking accuracy, and enhance real-time monitoring.

- **Implementation**: The firm deployed Power Platform to develop a compliance tracking system. Power Automate was used to streamline workflow approvals, automate notifications, and track documentation. Power BI was employed to create real-time compliance dashboards that provided visibility into key metrics and status updates.

- **Automation and Monitoring**: Power Automate ensured compliance tasks were completed on time, with automatic alerts for approvals and deadlines. Power BI offered real-time monitoring of compliance activities, allowing the firm to proactively identify and address potential issues.

- **Integration**: The system was integrated with the existing compliance tools and databases, providing a unified view of compliance status and facilitating better coordination across departments.

Outcome and Benefits

- **Regulatory Compliance**: The firm significantly reduced noncompliance risk by ensuring timely approvals and accurate tracking.
- **Efficiency**: Automating compliance workflows and real-time monitoring improved process efficiency and reduced the administrative burden on staff.
- **Transparency**: Real-time dashboards provided greater transparency into compliance activities, enabling more informed decision-making and quicker response to potential issues

Use Case: Manufacturing Industry

In this section, we will see how the Manufacturing Industry benefited from the revolutionary implementation of the Power Platform.

In one notable incident, the breakdown of a critical injection molder on a Friday afternoon resulted in a frantic weekend repair effort. The machine, used for producing high-precision automotive components, malfunctioned due to an overlooked issue with its hydraulic system. The repair team worked overtime, incurring extra costs and pushing the machine back into operation by Monday morning. However, due

CHAPTER 12   REAL-WORLD USE CASES AND SUCCESS STORIES

to the extended downtime, the company missed a critical shipment deadline for AutoTech Motors, leading to a strained client relationship and a potential financial penalty. This situation highlighted the urgent need for a more proactive and efficient approach to maintenance management.

Problem Statement

Precision Industries, a leading automotive parts manufacturer, operates a sprawling facility with advanced machinery. Despite their state-of-the-art equipment, they face significant operational challenges:

- **Frequent Equipment Breakdowns**: At Precision Industries, machinery such as CNC machines, injection molders, and conveyor systems are vital for production. However, these machines frequently break down due to unforeseen issues like mechanical failures or wear and tear. For example, CNC machines, crucial for precision cutting, have an average of three breakdowns per month, leading to costly production halts. This results in a backlog of orders and delays in delivering products to clients like AutoTech Motors and Speedy Autos, affecting client satisfaction and potentially leading to a loss of business. This potential loss of business underscores the need for a more proactive maintenance strategy. The firm's reactive approach to maintenance, led by John, the head of the maintenance department, is proving to be a costly strategy. Urgent repairs, often more expensive, are required when breakdowns occur. For instance, an unexpected breakdown of the injection molder last quarter required a rushed repair that cost the company an

635

additional $15,000 compared to routine maintenance. The cost of spare parts, overtime pay for maintenance staff, and production delays contribute significantly to these expenses, highlighting the urgent need for a more proactive and cost-effective maintenance strategy.

- **Production downtime**: Production downtime, a persistent issue at Precision Industries, not only halts production but also disrupts the entire supply chain. During a recent episode, a conveyor belt malfunction led to a 12-hour shutdown, causing a delay in the assembly line and forcing the company to push back delivery schedules. This downtime not only results in missed deadlines for important orders from clients such as Precision Automotive and Gear Works Inc., but it also impacts their trust and potentially results in lost contracts. This situation underscores the need for improved operational efficiency and client management, which can be achieved through the proposed changes.

Expected Solution

To address these challenges, Precision Industries needs a solution that offers

- **Real-Time Insights:** It is crucial to have a system that continuously monitors equipment performance and provides real-time data analysis. For example, tracking metrics like machine temperature, vibration levels, and usage hours can help identify patterns that precede equipment failures. With this real-time data, the company can pre-emptively address issues before they escalate into costly breakdowns.

- **Predictive Maintenance Capabilities**: Implementing predictive maintenance is essential to reduce the frequency and severity of equipment failures. Predictive analytics can analyze historical data and current performance to forecast potential failures. For instance, if the data indicates that a CNC machine's performance degrades over time, maintenance can be scheduled proactively. This shift from reactive to predictive maintenance would minimize unexpected downtime and reduce repair costs.

- **Streamlined Maintenance Management**: The company also needs a streamlined system for logging maintenance activities, tracking repairs, and scheduling preventive measures. John and his team use a mix of paper logs and basic spreadsheets, which leads to inefficiencies and errors. An integrated system would enable better tracking of maintenance history, resource allocation, and task management.

Transformation Journey Using Power Platform

In this section, we will go through various transformation stages and understand how the transformation is done.

Assessment and Planning

At the very first step, we must make sure about the clear objective—Identify and define the issues related to equipment maintenance and outline the goals for implementing Power Platform solutions.

CHAPTER 12　REAL-WORLD USE CASES AND SUCCESS STORIES

To achieve so, following are the activities:

- **Stakeholder Meetings**: Conduct meetings with key stakeholders, including John (Head of Maintenance), Lisa (Production Manager), and Mark (IT Specialist), to gather detailed requirements and pain points.

- **Data Analysis**: Review historical data on equipment performance, maintenance records, and downtime incidents to understand current challenges.

The following are the achievements:

- **Problem Identified**: Frequent CNC machine breakdowns, leading to unexpected downtime and high repair costs.

- **Goal Set**: Reduce downtime by 30% and maintenance costs by 25% within the next year.

Leveraging Power Platform

Based on the findings in previous sections, management decided to leverage the benefits of Power Platform for various requirements.

Usage of Power BI to Develop Data Analysis Dashboard

Use Power BI to analyze equipment performance data and create dashboards that provide actionable insights. It involves the following activities:

- **Data Integration**: Connect Power BI to data sources such as IoT sensors on machinery, maintenance logs, and historical performance data.

- **Dashboard Creation**: Develop interactive dashboards to visualize key performance indicators (KPIs) like machine temperature, vibration levels, and usage hours.

Table 12-1 provides example machine data.

Table 12-1. Machine Data for Analysis

MachineID	Timestamp	Temp. (°C)	Vibration (Hz)	Hours of Operation
CNC-001	2024-07-01 08:00:00	85	12	120
CNC-001	2024-07-01 09:00:00	87	13	121

Automate and Get the Alert Using Power Automate

Automate the process of generating maintenance alerts based on the data insights from Power BI. Following are the activities:

- **Trigger Setup**: Configure Power Automate to monitor data from Power BI dashboards. Set up triggers for predefined thresholds (e.g., temperature exceeding 90°C).

- **Alert Generation**: Create workflows that send notifications to maintenance teams and generate maintenance tickets.

CHAPTER 12   REAL-WORLD USE CASES AND SUCCESS STORIES

Following are the workflow step considerations:

- Monitor data feed from Power BI.
- If temperature is > 90°C, send an email notification to John.
- Create a maintenance ticket in the system with details of the equipment and issue.

Using Power Apps: Custom Maintenance Tracking and Management

Develop a custom Power Apps application to manage and track maintenance activities.

- **App Development**: Create a Power Apps application that allows maintenance staff to log activities, track repairs, and manage schedules.
- **Integration**: Integrate the app with Power BI for real-time data access and with Power Automate for automated task management.

Testing and Validation

Ensure that all components work together seamlessly and meet the defined goals.

- **Testing**: Conduct end-to-end testing of the Power BI dashboards, Power Automate workflows, and Power Apps functionalities.
- **Validation**: Validate the accuracy of data insights, effectiveness of alerts, and usability of the maintenance tracking app.

CHAPTER 12   REAL-WORLD USE CASES AND SUCCESS STORIES

Deployment and Training

Deploy the solution across the organization and train staff on its use.

- **Deployment**: Roll out the Power Platform solutions to all relevant teams.

- **Training**: Provide training sessions for maintenance staff, production managers, and IT personnel on using Power BI, Power Automate, and Power Apps.

Monitoring and Optimization

Continuously monitor the system's performance and optimize based on feedback and changing needs.

- **Monitoring**: Track system performance and user feedback to identify areas for improvement.

- **Optimization**: Make necessary adjustments to dashboards, workflows, and apps to enhance the efficiency and address any emerging issues.

Summary

In this chapter, we have delved into real-world use cases and success stories that vividly illustrate the transformative power of Microsoft Power Platform across various industries. We began by exploring how a manufacturing firm, which was struggling with frequent equipment breakdowns and high maintenance costs, leveraged Power Platform to implement a predictive maintenance system. This system significantly reduced equipment downtime and maintenance costs. In the healthcare sector, we examined how Power Platform was used to automate patient scheduling and streamline medical record management, addressing the challenge of manual scheduling and improving operational efficiency and patient satisfaction.

CHAPTER 12 REAL-WORLD USE CASES AND SUCCESS STORIES

These success stories collectively highlight Power Platform's versatile and impactful nature in addressing diverse business challenges. As organizations navigate the complexities of the digital era, the solutions provided by Power Platform not only drive innovation but also enhance operational efficiency.

Key Takeaways

- **Rapid Deployment**: Power Platform enables quick development and solutions deployment, helping businesses promptly address challenges.

- **Enhanced Efficiency**: The automation and analytics provided by Power Platform tools improve operational efficiency and reduce manual effort.

- **Customization and Flexibility**: Power Platform's low-code nature allows for tailored solutions that meet specific business needs, enhancing overall productivity.

Index

A

Accessibility
    Canvas apps, 325–327
    design principles, 324
    model-driven apps, 327, 328
    operable, 324
    perceivable, 324
    power platform apps, 330, 331
    robust, 325
    testing/validating tools, 329–330
    understandable, 325
Accessibility Checker, 329
Administration
    analytics
        data export to Data Lake, 107–109
        Power Apps, 102
        telemetry, 105–107
        tenant-level, 103–105
        types of reports, 101
    global admin, 60, 61
    governance and management, 57
    Managed Environments, 114
    Power Platform admin, 61, 62
    roles/responsibilities, 58, 59
    security layers, 63, 64
    use cases, 113
AI Builder
    accountability, 524
    architectural components, 525
    architecture
        core components, 511
        data sources, 512
        integration, 512
        no-code/low-code environment, 512
        training/deployment, 511
    Azure AI Studio, 485–487
    capabilities, 485
    customer interactions, 482
    decision-making, 482
    document processing, 484
    engineering process, 488–492
    features and capabilities, 18
    feedback analysis, 484
    home page screenshot, 481, 482
    hub, 21
    increased efficiency, 483
    integration, 525
        automated workflows, 513
        categorization text, 514, 515
        Copilot Studio, 519–521

INDEX

AI Builder (*cont.*)
    data-driven insights, 519
    data source, 515, 516
    Dataverse Plugins, 519
    demo screen, 516
    low-code plugins, 519
    Power apps, 514
  key features, 484
  key learning, 475–477
  Microsoft Power Platform, 18
  models
    benefits, 507
    business card reader, 510
    business processes, 507–510
    category classification, 508
    custom model, 506, 507
    descriptions/template
      mappings, 500–503
    document processing, 508
    entity extraction, 508
    features, 500
    key phrase extraction, 510
    language detection, 509
    object detection, 510
    prebuilt models, 504
    prediction, 509
    proprietary data, 505–507
    receipt processing, 508
    sentiment analysis, 504, 509
    text recognition, 510
    text translation, 509
    training process, 506
  model training/
    deployment, 484
  no-code AI cheat sheet, 21, 22
  Power Apps/Power
    Automate, 19, 20
  prebuilt models, 484
  predictive maintenance, 484
  prompts
    built-in knowledge, 498, 499
    business solutions, 497
    creation, 497
    customization, 496
    dataverse tables, 499
    demo screen, 498
    emails, 497
    features, 492, 495, 497
    filtering/references, 496
    hands-off automation, 493
    integration, 496
    prebuilt prompts, 494, 495
    prerequisites, 494
    tasks/business
      scenarios, 497
  real-world applications, 483
  real-world use cases, 19
  responsible, 524
  routine tasks, 482
  scalablility/flexibility, 485
  security/governance
    accessibility/
      permissions, 521
    capacity management, 523
    data security/privacy, 521
    DLP policies, 522
    lifecycle management, 522
    monitoring/compliance, 523

INDEX

overview, 520
personas/roles, 520
roles/permissions
    mapping, 522
unified environment, 485
Apache Parquet, 193
Application lifecycle management
    (ALM), 66, 75, 396, 527
  application development, 528
  benefits, 532, 533
  CI/CD platforms, 532
  complexity, 543
  comprehensive tools
    accelerator, 555
    benefits, 557
    Center of Excellence
      (CoE), 556
    collaboration, 557
    customizable templates, 556
    key features, 555
    organizations
      streamline, 557
    Power Platform makers, 556
    release phase, 559
    test phase, 558
  connection references, 554
  customizations/
    configurations, 543
  cyclic process, 529, 530
  data management, 544
  dataverse, 531
  definition, 527
  dependencies, 553, 554
  environment planning, 553
  governance, 528
  holistic approach, 533
  integration, 544
  layers, 554
  maintenance, 529
  pipelines, 547–551
  Power Platform (*see* Power
    Platform)
  publisher, 553
  robust environment, 530
  security/compliance, 544
  solutions, 531
  solution updates, 554
  source control systems, 531
  strategies, 543
  structured approach, 533
  testing, 553
  tooling/automation, 544
  unmanaged solutions, 553
  version control/source
      code, 545
    build phase, 545
    planning phase, 545
    release phase, 545
    strategies, 547
    systematic approach, 546
Application Programming
    Interfaces (APIs), 201,
    583, 609
Artificial general intelligence
    (AGI), 480
Artificial intelligence (AI), 372
  AI Builder, 475
  AlphaGo, 480

645

INDEX

Artificial intelligence (AI) (*cont.*)
   birth of, 478
   deep learning, 480
   ethical considerations/
      regulations, 480
   expert systems, 479
   GPT-3, 480
   history, 477, 481
   integration, 480
   machine learning, 479
   mythology/fiction, 477
   optimism/challenges, 479
   responsible, 524
   Twentieth century, 478
   see also Generative AI (GenAI)
Auditing
   data-level, 110
   events, 110
   granular control, 111
   platform-level, 110
   purpose, 109
   types, 110
Audit logs, 84, 110, 124, 150, 183, 370–372, 386
Autonumber columns, 134
Azure Active Directory (AAD), 64, 81, 593
Azure AI Studio
   comparison, 485
   customization/control, 487
   functionality/features, 486
   integration/ecosystem, 486
   target audience/usability, 485

Azure Blob Storage, 100, 227
Azure Synapse Analytics, 108, 184–189, 193, 196, 197, 487
Azure Synapse Link
   advantages, 187
   analytics, 189
   analytics platform, 188
   benefits, 185, 186, 193–196
   configuring/activating, 190
   definition, 186
   Delta Lake, 193
   enable change tracking, control data synchronization, 191, 192
   ETL processes, 188
   Microsoft Fabric, 198–201
   monitoring, 196–198

B

Business Process Flows (BPFs), 123, 142–144, 309, 418

C

Canvas apps, 11, 276, 281, 283
   access apps, 292
   building apps, 298–300
   business logic error, 355
   connected data source, 295
   controls, 294, 295
   creation, 293
   debugging, 354

INDEX

dragging and dropping
    controls, 289
  features, 289–292
  implement logic, 296
  performance issues, 354
  publish app, 297
  share/collaborate, 297
  test/design, 297
  testing
    types, 348, 349
  themes/branding
    accessibility, 323
    colors, 317
    consistency, 322
    media/images, 319
    model-driven apps, 319–321
    performance, 322
    readability, 322
    responsive design, 319
    setup theme, 317, 318
    styles to controls, apply, 318
    user experience, 323
  tools/techniques, 349, 350
  use case, 301
  user interface design, 294
  user interface issues, 354
Center of Excellence (COE)
  kit, 112–114
Chain-of-Thought prompting, 489
Columns
  autonumber, 133, 134
  calculations, 133
  choice
    global, 131
    local, 132
    yes/no, 131
  data types, 130
  definition, 130
  formula, 133
  lookup, 132
  properties, 130
  relationships, 132
  roll-up, 133
  validation rules, 131
Command line interface
  (CLI), 27, 549
Common Data Model (CDM), 117,
  162, 167, 284
Common Data Service, 116, 187,
  281, 303
Common Data Service for Apps
  (CDS), 5, 116
Component libraries, 277
Connector Gallery, 98
Connectors, 8, 15, 34
  action control, DLP, 99
  actions, 384
    CRM data, 385
    financial services, 385
    human resources (HR), 385
    technical
      support, 385
  architecture, 56
  benefits, 381, 382
  business applications, 52
  characteristics, 52, 53
  cloud-based data sources
    building applications, 237

Connectors (*cont.*)
    business process
      automation, 235
    composite data model, 235
    data-driven decision
      making, 236
    dataflows, 233
    data integration, 238
    ease of use, 235
    limitations, 236
    unified custom view, 235
    virtual tables, 234
connectivity, 56
Copilot Studio
    actions, 383
    configuration, 382
    mapping data, 383
    monitoring, 383, 384
    selection, 382
    testing/validation, 383
    data source connectivity issues,
      troubleshooting
    authentication/
      authorization issues, 252
    configure data source, 251
    gateway logs, analyze, 253
    identify service outages, 252
    issues users
      encounter, 248–250
    leverage dataverse
      diagnostic tools, 253
    monitor resource
      utilization, 252
    network tracing tools, 253
    validate gateway
      configuration, 250, 251
    verify network
      connectivity, 250
definition, 225
endpoint filtering, 100
enterprise systems, 380, 381
meaning, 380
nondevelopers, 225
real-world use cases
    business automation,
      262, 263
    customer data
      management, 263
    enterprise data
      integration, 261
    financial data
      consolidation, 264
    healthcare data
      integration, 265
    human resource
      management, 265, 266
    IoT data management, 266
    real-time analytics/
      reporting, 262
    supply chain
      management, 264
scaling
    capacity
      planning, 255
    high availability/
      reliability, 257
    performance, 256
security/governance, 386

INDEX

third-party applications and services, 96
types, 54, 96–98
   custom, 229
   standard, 226
use cases, 54, 55
Continuous integration/continuous delivery (CI/CD), 75, 532, 547
Continuous integration/continuous deployment (CI/CD), 556
Conversational Language Understanding (CLU), 393
Convolutional neural networks (CNNs), 480
Copilot Studio, 4, 7, 361
  architecture, 392
    analytics/management, 395
    authentication/authorization, 393
    component leverages, 394
    core AI services, 393
    data integration/management, 394
    lifecycle management, 396
    security/compliance, 395
  connectors, 380–386
  custom GPTs, 39
  features, 39, 40, 42
  Generative AI (*see* Generative AI (GenAI))
  integration, 40
    actions, 517
    functions/expertise, 517
    plugins action, 517
    prompt actions, 518, 519
  monitoring/diagnosing, 396
    analytics sessions, 399
    capabilities, 397
    comprehensive analysis, 399
    Customer Satisfaction (CSAT), 401
    description/details, 402–404
    events/auditing, 398
    summary charts, 400, 401
    tools/capabilities, 396, 397
    topic summary charts, 402
  Power Automate, 430–438
  Power CAT (*see* Power CAT Copilot Studio Kit)
  publication/integration
    auditing/troubleshooting, 408
    Bot Service Channels, 407
    Facebook, 406
    Live Website, 404
    Microsoft Teams, 405
    Mobile/Custom Apps, 407
    Power Pages, 405
    scenarios, 404–408
    tools, 408
  security/governance, 367–372
  See also Microsoft Copilot Studio
Create, Read, Update, Delete (CRUD), 122, 452

INDEX

Custom APIs
    API endpoints, 204
    features, 204
    implementation, 205, 206
    use cases, 205
Custom connectors, 97
    internal APIs, 230
    legacy systems, 230
    practices, 230–232
    user-defined, 229
Customer-Managed Keys (CMKs), 48, 71, 77, 84, 605
Customer relationship management (CRM), 127, 153, 280, 384

D

Data Analysis Expressions (DAX), 43
Dataflows
    automation, 179
    benefits, 162–164
    benefits, scheduling/automation, 180
    creation and configuration, 167–171
    data volumes, 159
    disadvantages, 164, 165
    enhance security, 161
    Excel and Power BI, 160
    features, 160
    monitoring and managing execution
        governance/compliance, 183, 184
        monitoring tools, 181
        performance optimization, 182
        troubleshooting/diagnostics, 181
    Power BI Desktop, 162
    Power BI service, 162
    reusable transformation, 161
    scheduling, 178
    transformation/data preparation
        advanced transformations, 173
        aggregation/grouping, 172
        data analysis, 173
        data cleaning, 172
        data refresh/scheduling, 174
        data sources, 171
        filtering/sorting, 172
        integartion, 174
        Power Query, 171
        practices, 175
        transforming data, 172
    use-case scenario, 166, 167
Data Loss Prevention (DLP), 77, 84, 367, 522
    blocking channels, 370
    capabilities, 369
    connector configuration, 368, 369
    event categories/descriptions, 370–372
    policies, 66, 69, 70, 93, 94, 367, 368, 395

INDEX

Power Automate, 421
skills, 369
Data profiling tools, 182
Dataverse, 4
   analytics/reporting, 155
   authentication layers, 36, 37
   automation/workflow
      management, 118, 119, 156
   benefits, 115
   BPFs, 142–144
   business applications, 32, 117
   business data, 115
   business rules, 141, 142
   capabilities, 38
   columns, 130
   components, 32
   connectors, 34
   cost-effective solution, 120
   CRM, 153, 154
   custom applications, 154
   data connectivity, 119
   data integration/
      consolidation, 155
   developers, 33
   ERP, 154
   extensibility, 119
   forms
      card, 137
      definition, 136
      main, 136, 138
      mobile, 137
      quick create, 136
      quick view, 137
   healthcare applications, 156
   import and export
      data, 151, 152
   integration, external
      services, 207
      APIs/webhooks, 208
      built-in connectors, 207
      custom connectors, 207
      data gateways, 208
      integration method, 208
      scenarios/solutions, 209, 210
   keys, 134, 135
   layers
      business logic, 122
      data, 123
      presentation, 120, 121
      security, 124, 125
      service, 122
   low-code/no-code
      development, 116
   Microsoft services, 157
   plugins, 34, 146, 147
   security, 35, 36, 150, 157
   security mechanisms, 32
   security roles
      access levels, 148
      hierarchical security, 149
      permissions, 148
      RBAC, 147
      sharing/team security, 149
      table-/column-level
         security, 149
   tables, 33, 34, 126
   views, 138
   workflows, 144–146

Dataverse accelerator
 benefits, 223, 224
 definition, 222
 features, 222, 223
Dataverse security
 features, 88
 hierarchy structure, 89, 90
 levels to control access, 92
 permissions/privileges, 90, 91
 security models, 87, 89
Data visualization
 Canvas Apps, controls, 341, 342
 data/audience, 346
 design patterns, 346
 JavaScript libraries, 344
 model-driven apps, controls, 342, 343
 performance, 347
 Power BI, 344
 testing/feedback, 347
 use cases, 345
Delta Lake, 193-196
Dynamics 365 Portals, 27

E

Electronic health records (EHR) system, 265, 630
Enterprise Resource Planning (ERP), 154, 166, 209, 263
EntityId, 135
Environment strategy
 access control/resource management, 68
 collaboration, 70
 development, 69
 elements, 64, 65
 optimize resource utilization, 70
 security, 69
 training and resources, 70
 types of environment, 66-68
External Websites, *see* Power Pages
Extract, transform and load (ETL), 159, 162, 187, 188

F

Few-shot learning, 489, 491
Financial services
 assessment/planning, 633
 automation/monitoring, 633
 implementation, 633
 integration, 634
 outcome/benefits, 634
 transfoemation, 633
Foreign keys, 135
Formula columns, 133

G

Gateway clusters
 components, 239
 features, 246, 247
 installation, 239-241
 limitations, 245, 246
 on-premises data, 238, 239, 242, 248, 267

scaling on-premises
data, 257–261
setting up configuration,
243, 244
strategic implementation, 268
use cases, 244, 261
General Data Protection
Regulation (GDPR), 194,
573, 579, 607, 608
Generative actions
action execution, 387
automatical slot-filling, 388
benefits, 391, 392
chaining plugins, 387
configuration/setup, 389
dynamics chain, 390
features, 387
flexibility/scalability, 388
handling multi-intent
queries, 388
HR assistance, 391
key feaatures, 387, 388
LangChain concepts, 388
natural language, 389
order processing, 391
technical support, 391
testing/optimization, 390
triggers, 389
user experience, 388
visual authoring tools, 389
Generative AI (GenAI)
comprehensive overview, 372
customer supports, 376, 377

data sources, 379, 380
features, 373–375
implementation, 377, 378
internal sources, 376
key features, 375, 376
knowledge sources, 377
order management, 377
primary/fallback
information, 375
prompting techniques, 378, 379
Globally Unique Identifier
(GUID), 135

H

Healthcare industry, 630
automation, 630
implementation, 630
integration, 631
outcome/benefits, 631
transformation, 630
Health Insurance Portability and
Accountability Act (HIPAA),
84, 259, 602, 604, 615

I

iFrames, 610, 611, 619
Information security management
system (ISMS), 24, 607
Integration testing, 348, 351
International Organization for
Standardization (ISO), 24

INDEX

J
JavaScript, 344, 611

K
Key performance indicators (KPIs), 155, 167, 400, 410, 639
Kusto Query Language (KQL), 397

L
Large language models (LLMs), 361, 394, 496
    Generative AI, 373
Lockbox, 48, 71, 77
Lookup columns, 132

M
Managed Environments
    admin center, 72
    capabilities
        advisor, 80
        CMK, 77
        components, 78
        data policies, 75
        DLP, 77, 78
        environment groups, 74
        environment routing, 79, 80
        insights, 75
        IP locations, 76
        lockbox, 77
        pipelines, 75, 76
        sharing permissions, 74
        solution checker, 76
    components, 71
    functionalities, 71
Manufacturing industry
    alerts
        activities, 639
        considerations, 640
        deployment/training, 641
        monitoring/
            optimization, 641
        testing/validation, 640
        tracking/management, 640
    frequent equipment
        breakdowns, 635
    leveraging information
        dashboard creation, 639
        integration, 638
        machine data, 639
        Power BI, 638
        requirements, 638
    operational challenges, 635, 636
    predictive maintenance, 637
    production downtime, 636
    real-time data analysis, 636, 637
    streamlined system, 637
    transformation
        achievements, 638
        activities, 638
        objective, 637
Microsoft Azure, 186
Microsoft Azure OpenAI Studio, 39
Microsoft Copilot Studio, 5, 361
    creation, 363
    custom Copilot, 362

delete option, 364, 365
development/integration, 365
generative actions, 365, 387–392
key features, 361, 362
monitoring/management, 366
publication process, 366
real-time data, 365
scenarios, 366
Microsoft Fabric, 198–201
Microsoft Teams or Slack, 209
Model-driven apps, 11
   access, 306, 307
   data-centric approach, 302
   debugging/testing, 355–357
   defined data model, 307, 308
   error handling, 313
   features, 303–306
   forms/views/charts, 308, 309
   monitoring/improvements, 314
   optimized data model, 311
   optimize performance, 312
   reusable components, 311
   security/compliance, 313
   test/publish, 310
   tools/techniques, 352, 353
   types of testing, 351
   use cases, 314, 315
   workflows/business logic, 309
Modern app design
   principles, 269, 270
   responsive design
      best practices, 277–280
      creating applications, 272

media queries, 274, 275
principles, 273
scalable images and media, 274
tools, Power Apps, 275–277
user engagement and satisfaction, 270, 271
Multifactor authentication (MFA), 85, 151, 579, 591

N

Natural Language Processing (NLP), 375, 377
Network Access Control (NAC) policies, 86

O

One-shot learning, 489
Open Data Protocol (OData), 122, 128, 204
Open SQL Server Management Studio (SSMS), 221

P

Payment Card Industry Data Security Standard (PCI DSS), 25–28, 573
Performance testing, 349, 352
Pipelines, 547
   built-in safeguards, 550
   centralized governance, 548

655

INDEX

Pipelines (*cont.*)
   control/customization
      options, 550
   cost savings, 551
   DevOps, 549
   extensibility, 549
   features, 547
   makers, 548
   overview, 548
   persona
      admins, 552
      makers, 551
      professional developers, 552
   personal pipelines, 549
   platform host, 549
   preconfigured pipelines, 549
   productivity, 550
   quality/compliance, 550
   scalability, 548
Plugins, 34, 146, 201
   business processes, 201
   features, 201, 202
   implementation, 203
   use cases, 202
Power Apps
   AI Builder, 283
   benefits, 287, 288
   building custom applications, 9
   Canvas apps, 11, 283
   capabilities, 281
   CDM, 284
   components, 10
   connectors, 283
   create custom applications, 281

   Dataverse, 282
   definition, 9
   development lifecycle, 285, 286
   feature, 10
   maker portal, 13
   model-driven apps, 11
   no-/low-code development, 12
   Power BI, 284
   SharePoint document, 284
   templates/connectors, 12
   user-friendly interface, 12
Power Apps Portals, 27
Power Automate, 411
   actions, 412
   AI Builder, 414
   approval workflows, 415
   auditing/compliance, 470
   automate workflows, 412
   Builder (*see* AI Builder)
   business processes, 13, 14
   cloud flows, 413
      action pane, 426
      creation, 425
      email action, 426
      save/testing process, 427
      sign-in, 425
      trigger, 425, 426
   connectors, 14, 15, 414
   Copilots
      conditions/loops, 432
      employee onboarding
         process, 433–435
      error detection, 431
      error handling, 436

INDEX

features, 429–431
flow creation process, 430
flow objective, 432, 433
modular design, 435
optimizations, 431, 436
real-time assistance, 430, 431
security/compliance, 437
services/applications, 433
triggers/actions, 432
data connectivity, 455
   capabilities, 446
   connectors, 446, 447
   Dataverse table, 448
   set up connections, 447, 448
data connectivity/ transformation, 446
debugging tools/techniques
   history, 463
   logging/notifications, 463
   outputs, 463
   testing, 464
desktop flows, 413
   creation, 427
   desktop, 427
   edit/customization, 428
   recording actions, 428
   run/save options, 428
documentation, 471
error handling, 457, 468
   API call options, 460
   configuration, 457
   data validation, 460
   documentation, 465

logging data, 464
notifications, 465
parallel branching, 459
proactive error, 464
regularly monitor, 465
scope action, 458
terminate action, 458
testing/validation, 466
features, 421, 422
integration
   scenarios, 440, 441
integration (Apps)
   applications/services, 438
   benefits, 438, 439
   business rules, 441
   data synchronization, 440
   design considerations, 443
   maintenance/updates, 444
   notifications, 440
   package, 445
   real-time data, 439
   security/compliance, 444
   steps, 441–443
key features, 411–415
manipulation, 452, 453, 456
modularization flows, 467
objectives, 467
performance, 468
permissions, 469
process flow, 467
secure authentication, 469
security and compliance, 15
templates, 414
testing, 470

INDEX

Power Automate (*cont.*)
    transformation, 449
        AI Builder models, 451
        built-in actions, 449
        Dataverse table, 452
        expressions, 450
        formatDateTime
          function, 451
        split function, 451
        string/int function, 450
    transformations, 455
    triggers, 412
    troubleshooting, 457
        authentication/
          permissions, 460
        connectors, 461
        incorrect data handling, 462
        timing out/delays, 461
        triggers, 462
    types
        automated flows, 415, 416
        business process, 415, 418
        desktop, 419, 420
        manual flows, 417
        scheduled flows, 416
    use cases, 422
        data collection, 423
        document approval
          process, 422
        notifications, 423
        onboarding process, 424
        SharePoint document, 422
        social media monitoring, 423
    users, 14
    validation, 468
    workflow automation, 16, 17, 453–455
Power Automate and AI Copilots
    AI Builder, 335
    AI models, 335
    connect Power Apps, 334
    features, 335
    model-driven apps, 332
    monitoring, 340
    performance, 338
    security, 339
    test/publish, 334
    test/refine, 336
    trigger, 333
    use cases, 332, 336–338
    user training, 339
Power BI, 344
    business analytics tool, 42, 211
    Dataverse
        connecting power, 213
        connectors, 217, 218
        dashboards, 214
        data transformation/
          modeling, 213
        practices, 216
        publishing/sharing
          reports, 214
        use cases, 214, 215
        visualizations, 214
    definition, 42
    features, 42–44
    reports, 218, 219
    TDS endpoint, 220, 221

INDEX

visualizing data, 212, 213
Power CAT Copilot Studio Kit
    comprehensive set, 409
    key performance indicators, 410
    testing capabilities, 409
Power FX
    benefits, 46
    characteristics, 44, 45
    definition, 44
    use cases, 45, 46
Power Pages, 282, 561
    addresses, 565
    advantage, 565
    benefits, 585
    business process
        advantages, 585
        cost-effectiveness, 586
        scalability/flexibility, 587
        seamless integration, 587
        website development, 586
    complexities, 616
    components
        backend, 583
        content management, 583
        custom code, 583
        database, 584
        frontend, 582
        responsive design, 582
        user interface (UI), 582
    cost management, 616
    cross-browser capabilities, 612–614, 619
        caching strategies, 613
        minification, 614
        performance optimization, 613
        responsive web design, 612
        testing tools, 613
    customization, 614
    dataverse, 23
    dependencies, 616
    documentation/support, 617
    dynamic/versatile tool, 617
    ecosystem tools, 566
    encryption, 572
    External Websites
        architecture, 562
        cross-browser, 563
        digital transformation, 563
        low-code approach, 562, 563
        primary benefits, 562
        security, 562
        unique tool, 561
    features, 565–568
        and capabilities, 28
        components/core elements, 567–576
        customization, 574–576
        drag-and-drop/prebuilt templates, 568
        healthcare, 574, 575
        integration, 571
        low-code development, 568–570
        reliability, 574
        scalability, 573, 574
        seamless integration, 570, 571

INDEX

Power Pages (*cont.*)
    security, 571–573
  flexibility, 574
  flexible tool, 567
  functional websites, 23
  high-level architecture
    components, 582–584
    scalability/availability, 582
    structure, 581
    visualization, 580, 581
  information security policy, 27
  integration, 618
    capabilities, 608
    external content, 610, 611
    third-party services, 609, 610
  ISO, 24
  low-code design, 618
    principles, 576, 577
    user-centric design, 577
  modular/reusable
    components, 578
    data-driven approach, 578
    educational institution, 578
    integration, 579
    online learning platform, 580
    responsive, 578, 579
    scalability/performance, 579
    security, 579
    updation, 580
  offline scenarios, 616
  PCI DSS, 25–27
  platform (*see* Power Platform)
  professional developers, 615
  scalability, 615
  seamless integration, 615
  security, 566, 589, 618 (*see also* Security governance)
  security and governance, 23, 30, 31
  security/compliance management, 615
  site creation, 28–30
  SOC, 24, 25
  templates, 28
  transition, 619
  user experience
    e-commerce company, 589
    intuitive user interface, 588
    responsive layouts, 589
    unique features, 588
  versatility, 567
Power Platform, 533
  AI Builder, 475
  core components, 3, 7, 8
  definition, 5
  environments
    components, 537–539
    default, 534
    dependencies, 537
    developer plan, 534
    development/testing/production, 534, 535
    geographic location, 536
    layering, 540–542
    lifecycle, 537
    managed solutions, 538
    production, 534
    publisher, 537

sandbox environments, 534
solutions, 536
strategy, 535
types, 533, 534
unmanaged solutions, 538
history/evolution, 5
layering, 540
   components, 540
   creation, 540
   dependency chain, 540
   scenarios, 541
   uninstallation, 542
   working process, 541
Managed Environments, 47–51
organizations, 6, 7
products, 9
real-world (*see* Real-world application)
segmentation, 542
upgrades, 542
Power Query, 171
   advanced dataflow scenarios, 176, 177
   dataflows, 175
   data transformation/cleansing, 176
   definition, 175
Premium connectors, 54, 96
Primary Key, 135
Prompt engineering
   balance/neutrality, 491
   capabilities, 488
   clarity/specificity, 490
   consistency, 491
context provision, 490
feedback/adaptation, 492
iteration/refinement, 490
key elements, 488
testing/validation, 492
types, 489

Q

Quality management systems (QMS), 24

R

Real-world application, 623
   AI Builder, 483
   manufacturing industry (*see* Manufacturing industry)
   success stories
      financial services, 633, 634
      healthcare, 630, 631
      retail chain, 631–633
      transformation, 629
   unveiling Power Platform, 624–627
Recurrent neural networks (RNNs), 480
Retail industry
   assessment/planning, 632
   data integration, 632
   insights, 632
   operational efficiency, 633
   outcome/benefits, 632
   transformation, 631

INDEX

Retrieval Augmented Generation (RAG), 490, 496, 499
Robotic Process Automation (RPA), 419, 420, 428
Role-based access control (RBAC), 30, 83, 124, 129, 147, 149, 231, 243, 259, 395, 572, 597, 606, 616
Roll-up columns, 133

S

Screen readers, 329
Security and data governance
    access and data protection, 85
    access control, 83
    audit logs, 84
    CMK, 84
    compliance, 84
    data protection, 83
    DLP, 84, 93–96
    environments, 84
    environment security, managing, 86
    layers of security, 83
    organizational data, 81, 82
Security governance
    authentication (OAuth)
        compliance, 596
        configuration, 595
        definition, 593
        experience, 596
        fundamental access, 594
        general settings, 595
        identity providers, 595
        security, 596
        social media platforms, 594
        support, 594
        user permissions/access levels, 596
    authorization
        assignment, 600
        entity permissions, 598
        implementation, 601
        page permissions, 598
        RBAC models, 597
        responsibilities, 597
        users/roles, 601
        web roles, 597, 600
    built-in security
        authentication, 593–596
        authorization, 597–599
        encryption, 602–606
        features, 593
        setting up authorization, 599–602
    compliance/regulatory standards, 607
        GDPR guidelines, 607
        ISO/IEC 27001, 607
    elements, 589
    encryption
        CMKs models, 605
        comprehensive data security, 606
        healthcare website, 602
        key vault integration, 605
        RBAC security model, 606

rest, 603
SQL TDE, 604
storage, 604
TLS protocol, 605
transit, 604
web roles/table permissions, 606
least privilege access, 590
resources/training materials, 608
zero trust, 590
assumption, 592
least privilege limits, 592
micro-segmentation, 592
principles, 590, 591
verification, 591
Software Development Kit (SDK), 122, 407
SQL Server Management Studio (SSMS), 220, 221
Standard connectors
Azure services, 227
content generation services, 229
Dynamics 365, 227
e-signature services, 229
Google services, 228
Microsoft 365, 228
services, 226
SharePoint, 227
System and Organization Controls (SOC), 24–25
System Integration Testing (SIT), 538

T

Tables
types
activity, 127
custom, 126
elastic, 129
intersect, 127
metadata, 127
standard, 126
virtual, 128, 129
types of data, 126
Tabular Data Stream (TDS) endpoint, 220, 221
Transparent Data Encryption (TDE), 604
Transport Layer Security (TLS), 23, 31, 603, 605

U

Unit testing, 348, 351
Unveiling Power Platform
automation, 628
business scenarios, 625
collaboration/innovation, 628
complex/dynamic environment, 625
cost efficiency, 627
data-driven insights, 628
development tools, 626
flexibility/customization, 627
low-code approach, 625
low-code development, 626

Unveiling Power Platform (*cont.*)
    nontechnical users, 627
    transformative impact, 625, 626
User Acceptance Testing (UAT), 349, 351, 538
User-centric approach, 358

V

Version control mechanisms, 31
Views
    types, 138
        custom, 140
        looukup, 140

    personal, 139
    system, 138
    system chart, 139
    system dashboard, 139

W, X, Y

WCAG Color Contrast Checker, 329
Webhooks, 207–208, 610
Workflow automation, *see* Power Automate

Z

Zero-shot learning, 489

GPSR Compliance

The European Union's (EU) General Product Safety Regulation (GPSR) is a set of rules that requires consumer products to be safe and our obligations to ensure this.

If you have any concerns about our products, you can contact us on

ProductSafety@springernature.com

In case Publisher is established outside the EU, the EU authorized representative is:

Springer Nature Customer Service Center GmbH
Europaplatz 3
69115 Heidelberg, Germany